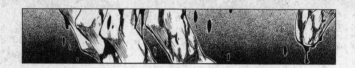

Every time we set aside our pride
We take a step closer to the beast
Every time we kill an emotion
We take a step away from the beast

BLEACH13 THE UNDEAD

Shonen Jump Manga

STARS AND

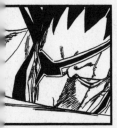

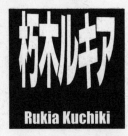

Rukia Kuchiki

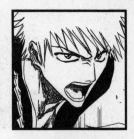

Ichigo Kurosaki

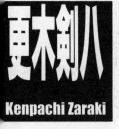

Kenpachi Zaraki

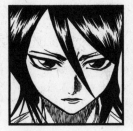

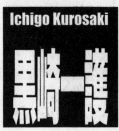

plot

After a fateful encounter with Soul Reaper Rukia Kuchiki, Ichigo Kurosaki himself becomes a Soul Reaper. Now, Ichigo and his friends have infiltrated the stronghold of the Soul Reapers to save Rukia. But the formidable Kenpachi Zaraki blocks Ichigo just steps away from Rukia's cell, and while Ichigo is struggling against Kenpachi's tremendous spiritual pressure, Chad faces a fearsome enemy of his own in Shunsui Kyôraku.

Meanwhile, the Soul Reapers are shocked to learn that Captain Aizen has been murdered!

BLEACH ALL

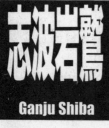

志波岩鷲

Ganju Shiba

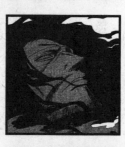

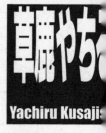

草鹿やち

Yachiru Kusaji

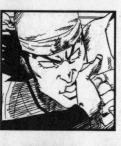

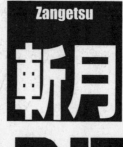

Zangetsu

斬月

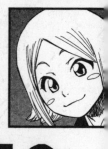

STORIES

LEACH13

THE UNDEAD

Contents

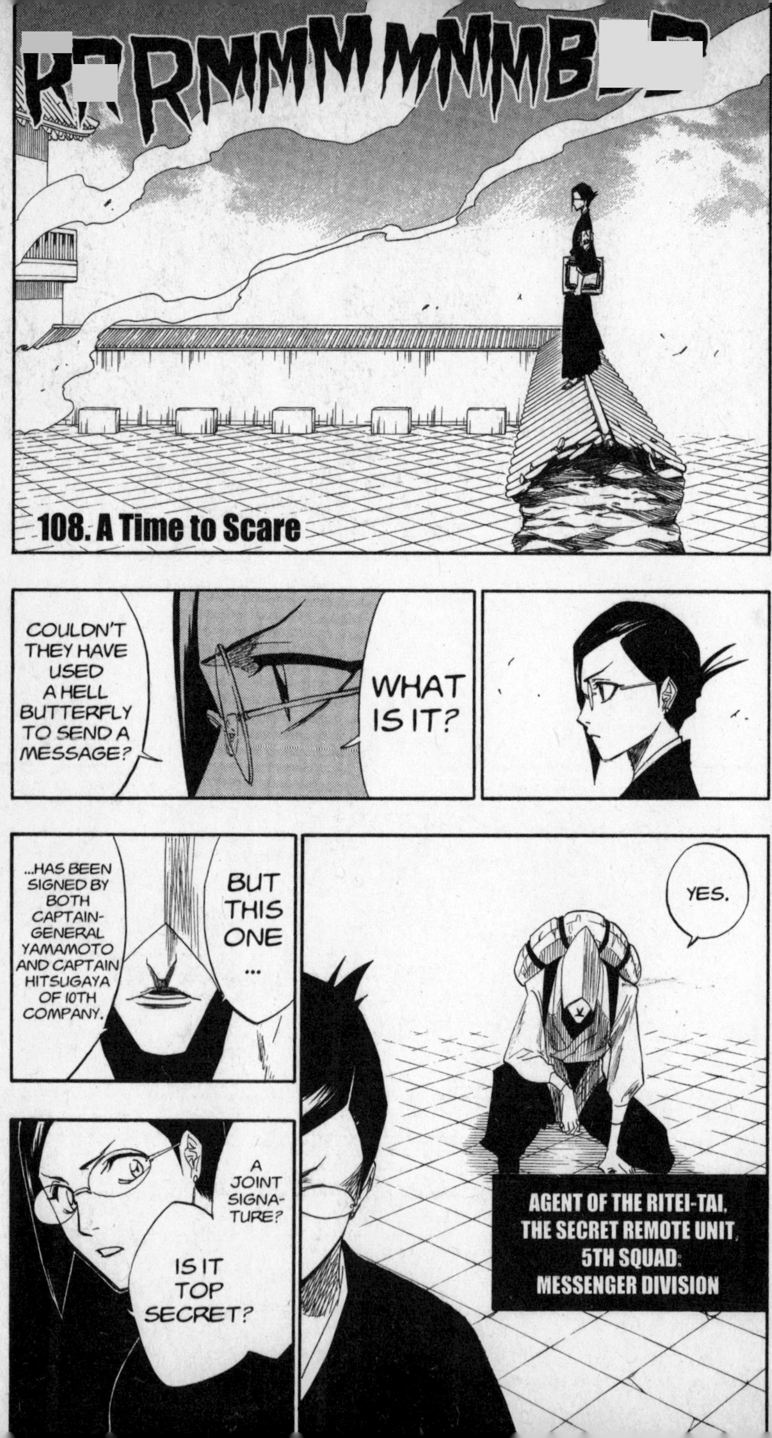
RRMMMM MMMMB
108. A Time to Scare
WHAT IS IT?
COULDN'T THEY HAVE USED A HELL BUTTERFLY TO SEND A MESSAGE?
YES.
AGENT OF THE RITEI-TAI, THE SECRET REMOTE UNIT 5TH SQUAD: MESSENGER DIVISION
BUT THIS ONE ...
...HAS BEEN SIGNED BY BOTH CAPTAIN-GENERAL YAMAMOTO AND CAPTAIN HITSUGAYA OF 10TH COMPANY.
A JOINT SIGNATURE?
IS IT TOP SECRET?

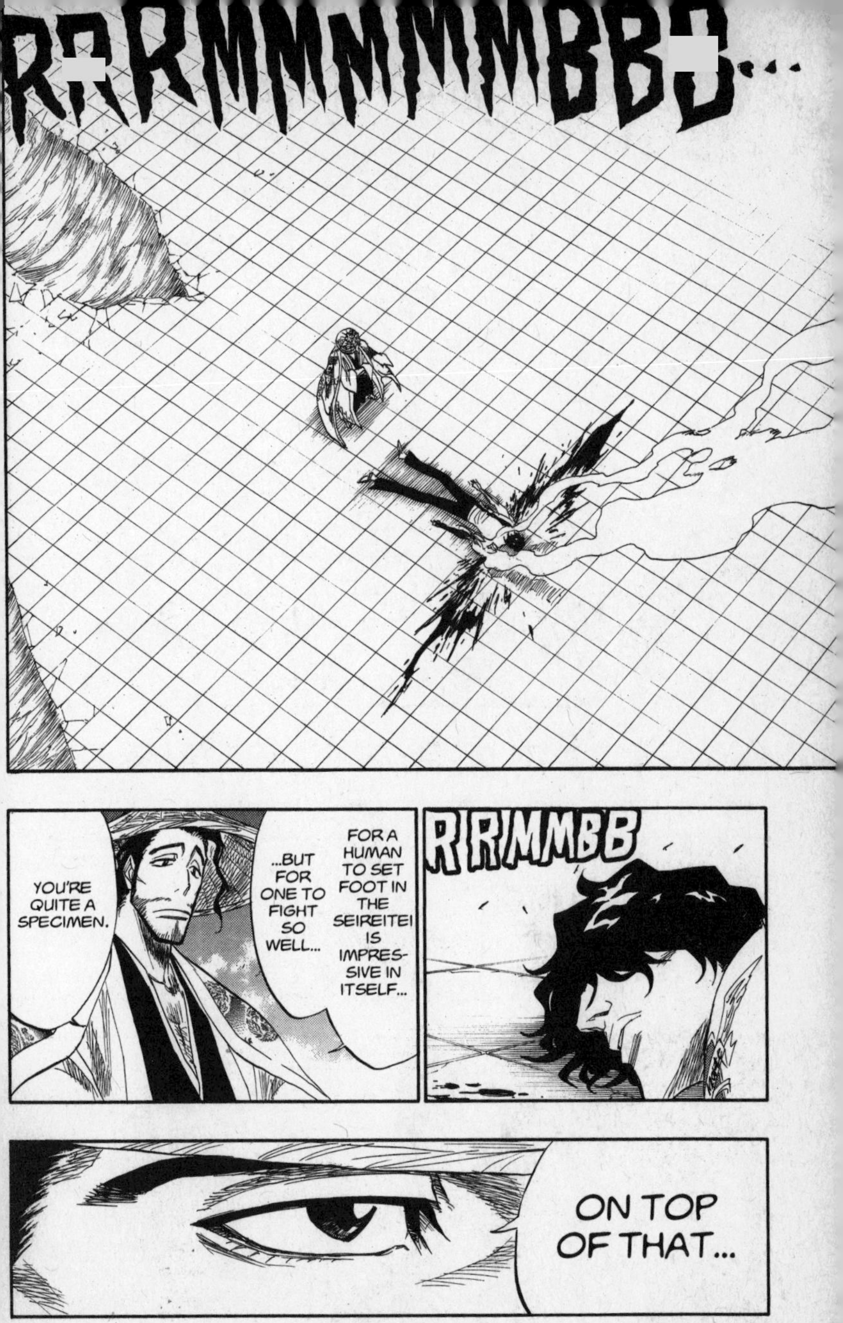
RRRMMMMMMBBB...
RRMMBB
FOR A HUMAN TO SET FOOT IN THE SEIREITEI IS IMPRESSIVE IN ITSELF...
...BUT FOR ONE TO FIGHT SO WELL...
YOU'RE QUITE A SPECIMEN.
ON TOP OF THAT...

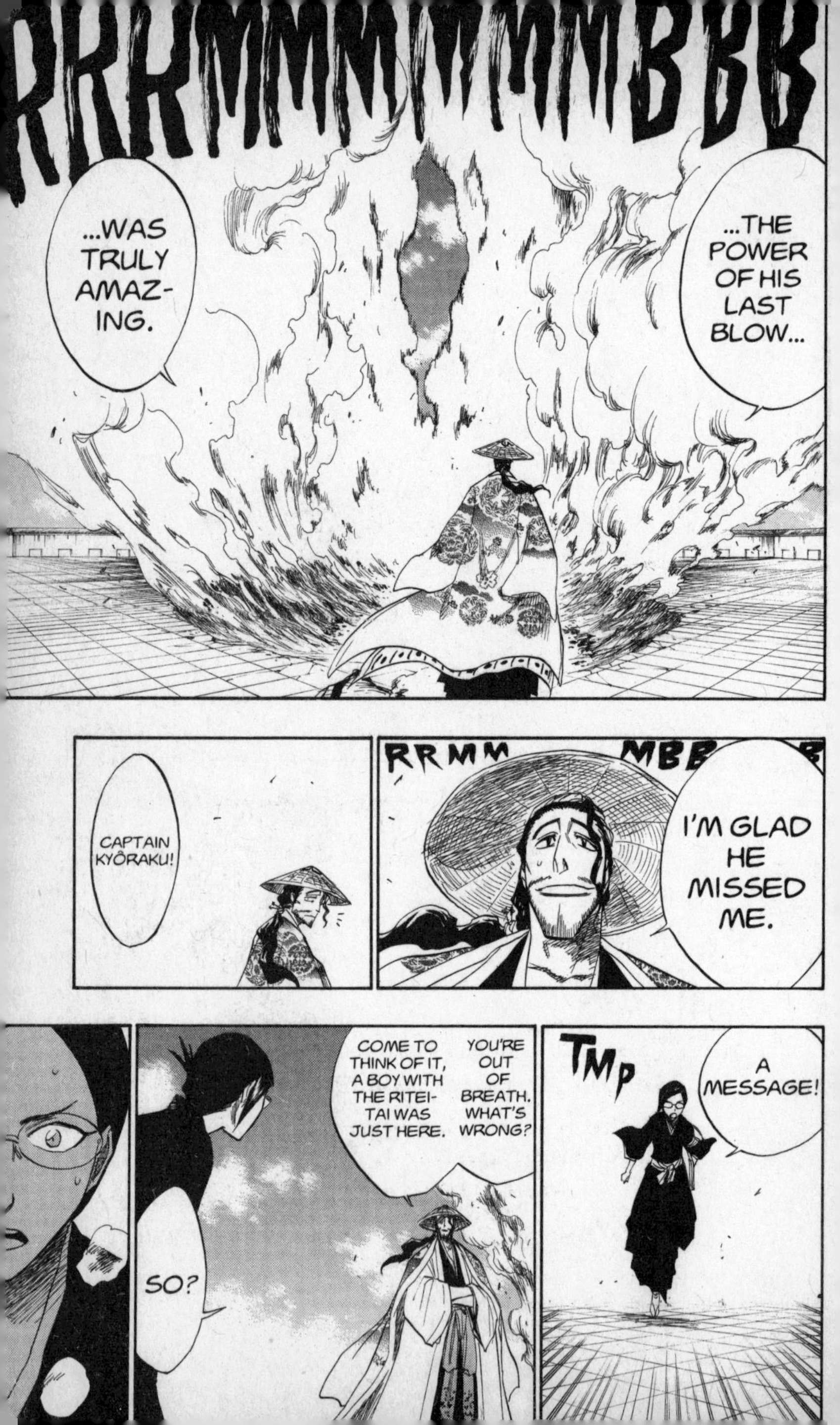
RRMMMMMMBBB
...THE POWER OF HIS LAST BLOW...
...WAS TRULY AMAZ-ING.
RRMM MBB B
I'M GLAD HE MISSED ME.
CAPTAIN KYÔRAKU!
TMP
A MESSAGE!
YOU'RE OUT OF BREATH. WHAT'S WRONG?
COME TO THINK OF IT, A BOY WITH THE RITEI-TAI WAS JUST HERE.
SO?

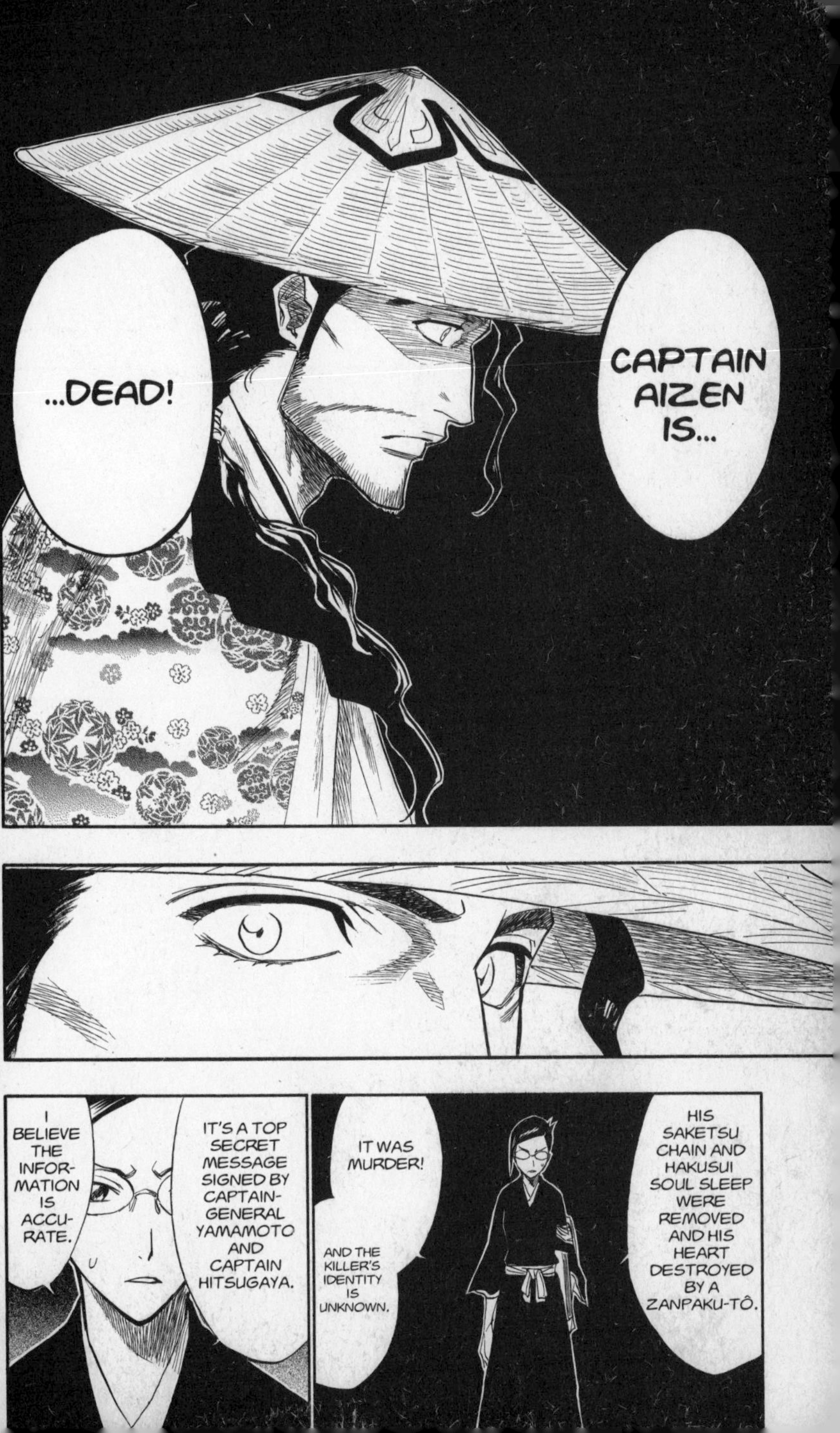
CAPTAIN AIZEN IS...
...DEAD!
HIS SAKETSU CHAIN AND HAKUSUI SOUL SLEEP WERE REMOVED AND HIS HEART DESTROYED BY A ZANPAKU-TÔ.
IT WAS MURDER!
AND THE KILLER'S IDENTITY IS UNKNOWN.
IT'S A TOP SECRET MESSAGE SIGNED BY CAPTAIN-GENERAL YAMAMOTO AND CAPTAIN HITSUGAYA.
I BELIEVE THE INFOR-MATION IS ACCU-RATE.

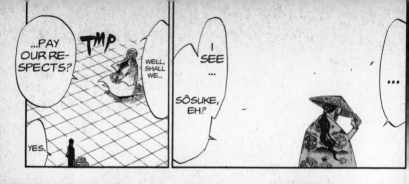

...PAY OUR RESPECTS?

TMP

WELL, SHALL WE...

YES.

I SEE ... SÔSUKE, EH?

...

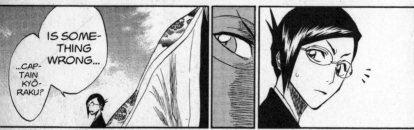

IS SOMETHING WRONG...

...CAPTAIN KYÔRAKU?

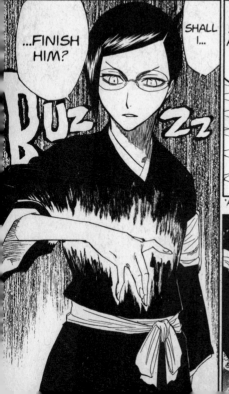

...FINISH HIM?

SHALL I...

BUZZZZ

...IS STILL ALIVE.

THIS RYOKA*...

*A SOUL THAT ENTERS THE SOUL SOCIETY ILLEGALLY

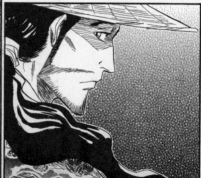

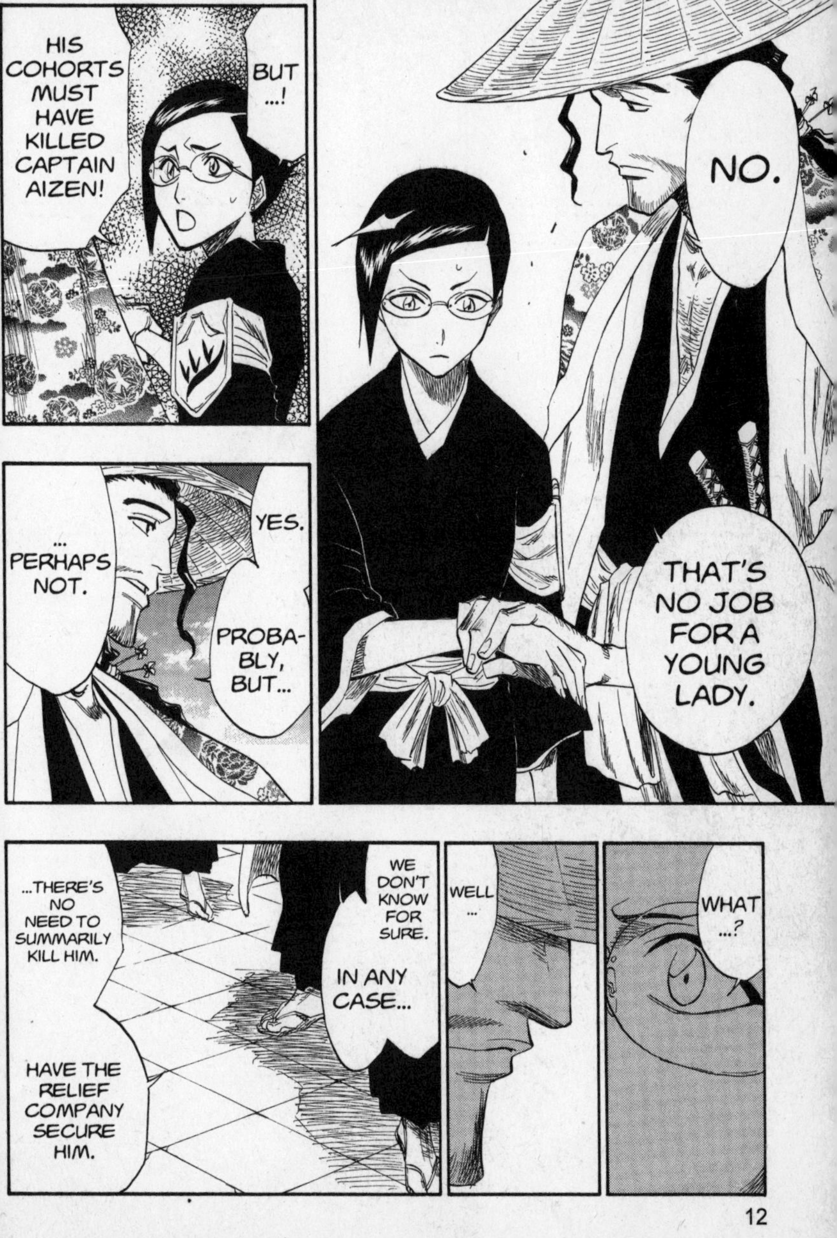
NO.
THAT'S NO JOB FOR A YOUNG LADY.
BUT ...!
HIS COHORTS MUST HAVE KILLED CAPTAIN AIZEN!
YES.
PROBABLY, BUT...
... PERHAPS NOT.
WHAT ...?
WELL ...
WE DON'T KNOW FOR SURE.
IN ANY CASE...
...THERE'S NO NEED TO SUMMARILY KILL HIM.
HAVE THE RELIEF COMPANY SECURE HIM.

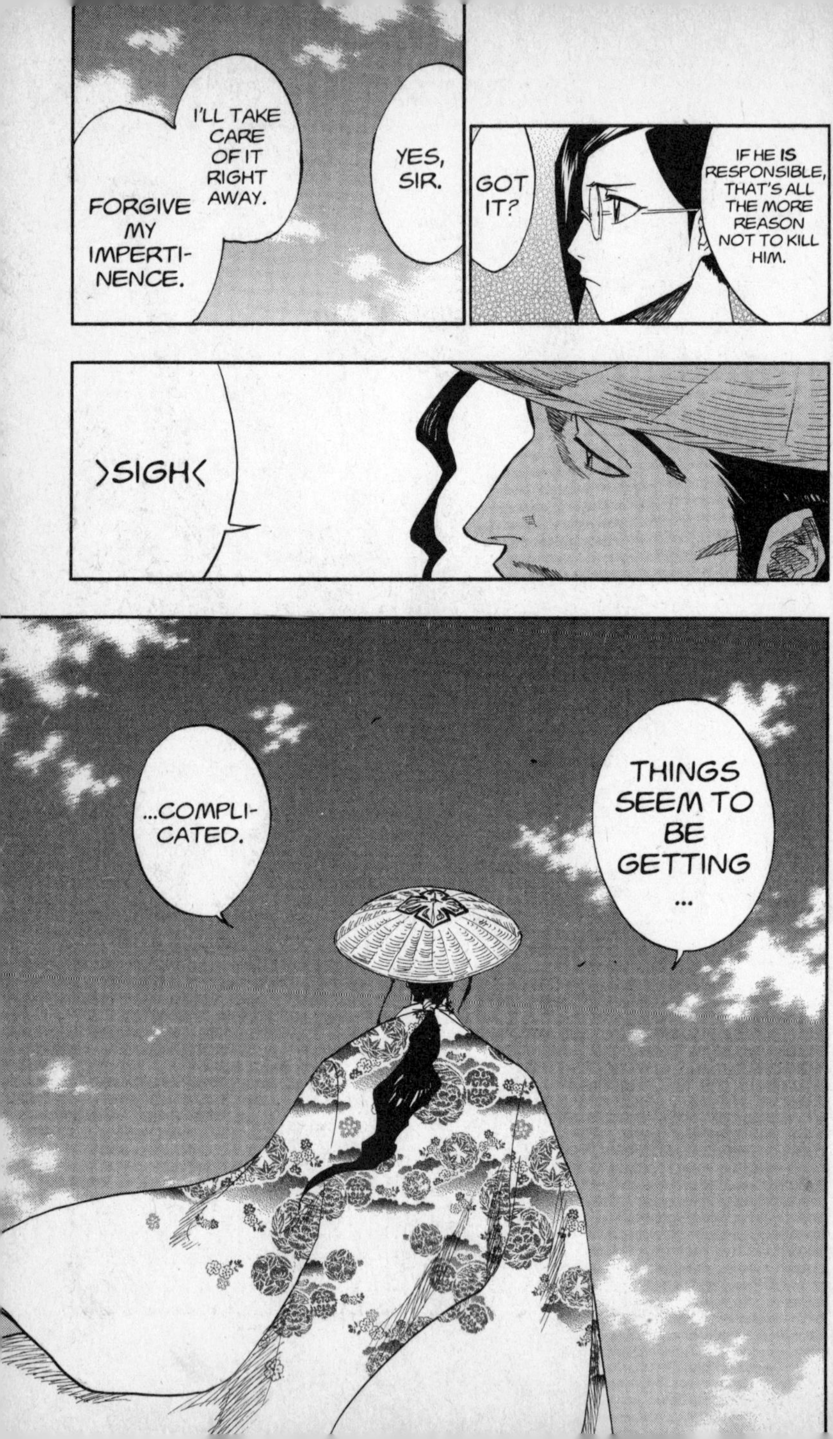
IF HE IS RESPONSIBLE, THAT'S ALL THE MORE REASON NOT TO KILL HIM.
GOT IT?
YES, SIR.
I'LL TAKE CARE OF IT RIGHT AWAY.
FORGIVE MY IMPERTINENCE.
>SIGH<
THINGS SEEM TO BE GETTING ...
...COMPLICATED.

108. A Time to Scare

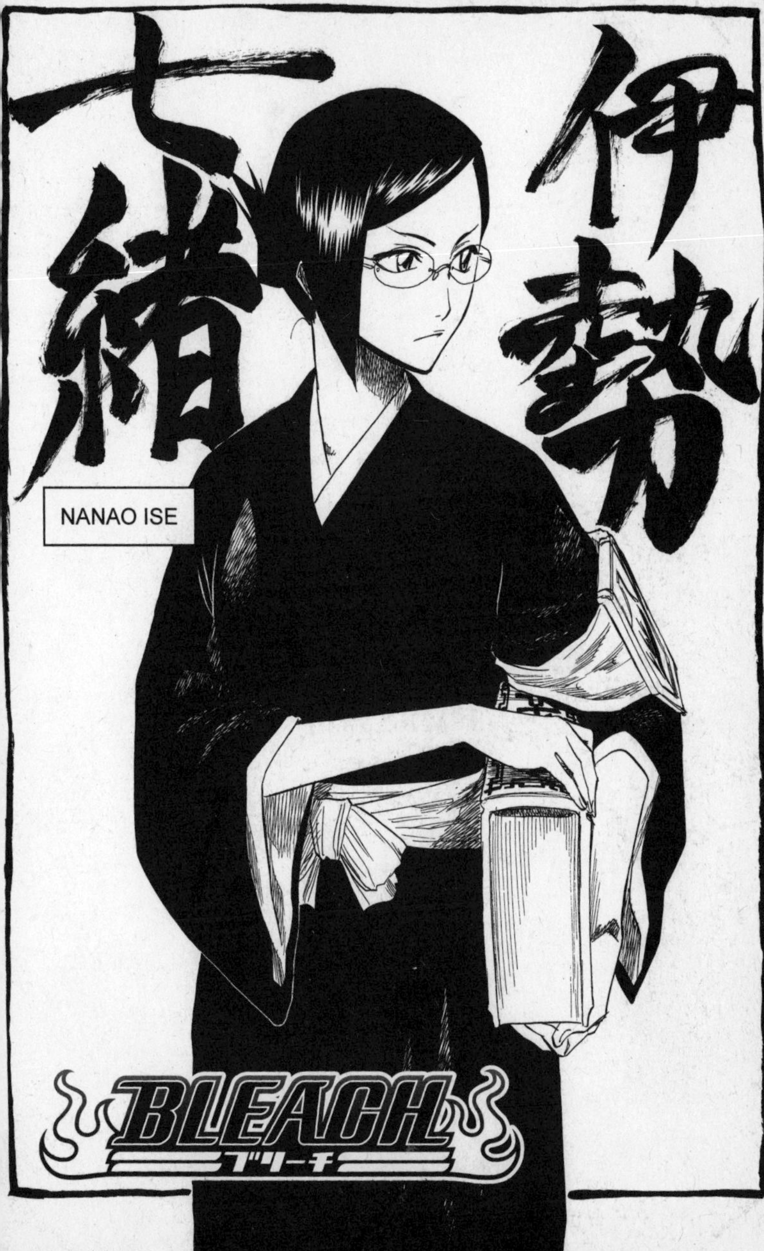
伊勢
七緒
NANAO ISE
BLEACH
ブリーチ

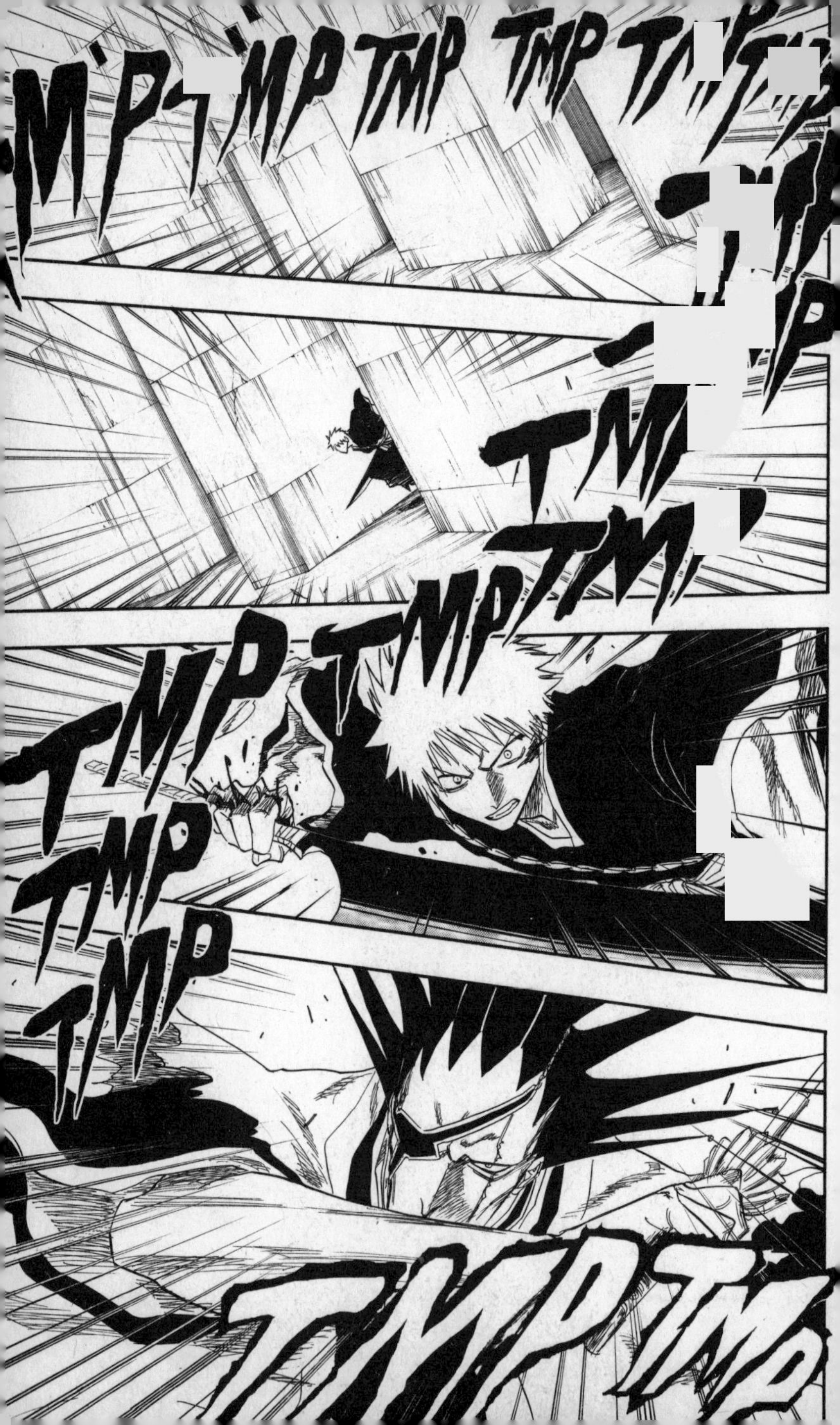
TMP TMP
TMP
TMP
TMP TMP
TMP
TMP
TMP
TMP TMP

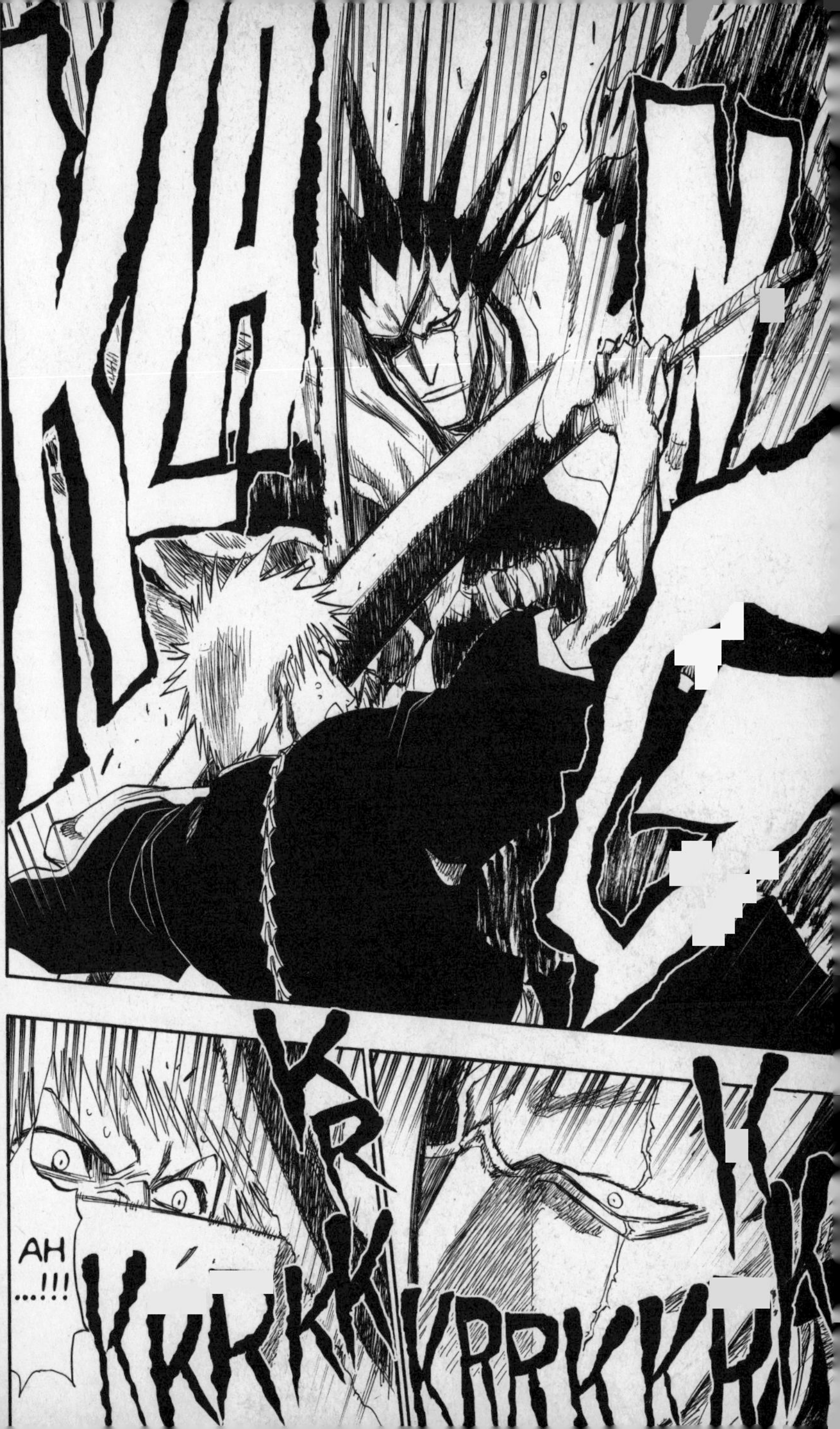
AH
...!!!

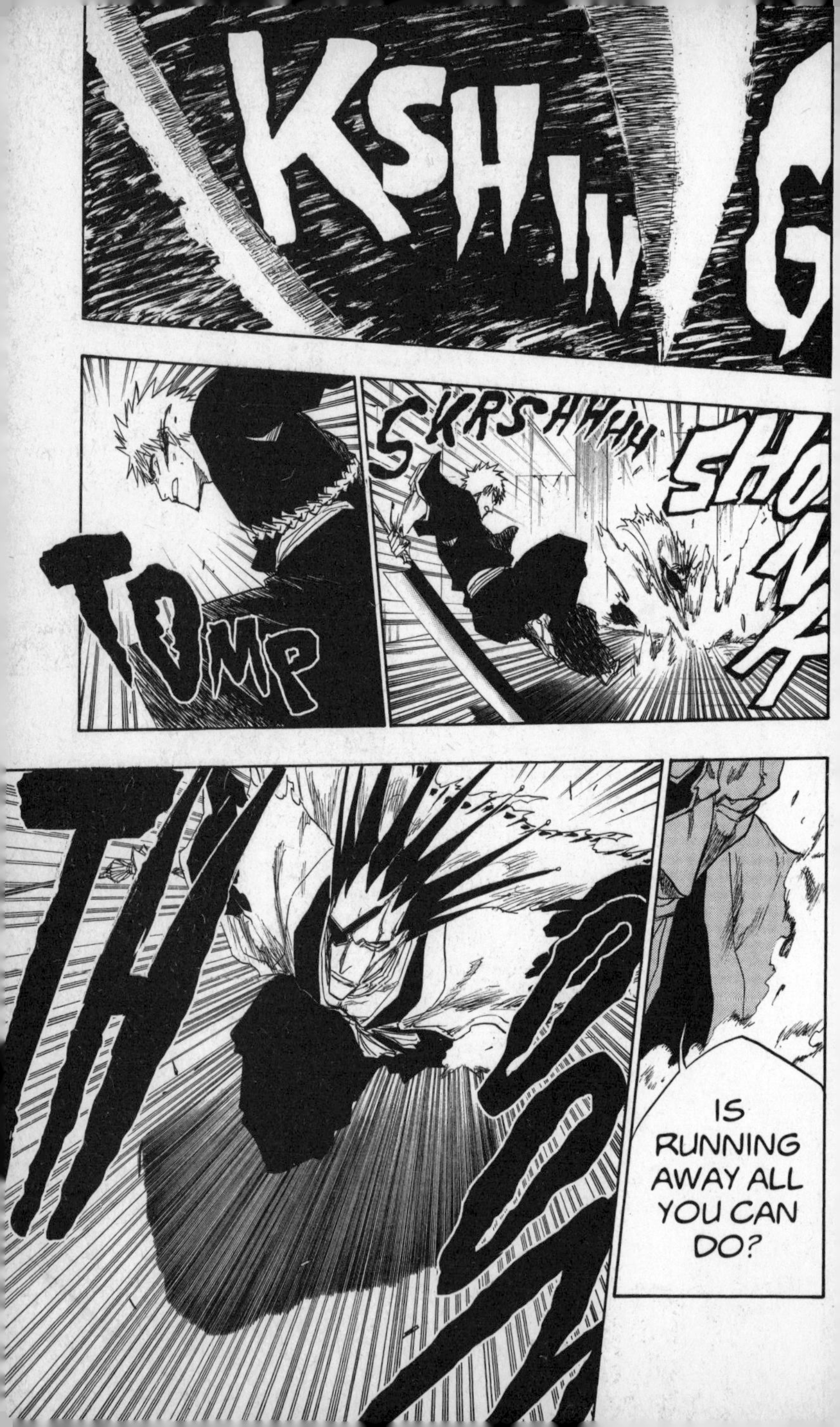
KSHING
SKRSHHHH
TOMP
IS RUNNING AWAY ALL YOU CAN DO?

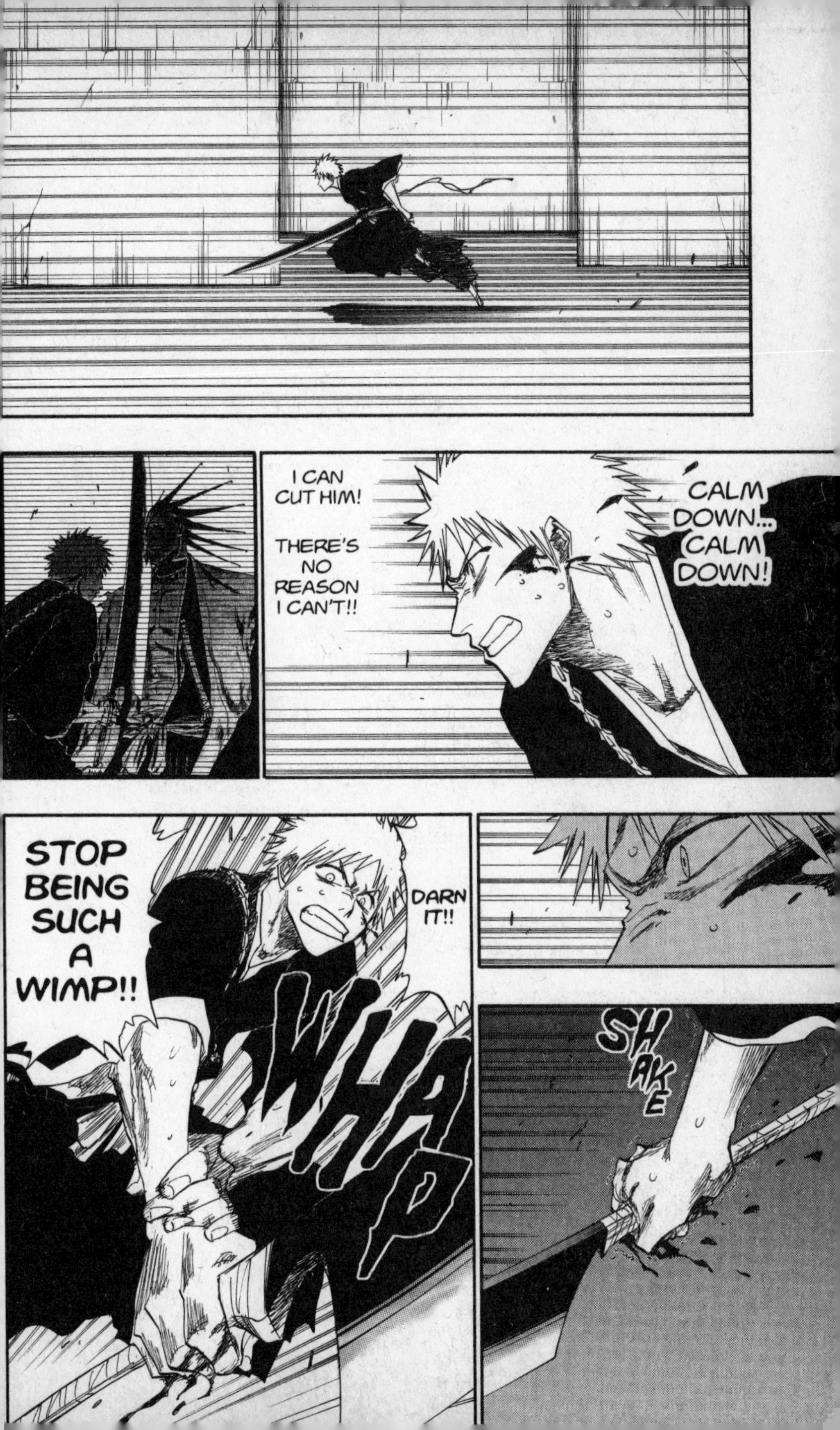
CALM DOWN... CALM DOWN!
I CAN CUT HIM!
THERE'S NO REASON I CAN'T!!
SHAKE
DARN IT!!
STOP BEING SUCH A WIMP!!
WHAP

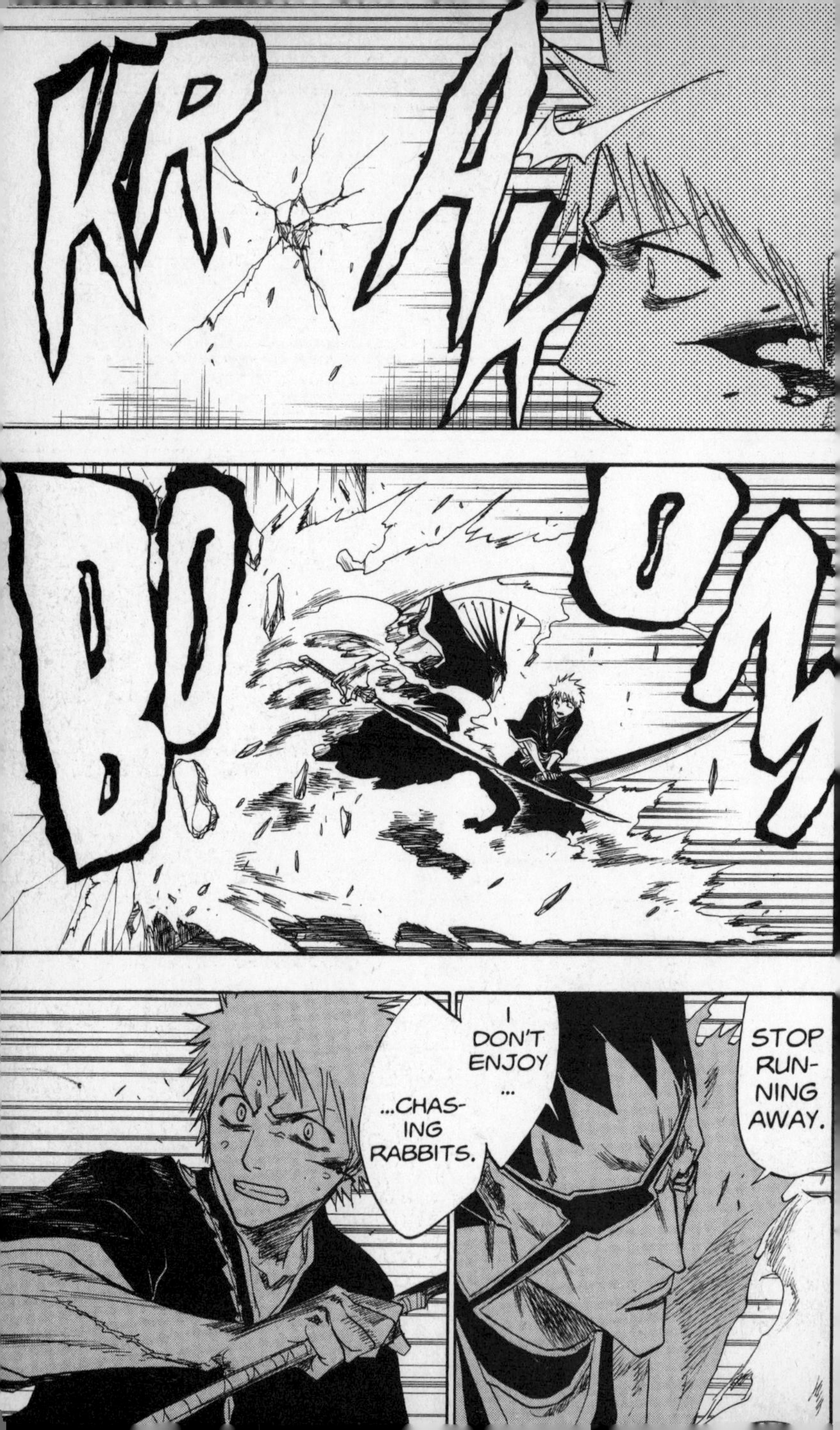
KRAK
BOOM
STOP RUN-NING AWAY.
I DON'T ENJOY ...
...CHAS-ING RABBITS.

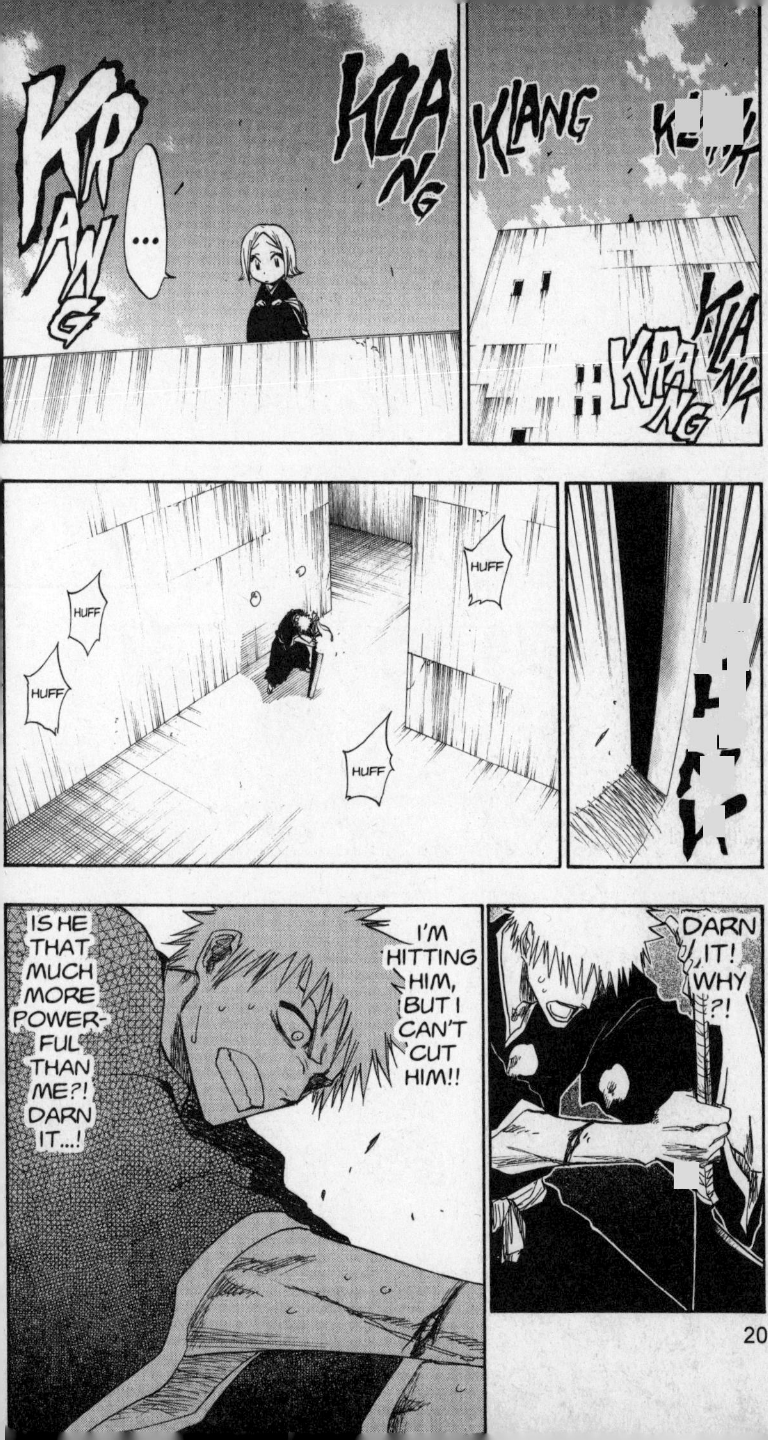
KLANG
KLANK
KRANG
KRANG
...
KRANG
HUFF
HUFF
HUFF
HUFF
DARN IT! WHY?!
I'M HITTING HIM, BUT I CAN'T CUT HIM!!
IS HE THAT MUCH MORE POWERFUL THAN ME?! DARN IT...!

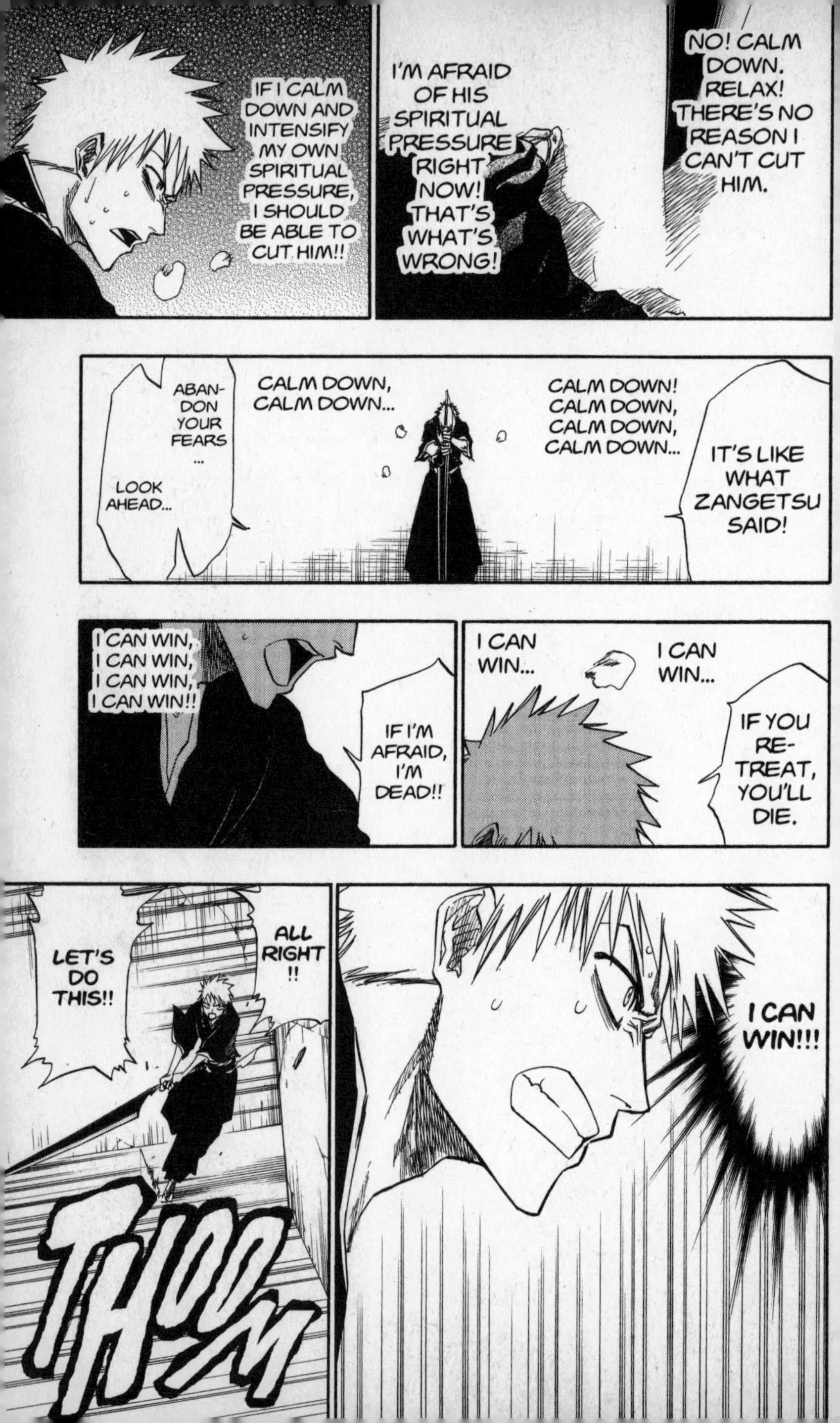
NO! CALM DOWN. RELAX! THERE'S NO REASON I CAN'T CUT HIM.
I'M AFRAID OF HIS SPIRITUAL PRESSURE RIGHT NOW! THAT'S WHAT'S WRONG!
IF I CALM DOWN AND INTENSIFY MY OWN SPIRITUAL PRESSURE, I SHOULD BE ABLE TO CUT HIM!!
IT'S LIKE WHAT ZANGETSU SAID!
CALM DOWN! CALM DOWN, CALM DOWN, CALM DOWN...
CALM DOWN, CALM DOWN...
ABAN-DON YOUR FEARS ... LOOK AHEAD...
IF YOU RE-TREAT, YOU'LL DIE.
I CAN WIN...
I CAN WIN...
IF I'M AFRAID, I'M DEAD!!
I CAN WIN, I CAN WIN, I CAN WIN, I CAN WIN!!
I CAN WIN!!!
ALL RIGHT !!
LET'S DO THIS!!
THOOM

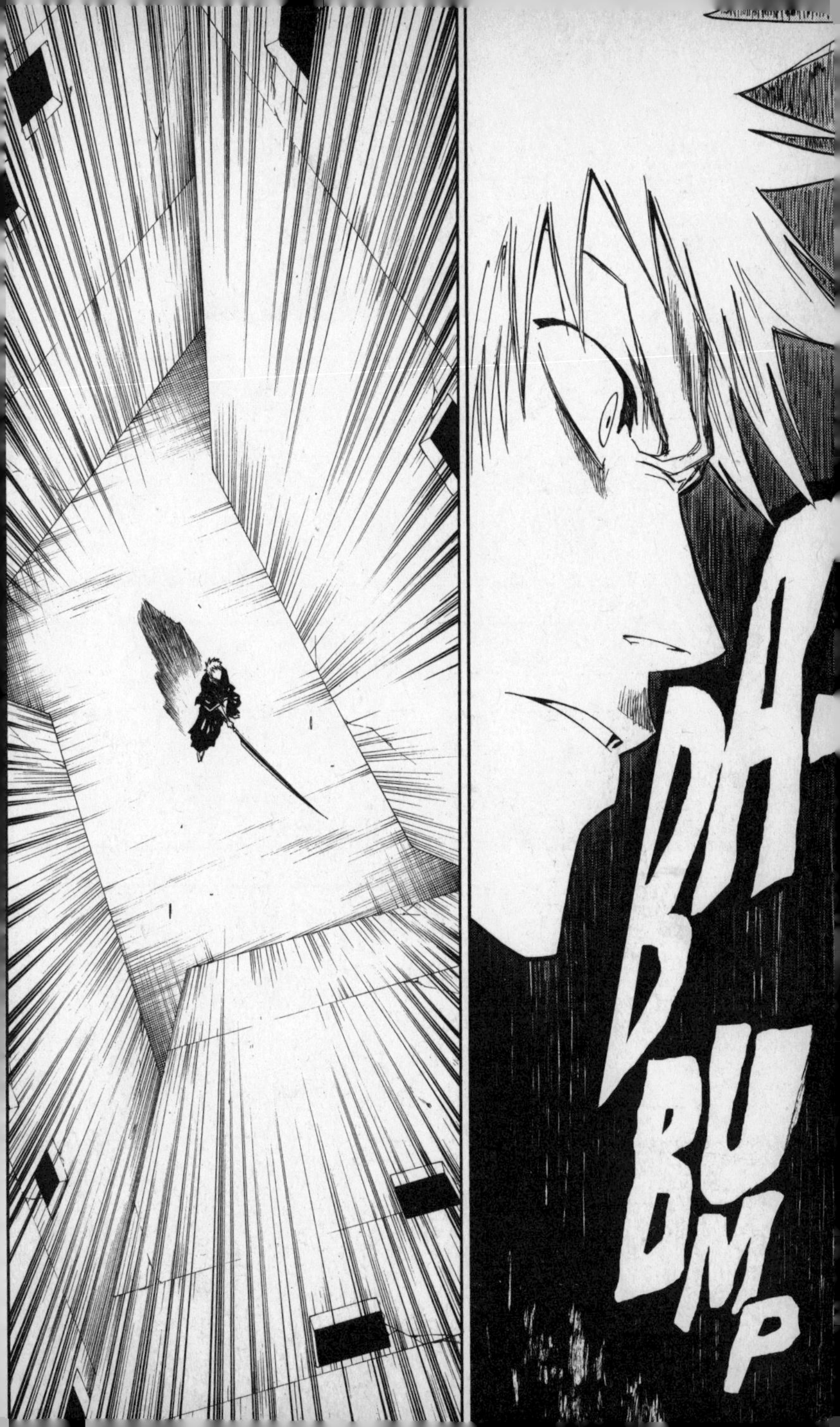

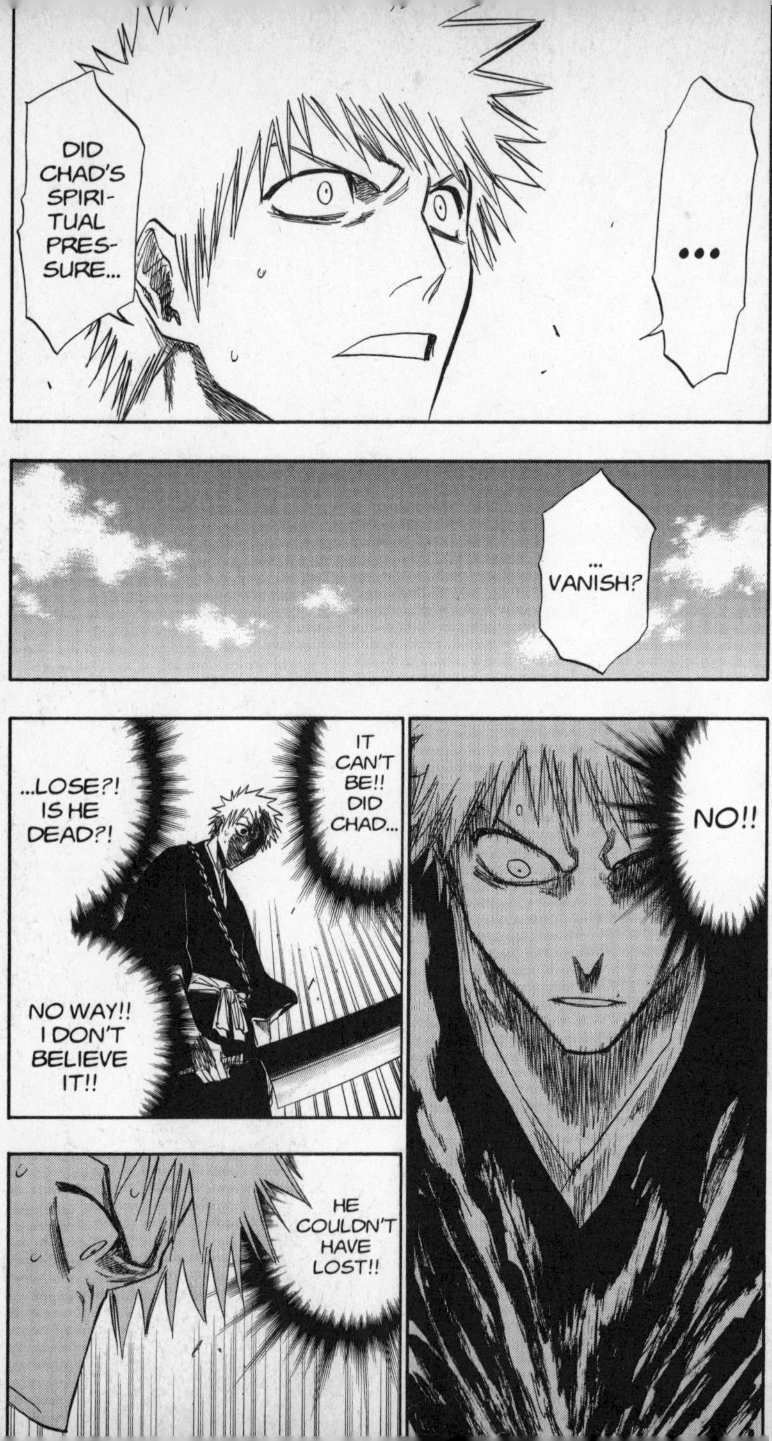
...
DID CHAD'S SPIRI- TUAL PRES- SURE...
... VANISH?
NO!!
IT CAN'T BE!! DID CHAD...
...LOSE?! IS HE DEAD?!
NO WAY!! I DON'T BELIEVE IT!!
HE COULDN'T HAVE LOST!!

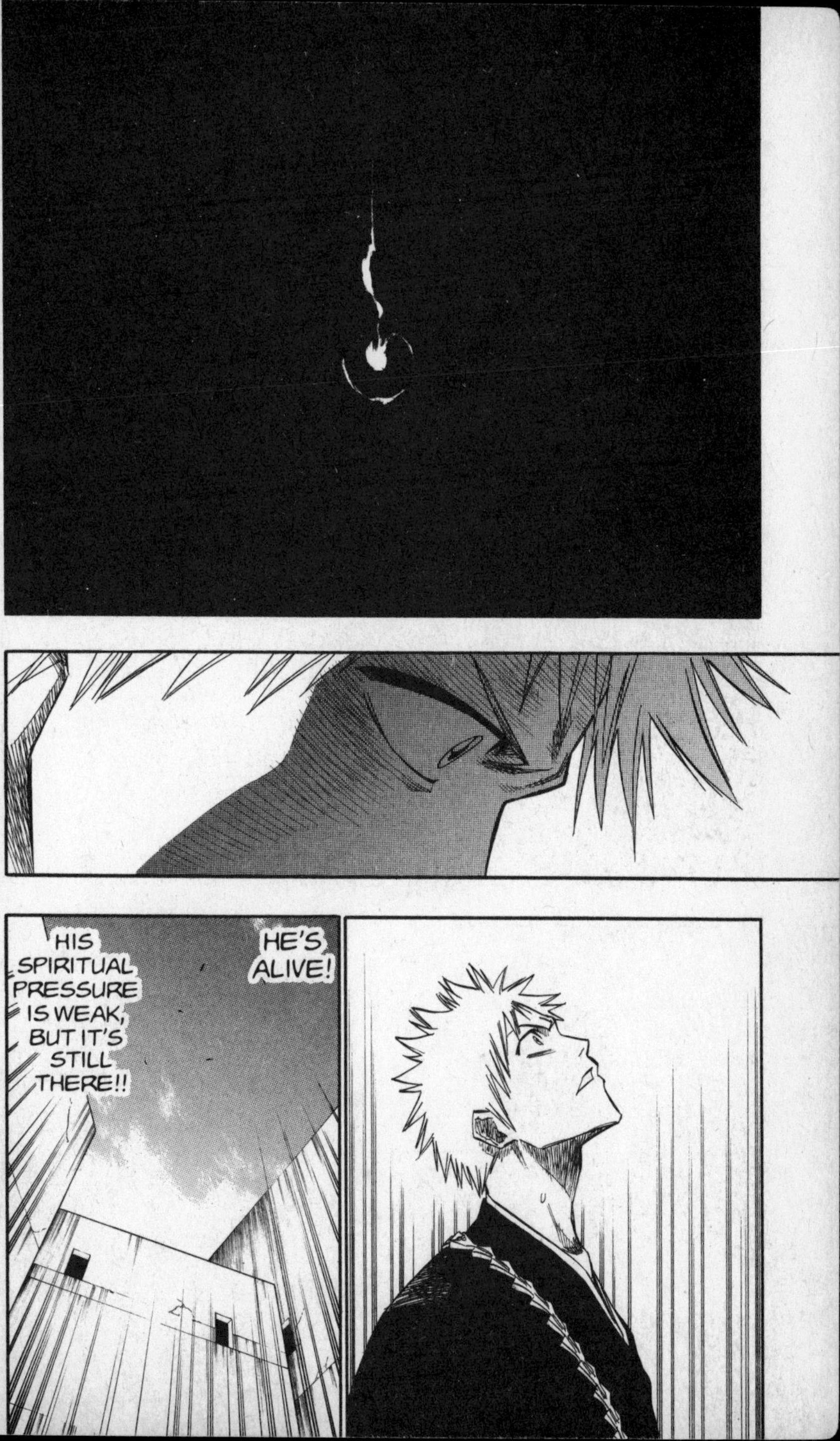
HE'S ALIVE!
HIS SPIRITUAL PRESSURE IS WEAK, BUT IT'S STILL THERE!!

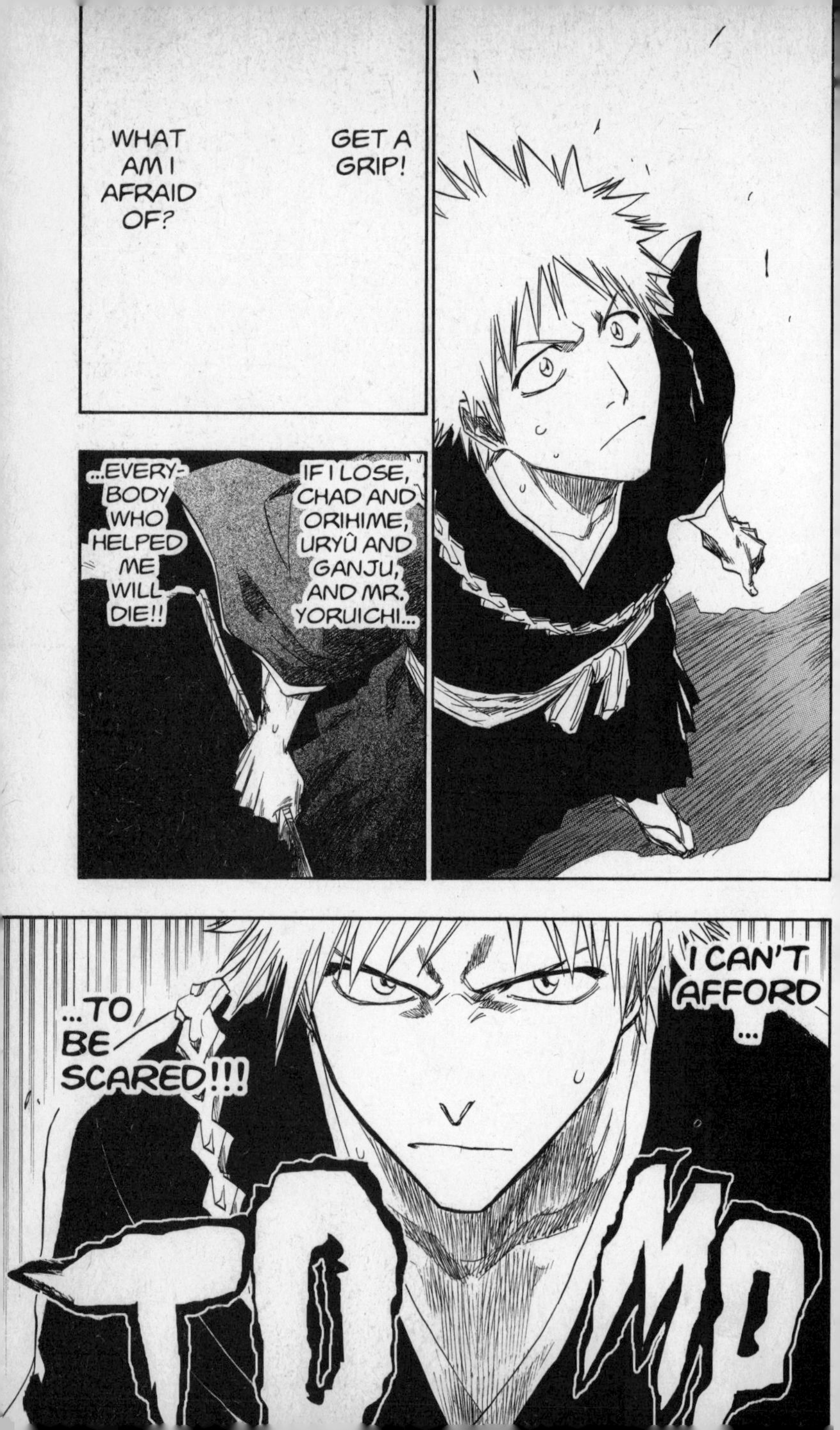
GET A GRIP!
WHAT AM I AFRAID OF?
IF I LOSE, CHAD AND ORIHIME, URYÛ AND GANJU, AND MR. YORUICHI...
...EVERYBODY WHO HELPED ME WILL DIE!!
I CAN'T AFFORD...
...TO BE SCARED!!!
TOMP

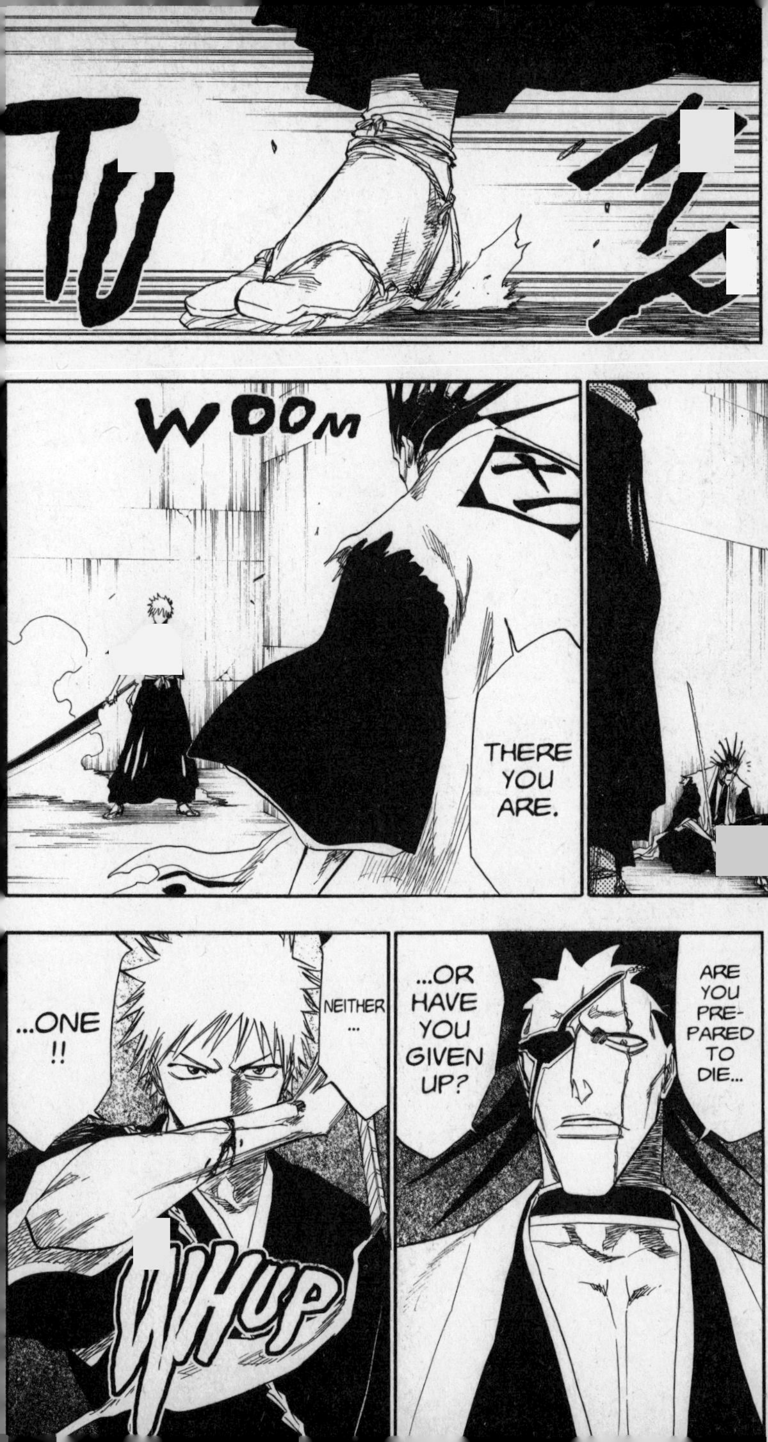
TU
WOOM
THERE YOU ARE.
ARE YOU PRE-PARED TO DIE...
...OR HAVE YOU GIVEN UP?
NEITHER...
...ONE !!
WHUP

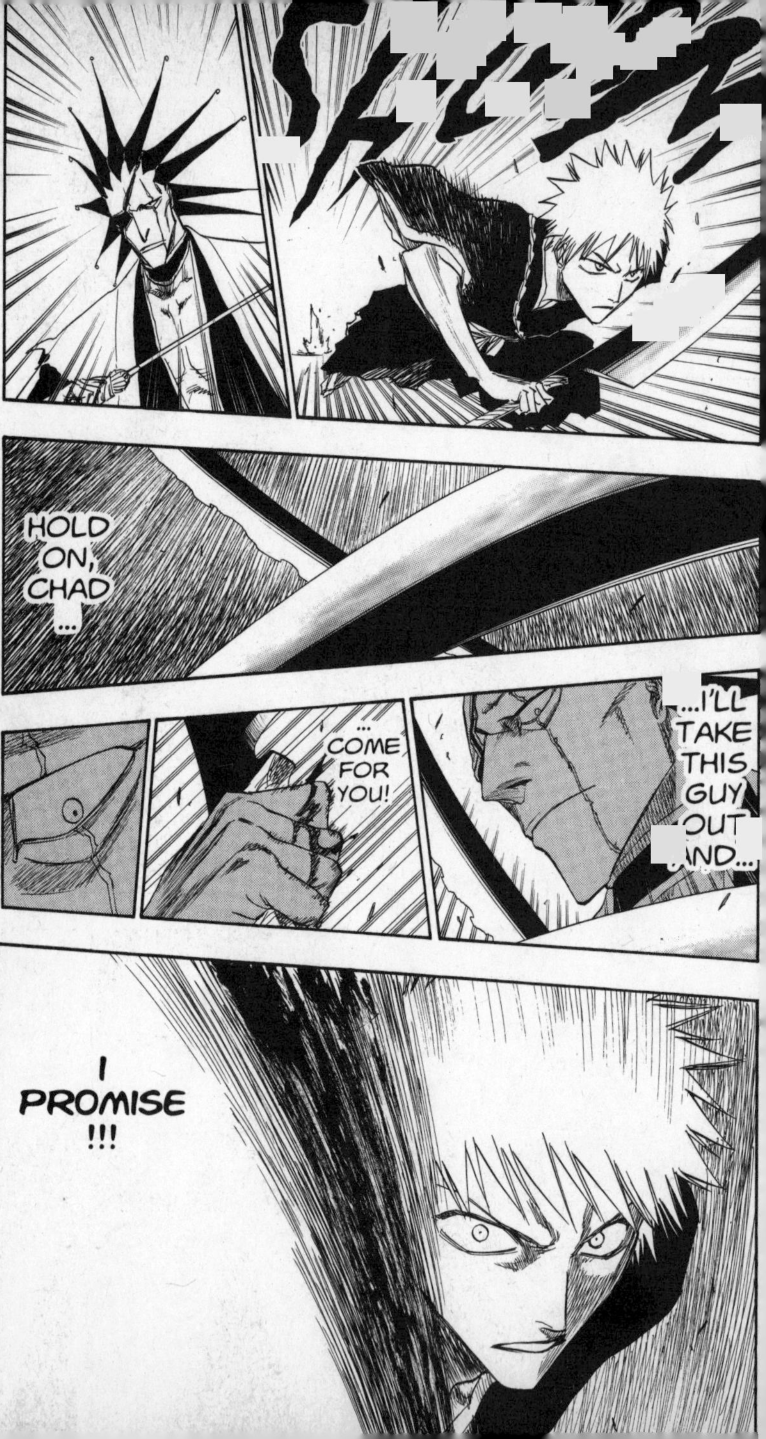
HOLD ON, CHAD ...
...I'LL TAKE THIS GUY OUT AND...
... COME FOR YOU!
I PROMISE !!!

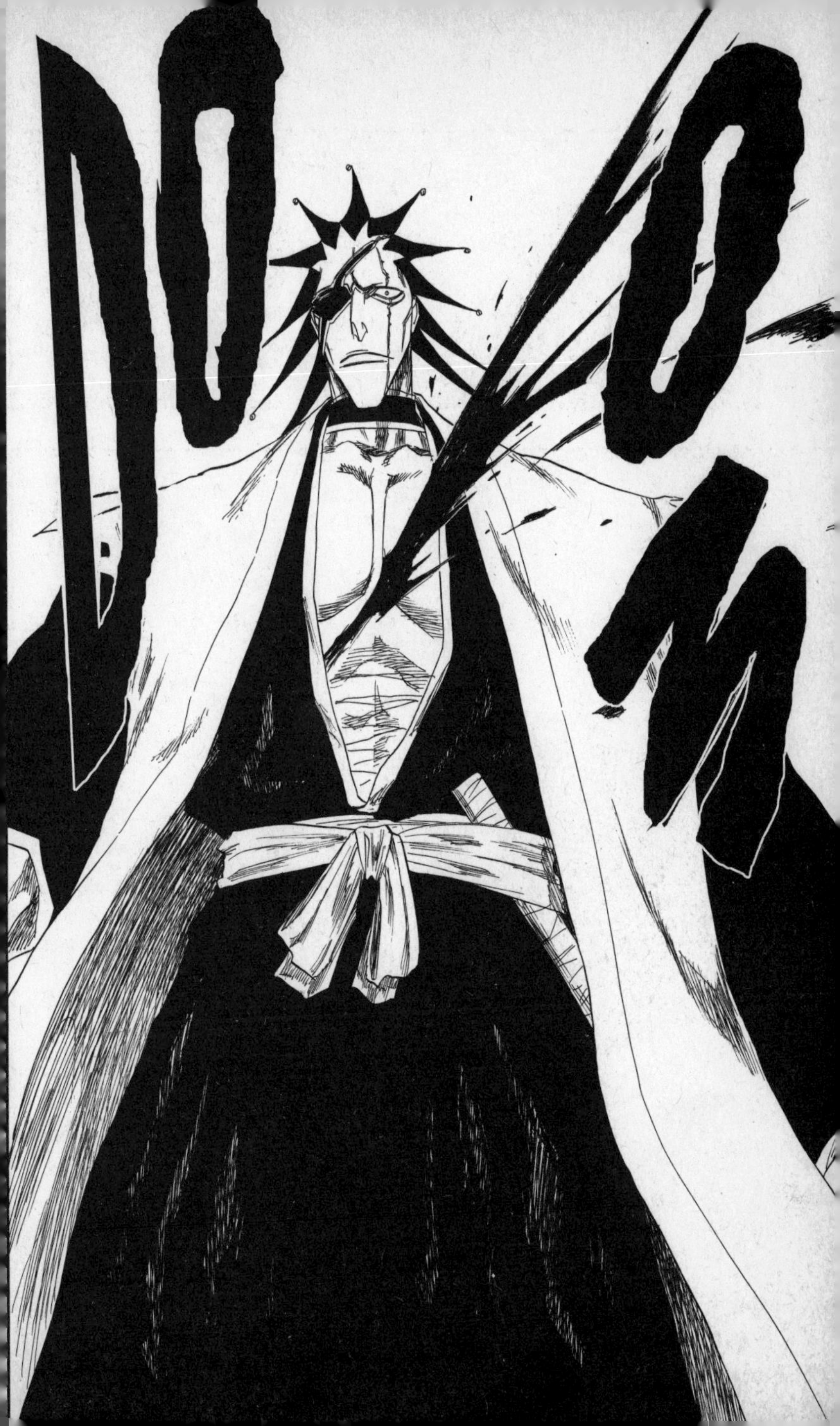
DOOM

READ THIS WAY

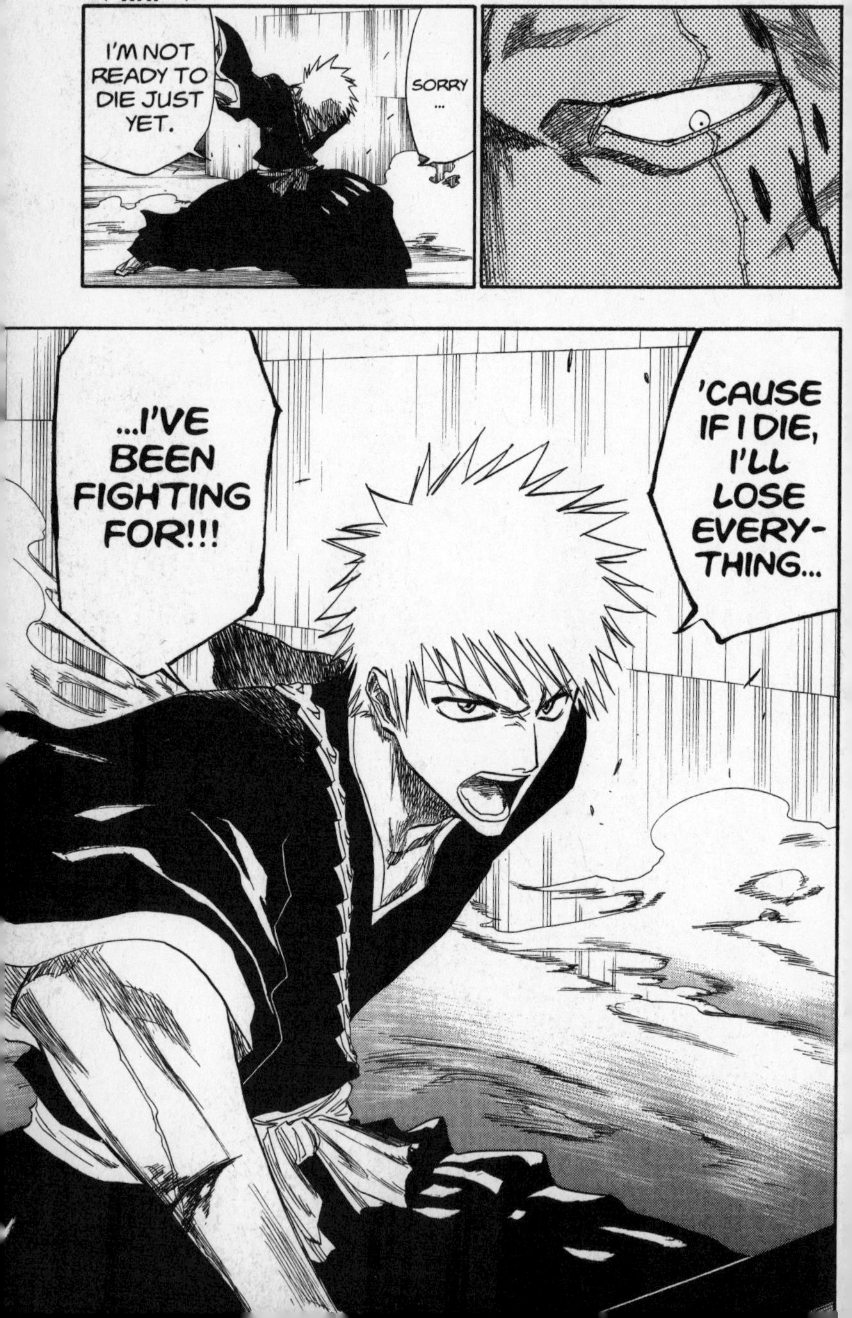
SORRY ...
I'M NOT READY TO DIE JUST YET.
'CAUSE IF I DIE, I'LL LOSE EVERY-THING...
...I'VE BEEN FIGHTING FOR!!!

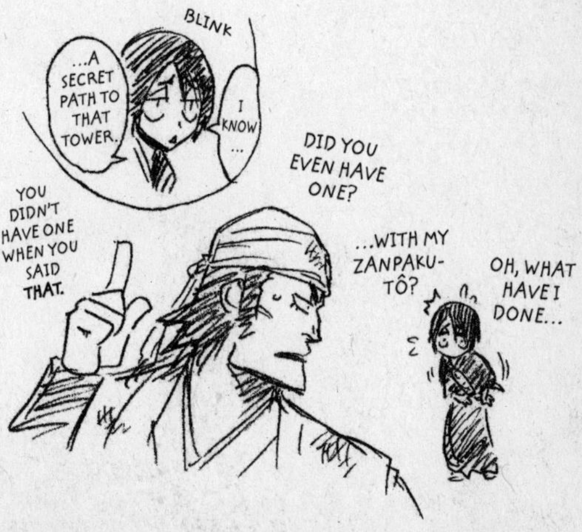
BLINK
I KNOW...
...A SECRET PATH TO THAT TOWER.
DID YOU EVEN HAVE ONE?
OH, WHAT HAVE I DONE...
...WITH MY ZANPAKU-TÔ?
YOU DIDN'T HAVE ONE WHEN YOU SAID **THAT.**

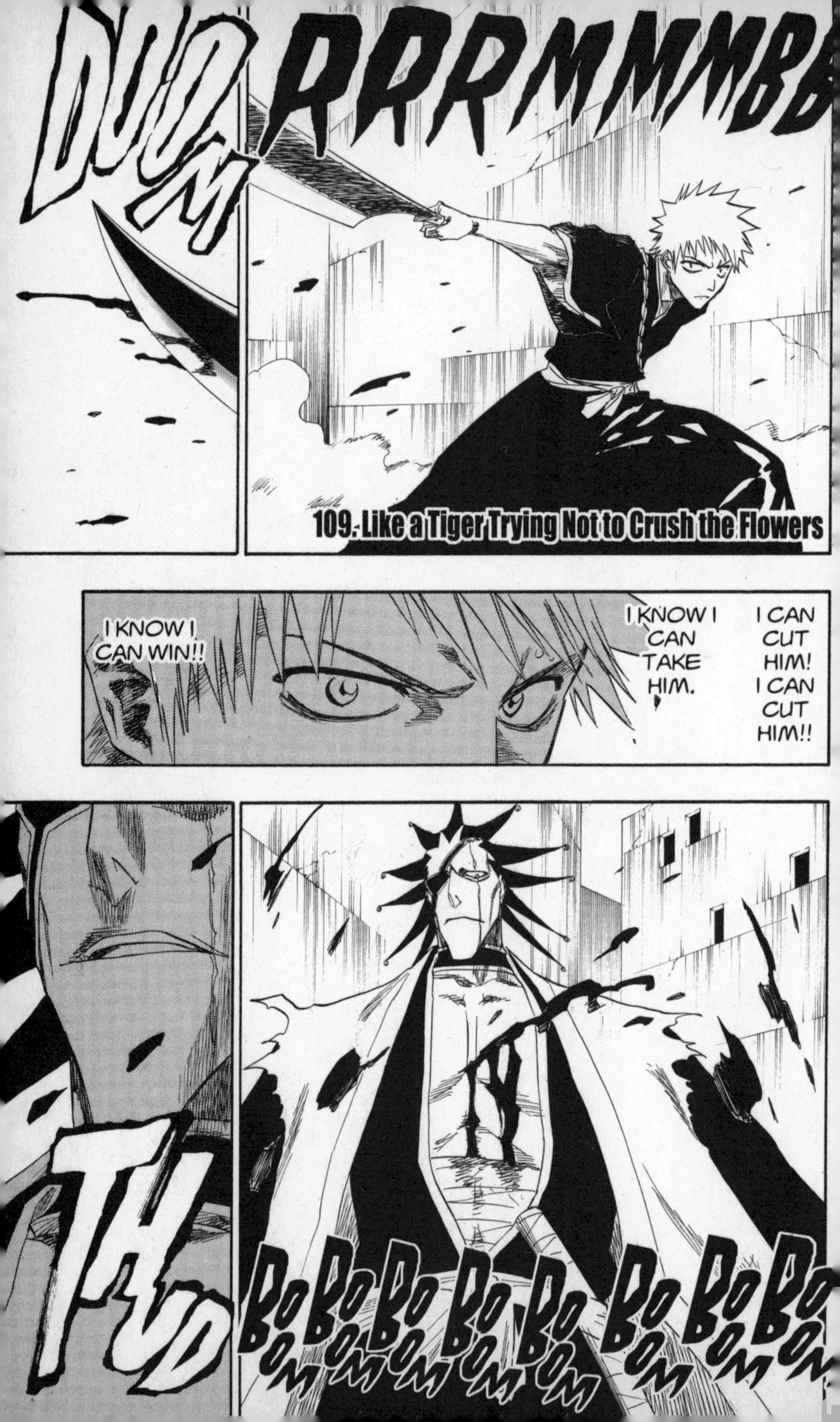
RRRMMMBB
109. Like a Tiger Trying Not to Crush the Flowers
I CAN CUT HIM! I CAN CUT HIM!!
I KNOW I CAN TAKE HIM.
I KNOW I CAN WIN!!

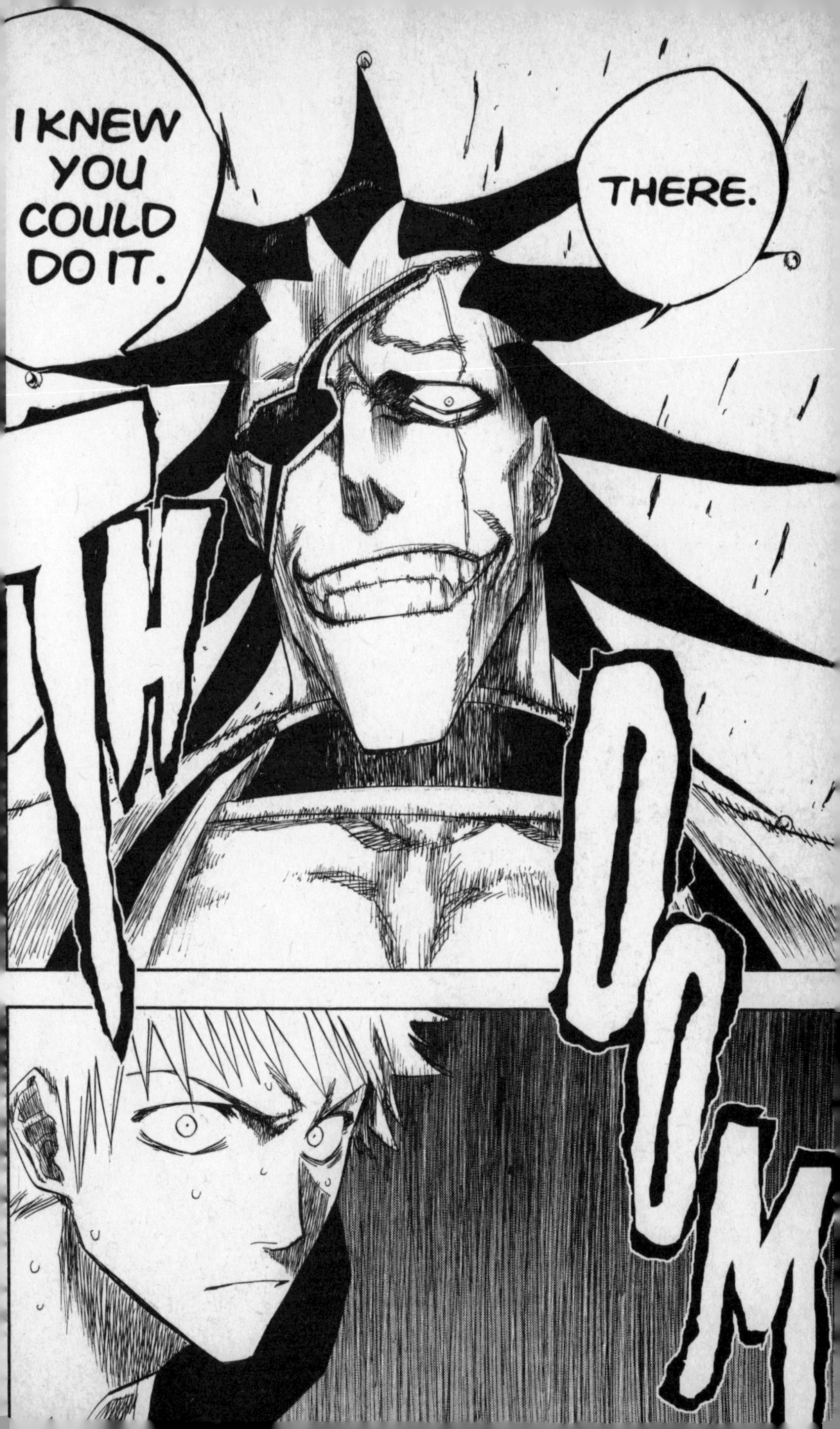
THERE.
I KNEW YOU COULD DO IT.
WHOOM

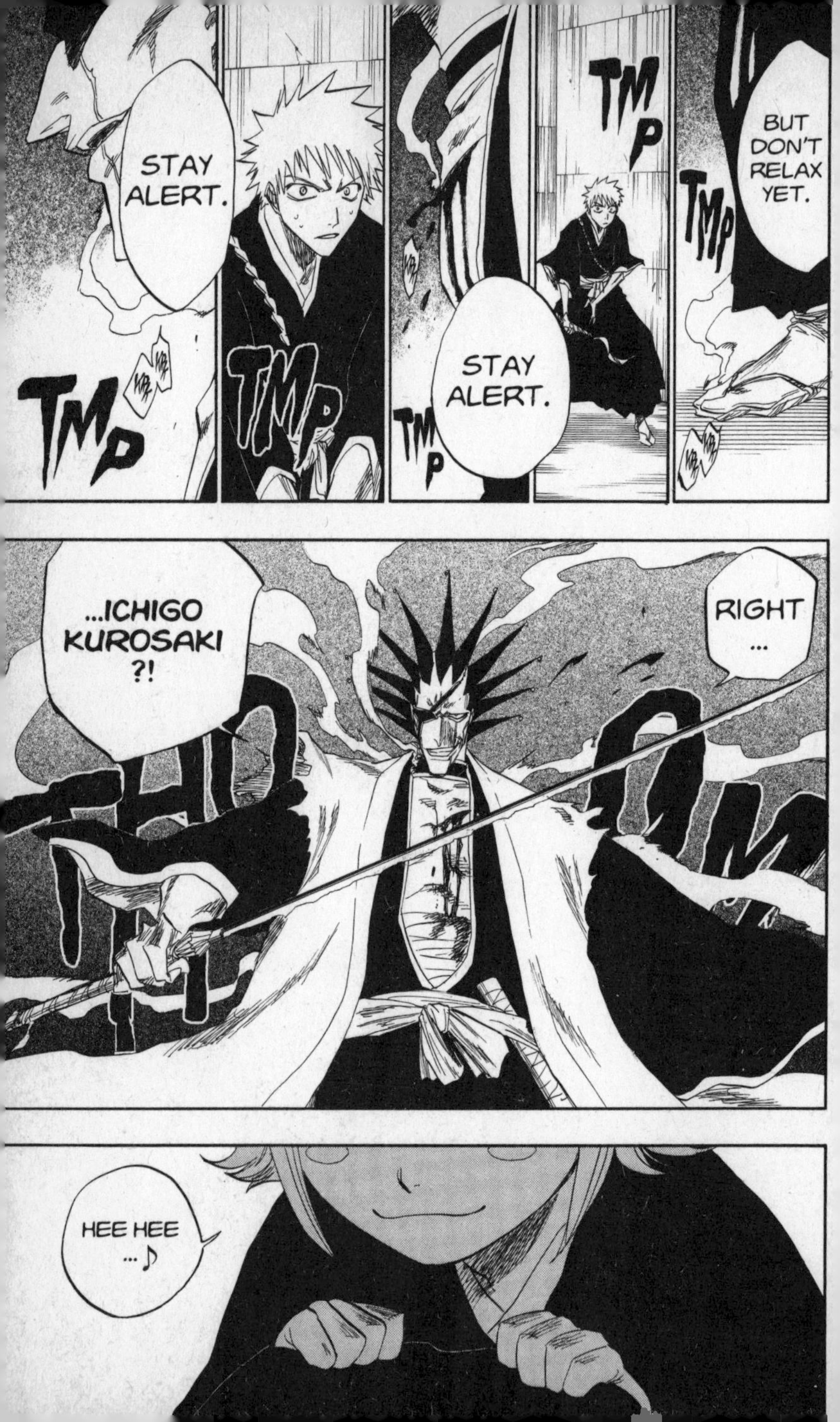
BUT DON'T RELAX YET.
TMP
TMP
TMP
STAY ALERT.
TMP
TMP
STAY ALERT.
TMP
RIGHT ...
...ICHIGO KUROSAKI ?!
HEE HEE ...♪

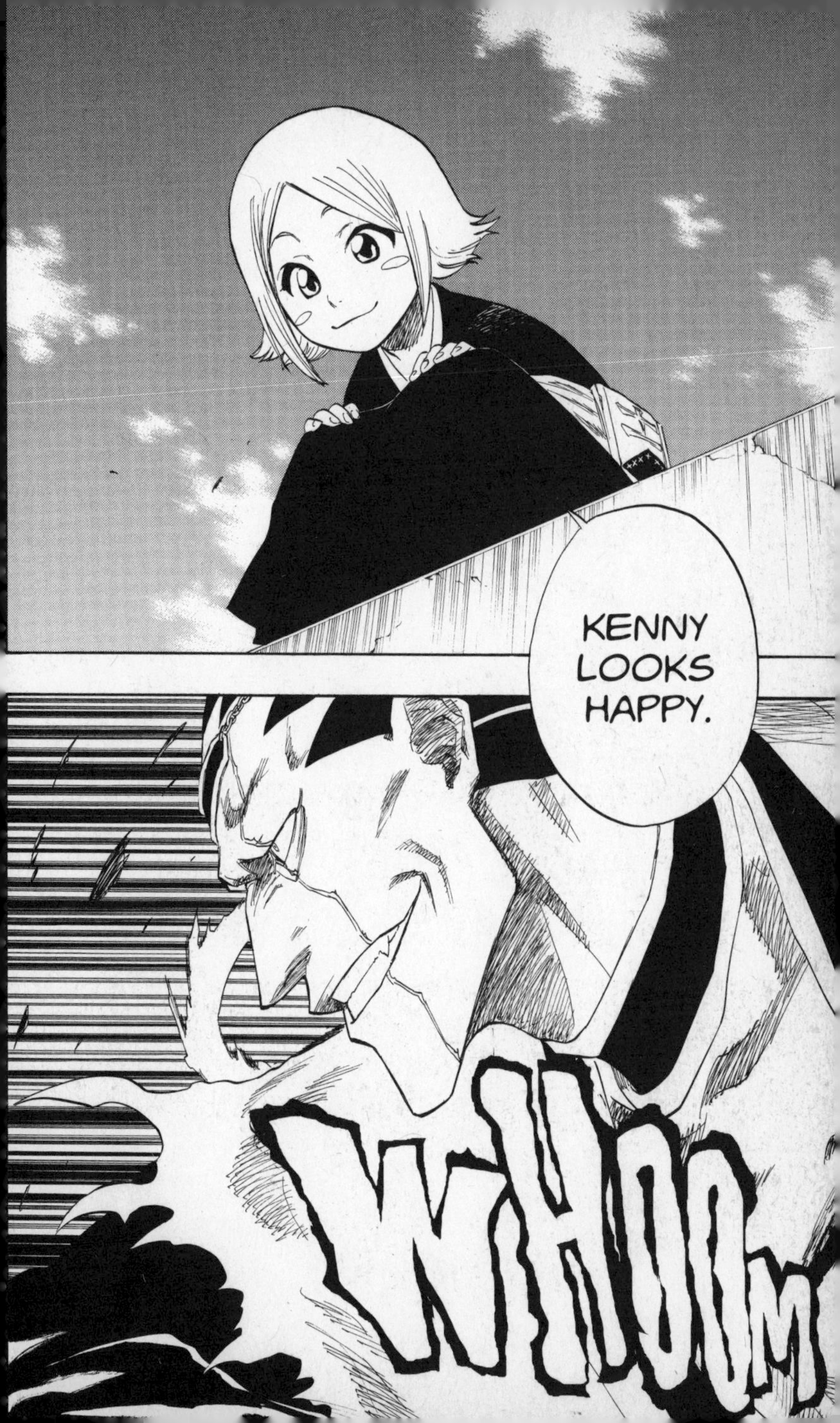
KENNY LOOKS HAPPY.
WHOOM

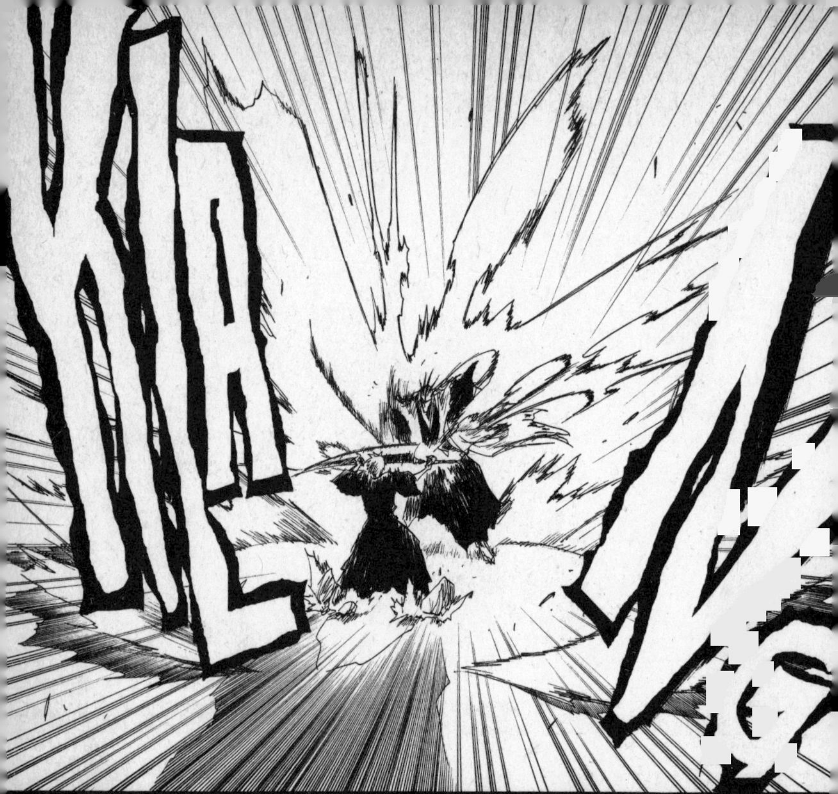

BLEACH

109. Like a Tiger Trying Not to Crush the Flowers

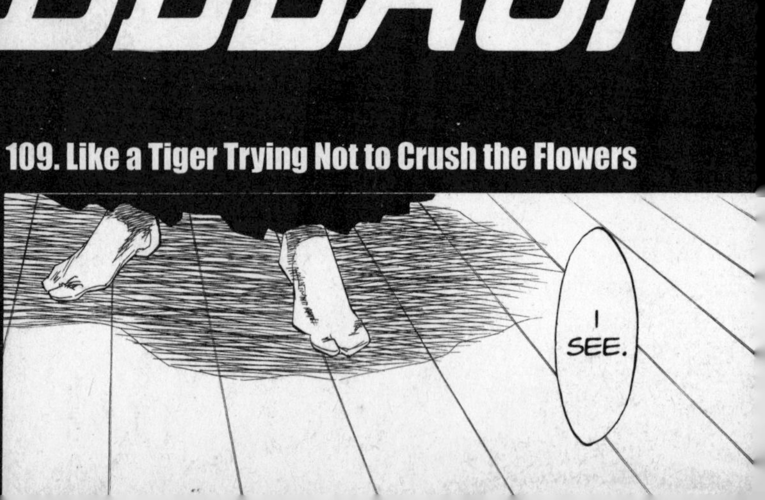
I SEE.

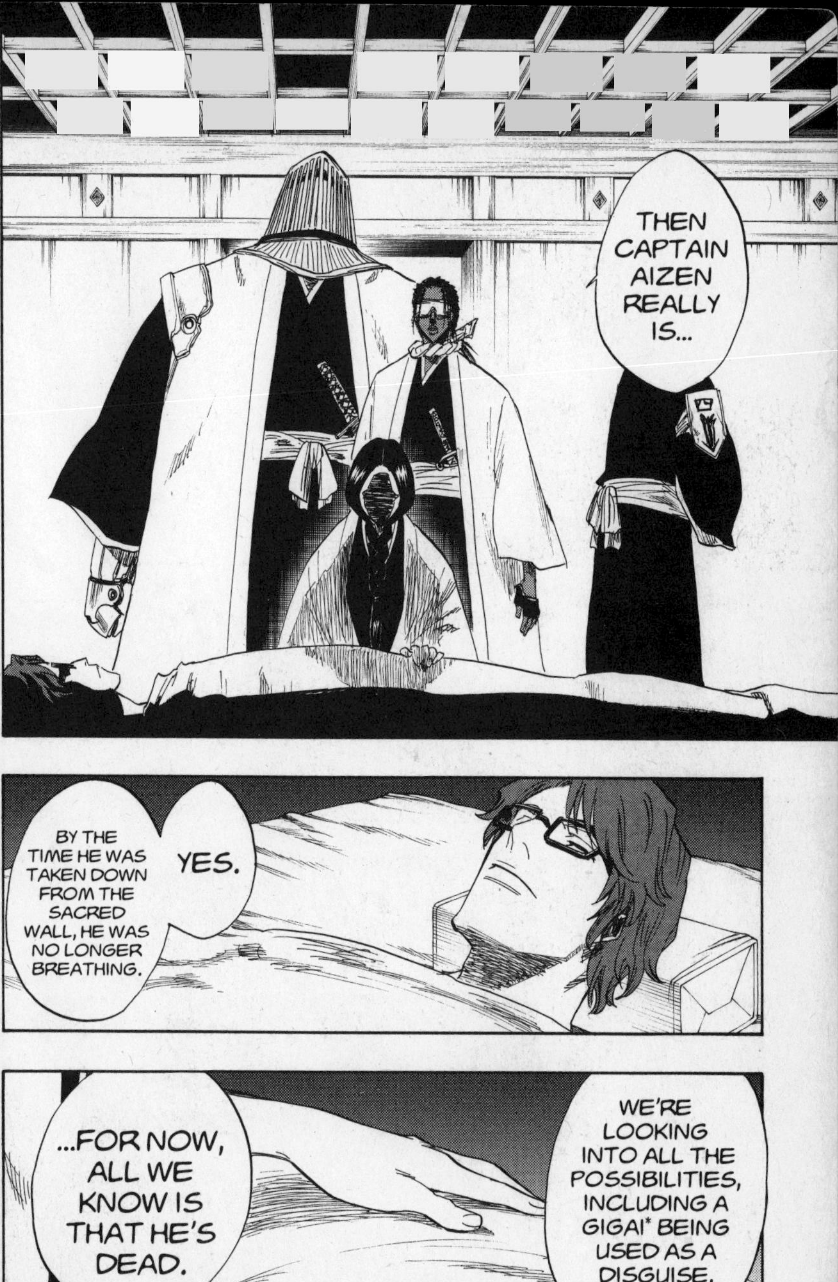
THEN CAPTAIN AIZEN REALLY IS...
YES.
BY THE TIME HE WAS TAKEN DOWN FROM THE SACRED WALL, HE WAS NO LONGER BREATHING.
WE'RE LOOKING INTO ALL THE POSSIBILITIES, INCLUDING A GIGAI* BEING USED AS A DISGUISE, BUT...
...FOR NOW, ALL WE KNOW IS THAT HE'S DEAD.

* A GIGAI IS A TEMPORARY BODY USED BY SOUL REAPERS IN EMERGENCIES.

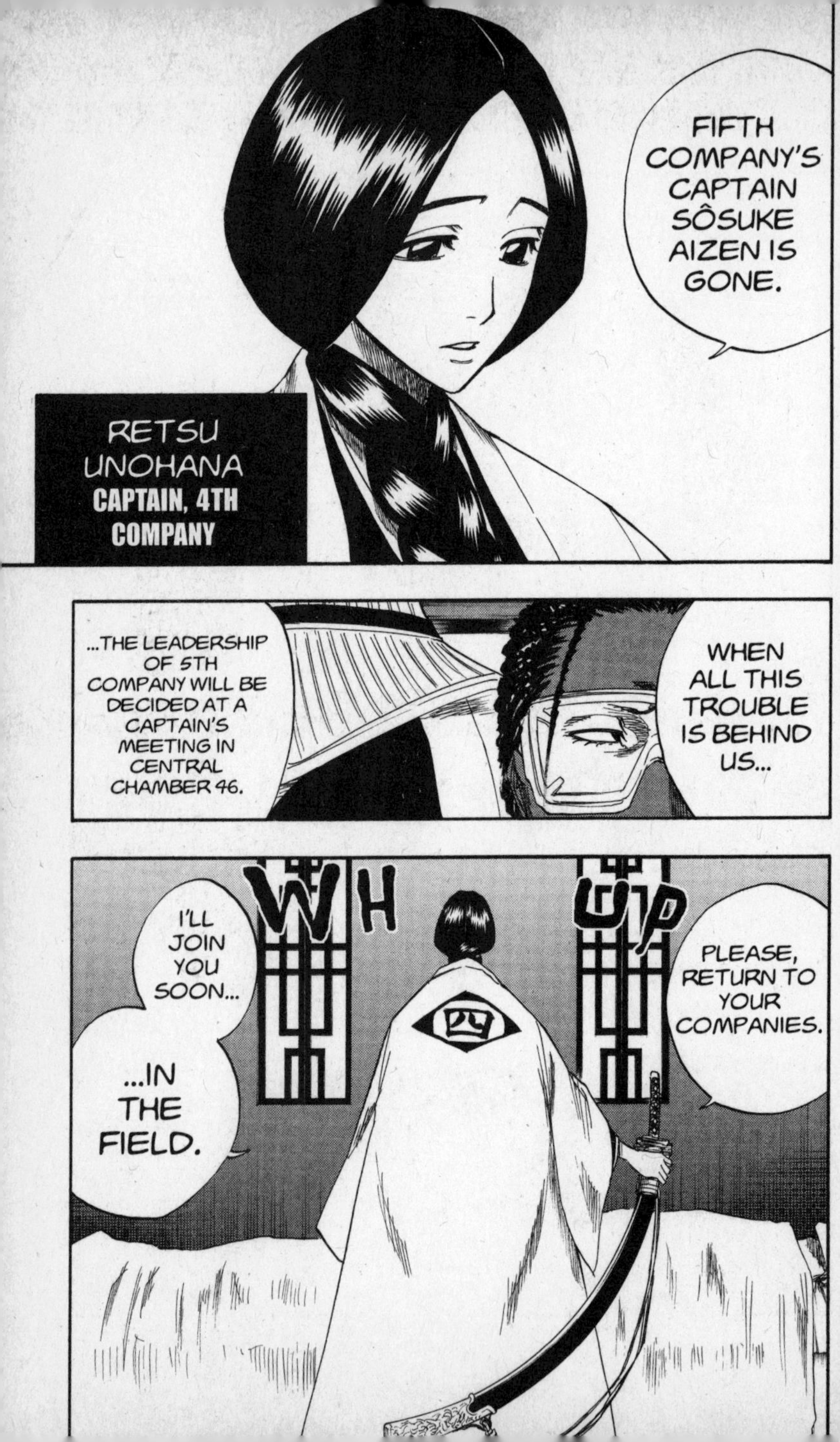
FIFTH COMPANY'S CAPTAIN SÔSUKE AIZEN IS GONE.
RETSU UNOHANA
CAPTAIN, 4TH COMPANY
WHEN ALL THIS TROUBLE IS BEHIND US...
...THE LEADERSHIP OF 5TH COMPANY WILL BE DECIDED AT A CAPTAIN'S MEETING IN CENTRAL CHAMBER 46.
PLEASE, RETURN TO YOUR COMPANIES.
WHUP
I'LL JOIN YOU SOON...
...IN THE FIELD.

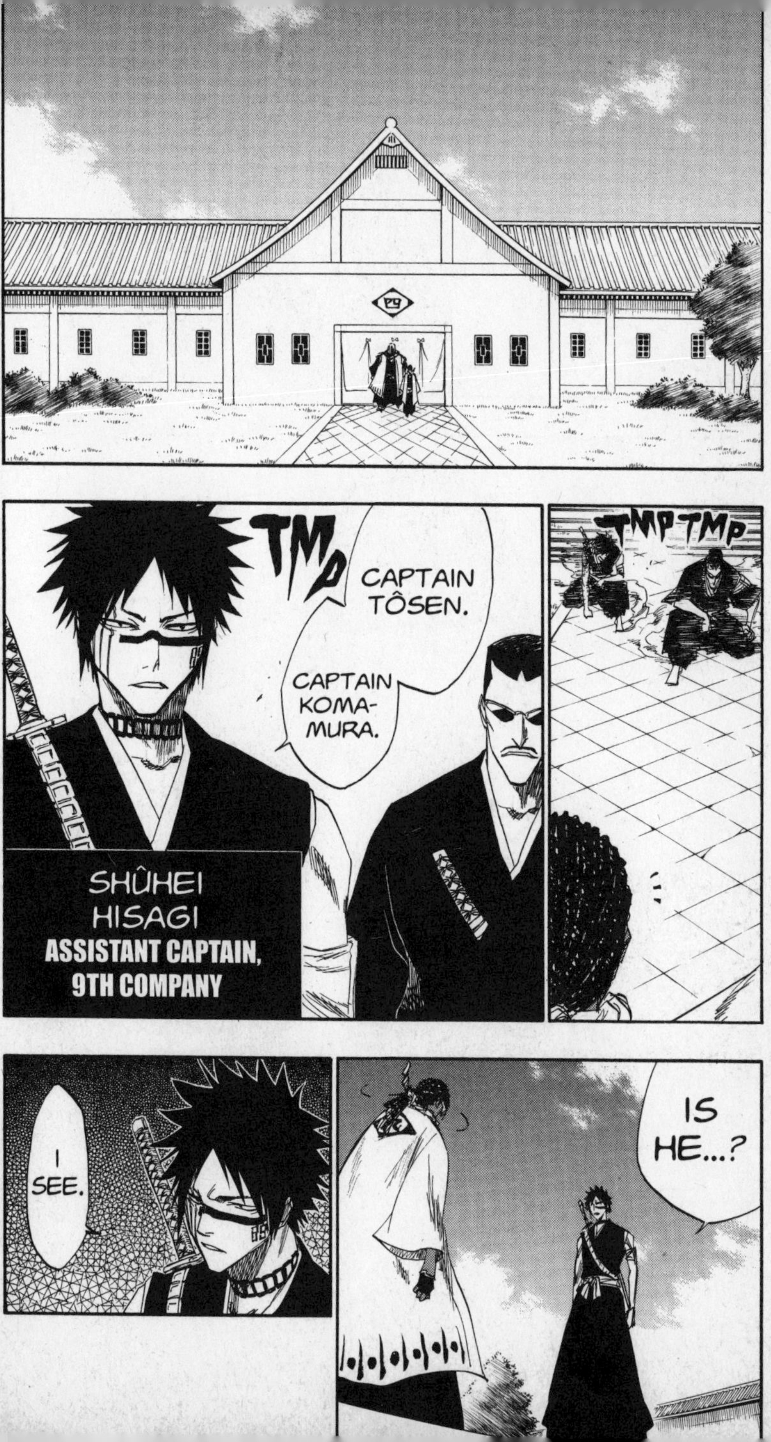
TMP TMP
TMP
CAPTAIN TÔSEN.
CAPTAIN KOMA-MURA.
SHÛHEI HISAGI
ASSISTANT CAPTAIN, 9TH COMPANY
IS HE...?
I SEE.

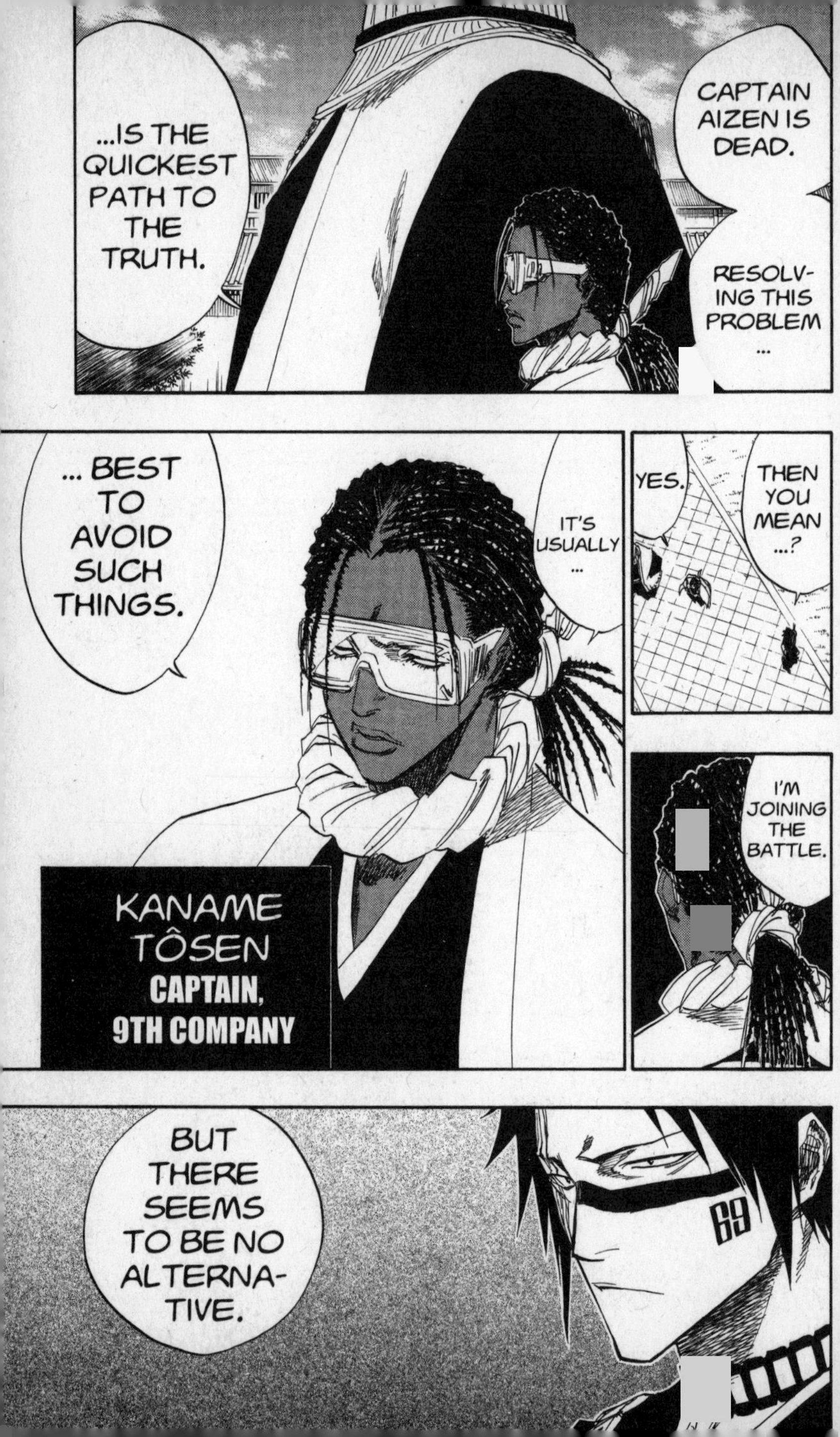
CAPTAIN AIZEN IS DEAD.
RESOLV-ING THIS PROBLEM ...
...IS THE QUICKEST PATH TO THE TRUTH.
THEN YOU MEAN ...?
YES.
I'M JOINING THE BATTLE.
IT'S USUALLY ...
... BEST TO AVOID SUCH THINGS.
KANAME TÔSEN CAPTAIN, 9TH COMPANY
BUT THERE SEEMS TO BE NO ALTERNA-TIVE.

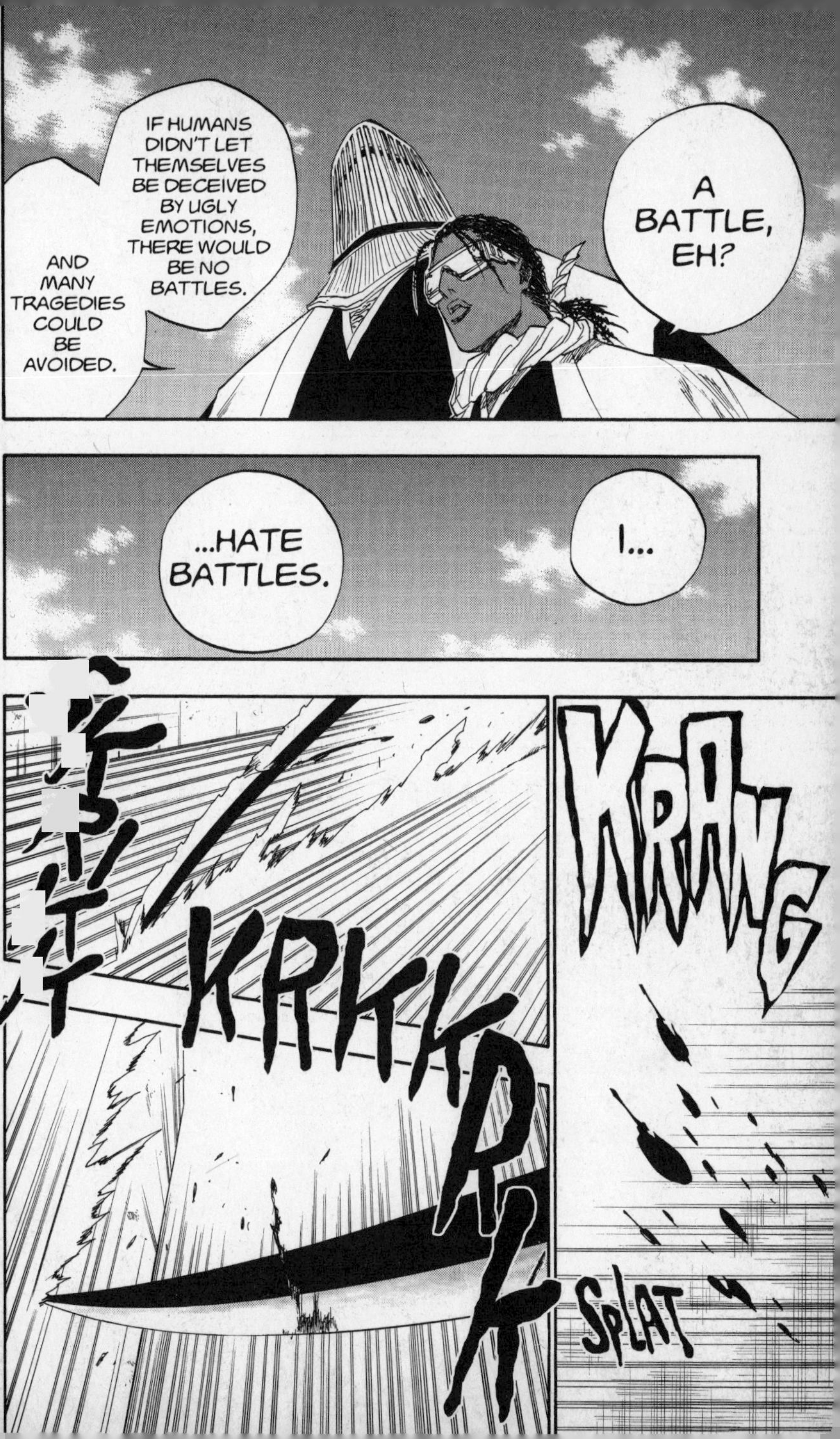
A BATTLE, EH?
IF HUMANS DIDN'T LET THEMSELVES BE DECEIVED BY UGLY EMOTIONS, THERE WOULD BE NO BATTLES.
AND MANY TRAGEDIES COULD BE AVOIDED.
I...
...HATE BATTLES.
KRANG
SPLAT
KRKKK

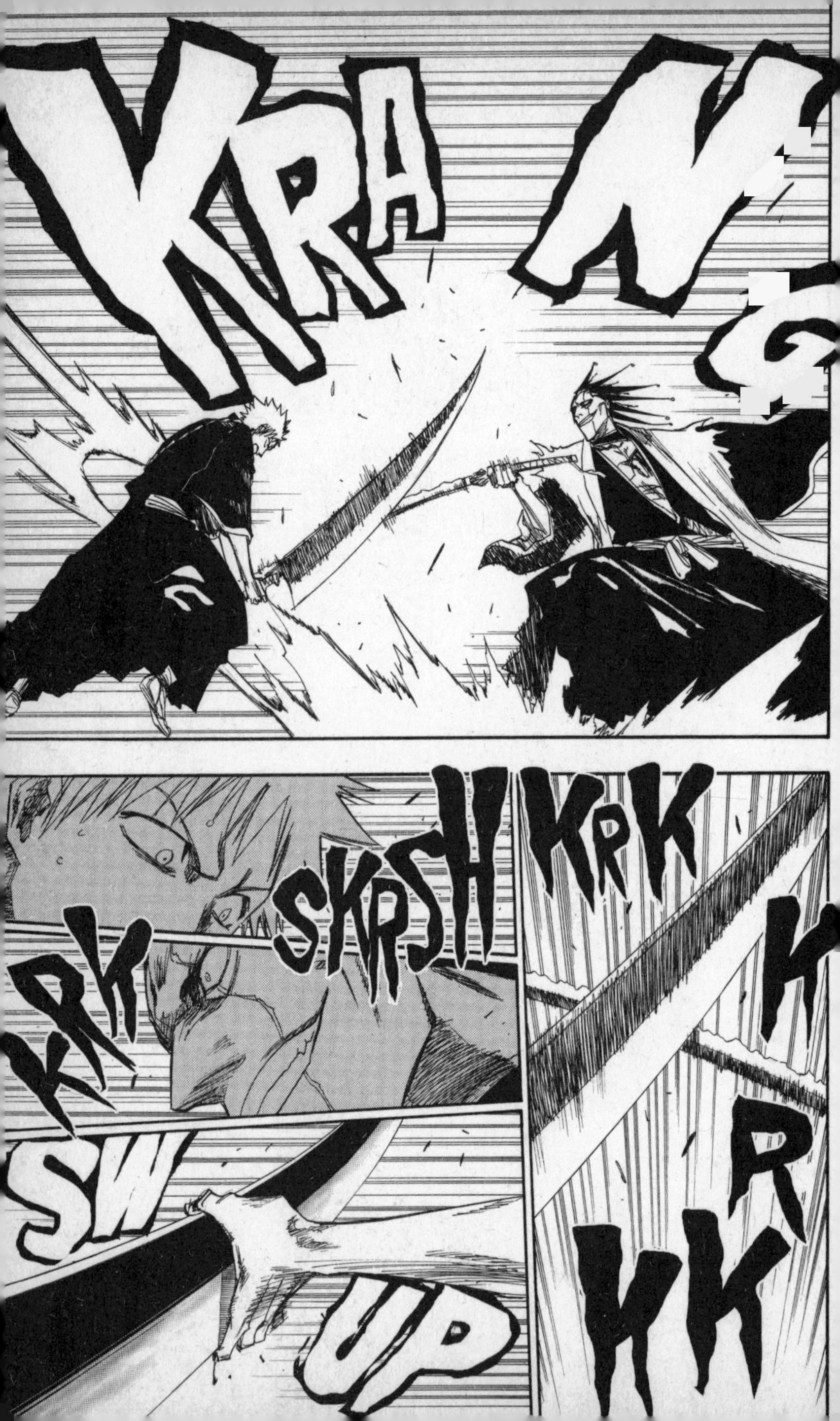
KRA
KRK
K
R
KK
SKRSH
KRK
SW
UP

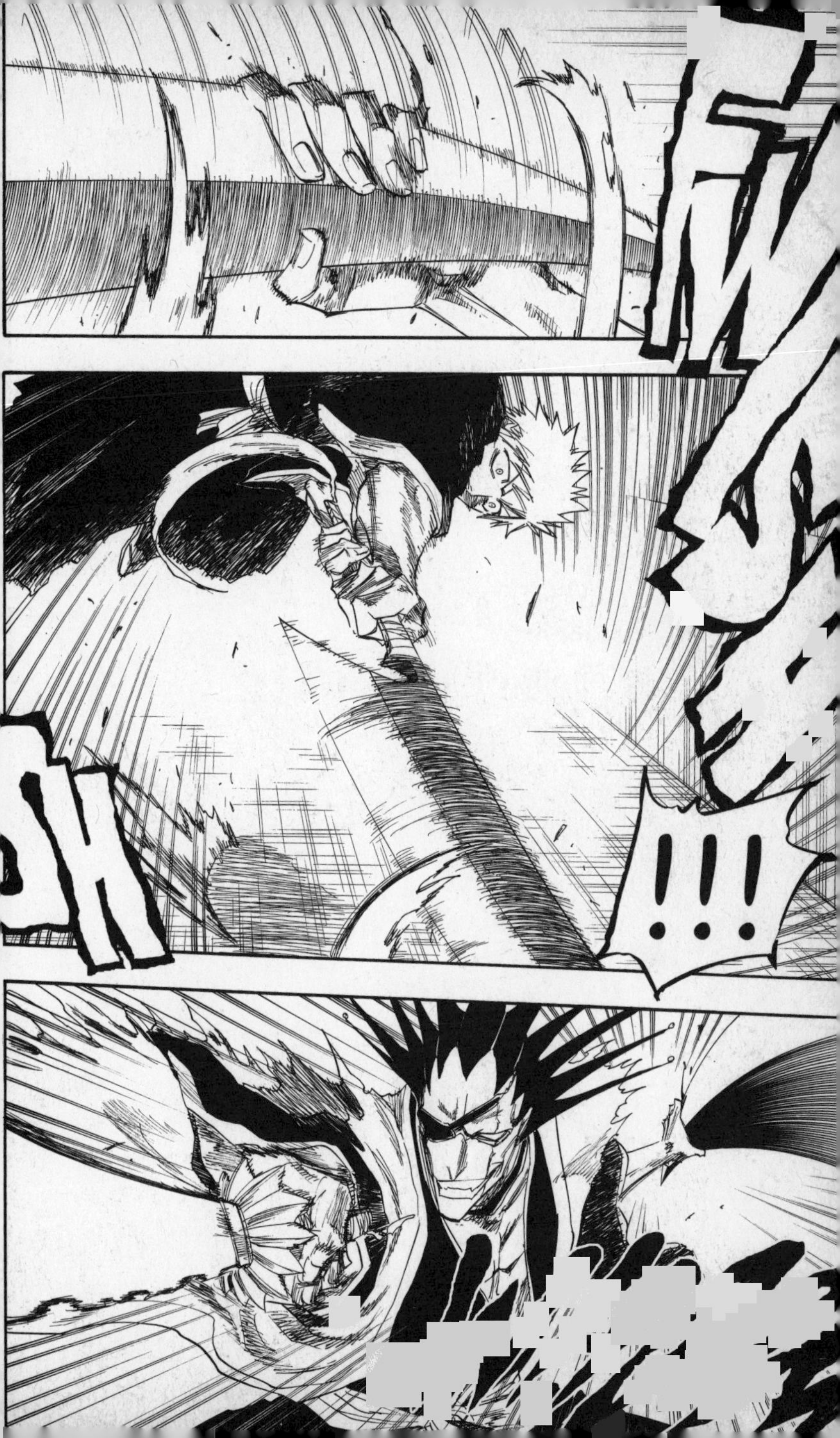
!!!

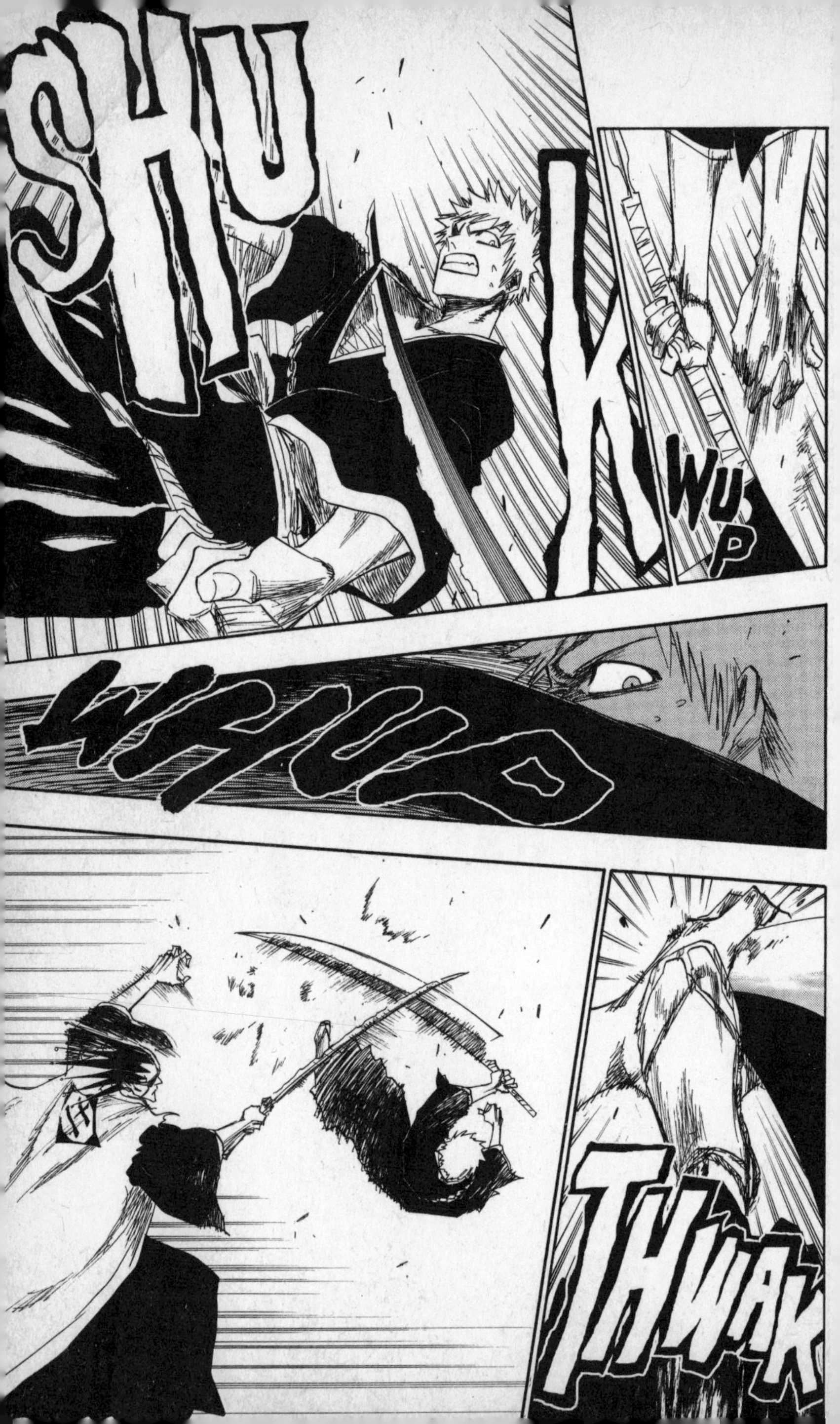
WUP
SHUK
WHUD
THWAK

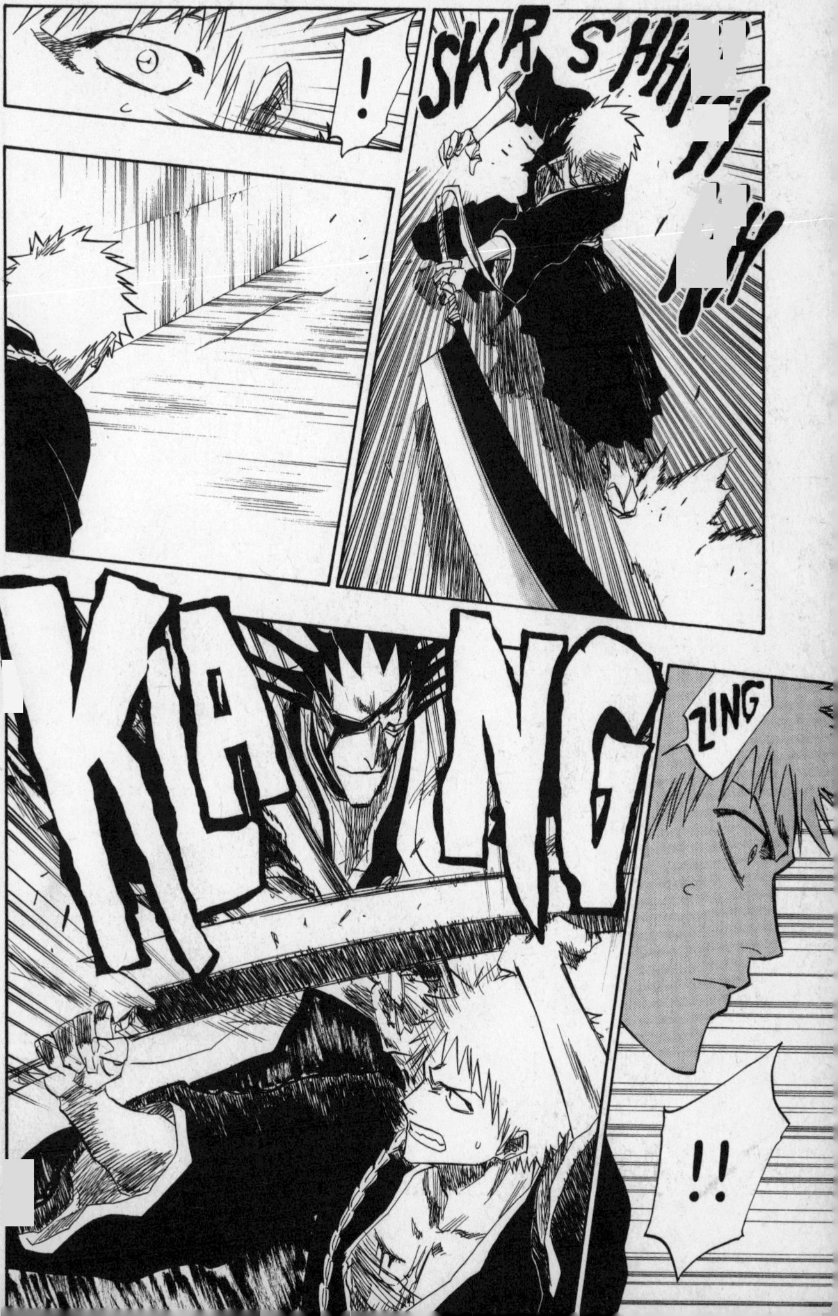
SKRSHH
!
ZING
!!
KLANG

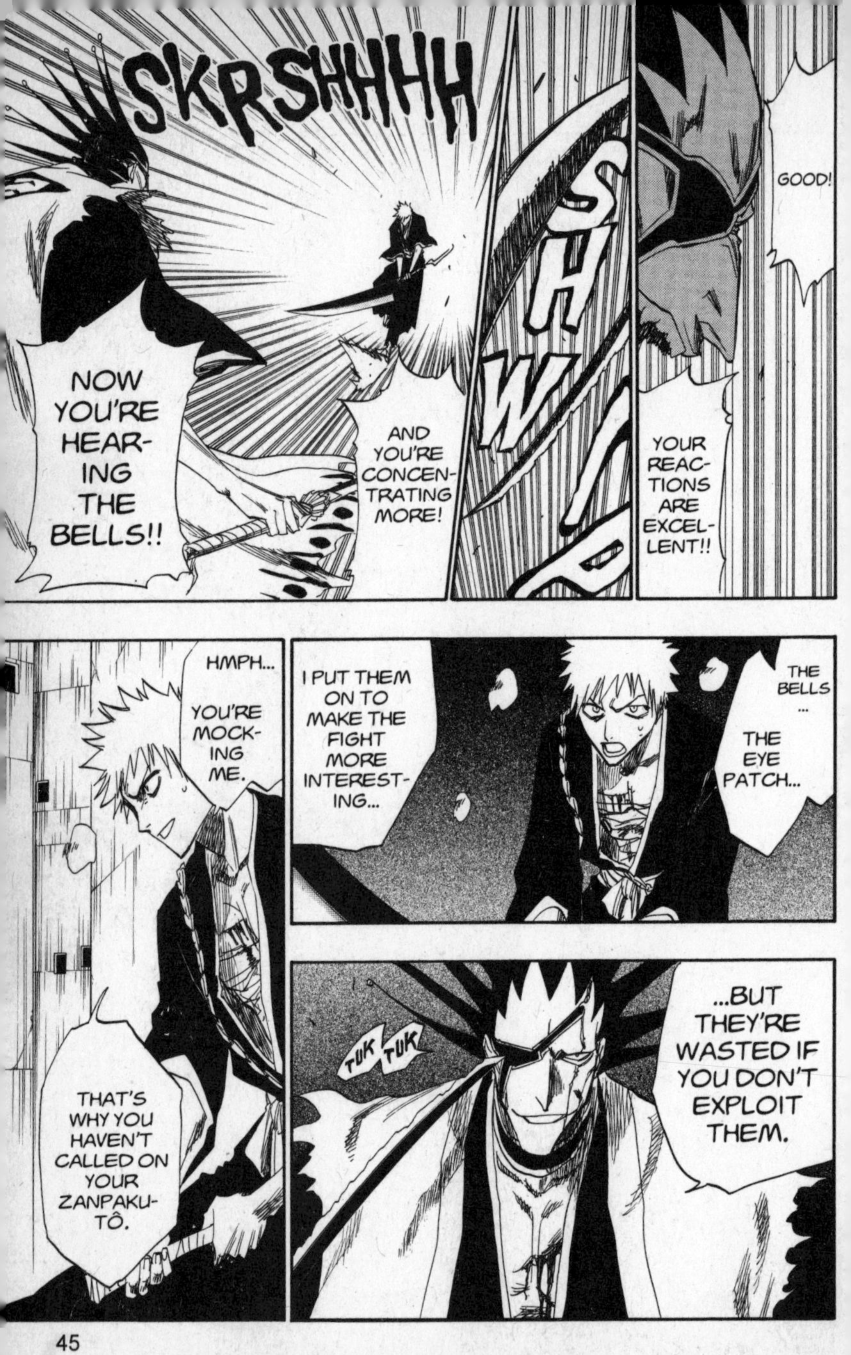
GOOD!
YOUR REACTIONS ARE EXCELLENT!!
SHWIP
SKRSHHHH
NOW YOU'RE HEARING THE BELLS!!
AND YOU'RE CONCENTRATING MORE!
THE BELLS... THE EYE PATCH...
I PUT THEM ON TO MAKE THE FIGHT MORE INTERESTING...
...BUT THEY'RE WASTED IF YOU DON'T EXPLOIT THEM.
TUK TUK
HMPH...
YOU'RE MOCKING ME.
THAT'S WHY YOU HAVEN'T CALLED ON YOUR ZANPAKU-TÔ.

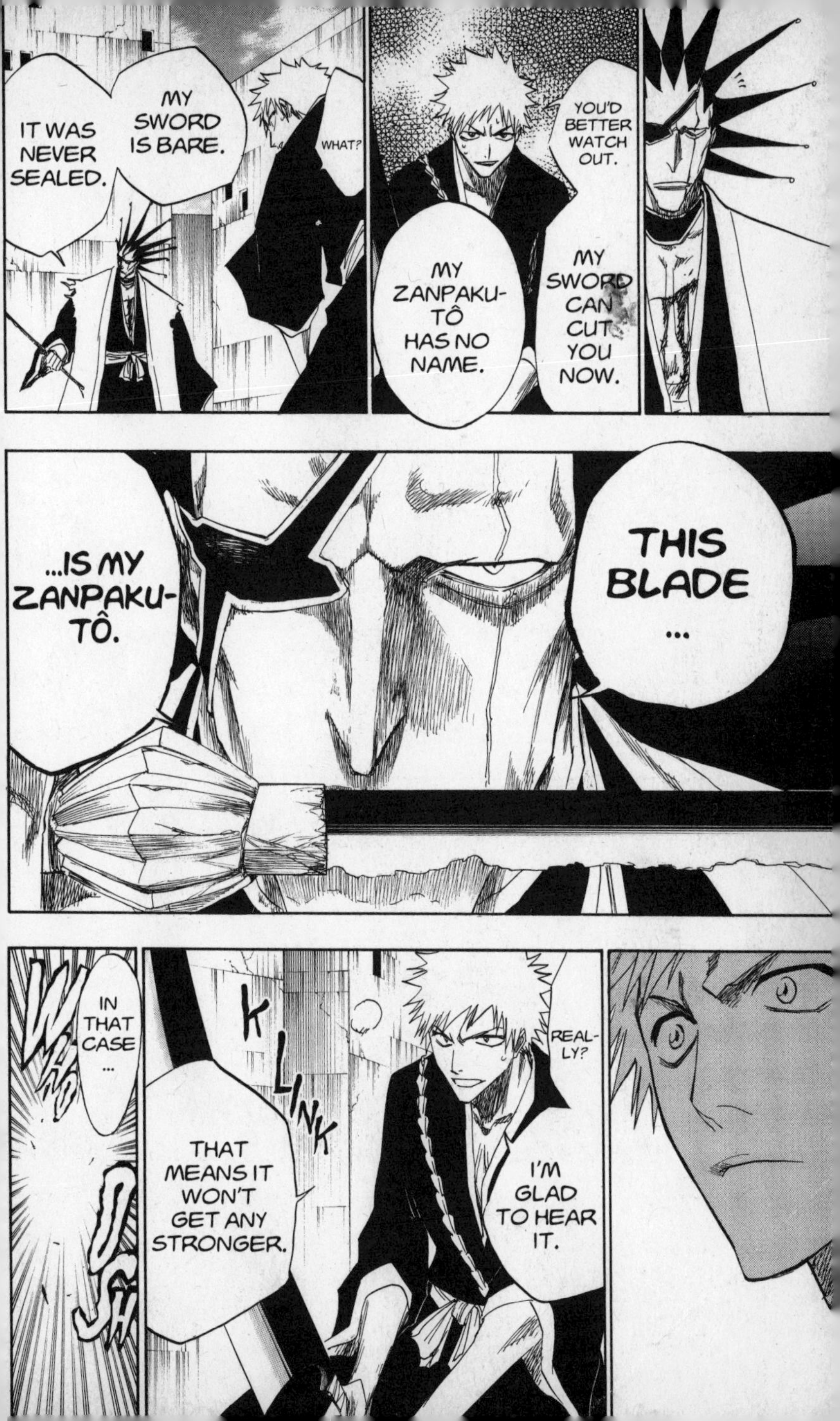
YOU'D BETTER WATCH OUT.
MY SWORD CAN CUT YOU NOW.
MY ZANPAKU-TÔ HAS NO NAME.
WHAT?
MY SWORD IS BARE.
IT WAS NEVER SEALED.
THIS BLADE ...
...IS MY ZANPAKU-TÔ.
REAL-LY?
I'M GLAD TO HEAR IT.
KLINK
THAT MEANS IT WON'T GET ANY STRONGER.
IN THAT CASE ...
WHOOSH

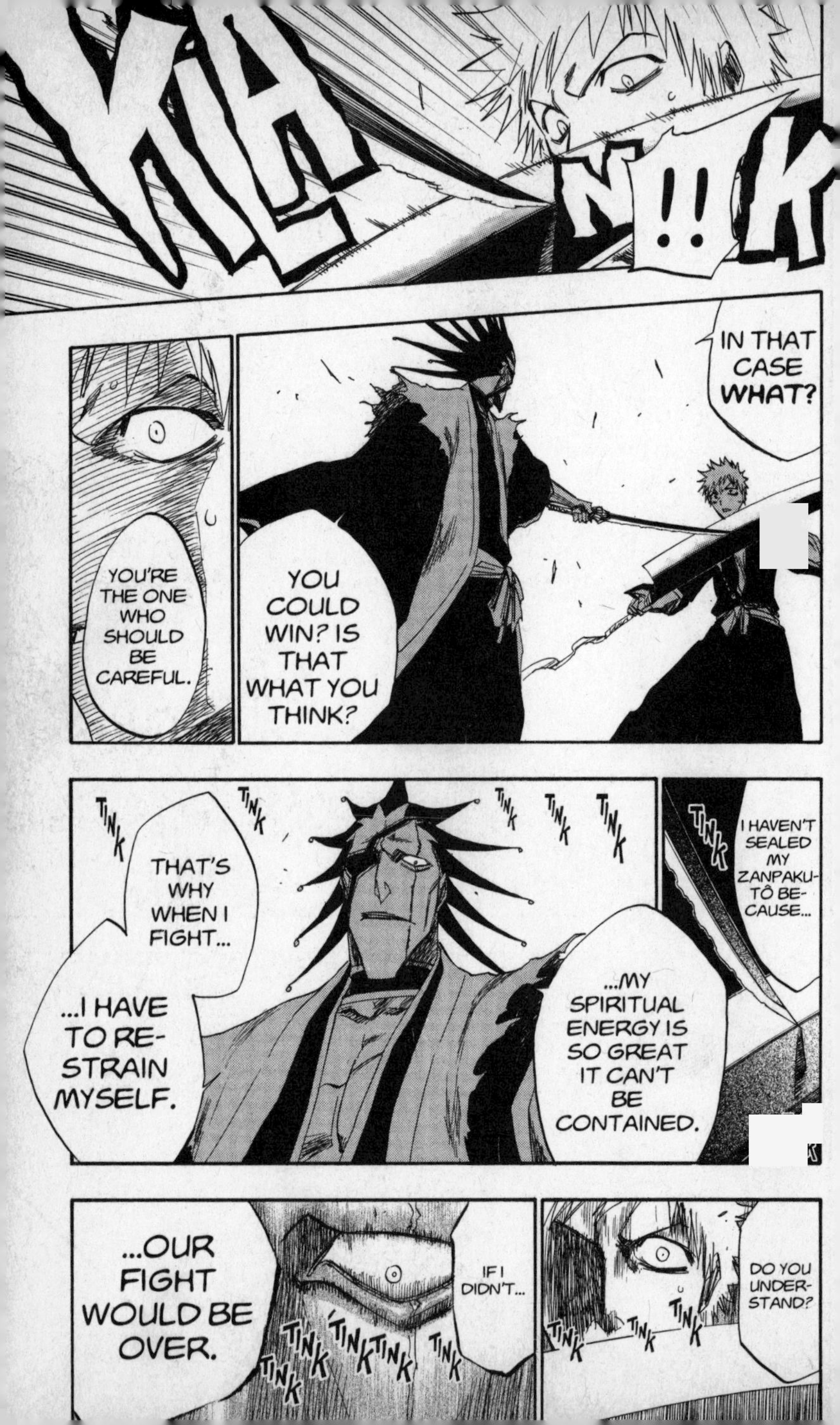
IN THAT CASE WHAT?
YOU COULD WIN? IS THAT WHAT YOU THINK?
YOU'RE THE ONE WHO SHOULD BE CAREFUL.
I HAVEN'T SEALED MY ZANPAKU-TÔ BE-CAUSE...
...MY SPIRITUAL ENERGY IS SO GREAT IT CAN'T BE CONTAINED.
THAT'S WHY WHEN I FIGHT...
...I HAVE TO RE-STRAIN MYSELF.
DO YOU UNDERSTAND?
IF I DIDN'T...
...OUR FIGHT WOULD BE OVER.

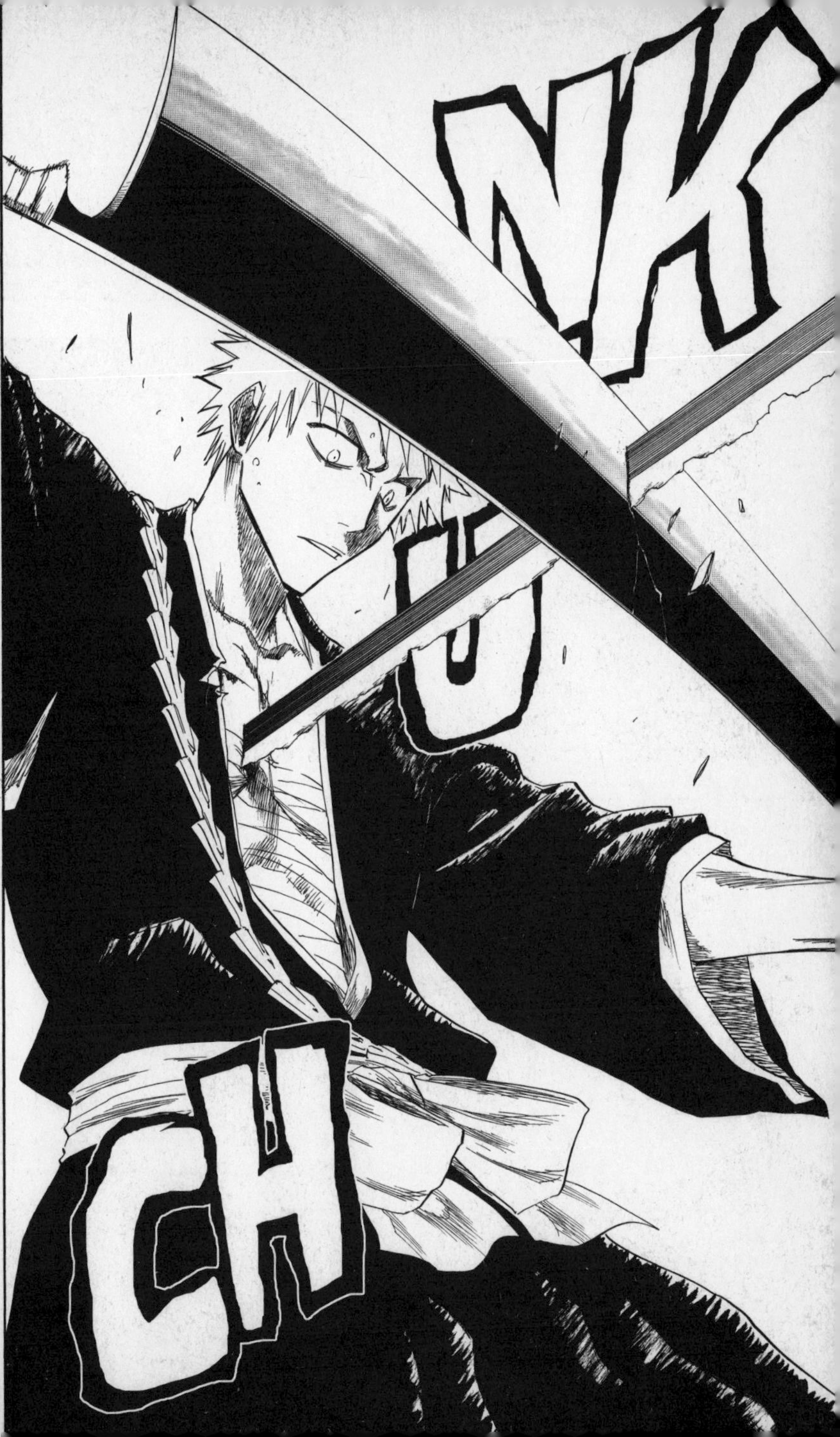
CHUNK

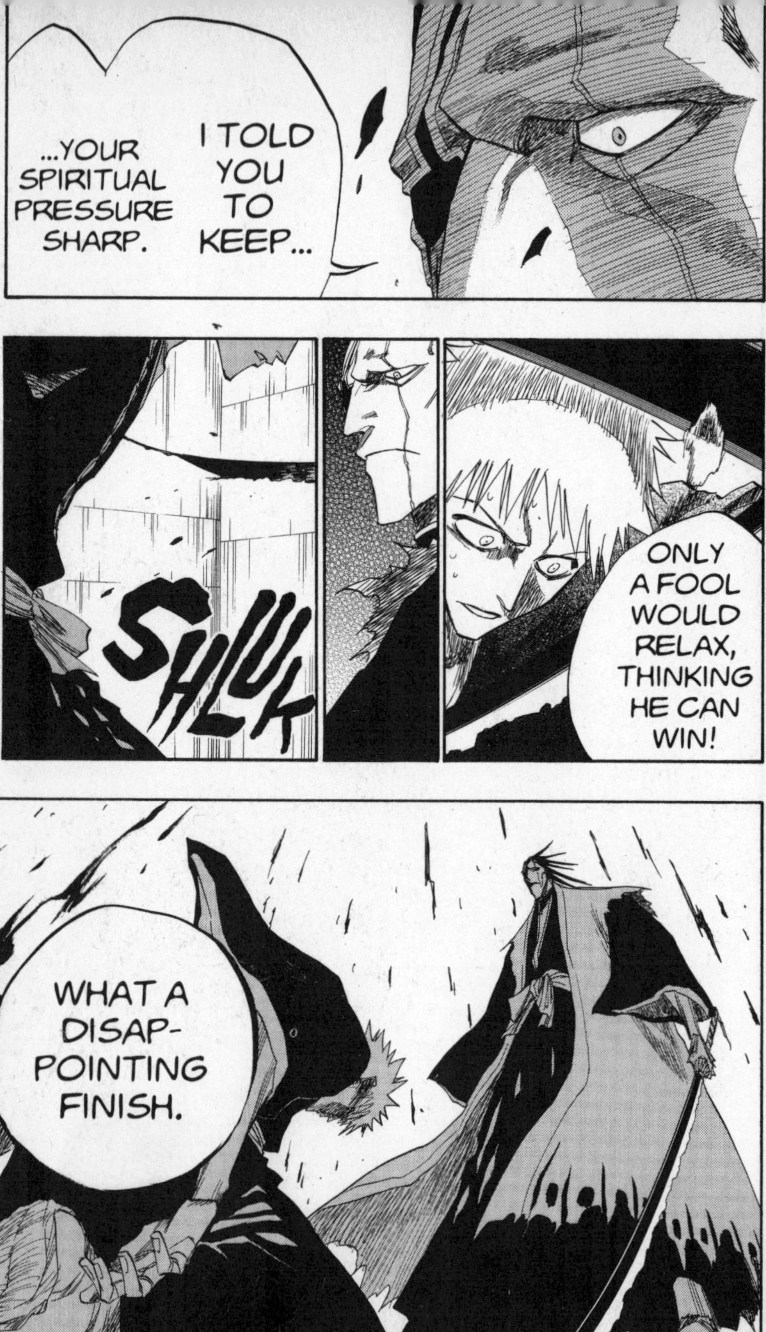
I TOLD YOU TO KEEP...
...YOUR SPIRITUAL PRESSURE SHARP.
ONLY A FOOL WOULD RELAX, THINKING HE CAN WIN!
SHLUK
WHAT A DISAP-POINTING FINISH.

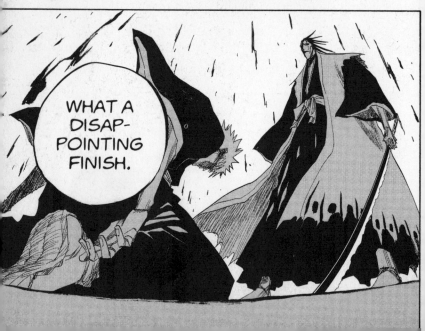

HELLO EVERYBODY, I'M YASOCHIKA IEMURA, THIRD SEAT OF 4TH COMPANY, WHO MANY SAY IS BETTER LOOKING WITHOUT GLASSES!

WITH PEN IN HAND, I EXPRESS THE ANGUISH OF MIDDLE MANAGEMENT PERSONNEL IN THE FORM OF A DAILY CLINICAL LOG. I HOPE YOU WILL READ THIS ALL THE WAY TO THE END.

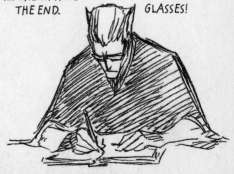

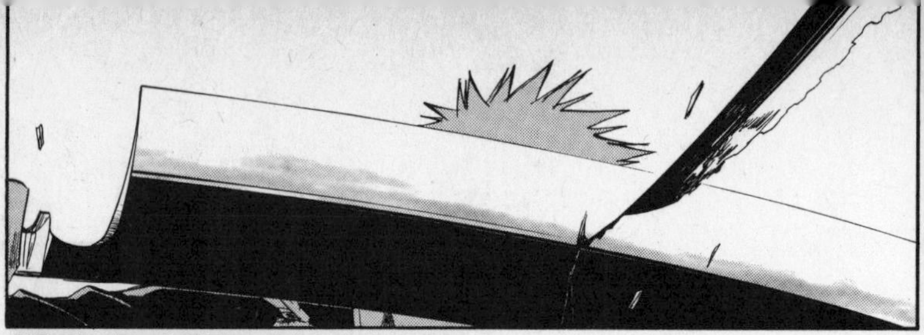

110. The Dark Side of the Universe

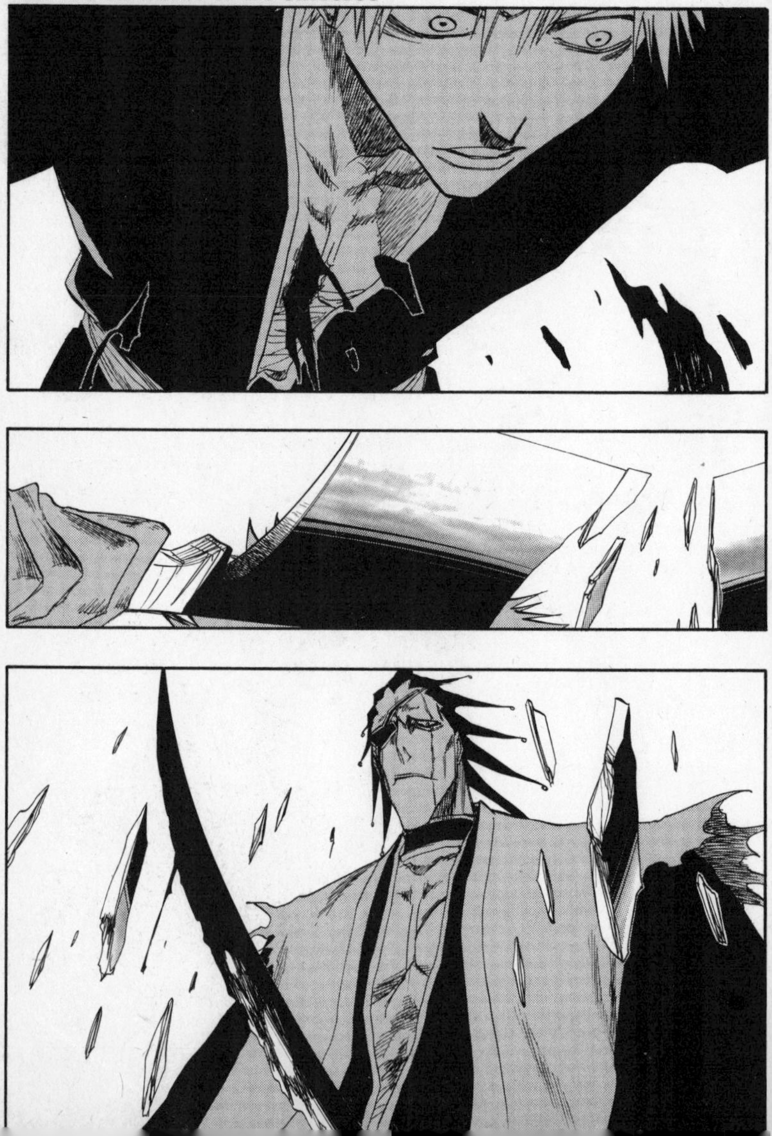

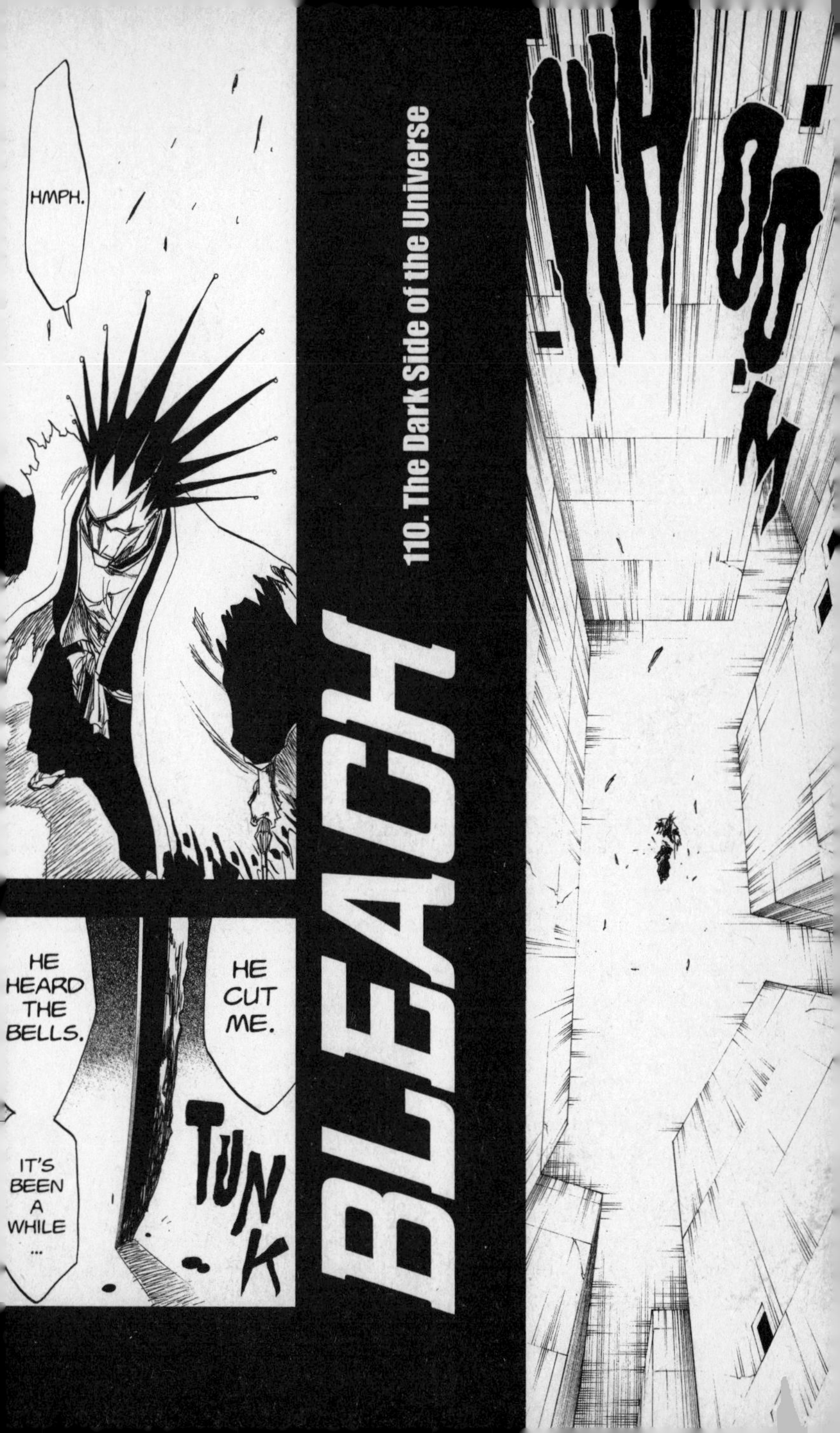
WHOOM
BLEACH
110. The Dark Side of the Universe
HMPH.
HE CUT ME.
TUNK
HE HEARD THE BELLS.
IT'S BEEN A WHILE ...

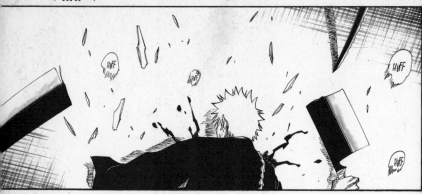

HUFF

HUFF

HUFF

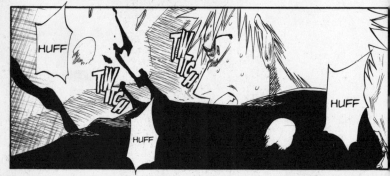

HUFF

TWITCH

TWITCH

HUFF

HUFF

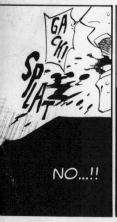

GA CK!

SP LA

NO...!!

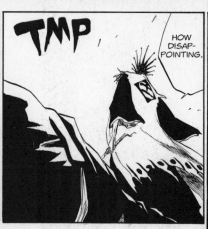

TMP

HOW DISAP-POINTING.

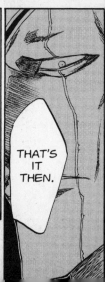

THAT'S IT THEN.

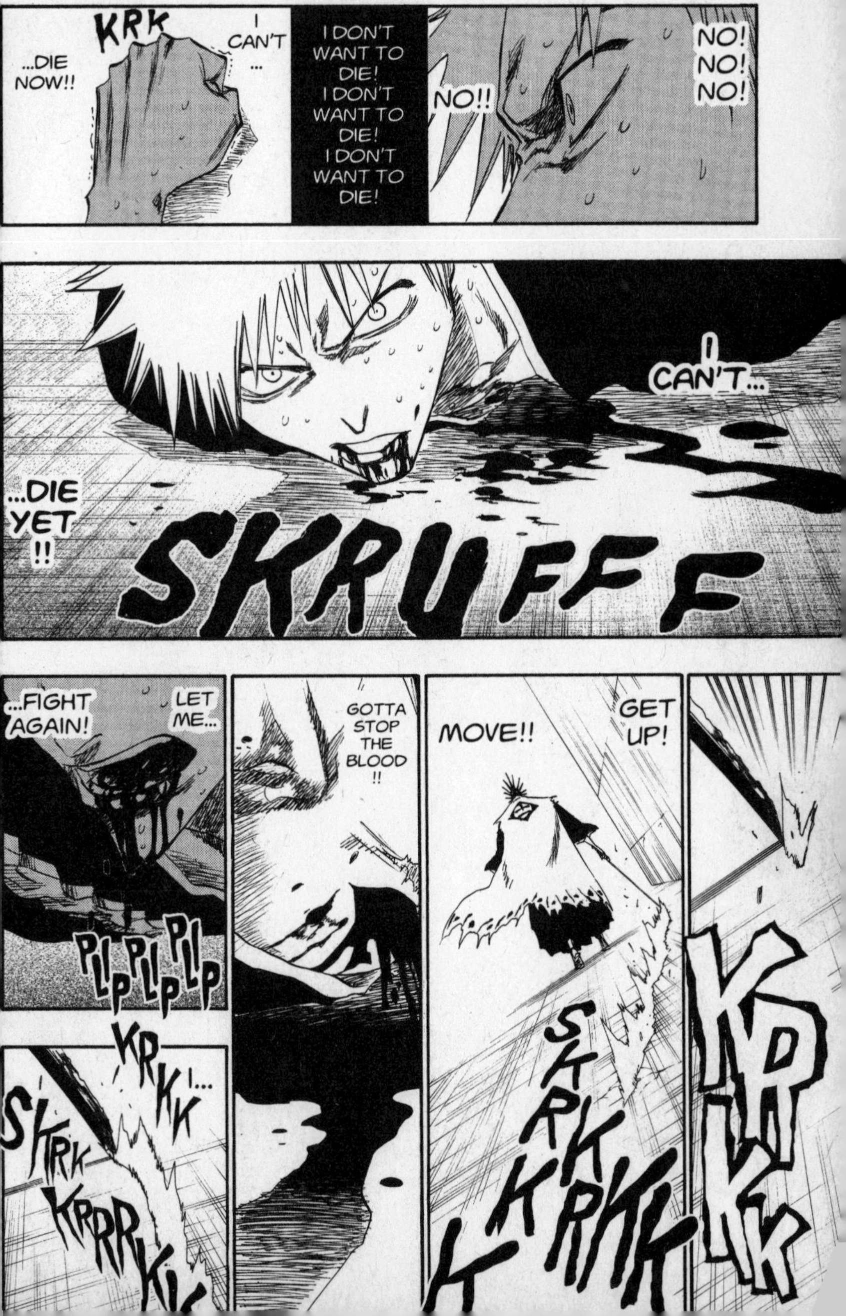
NO! NO! NO!
NO!!
I DON'T WANT TO DIE! I DON'T WANT TO DIE! I DON'T WANT TO DIE!
I CAN'T...
KRK
...DIE NOW!!
I CAN'T...
SKRUFFF
...DIE YET!!
GET UP!
MOVE!!
SKRK KRK KRKK
GOTTA STOP THE BLOOD!!
LET ME...
...FIGHT AGAIN!
PLIP PLIP PLIP
I...
KRKK
SKRK KRRRK

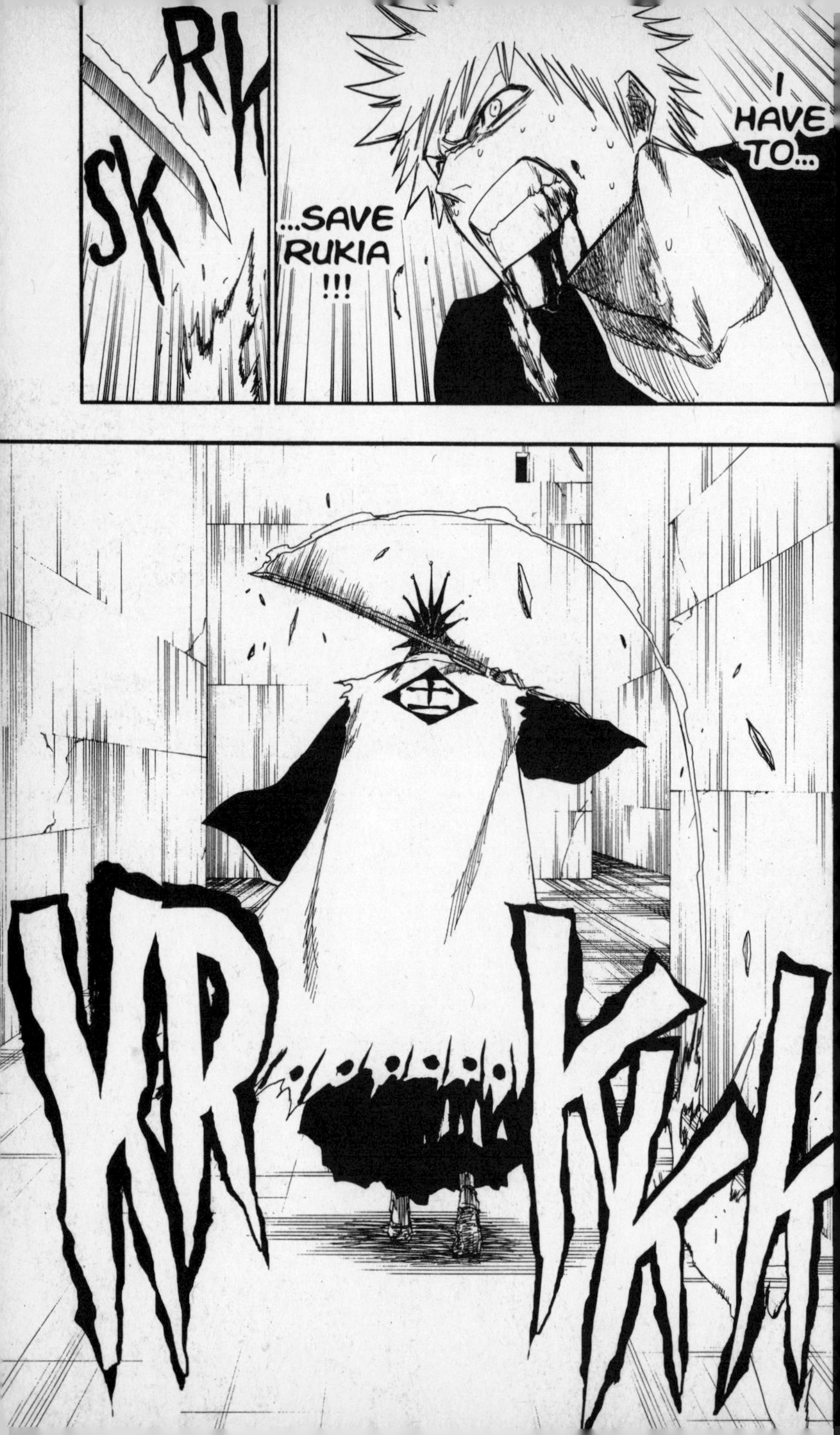
I HAVE TO...
...SAVE RUKIA!!!

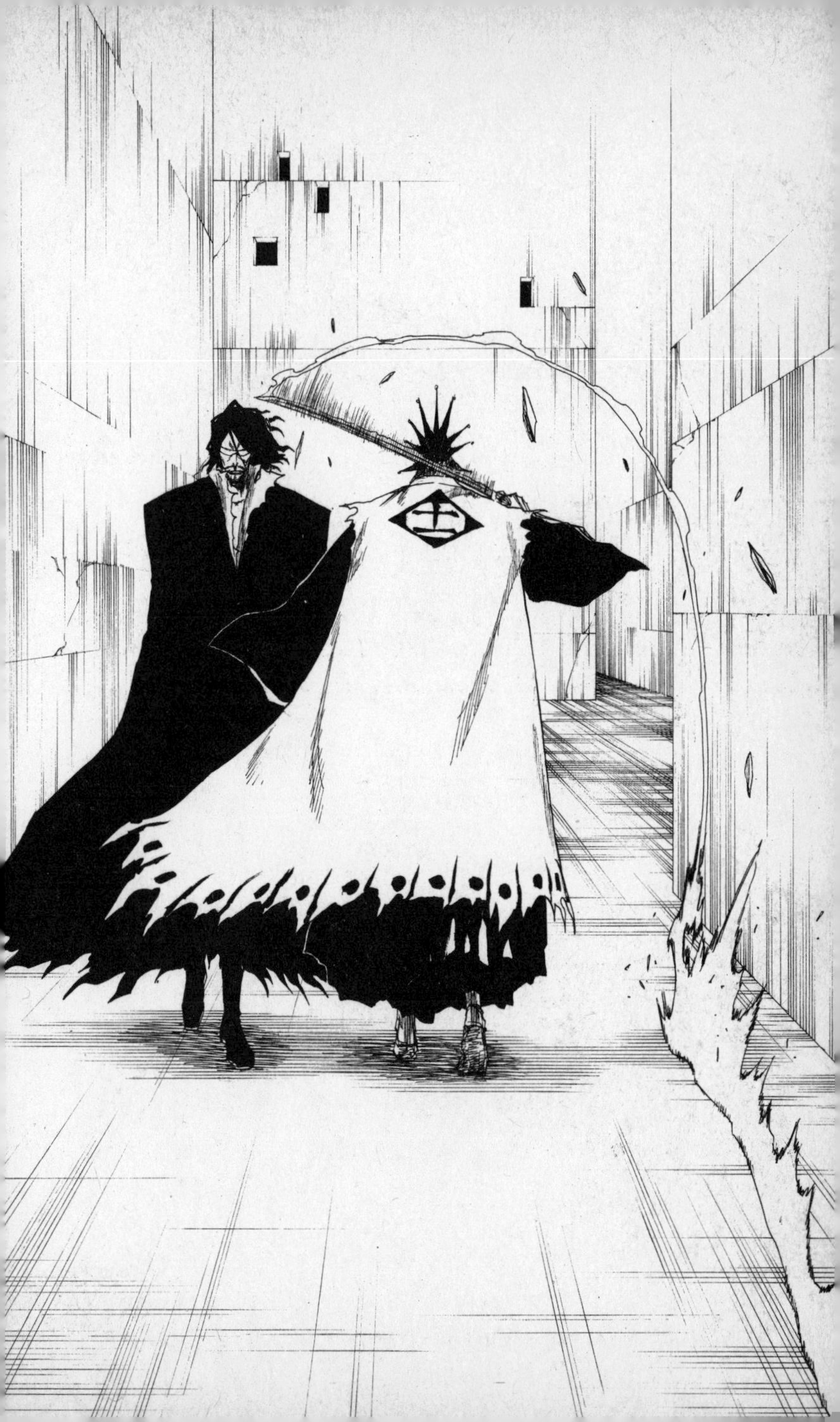

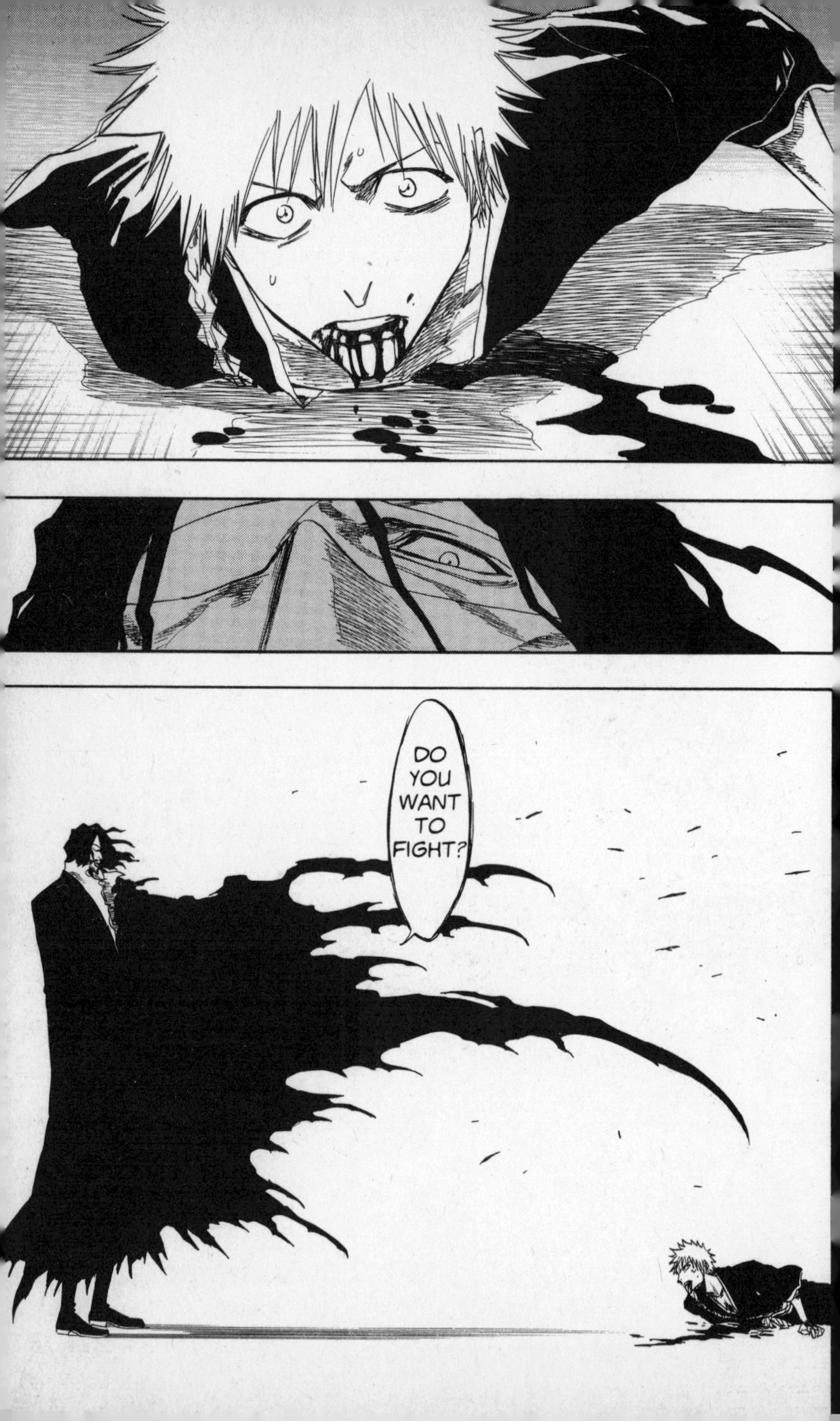
DO YOU WANT TO FIGHT?

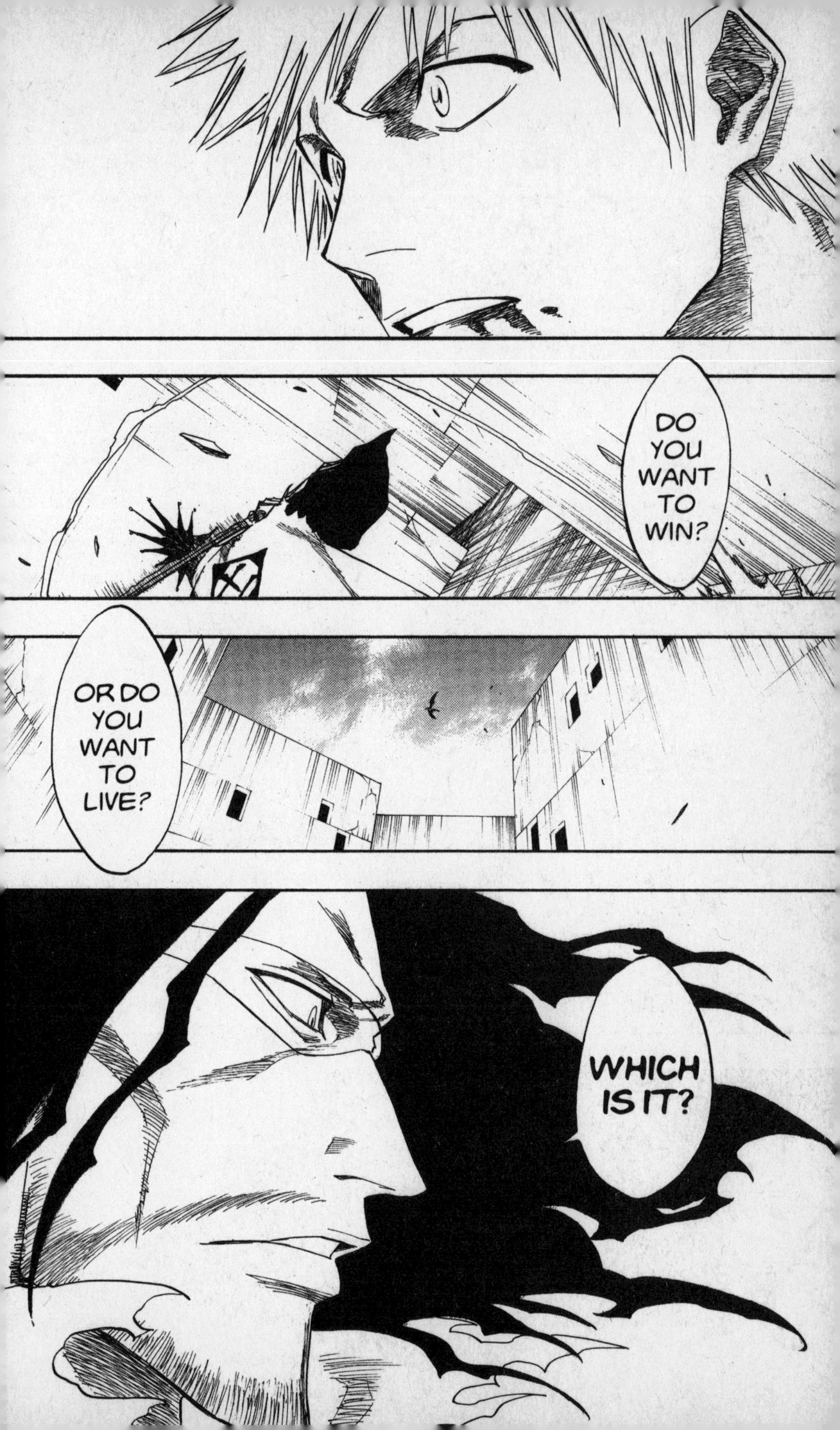
DO YOU WANT TO WIN?
OR DO YOU WANT TO LIVE?
WHICH IS IT?

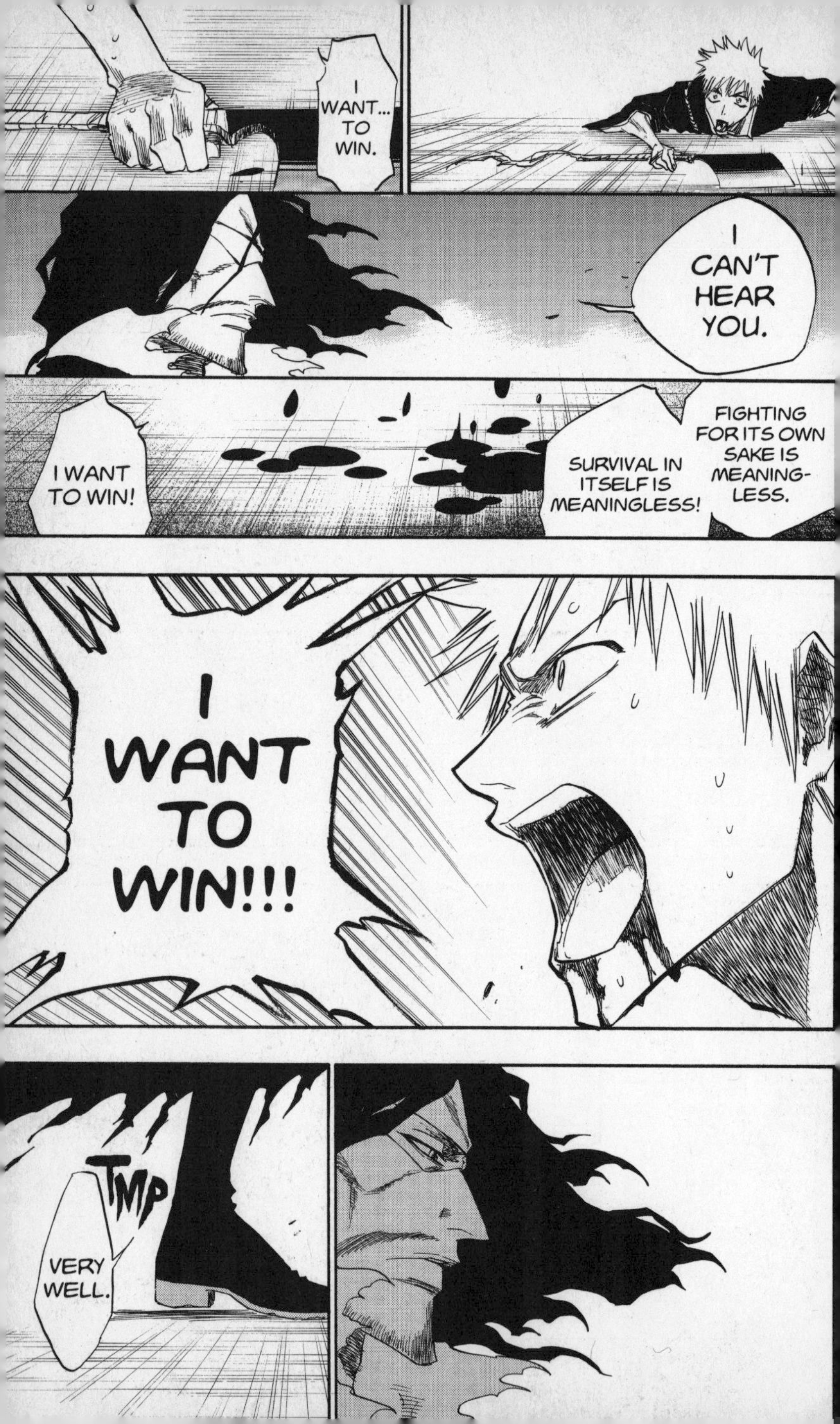
I WANT... TO WIN.
I CAN'T HEAR YOU.
FIGHTING FOR ITS OWN SAKE IS MEANING-LESS.
SURVIVAL IN ITSELF IS MEANINGLESS!
I WANT TO WIN!
I WANT TO WIN!!!
TMP
VERY WELL.

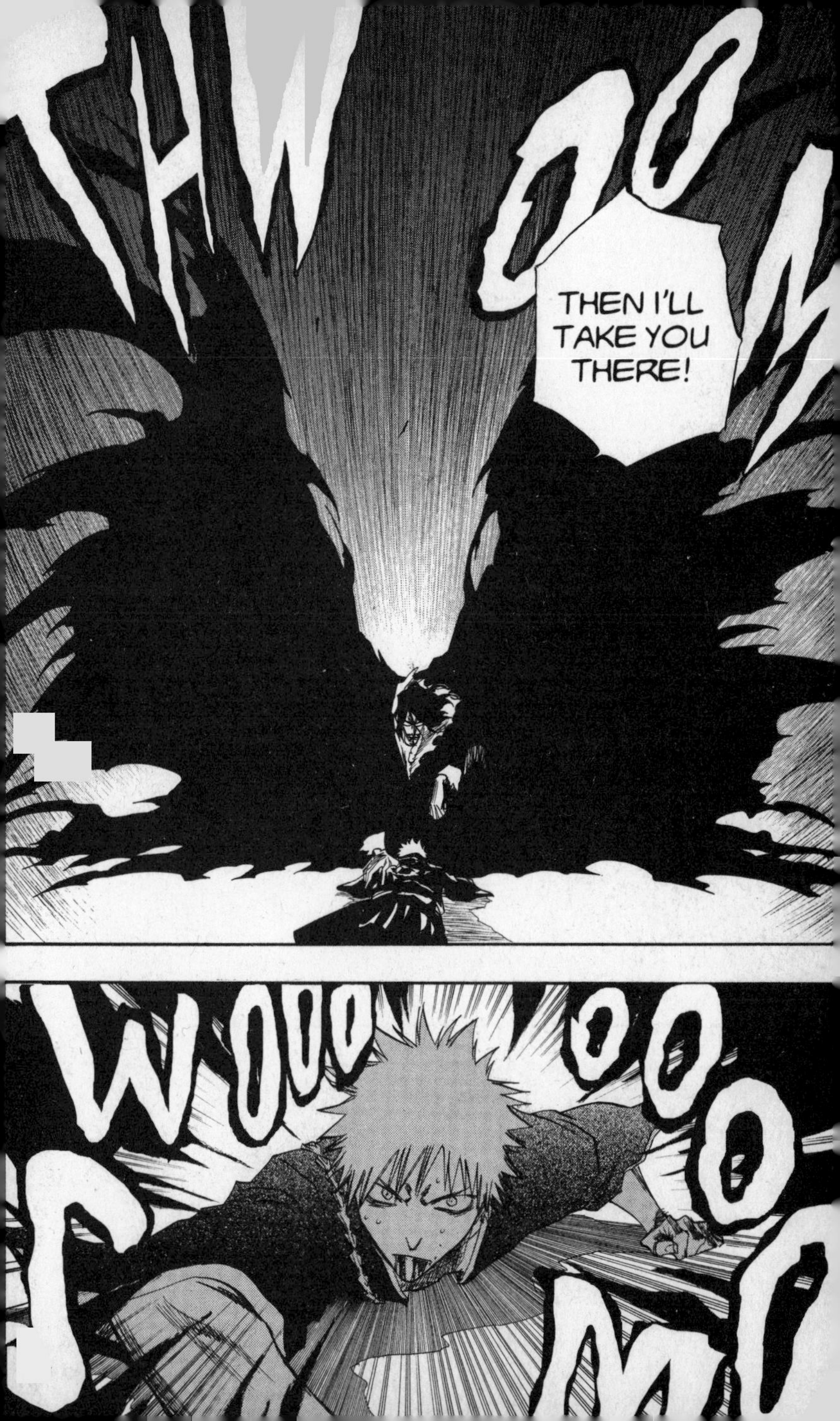
THWOOM
THEN I'LL TAKE YOU THERE!

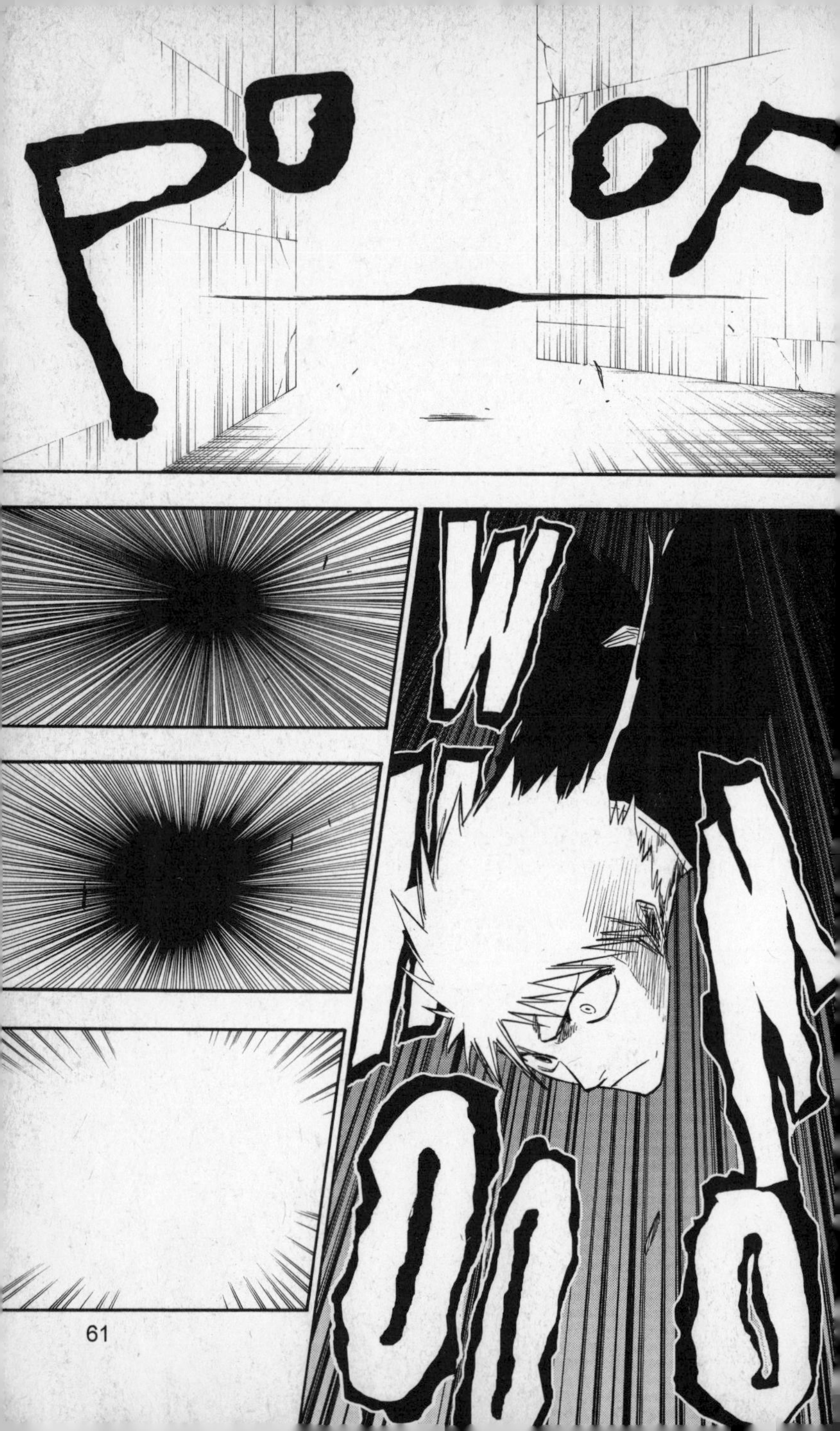
POOF

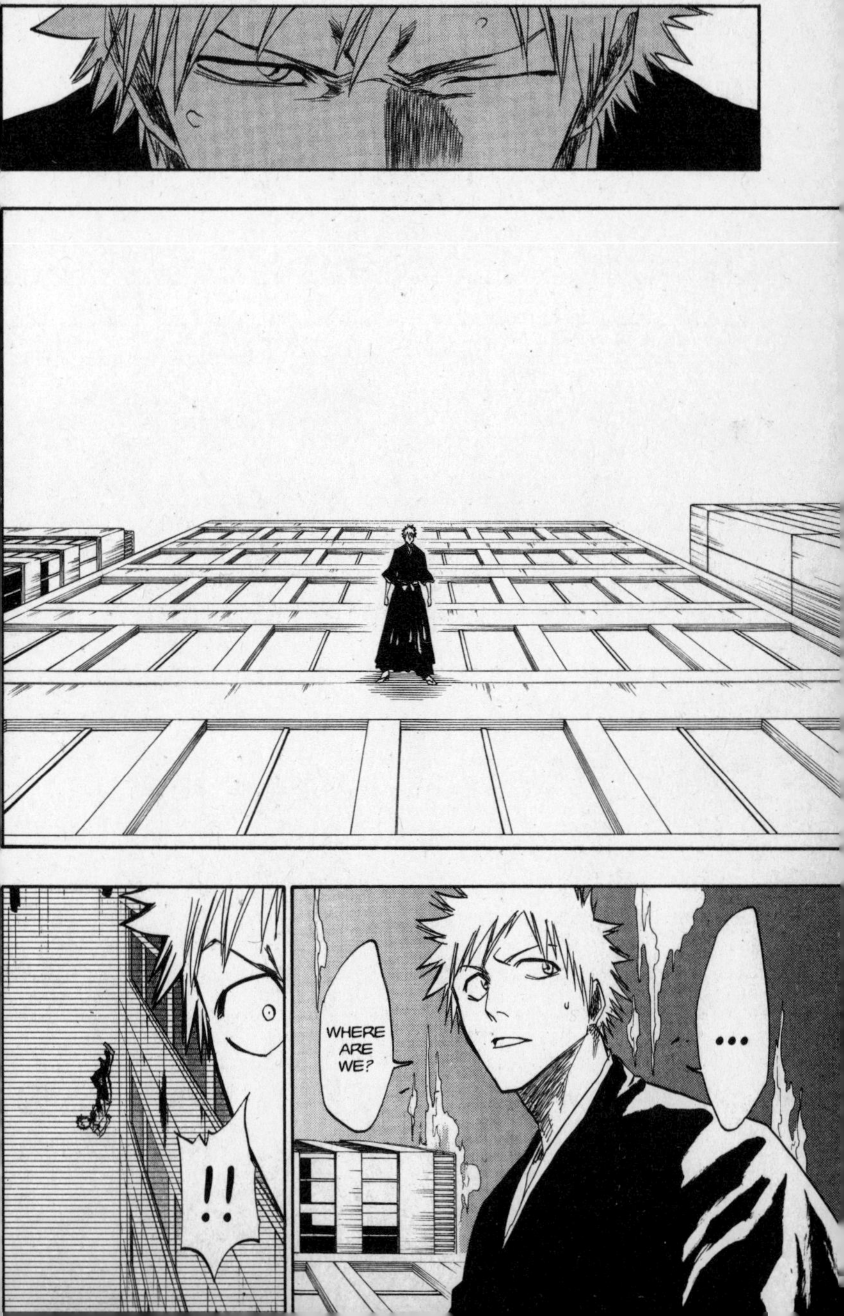
...
WHERE ARE WE?
!!

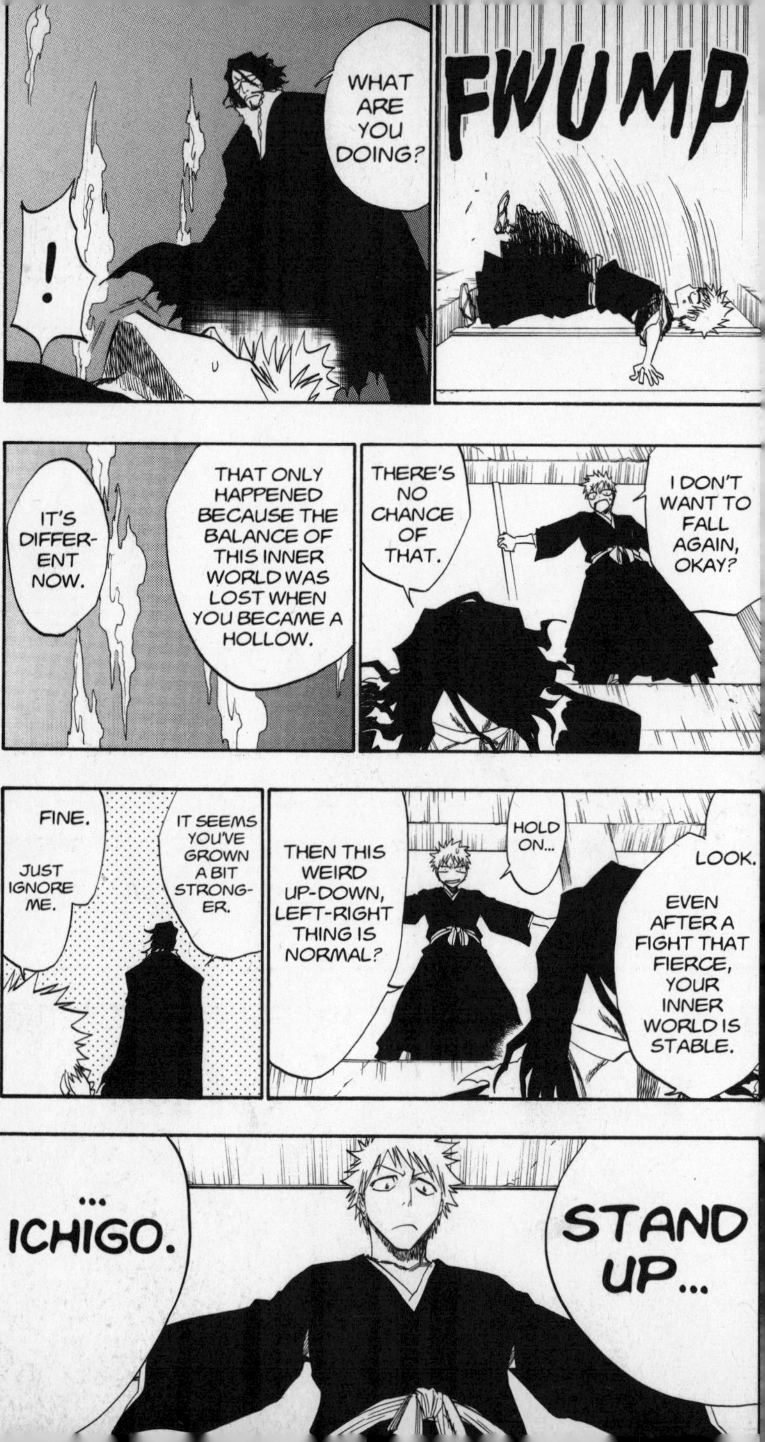
FWUMP
WHAT ARE YOU DOING?
!
I DON'T WANT TO FALL AGAIN, OKAY?
THERE'S NO CHANCE OF THAT.
THAT ONLY HAPPENED BECAUSE THE BALANCE OF THIS INNER WORLD WAS LOST WHEN YOU BECAME A HOLLOW.
IT'S DIFFER-ENT NOW.
LOOK.
EVEN AFTER A FIGHT THAT FIERCE, YOUR INNER WORLD IS STABLE.
HOLD ON...
THEN THIS WEIRD UP-DOWN, LEFT-RIGHT THING IS NORMAL?
IT SEEMS YOU'VE GROWN A BIT STRONG-ER.
FINE.
JUST IGNORE ME.
STAND UP...
...ICHIGO.

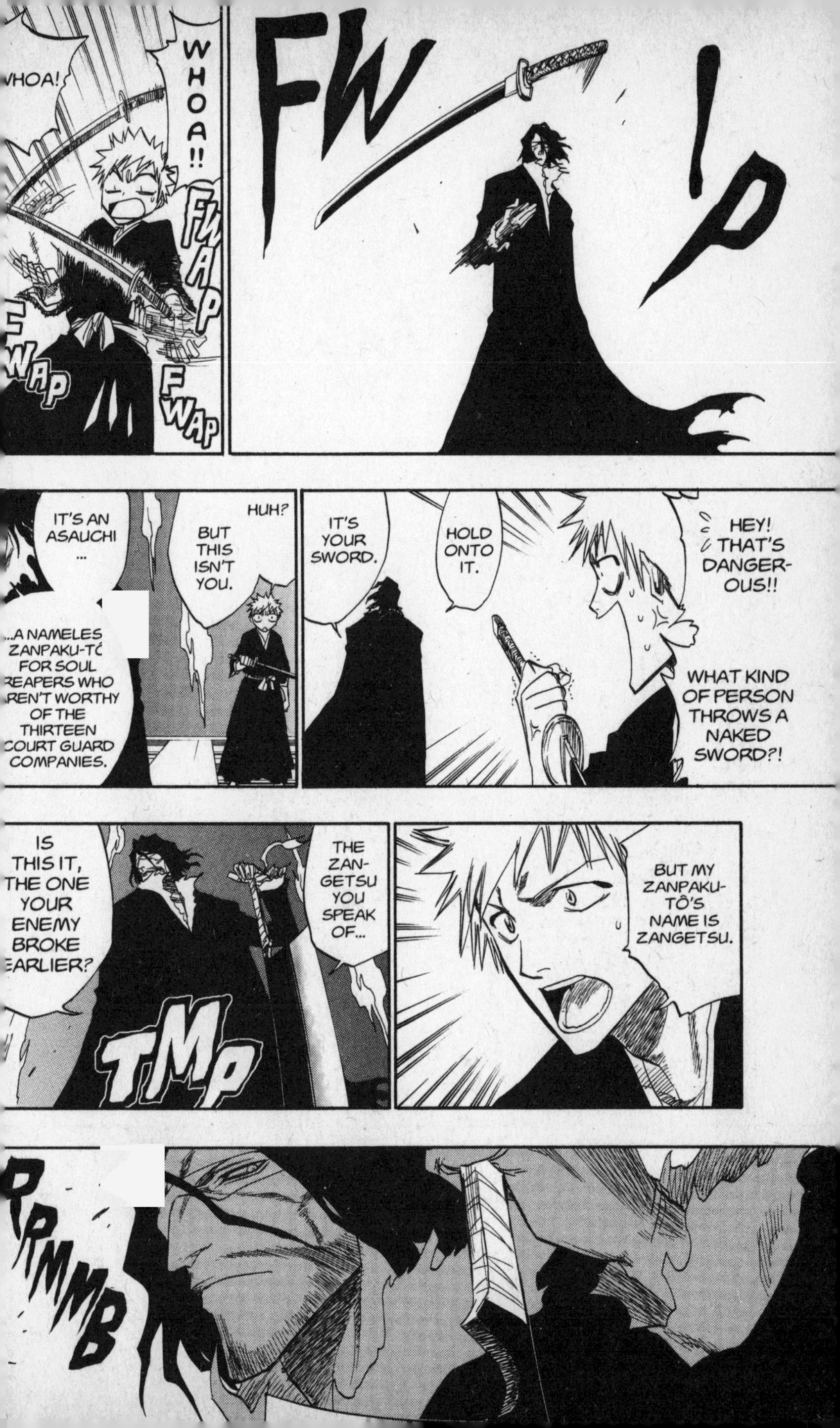
FWIP
WHOA!!
WHOA!
FWAP
FWAP
FWAP
HEY! THAT'S DANGER-OUS!!
HOLD ONTO IT.
IT'S YOUR SWORD.
WHAT KIND OF PERSON THROWS A NAKED SWORD?!
HUH?
BUT THIS ISN'T YOU.
IT'S AN ASAUCHI...
...A NAMELES ZANPAKU-TŌ FOR SOUL REAPERS WHO REN'T WORTHY OF THE THIRTEEN COURT GUARD COMPANIES.
BUT MY ZANPAKU-TÔ'S NAME IS ZANGETSU.
THE ZAN-GETSU YOU SPEAK OF...
IS THIS IT, THE ONE YOUR ENEMY BROKE ARLIER?
TMP
RRMMB

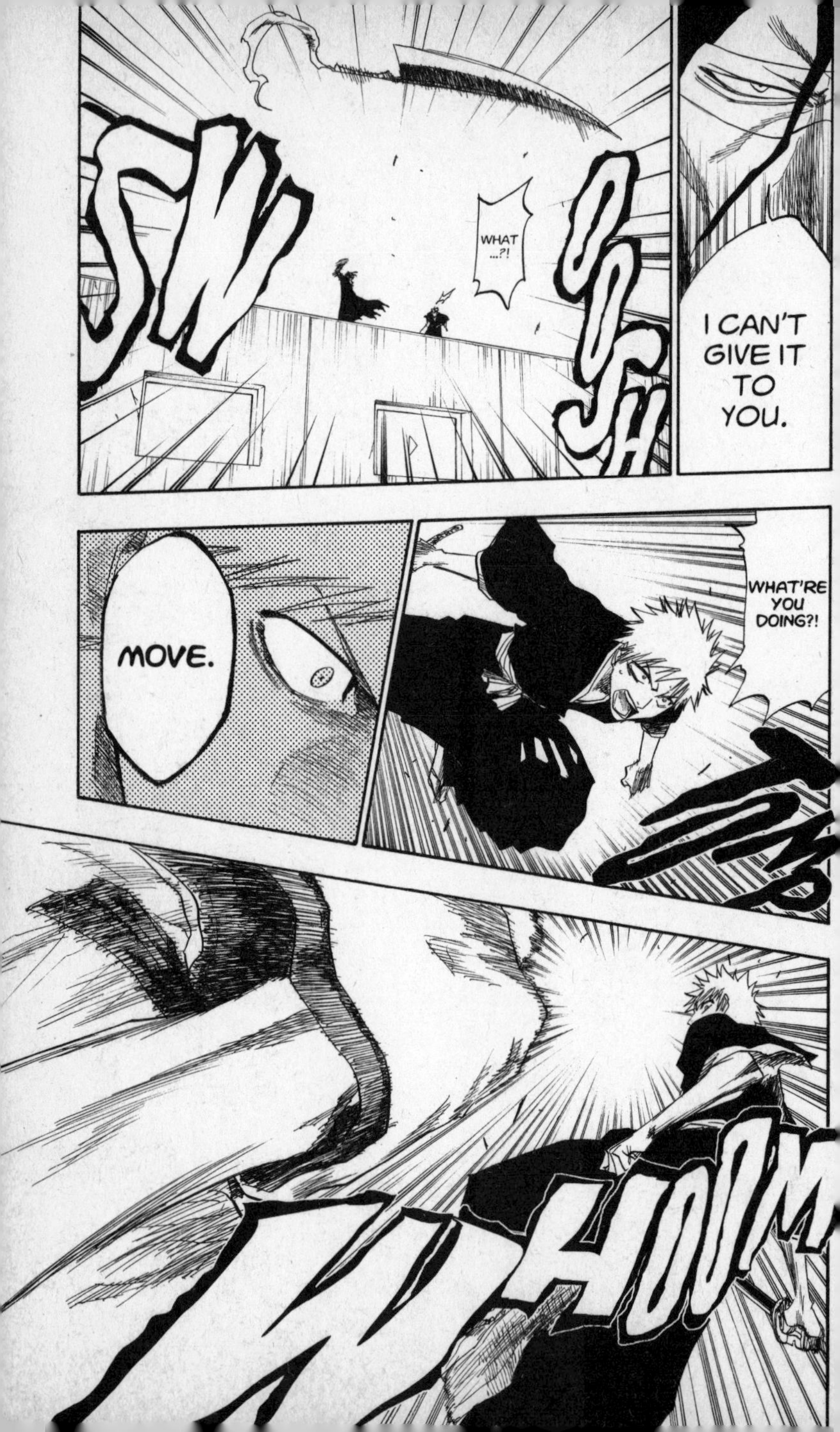
I CAN'T GIVE IT TO YOU.
SWOOSH
WHAT ...?!
WHAT'RE YOU DOING?!
MOVE.

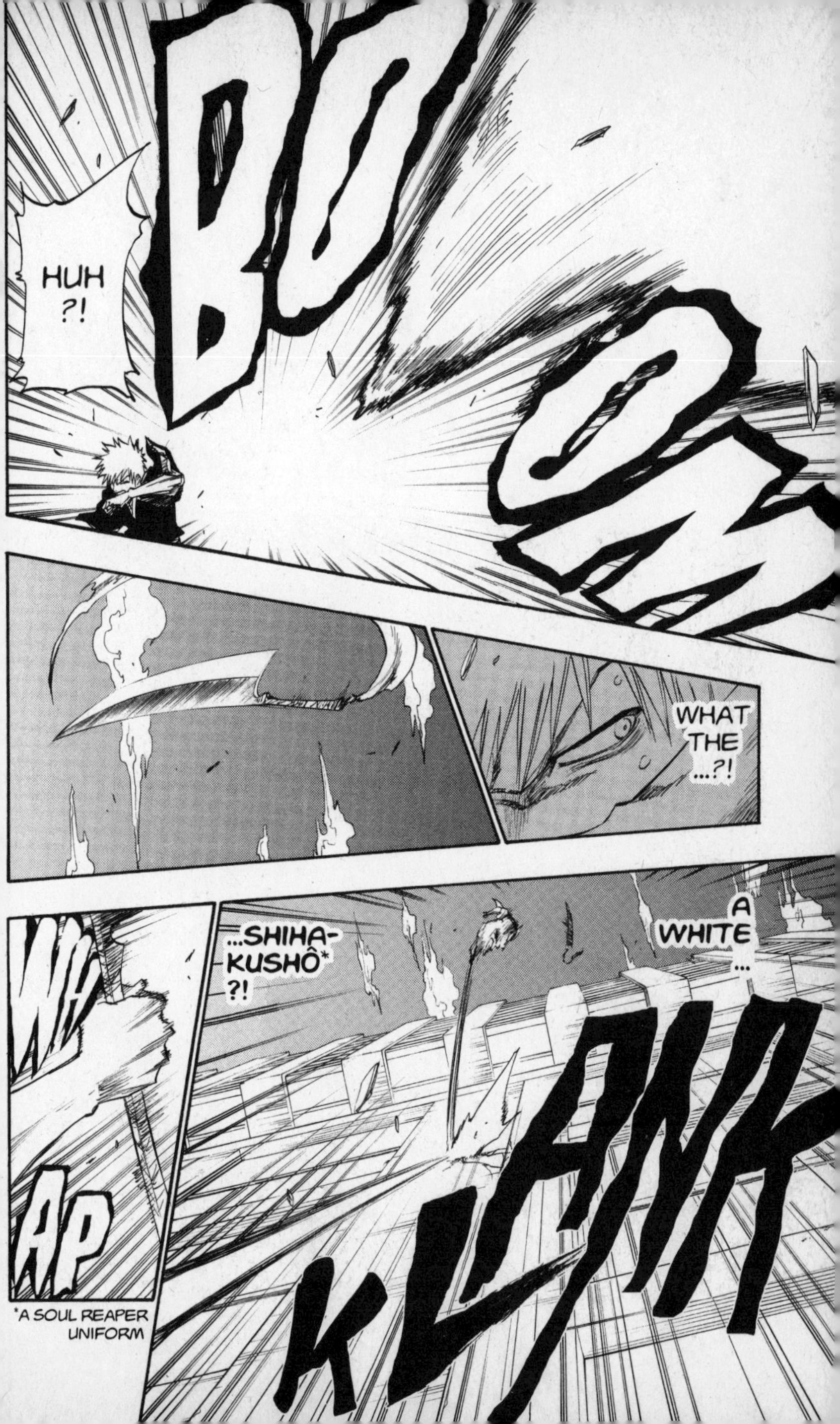
BOOM
HUH ?!
WHAT THE ...?!
A WHITE ...
...SHIHA-KUSHÔ* ?!
KLANK
WHAP

*A SOUL REAPER UNIFORM

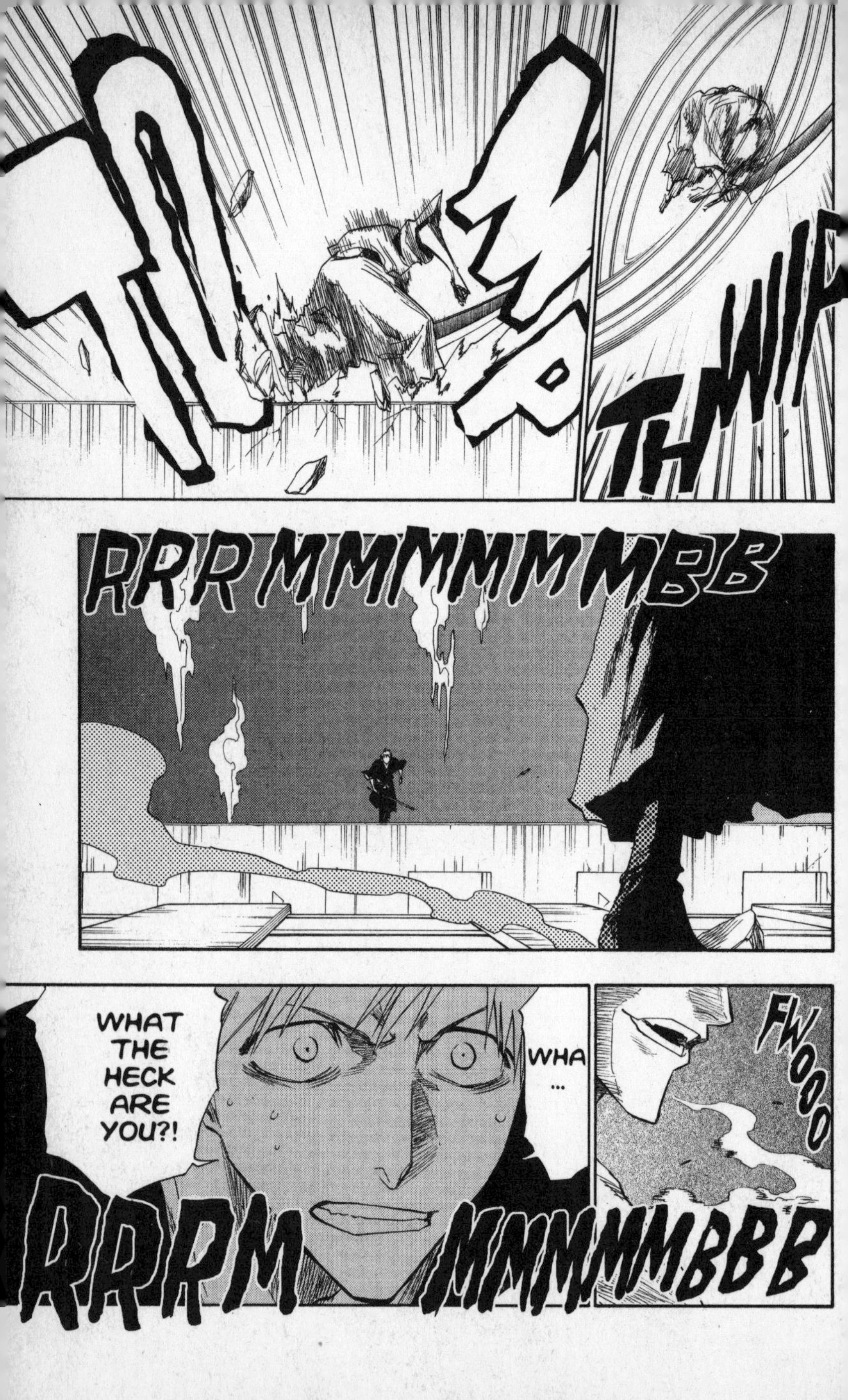
THWIP
RRRMMMMMMBB
FWOOO
WHA...
WHAT THE HECK ARE YOU?!
RRRMMMMMMBBB

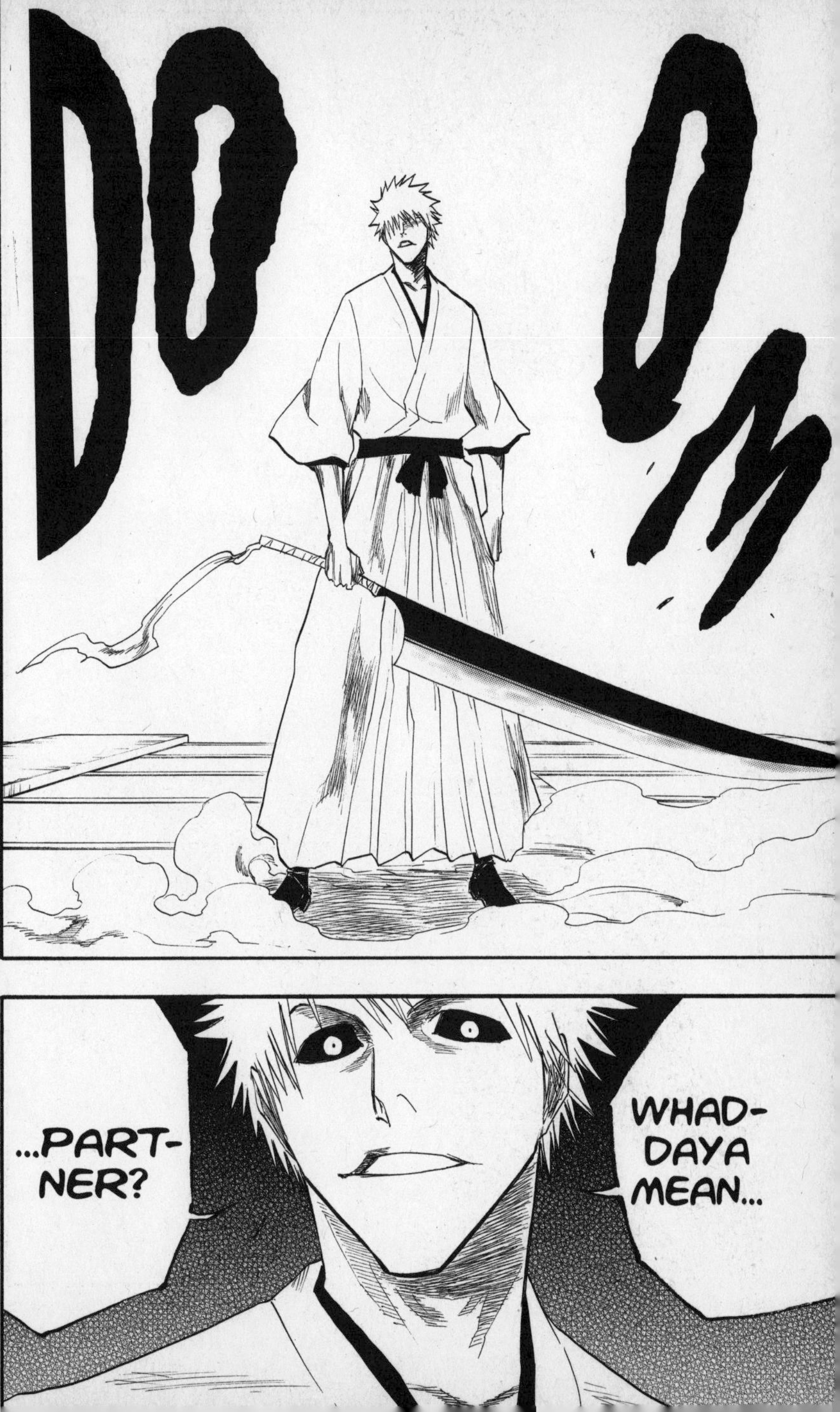
DOOM
WHAD-DAYA MEAN...
...PART-NER?

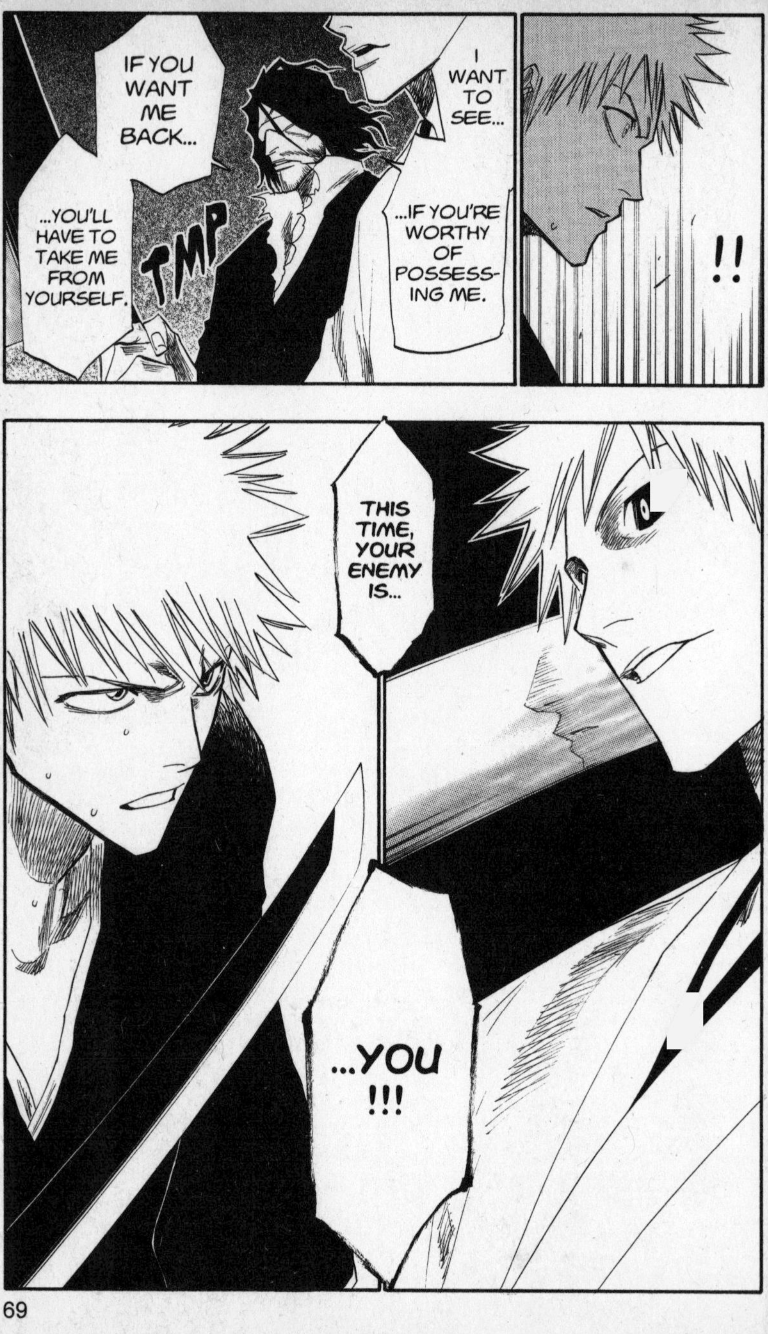
!!
I WANT TO SEE...
...IF YOU'RE WORTHY OF POSSESSING ME.
IF YOU WANT ME BACK...
TMP
...YOU'LL HAVE TO TAKE ME FROM YOURSELF.
THIS TIME, YOUR ENEMY IS...
...YOU !!!

THE 4TH COMPANY GENERAL RELIEF STATION HAS BEEN BUSY
EVER SINCE THE RYOKA PROBLEM STARTED. THE ~~GUYS~~ GENTLEMEN
OF 11TH COMPANY, IN PARTICULAR, HAVE BEEN HARD TO
HANDLE. AND ON TOP OF EVERYTHING, I RECEIVED A REQUEST
FROM 8TH COMPANY TO ADMIT A RYOKA. WE CAN BARELY
MANAGE AS IT IS, AND NOW I HAVE TO ADMIT A RYOKA?
I WISH THEY'D GIVE ME A BREAK. FIRST OF ALL, I DON'T
UNDERSTAND THE PURPOSE OF
TREATING A DEFEATED RYOKA.
~~CAPTAIN KYŌRAKU IS ALWAYS CHASING~~
~~GIRLS, WEARING GAUDY CLOTHES, AND~~
~~SLEEPING WHILE EVERYONE ELSE IS~~
~~WORKING. I DON'T KNOW HOW~~
~~SOMEONE LIKE HIM EVER GOT TO~~
~~BE A CAPTAIN~~ BUT I'D LIKE TO
EXPRESS MY GREAT RESPECT
FOR HIM.

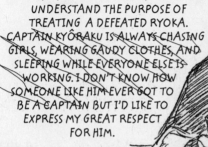

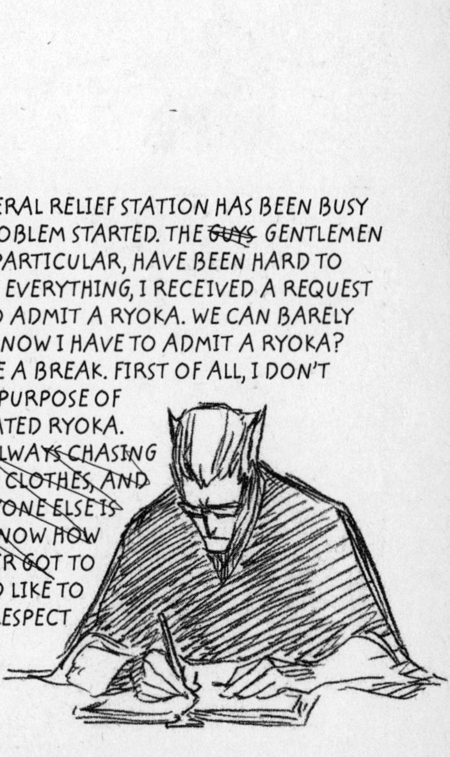

111. Black and White

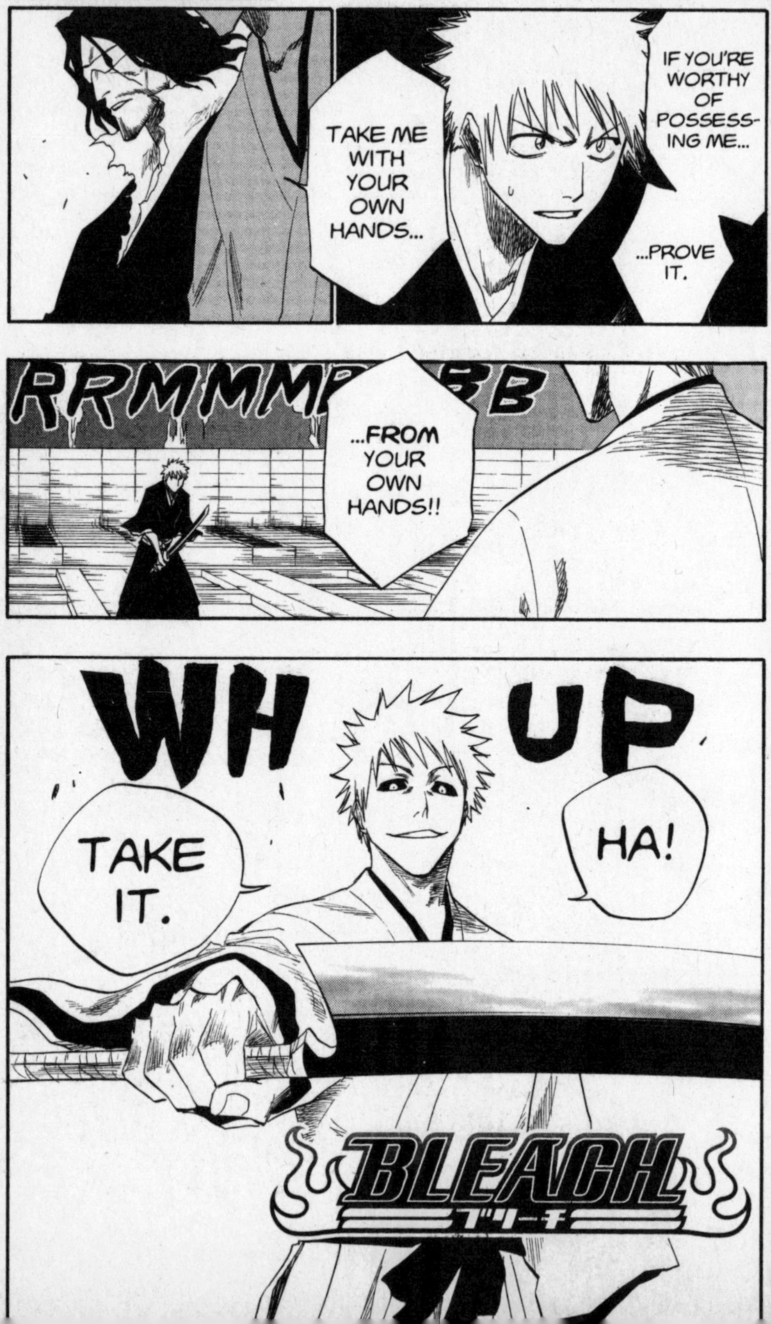
IF YOU'RE WORTHY OF POSSESS-ING ME...
TAKE ME WITH YOUR OWN HANDS...
...PROVE IT.
RRMMM BB
...FROM YOUR OWN HANDS!!
WH UP
HA!
TAKE IT.
BLEACH

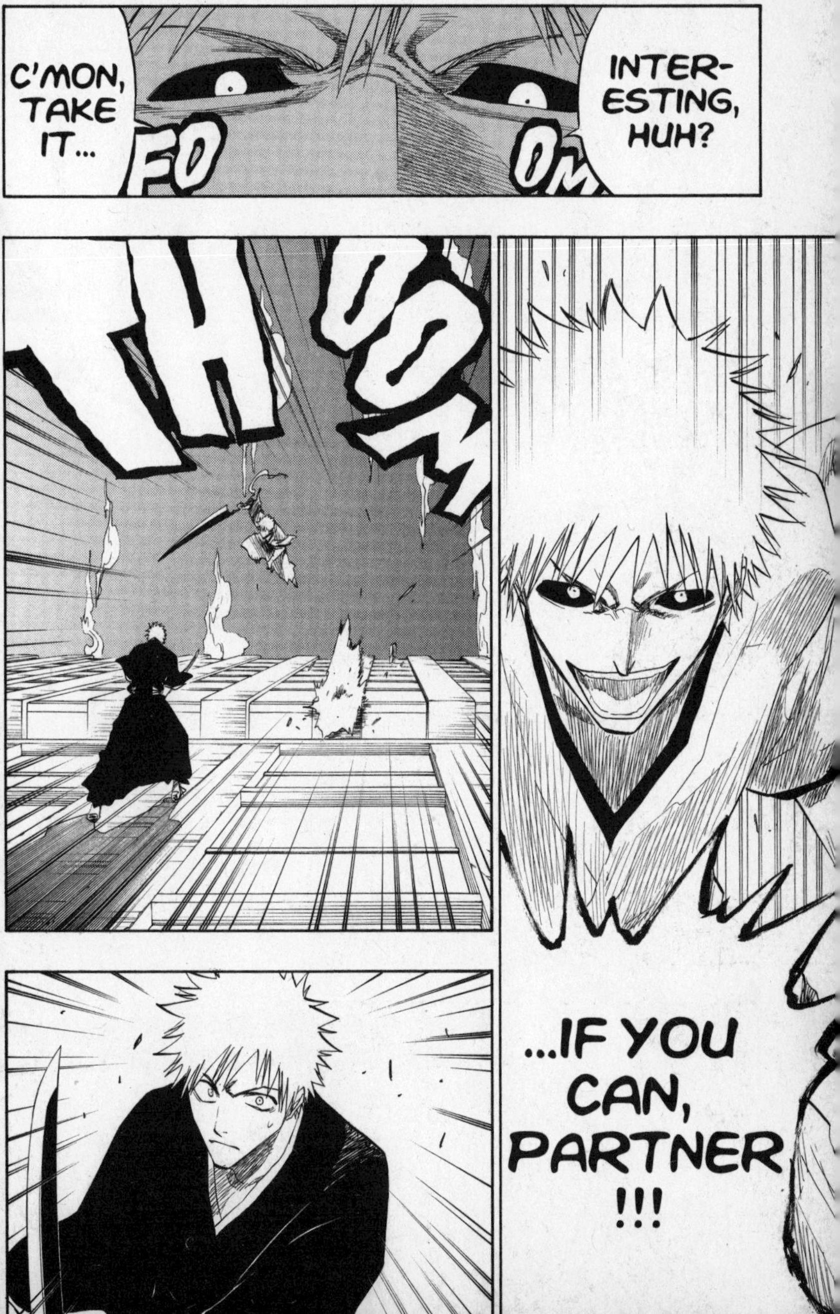
INTER-ESTING, HUH?
C'MON, TAKE IT...
FOOM
...IF YOU CAN, PARTNER!!!
THOOM

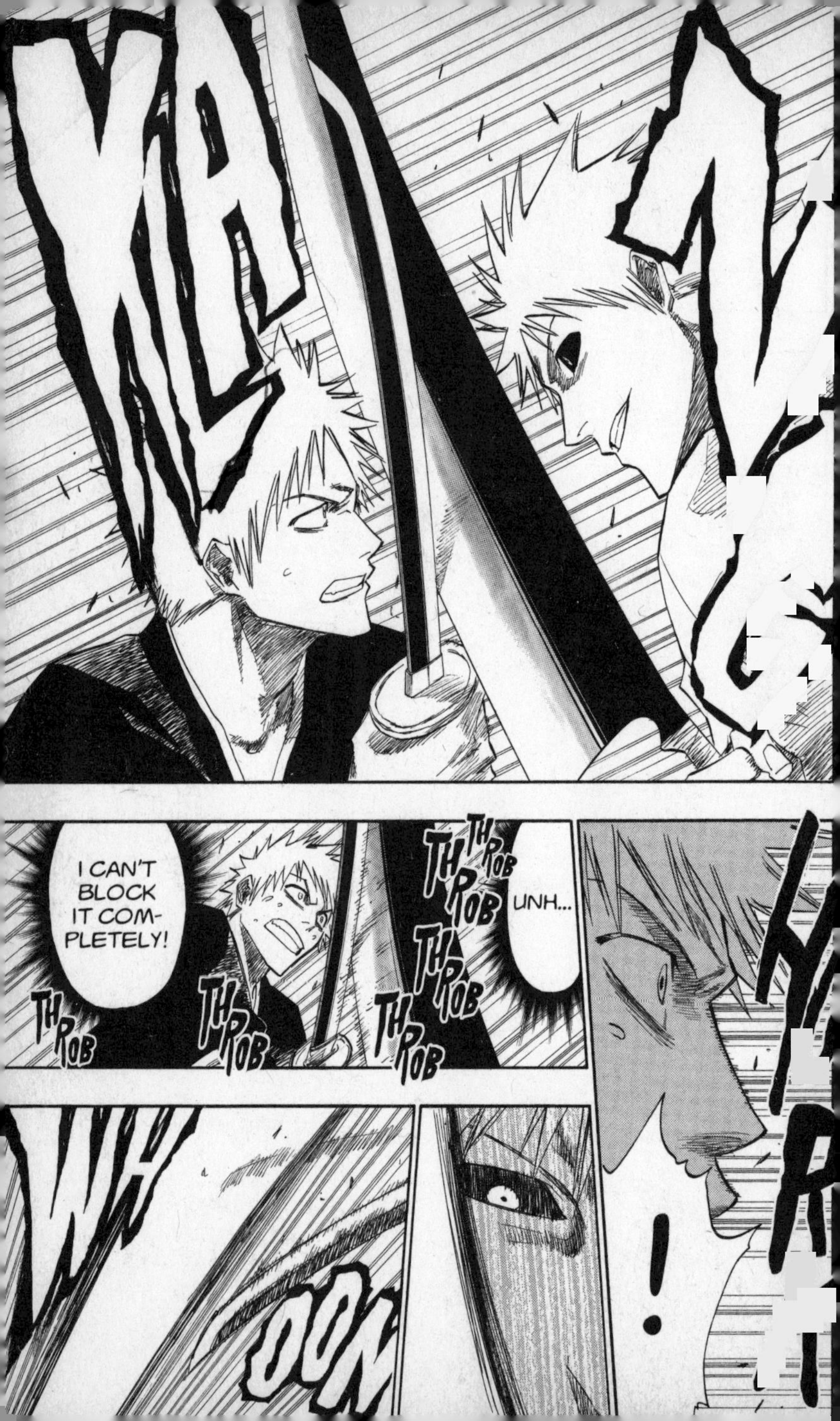
THROB
THROB
UNH...
THROB
THROB
I CAN'T BLOCK IT COMPLETELY!
THROB
THROB

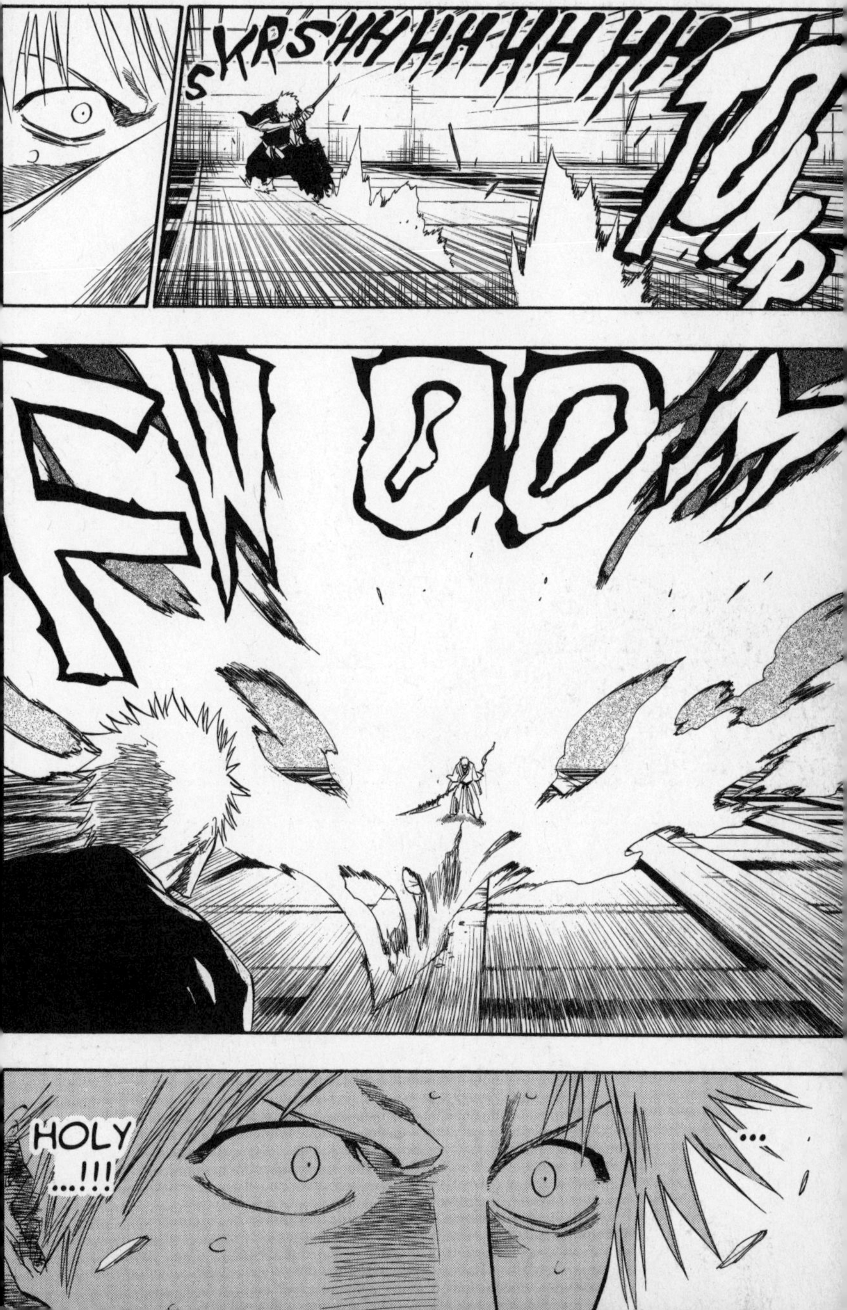
SKRSHHHHHHHHHH
TUMP
FWOOM
...
HOLY ...!!!

READ THIS WAY

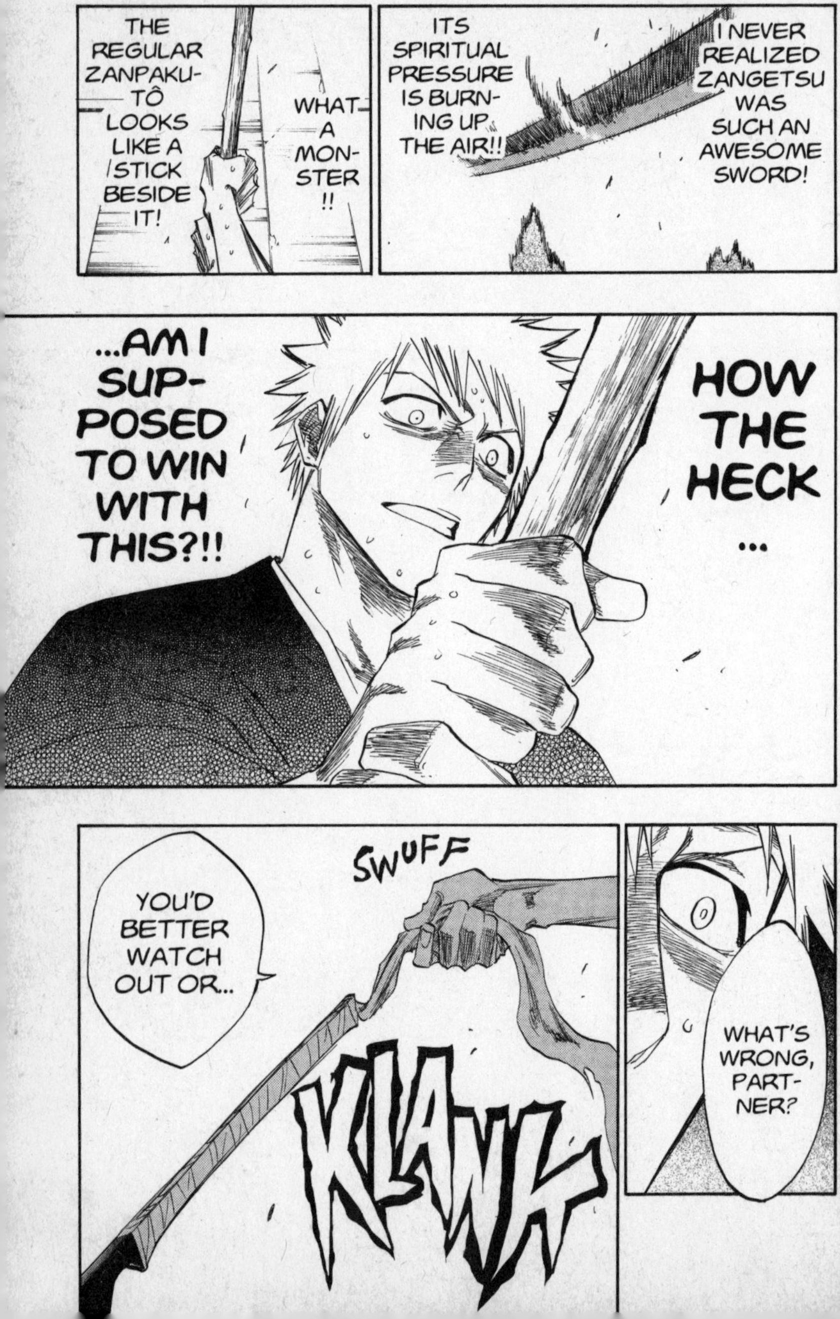
I NEVER REALIZED ZANGETSU WAS SUCH AN AWESOME SWORD!
ITS SPIRITUAL PRESSURE IS BURNING UP THE AIR!!
WHAT A MONSTER!!
THE REGULAR ZANPAKU-TÔ LOOKS LIKE A STICK BESIDE IT!
HOW THE HECK...
...AM I SUPPOSED TO WIN WITH THIS?!!
WHAT'S WRONG, PARTNER?
SWUFF
YOU'D BETTER WATCH OUT OR...
KLANK

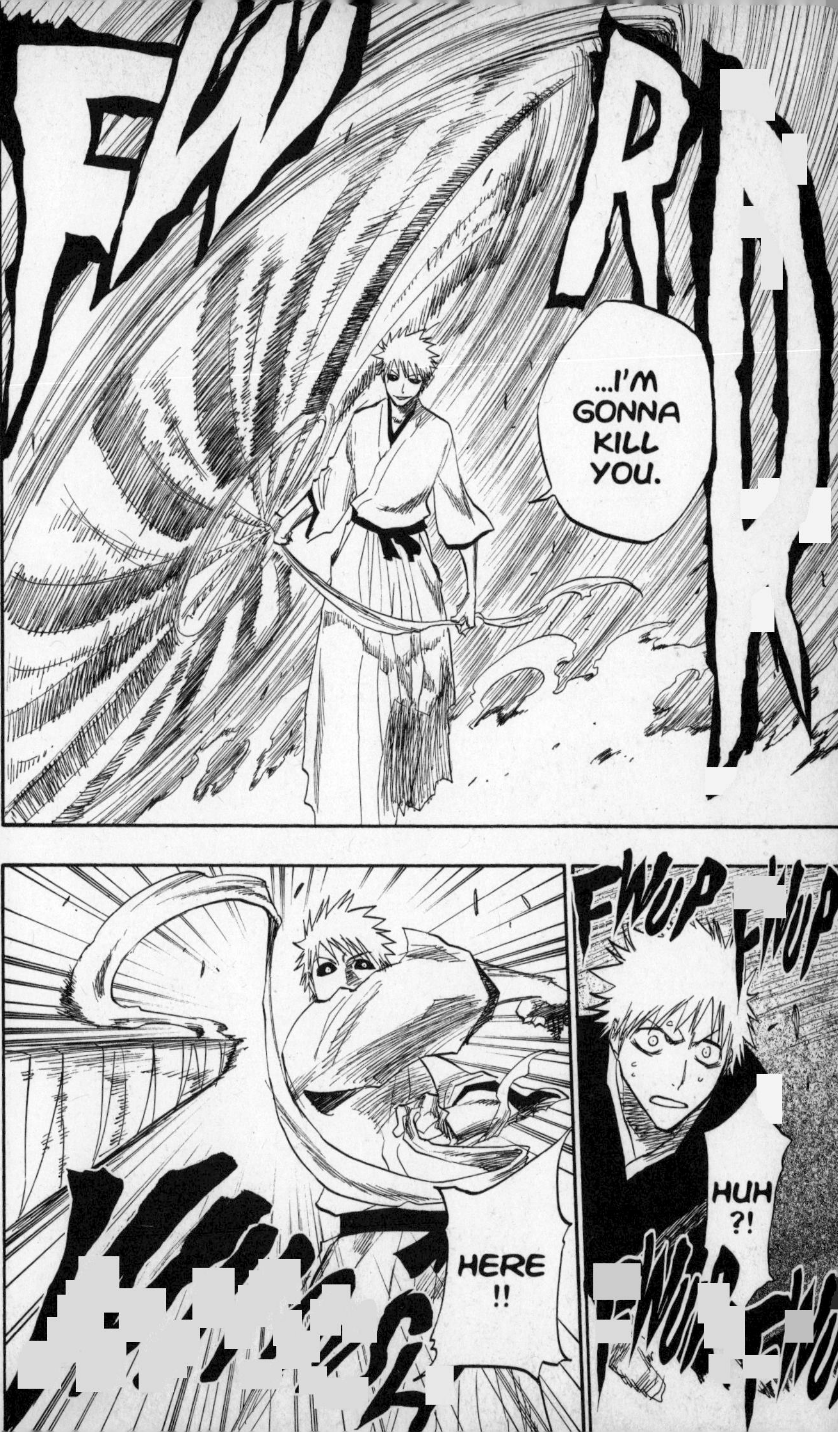
...I'M GONNA KILL YOU.
FWUP
HUH ?!
HERE !!

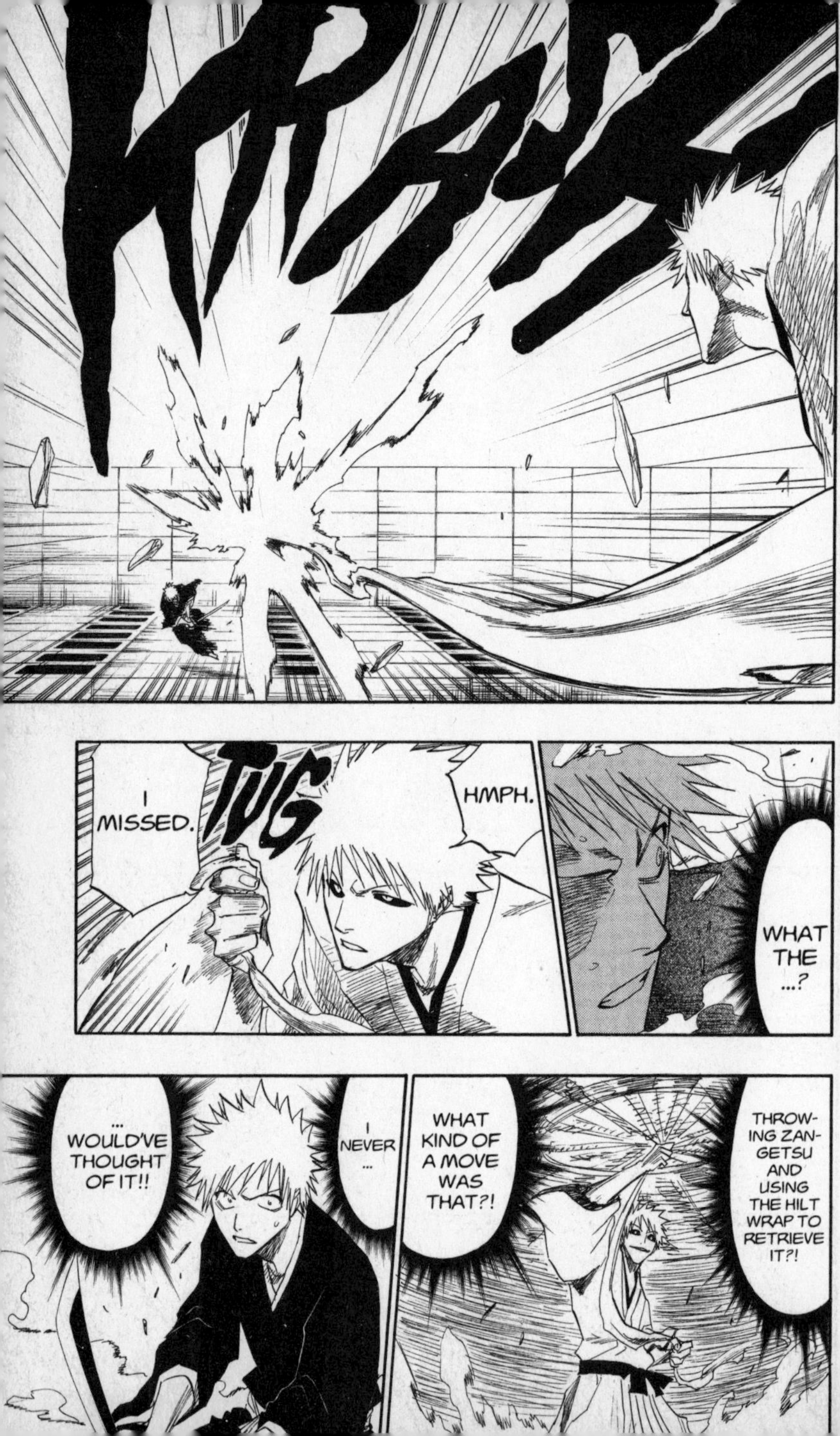
WHAT THE ...?
HMPH.
TUG
I MISSED.
THROW-ING ZAN-GETSU AND USING THE HILT WRAP TO RETRIEVE IT?!
WHAT KIND OF A MOVE WAS THAT?!
I NEVER ...
... WOULD'VE THOUGHT OF IT!!

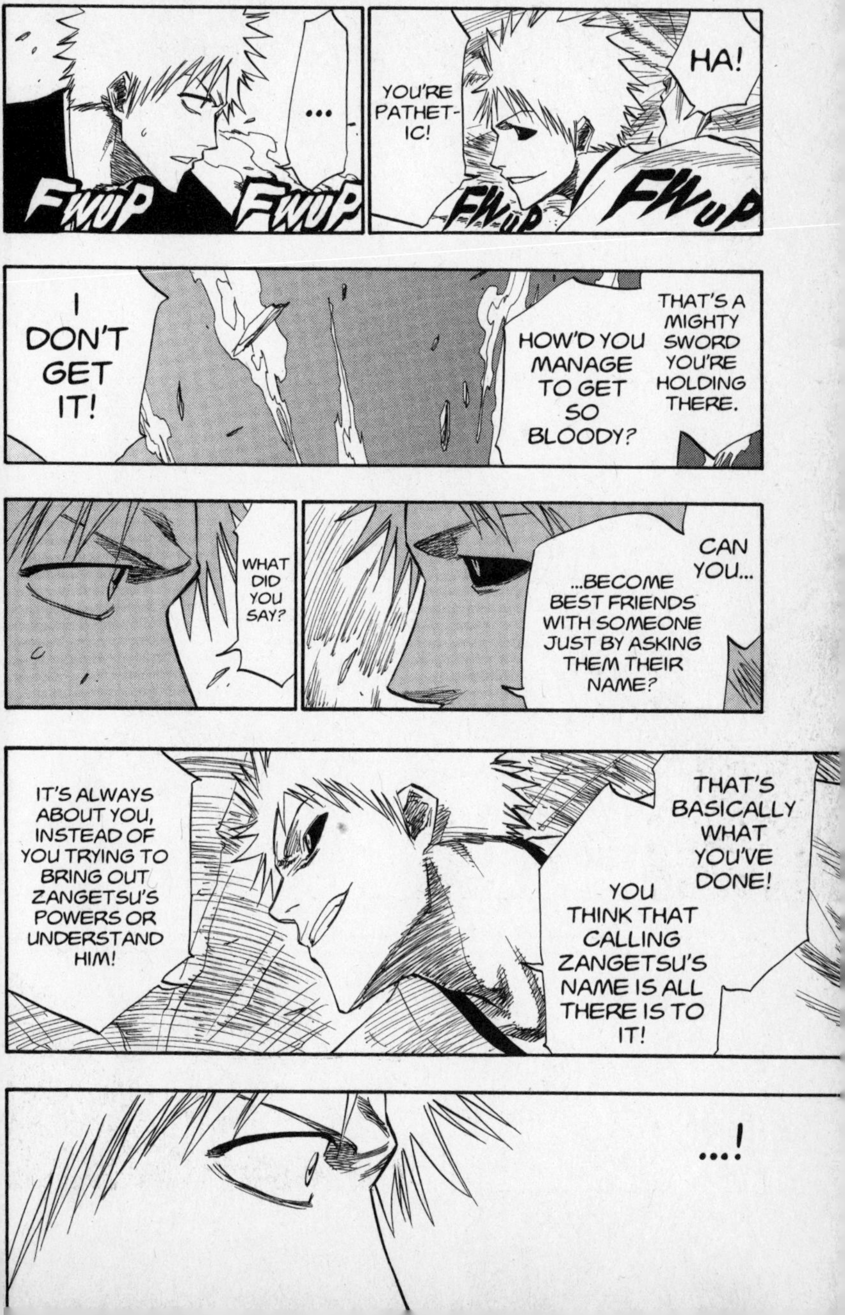
HA!
YOU'RE PATHETIC!
FWUP
FWUP
...
FWUP
FWUP
THAT'S A MIGHTY SWORD YOU'RE HOLDING THERE.
HOW'D YOU MANAGE TO GET SO BLOODY?
I DON'T GET IT!
CAN YOU...
...BECOME BEST FRIENDS WITH SOMEONE JUST BY ASKING THEM THEIR NAME?
WHAT DID YOU SAY?
THAT'S BASICALLY WHAT YOU'VE DONE!
YOU THINK THAT CALLING ZANGETSU'S NAME IS ALL THERE IS TO IT!
IT'S ALWAYS ABOUT YOU, INSTEAD OF YOU TRYING TO BRING OUT ZANGETSU'S POWERS OR UNDERSTAND HIM!
...!

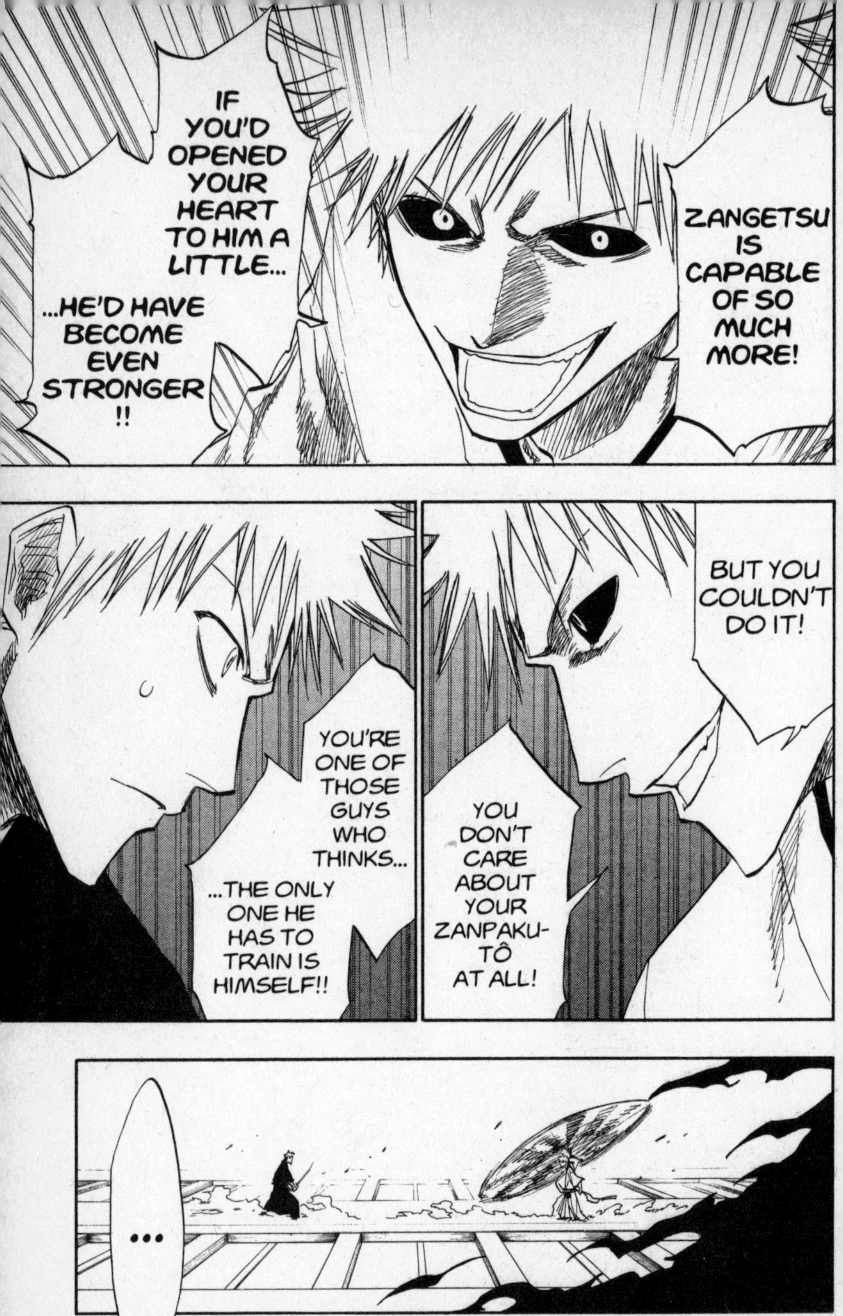
ZANGETSU IS CAPABLE OF SO MUCH MORE!
IF YOU'D OPENED YOUR HEART TO HIM A LITTLE...
...HE'D HAVE BECOME EVEN STRONGER!!
BUT YOU COULDN'T DO IT!
YOU DON'T CARE ABOUT YOUR ZANPAKU-TÔ AT ALL!
YOU'RE ONE OF THOSE GUYS WHO THINKS...
...THE ONLY ONE HE HAS TO TRAIN IS HIMSELF!!
...

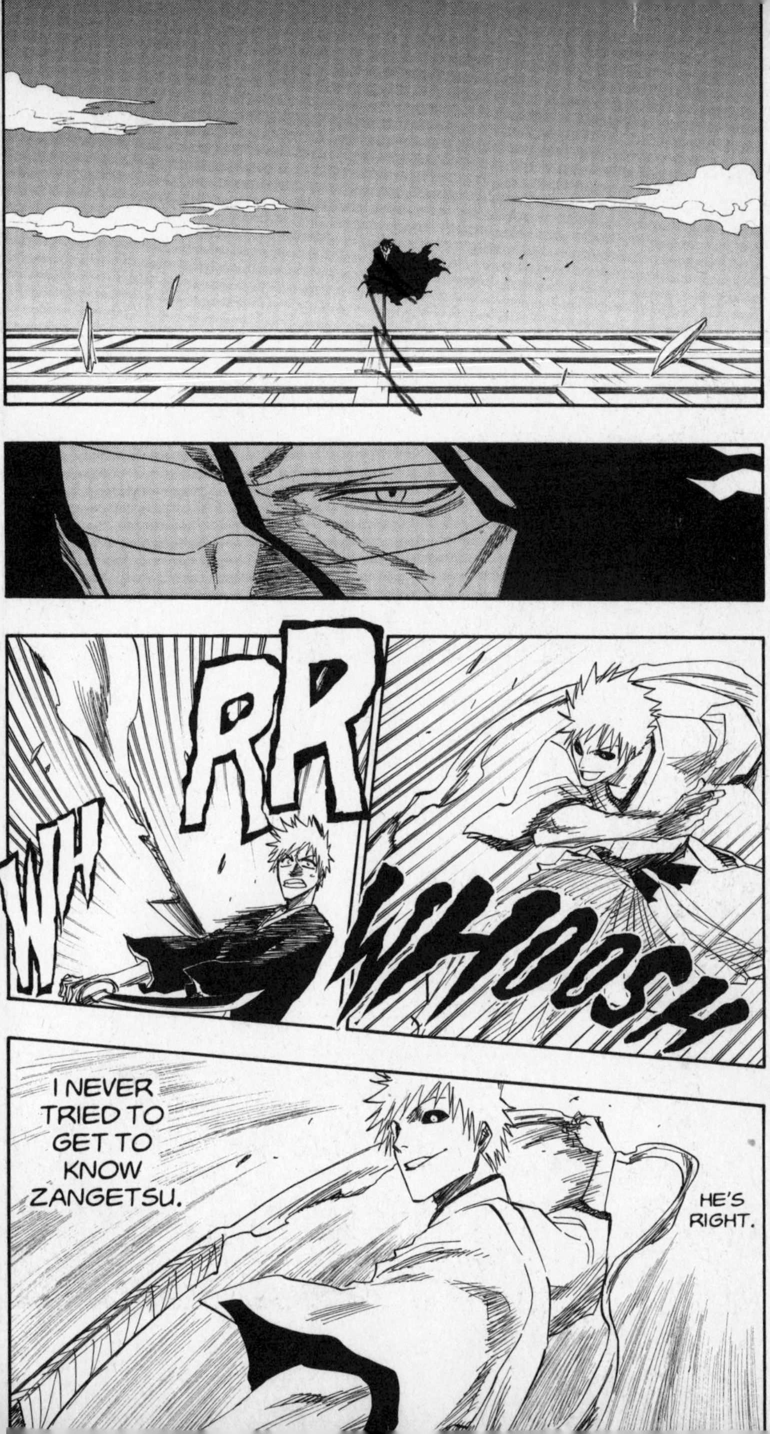
WHOOSH
WH
RR
HE'S RIGHT.
I NEVER TRIED TO GET TO KNOW ZANGETSU.

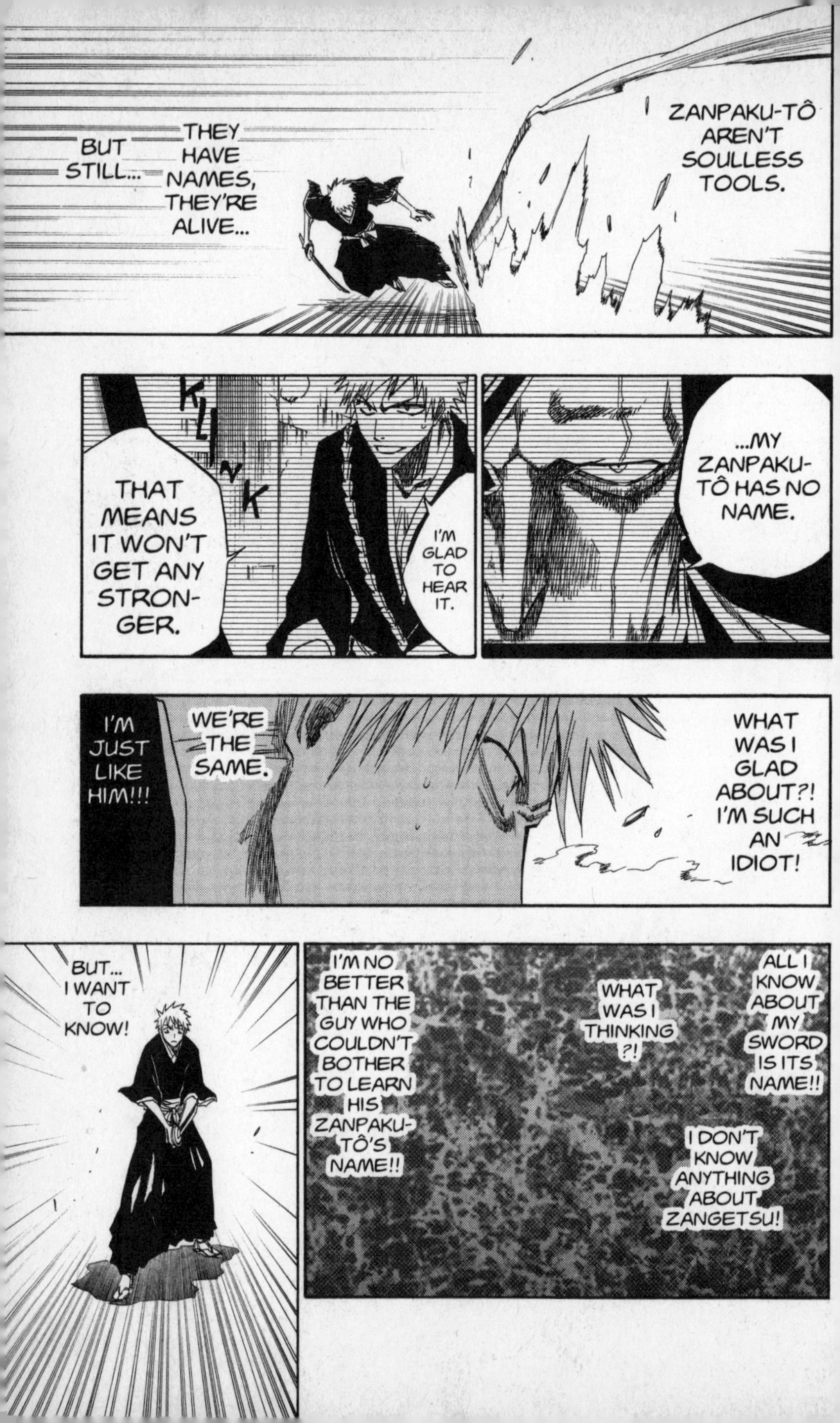

ZANPAKU-TÔ AREN'T SOULLESS TOOLS.
THEY HAVE NAMES, THEY'RE ALIVE...
BUT STILL...
...MY ZANPAKU-TÔ HAS NO NAME.
I'M GLAD TO HEAR IT.
KLINK
THAT MEANS IT WON'T GET ANY STRONGER.
WHAT WAS I GLAD ABOUT?! I'M SUCH AN IDIOT!
WE'RE THE SAME.
I'M JUST LIKE HIM!!!
ALL I KNOW ABOUT MY SWORD IS ITS NAME!!
WHAT WAS I THINKING?!
I DON'T KNOW ANYTHING ABOUT ZANGETSU!
I'M NO BETTER THAN THE GUY WHO COULDN'T BOTHER TO LEARN HIS ZANPAKU-TÔ'S NAME!!
BUT... I WANT TO KNOW!

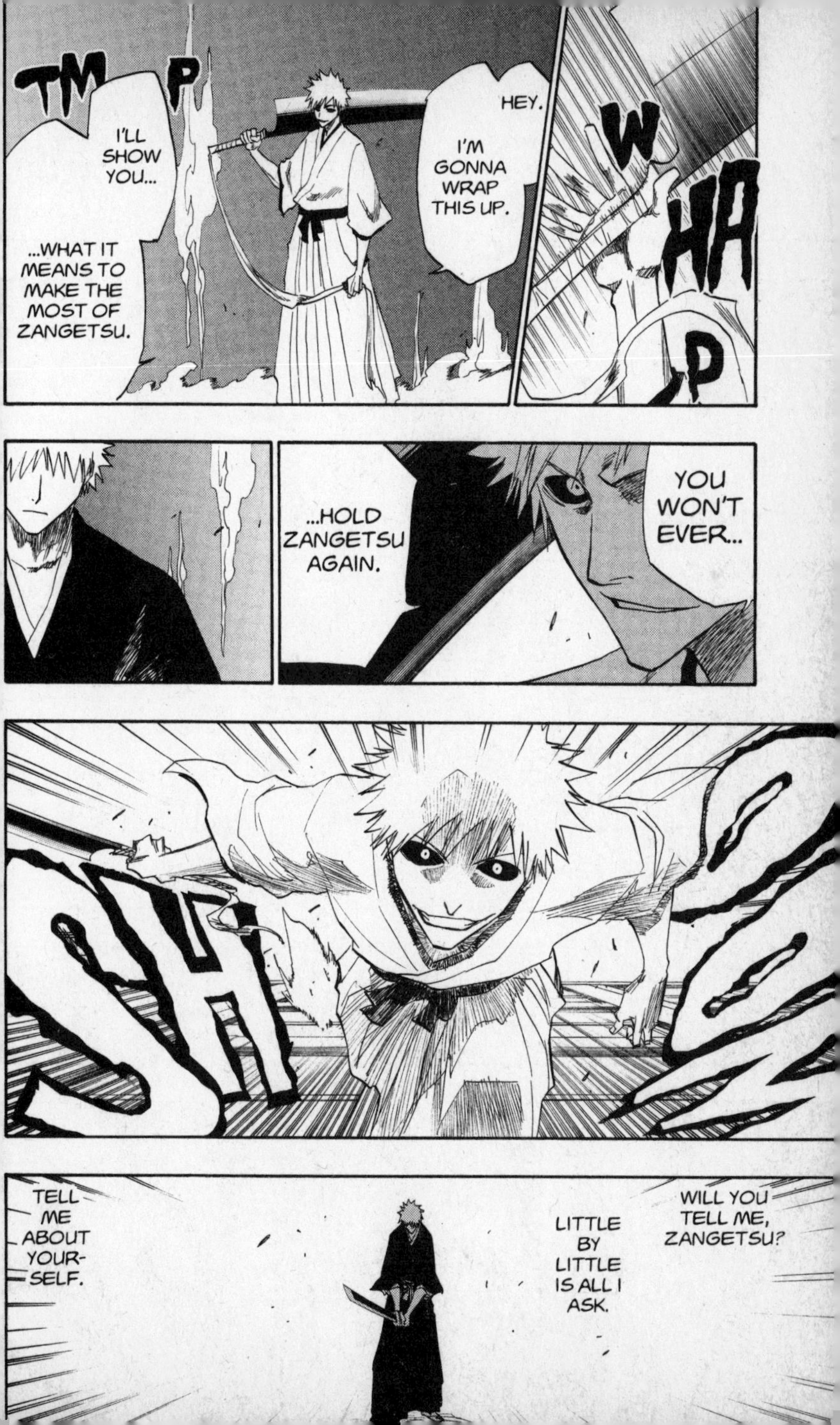
WHAP
HEY.
I'M GONNA WRAP THIS UP.
TMP
I'LL SHOW YOU...
...WHAT IT MEANS TO MAKE THE MOST OF ZANGETSU.
YOU WON'T EVER...
...HOLD ZANGETSU AGAIN.
WILL YOU TELL ME, ZANGETSU?
LITTLE BY LITTLE IS ALL I ASK.
TELL ME ABOUT YOUR-SELF.

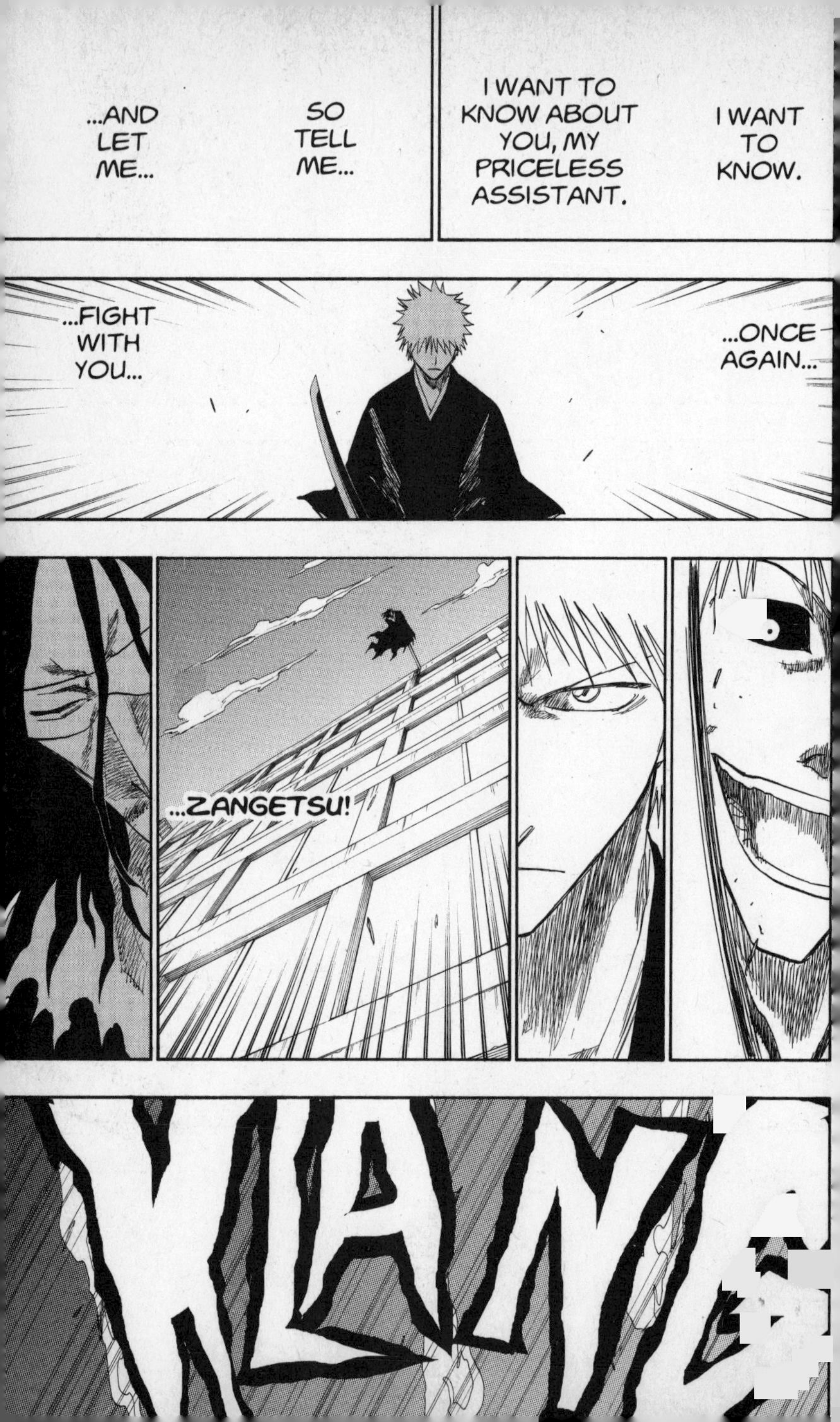
I WANT TO KNOW.
I WANT TO KNOW ABOUT YOU, MY PRICELESS ASSISTANT.
SO TELL ME...
...AND LET ME...
...FIGHT WITH YOU...
...ONCE AGAIN...
...ZANGETSU!

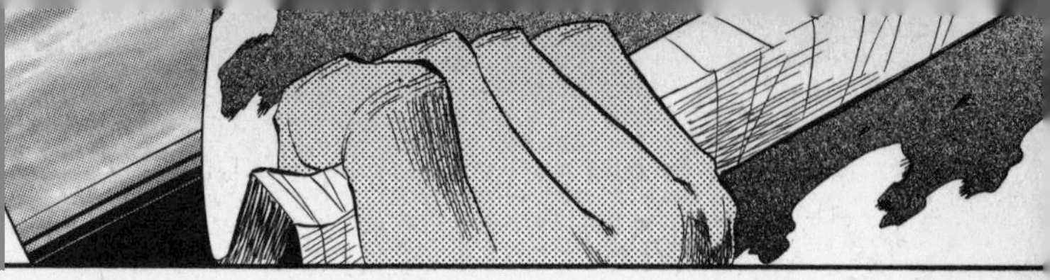

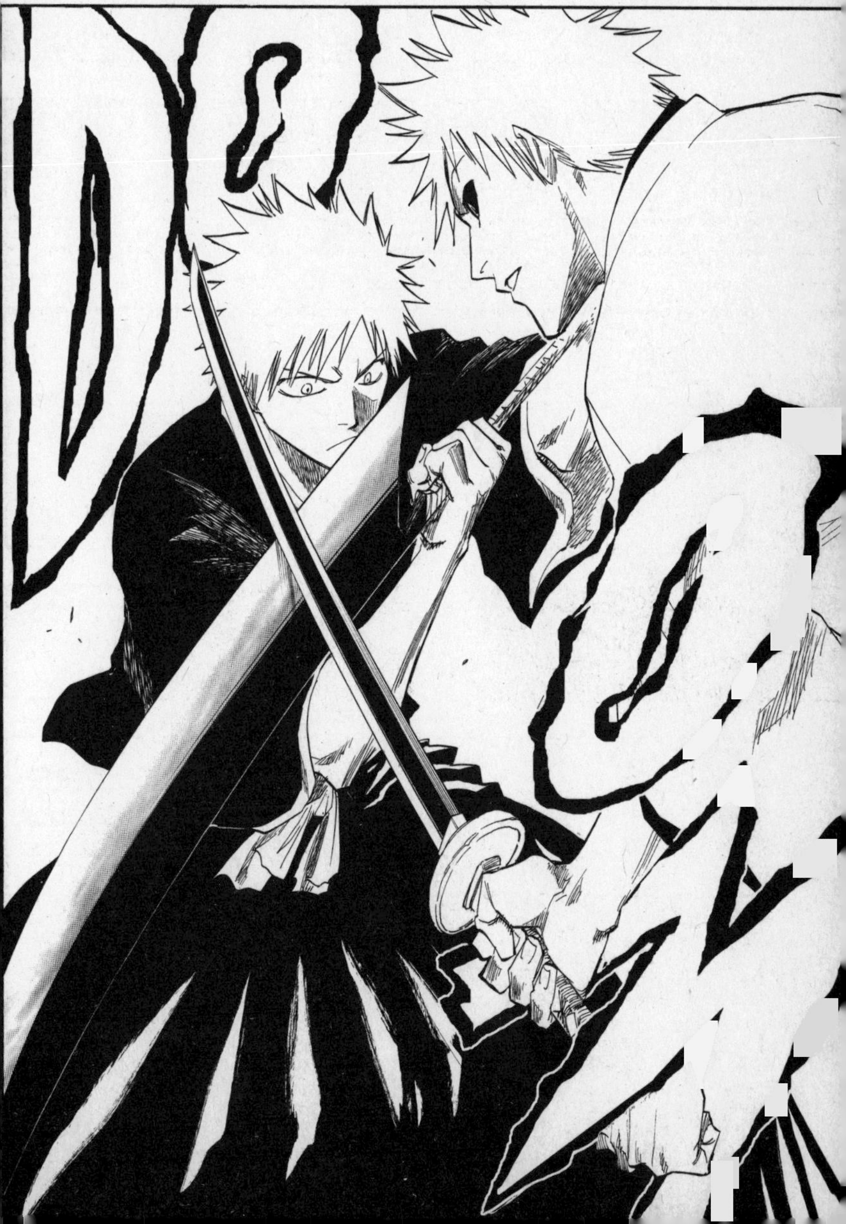

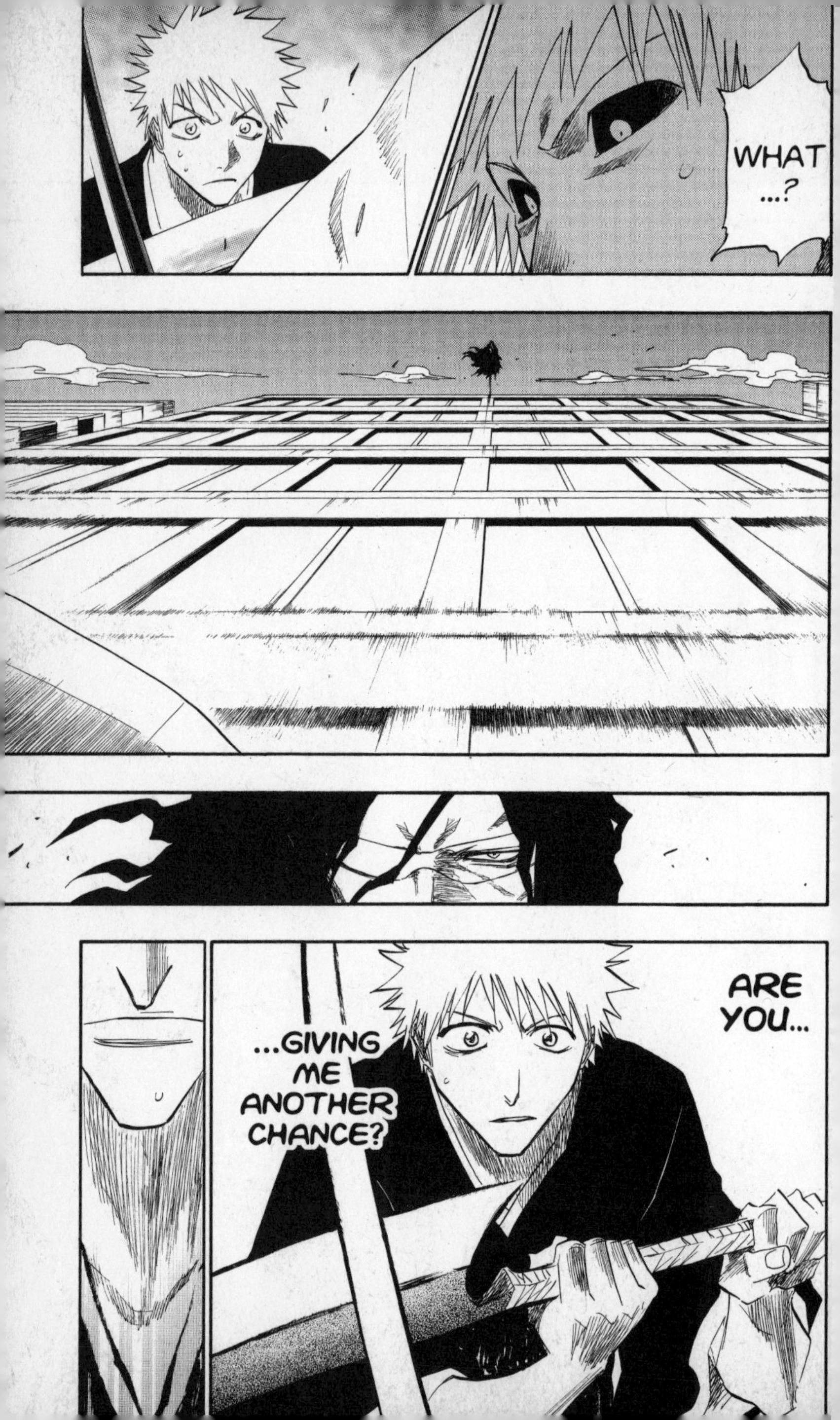
WHAT ...?
ARE YOU...
...GIVING ME ANOTHER CHANCE?

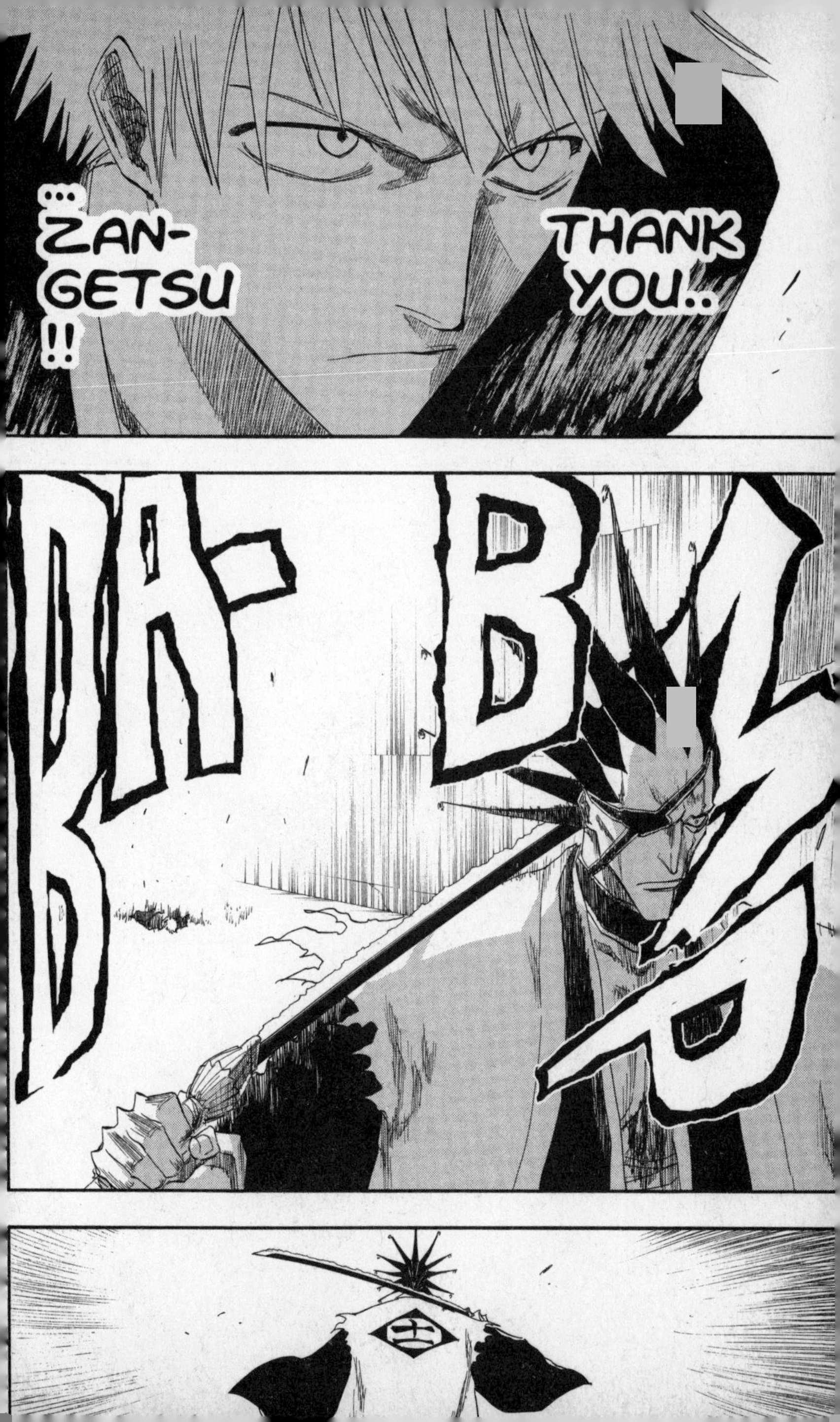
THANK YOU..
...ZAN-GETSU!!

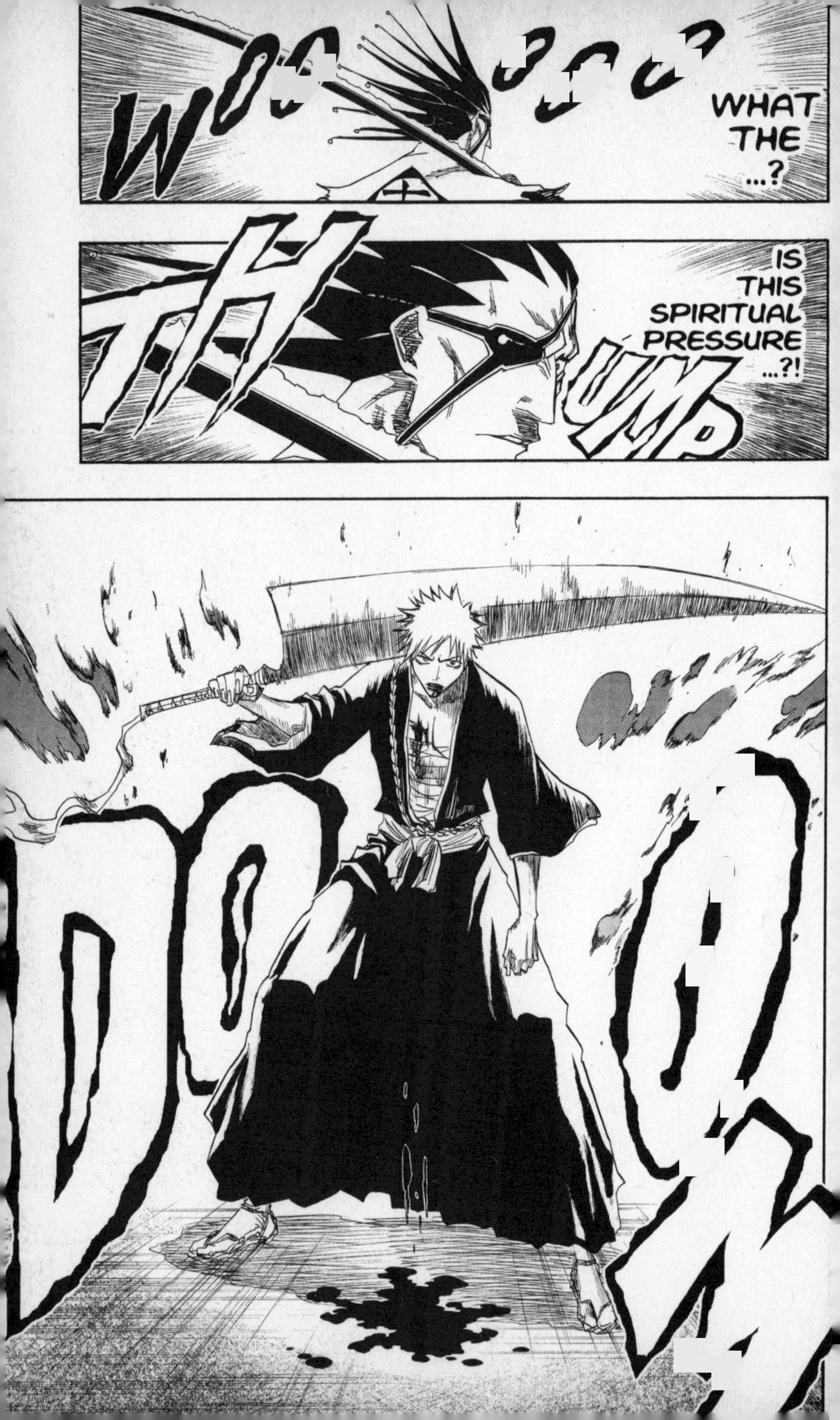
WHAT THE ...?
IS THIS SPIRITUAL PRESSURE ...?!
THUMP

~~THE DETRITUS~~
SURVIVORS OF 11TH COMPANY VISITED OUR
RELIEF STATION TODAY OUT OF THE BLUE.
THEY CAME TO SEE THEIR FELLOW COMPANY
MEN IKKAKU MADARAME AND YUMICHIKA
AYASEGAWA. THEY STARTED DRINKING AND
STRIPPING INSIDE THE RELIEF STATION. IT
WAS BEYOND MY
CONTROL. THAT'S
WHY I HATE THEIR
COMPANY. I WISH
ALL OF THEM
~~HAD BEEN~~
~~DEFEATED BY~~
~~THE RYOKA~~
GOOD HEALTH.

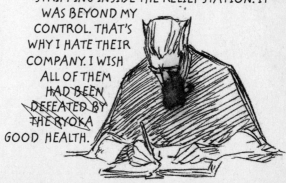

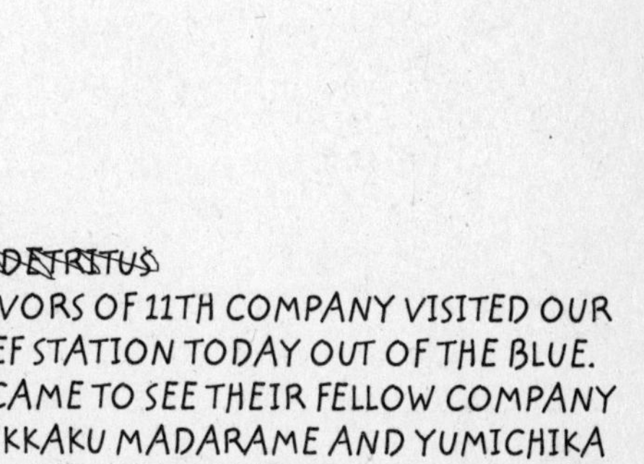

112. The Undead 2 (Rise & Rage)

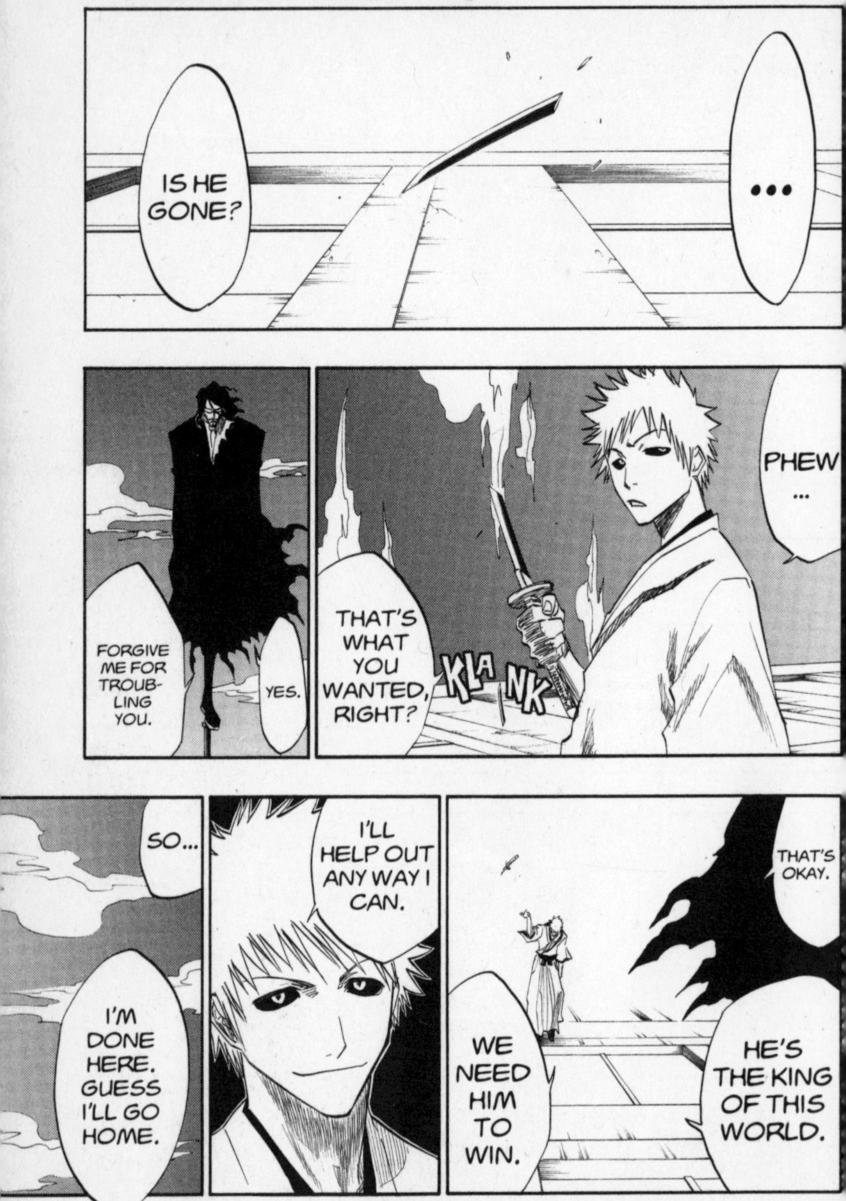
...
IS HE GONE?
PHEW...
THAT'S WHAT YOU WANTED, RIGHT?
KLANK
YES.
FORGIVE ME FOR TROUB-LING YOU.
THAT'S OKAY.
HE'S THE KING OF THIS WORLD.
WE NEED HIM TO WIN.
I'LL HELP OUT ANY WAY I CAN.
SO...
I'M DONE HERE. GUESS I'LL GO HOME.

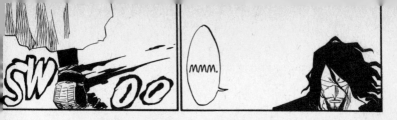

MMM.
SWOO
WOOOOOOOOOOOO
HE'S STRONG.
ZANGETSU...
...RAISE HIM WELL...
'CAUSE HIS POWER...
...WILL EVENTUALLY BE MINE.
ICHIGO...
I HATE RAIN.
IT RAINS IN THIS WORLD TOO.
WHEN YOU'RE UPSET, THE SKIES GROW CLOUDY.
WHEN YOU'RE SAD, IT RAINS.

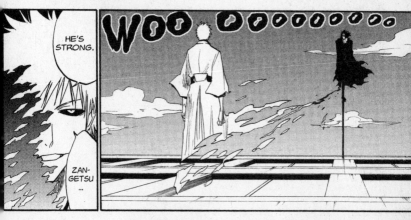

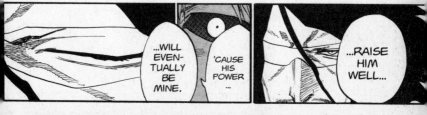

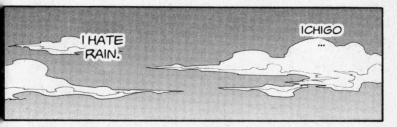

READ THIS WAY

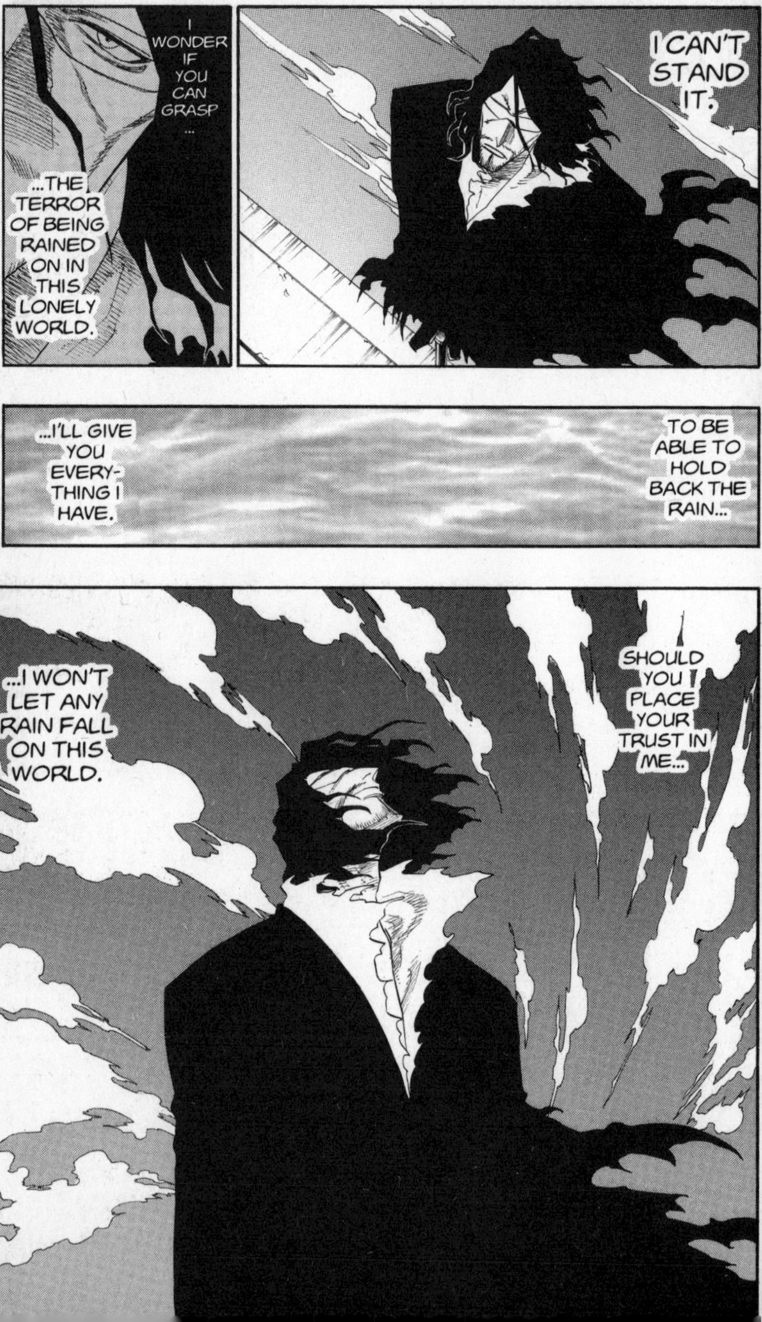
I CAN'T STAND IT.
I WONDER IF YOU CAN GRASP...
...THE TERROR OF BEING RAINED ON IN THIS LONELY WORLD.
TO BE ABLE TO HOLD BACK THE RAIN...
...I'LL GIVE YOU EVERYTHING I HAVE.
SHOULD YOU PLACE YOUR TRUST IN ME...
...I WON'T LET ANY RAIN FALL ON THIS WORLD.

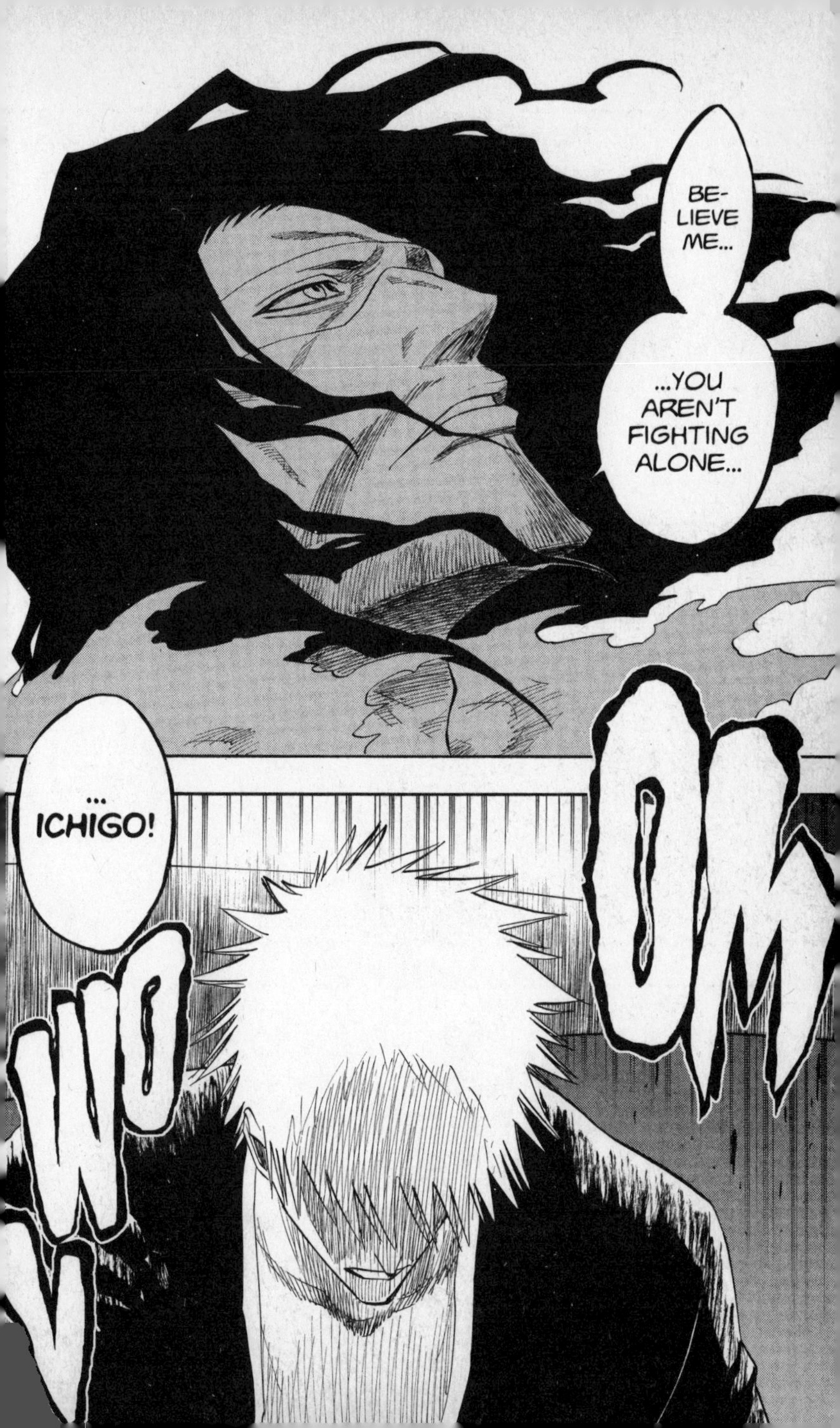
BE-LIEVE ME...
...YOU AREN'T FIGHTING ALONE...
...ICHIGO!
WOOM

READ THIS WAY

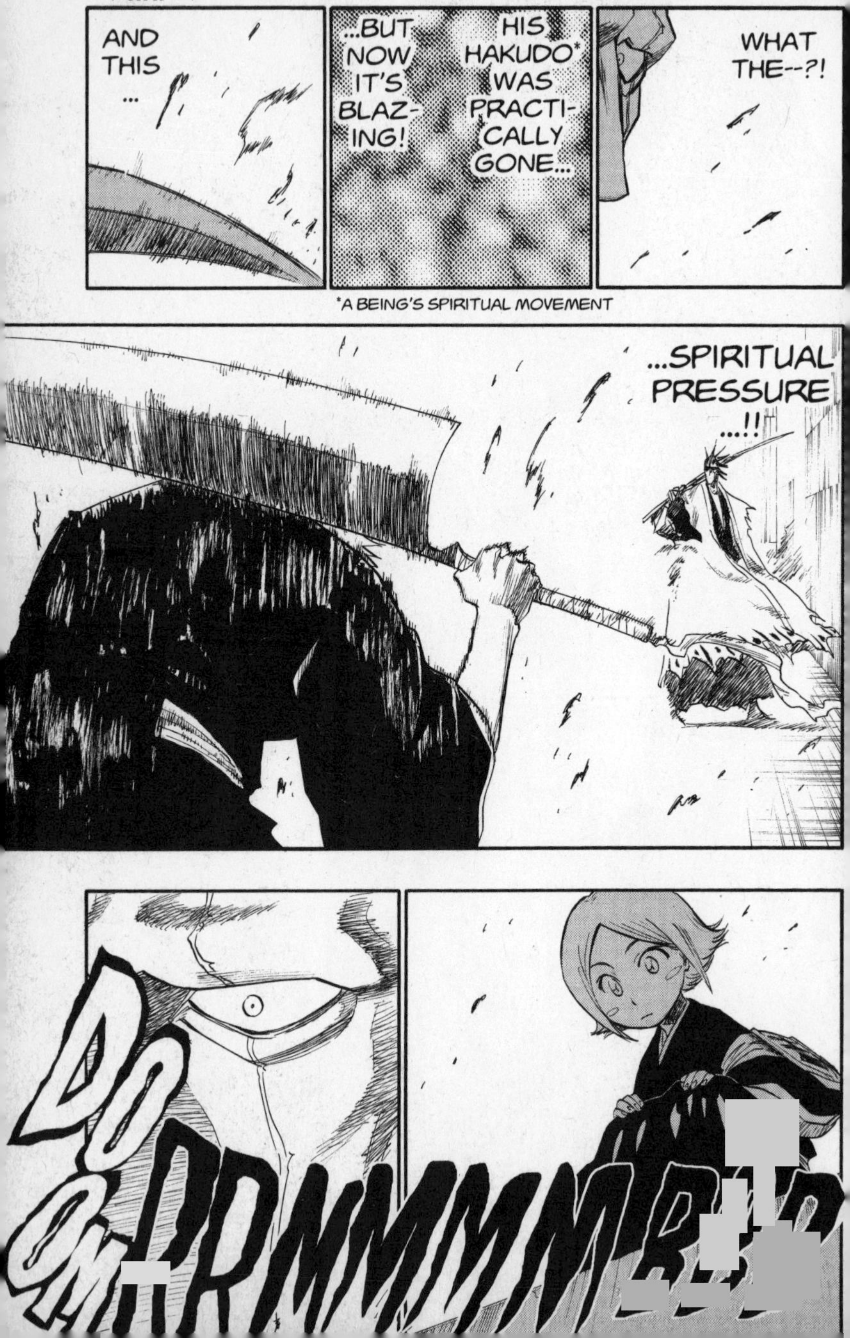
WHAT THE--?!
HIS HAKUDO* WAS PRACTICALLY GONE...
...BUT NOW IT'S BLAZING!
AND THIS ...
*A BEING'S SPIRITUAL MOVEMENT
...SPIRITUAL PRESSURE ...!!

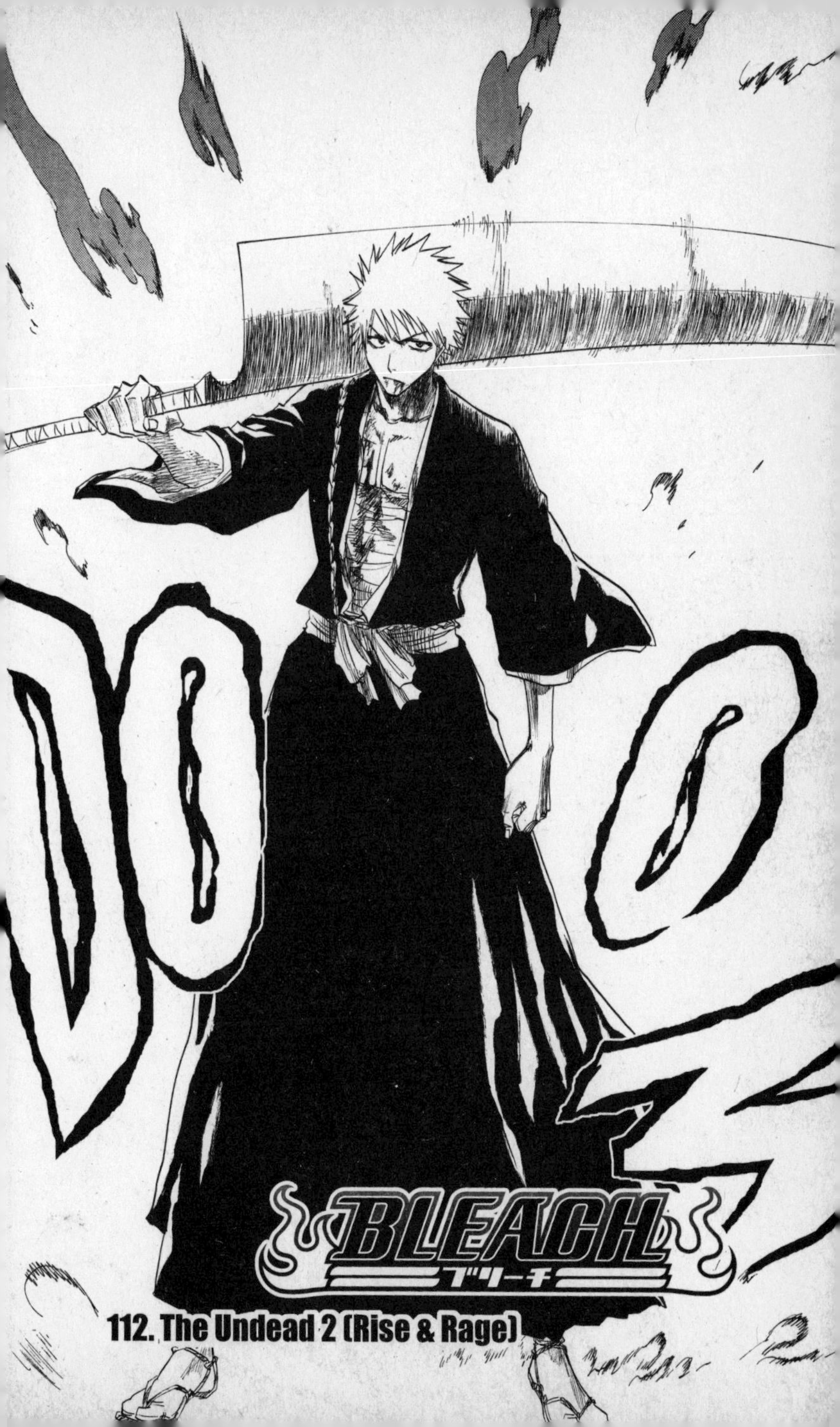
DOOOO
BLEACH
ブリーチ
112. The Undead 2 (Rise & Rage)

READ THIS WAY

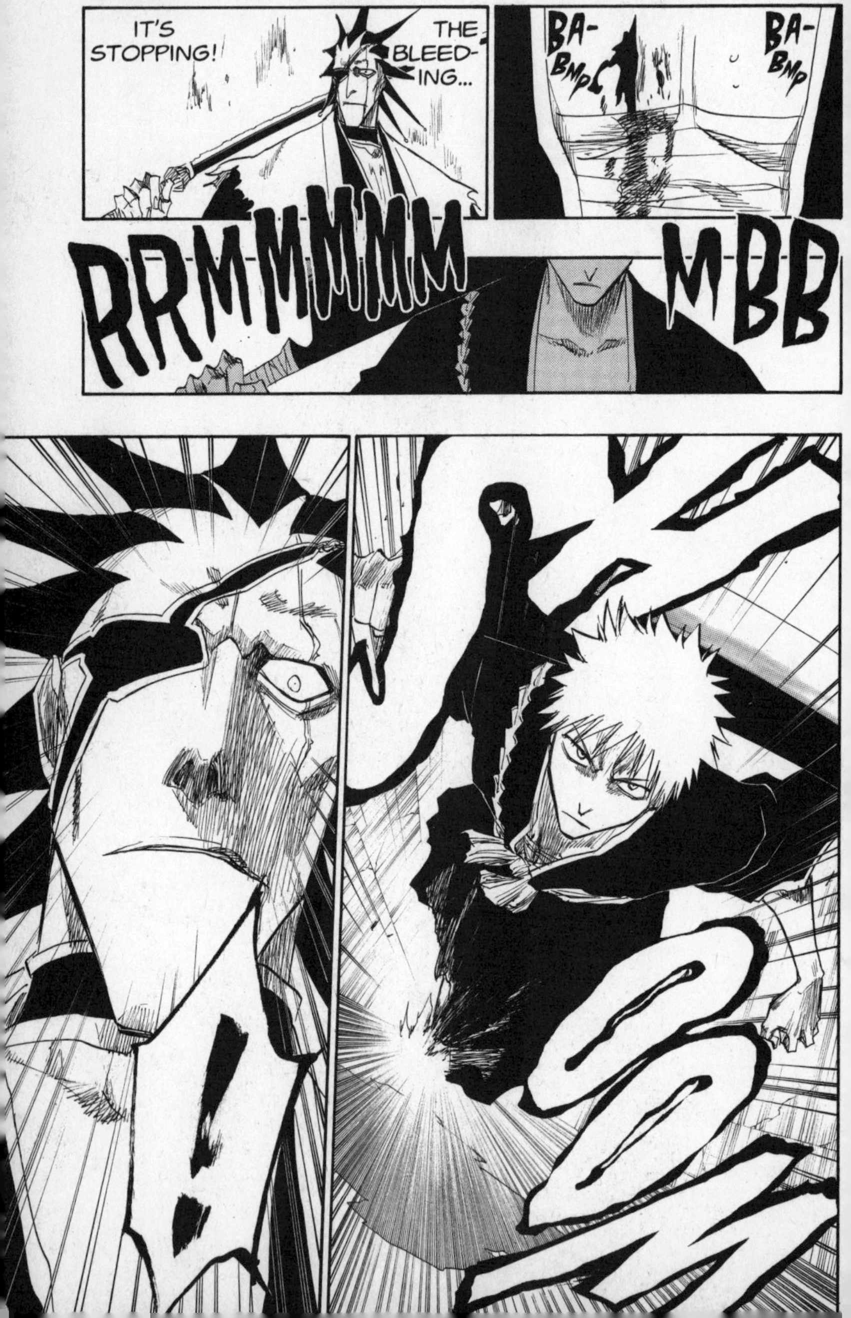
BA-BMP
BA-BMP
THE BLEEDING...
IT'S STOPPING!
RRMMMMMMMBB
!

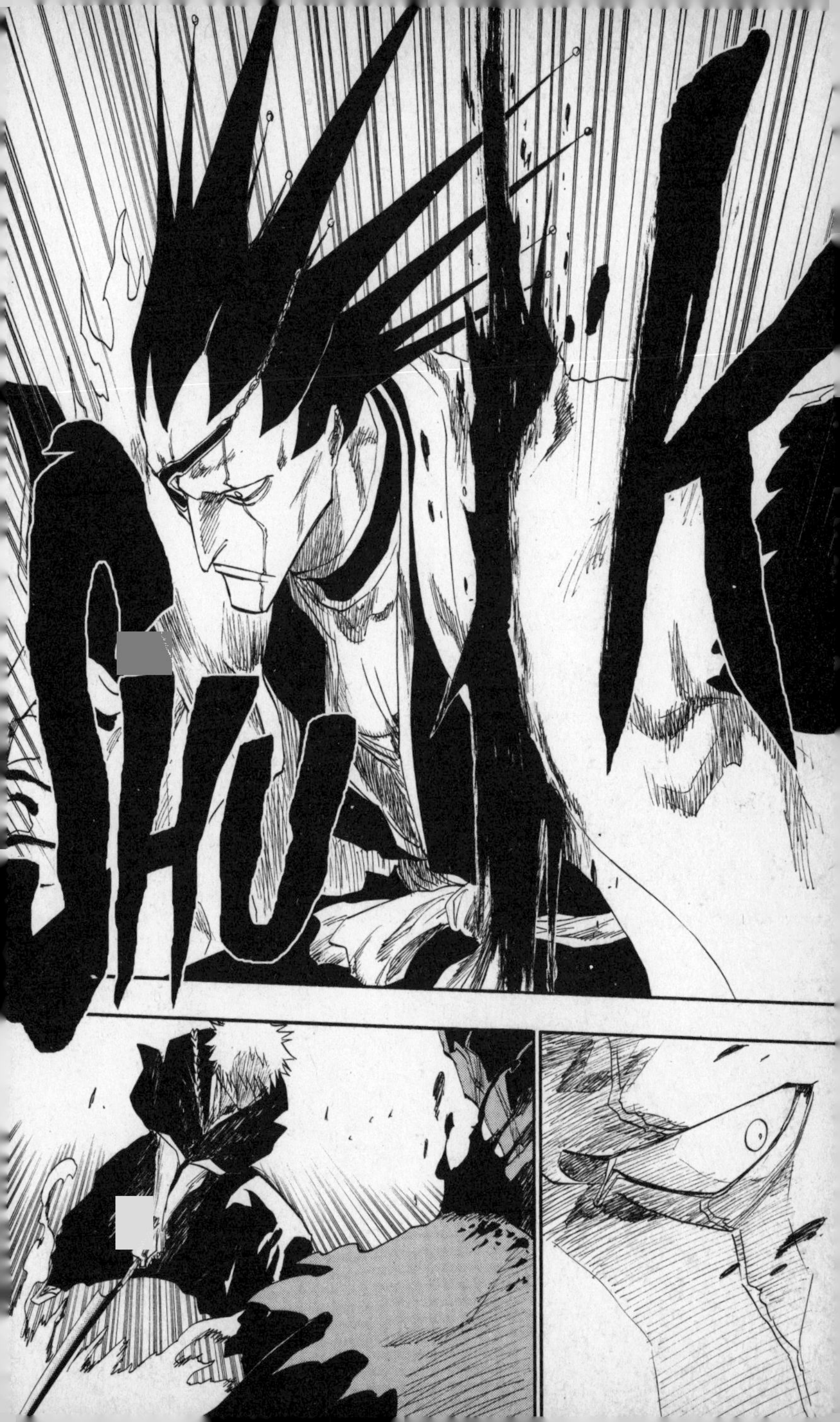
SHU

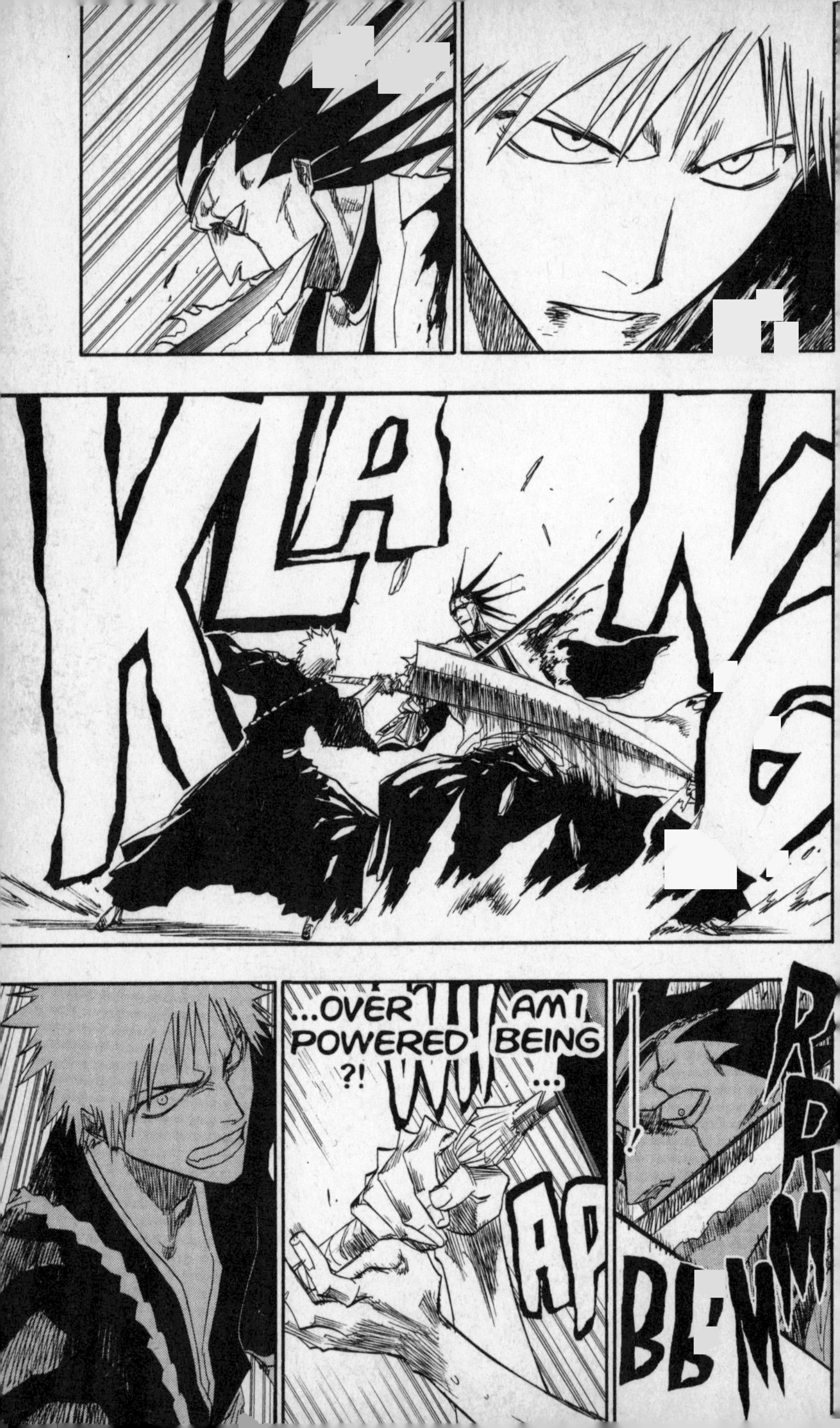
AM I BEING ...
...OVER POWERED ?!

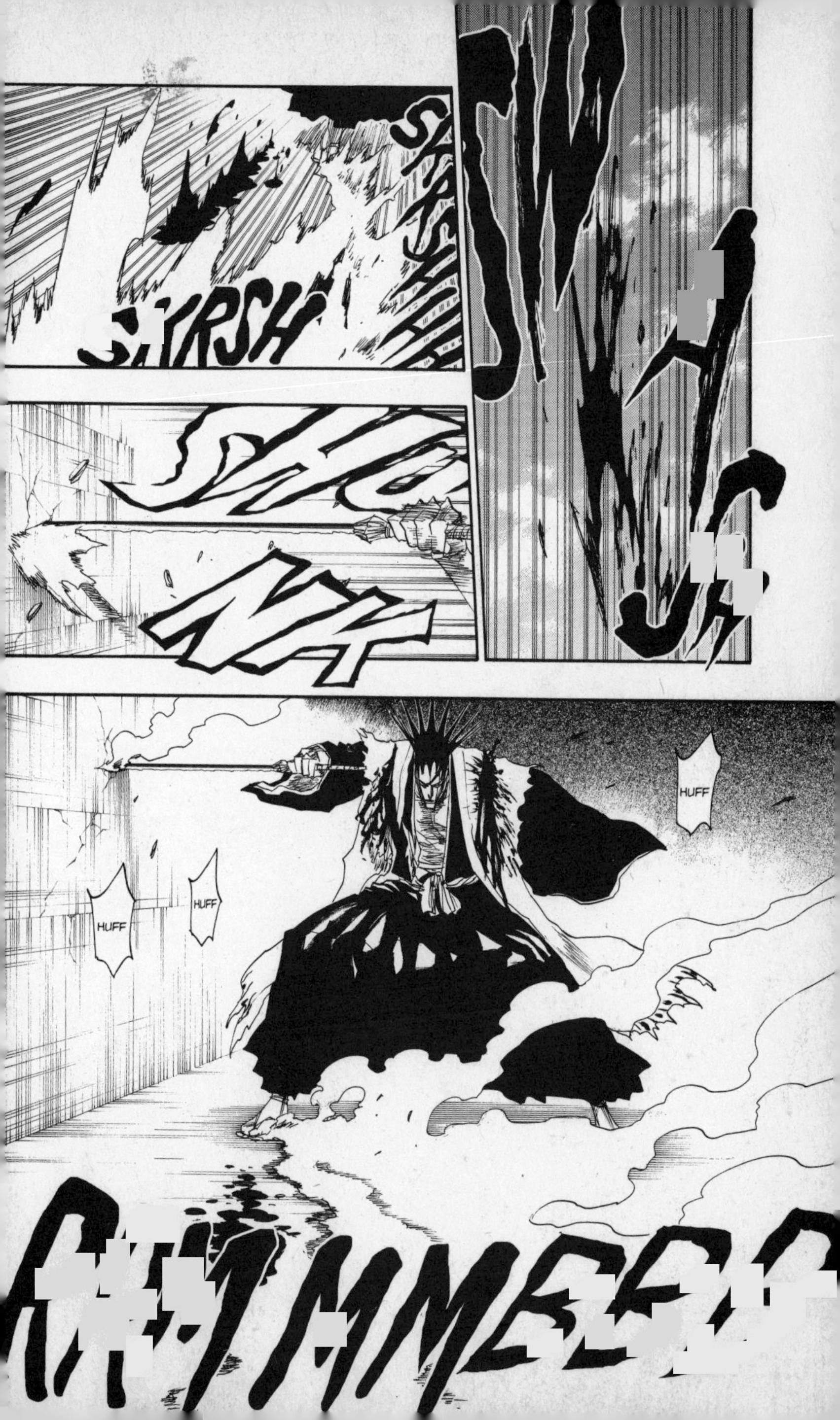
SHUNK
HUFF
HUFF
HUFF

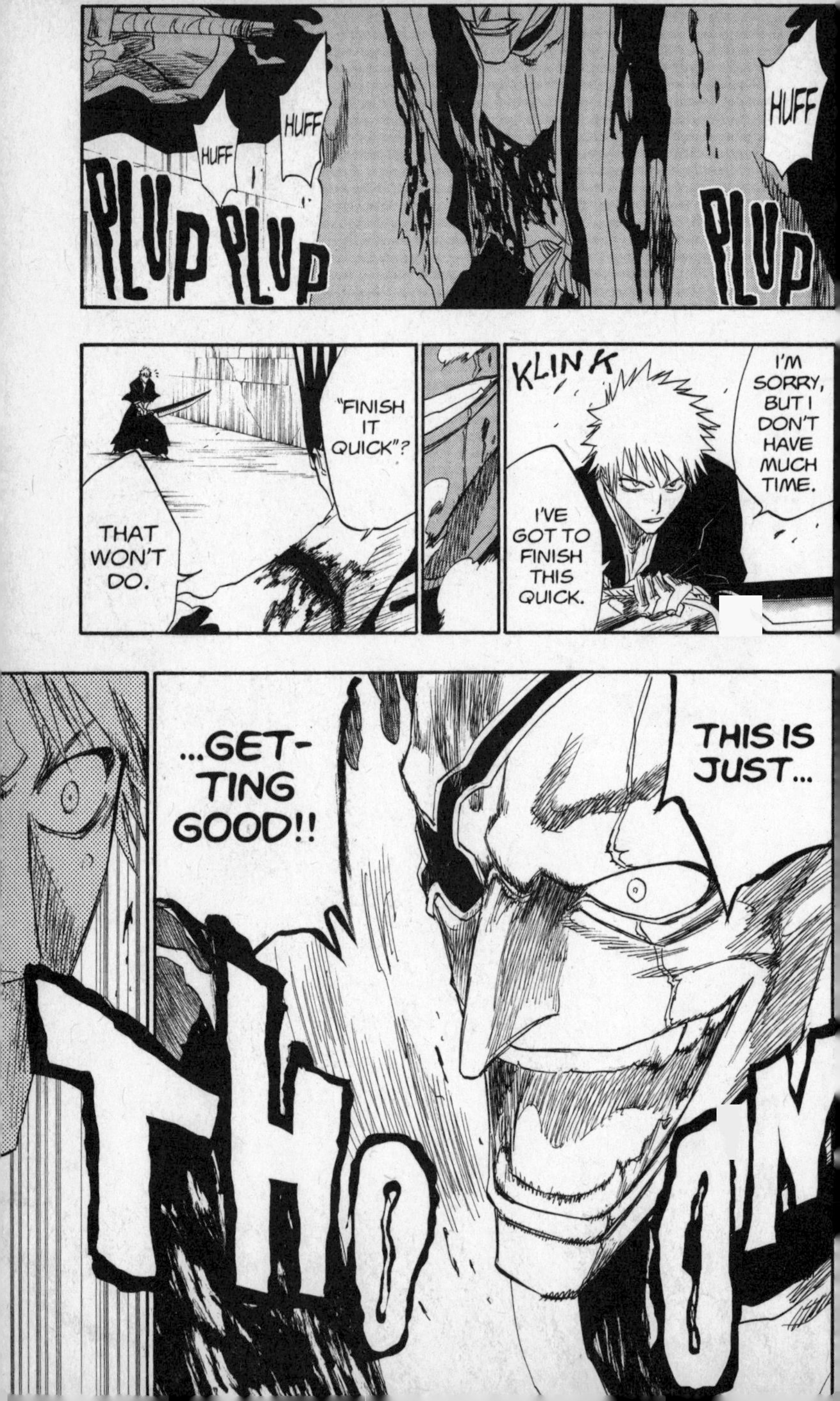
HUFF
PLUP
HUFF
HUFF
PLUP PLUP
I'M SORRY, BUT I DON'T HAVE MUCH TIME.
KLINK
I'VE GOT TO FINISH THIS QUICK.
"FINISH IT QUICK"?
THAT WON'T DO.
THIS IS JUST...
...GET-TING GOOD!!
THOOM

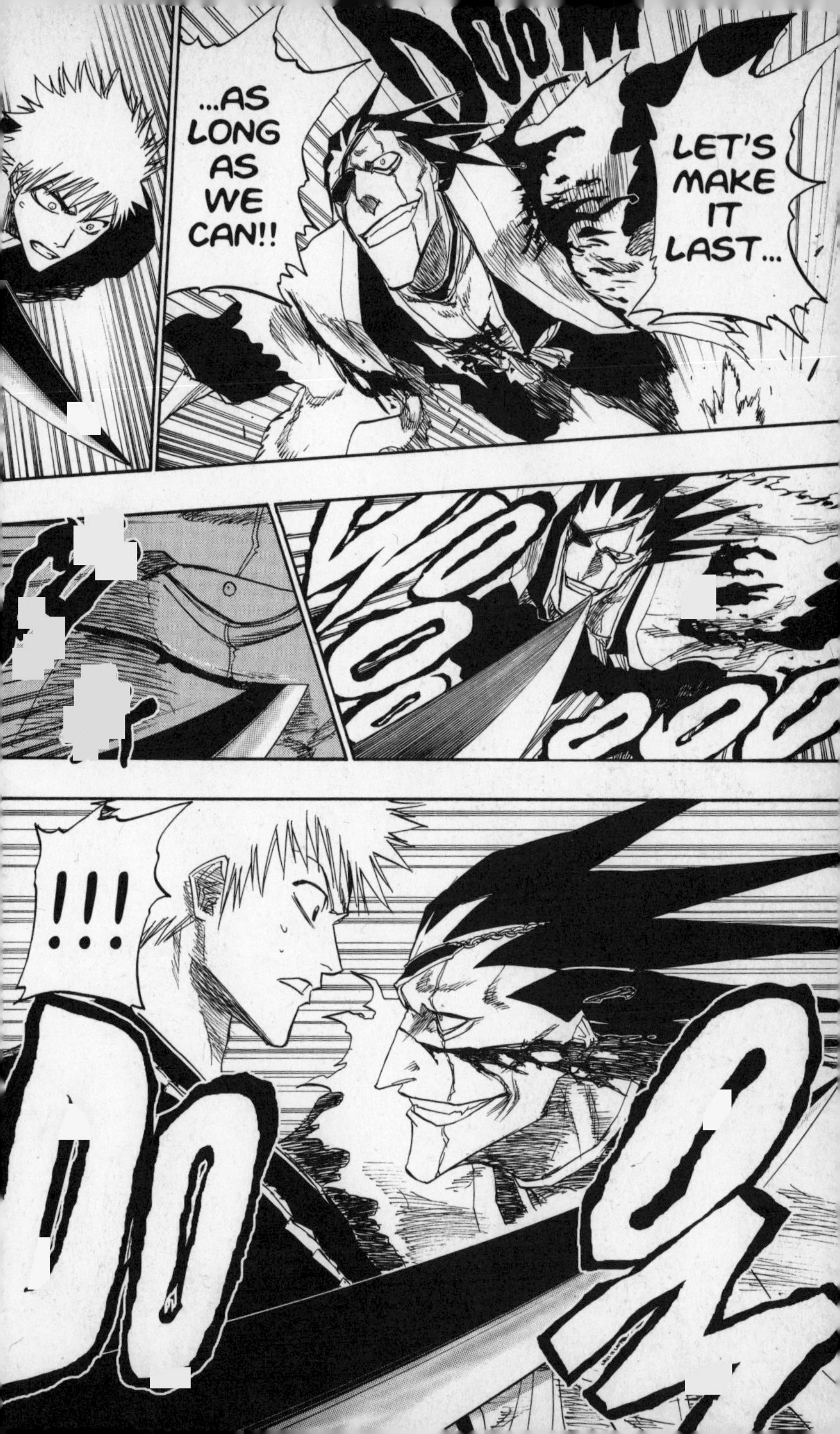
DOOM
LET'S MAKE IT LAST...
...AS LONG AS WE CAN!!
!!!

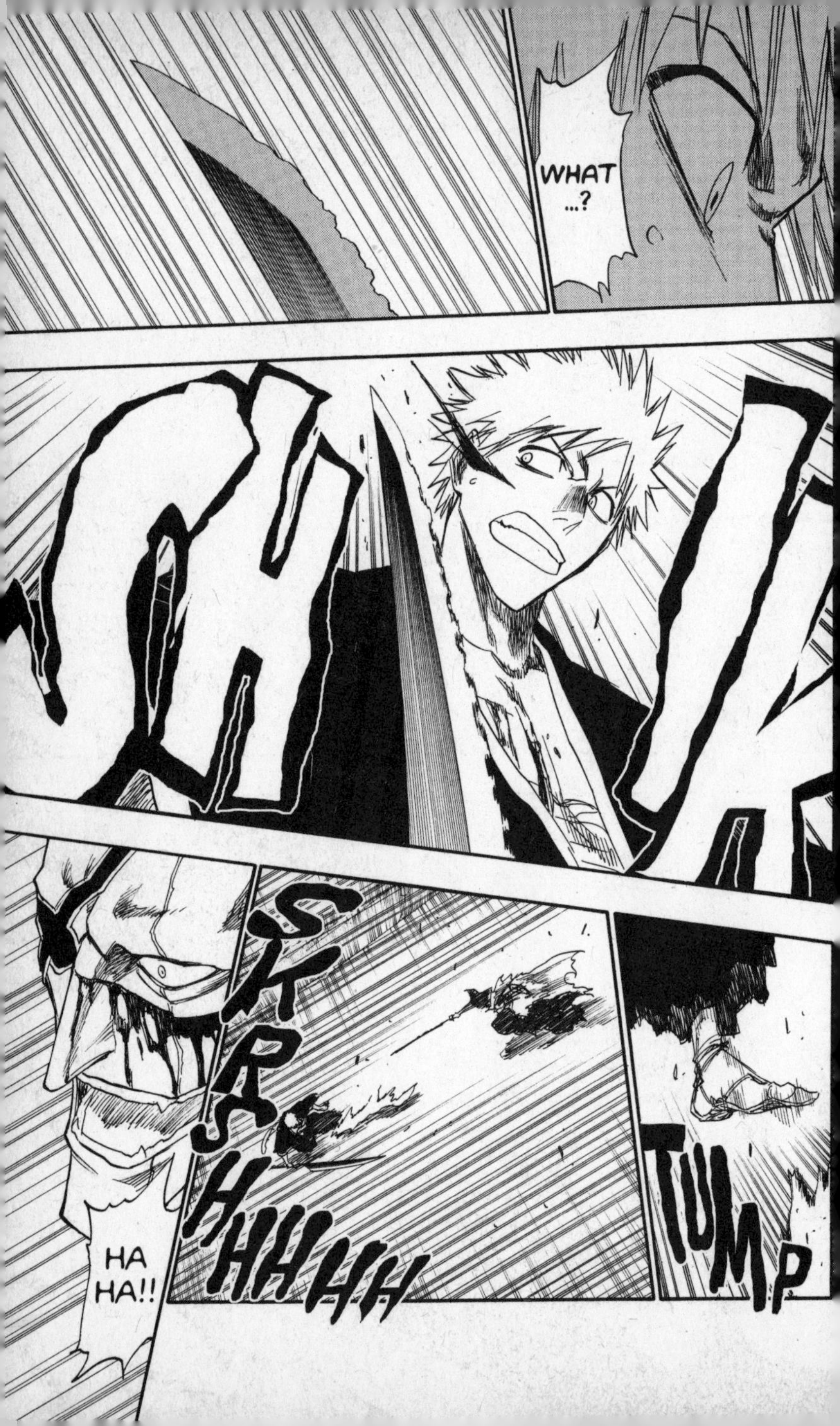
WHAT ...?
TUMP
SKRASHHHHHH
HA HA!!

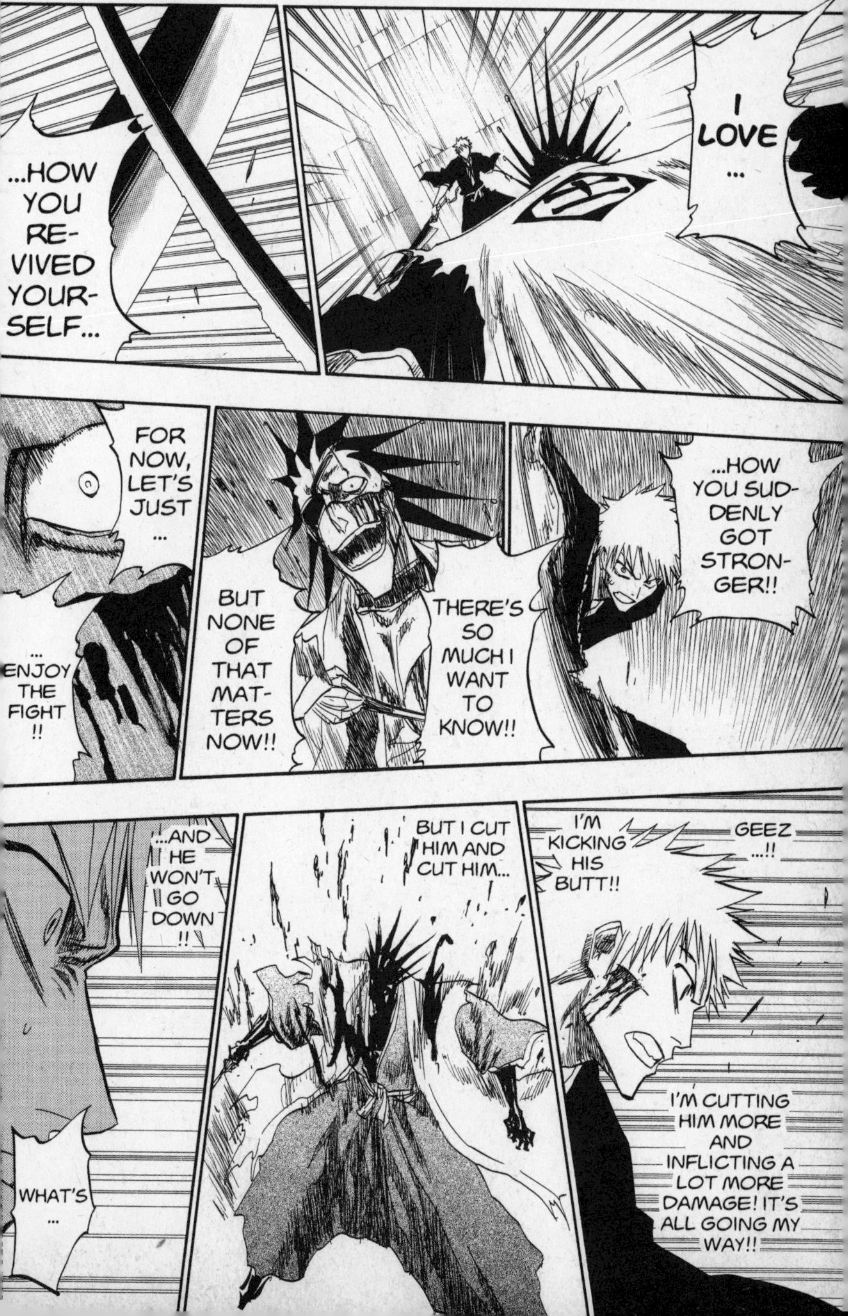
I LOVE ...
...HOW YOU RE-VIVED YOUR-SELF...
...HOW YOU SUD-DENLY GOT STRON-GER!!
THERE'S SO MUCH I WANT TO KNOW!!
BUT NONE OF THAT MAT-TERS NOW!!
FOR NOW, LET'S JUST ...
... ENJOY THE FIGHT !!
GEEZ ...!!
I'M KICKING HIS BUTT!!
I'M CUTTING HIM MORE AND INFLICTING A LOT MORE DAMAGE! IT'S ALL GOING MY WAY!!
BUT I CUT HIM AND CUT HIM...
...AND HE WON'T GO DOWN !!
WHAT'S ...

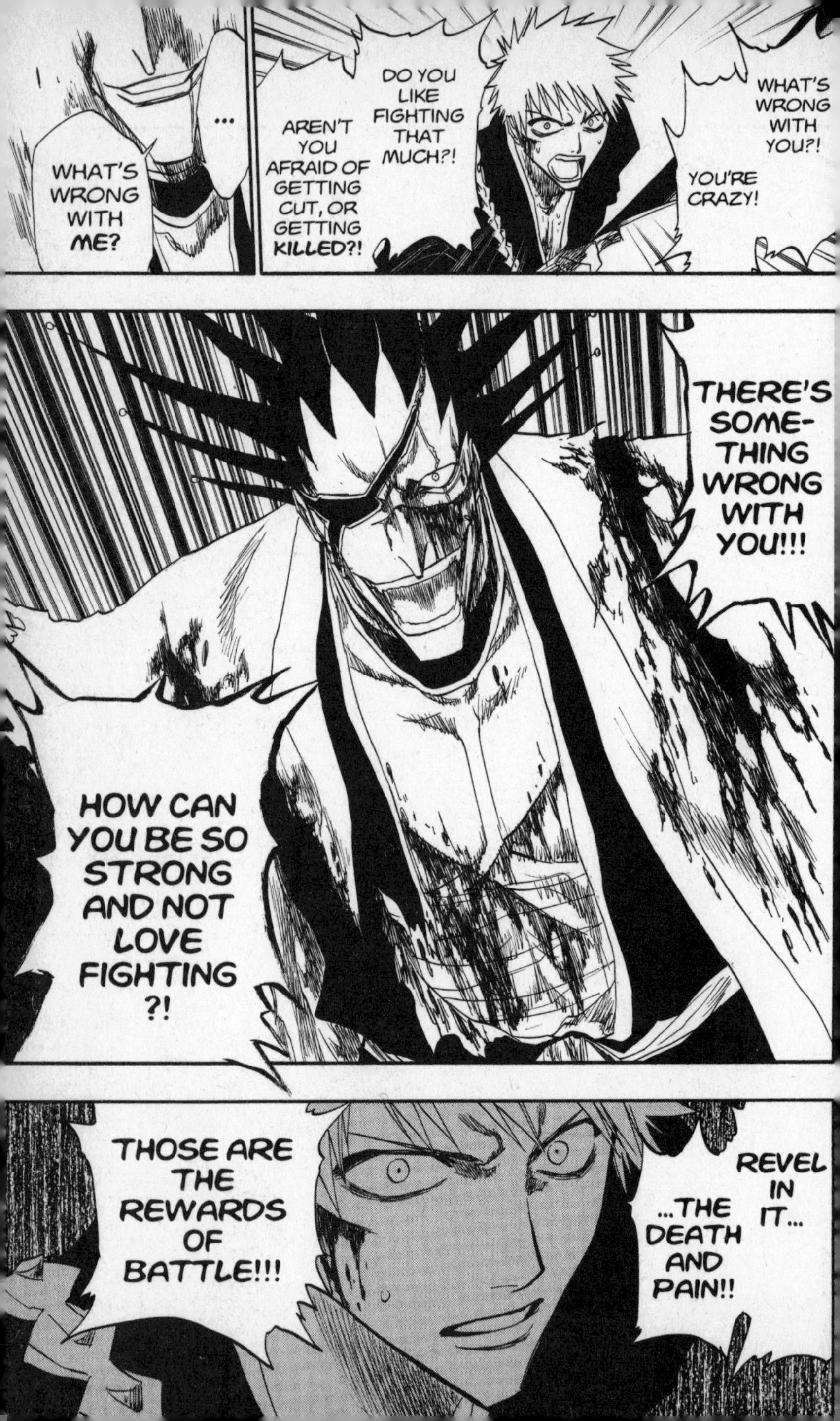
WHAT'S WRONG WITH YOU?!
YOU'RE CRAZY!
DO YOU LIKE FIGHTING THAT MUCH?!
AREN'T YOU AFRAID OF GETTING CUT, OR GETTING KILLED?!
...
WHAT'S WRONG WITH ME?
THERE'S SOME-THING WRONG WITH YOU!!!
HOW CAN YOU BE SO STRONG AND NOT LOVE FIGHTING ?!
REVEL IN IT...
...THE DEATH AND PAIN!!
THOSE ARE THE REWARDS OF BATTLE!!!

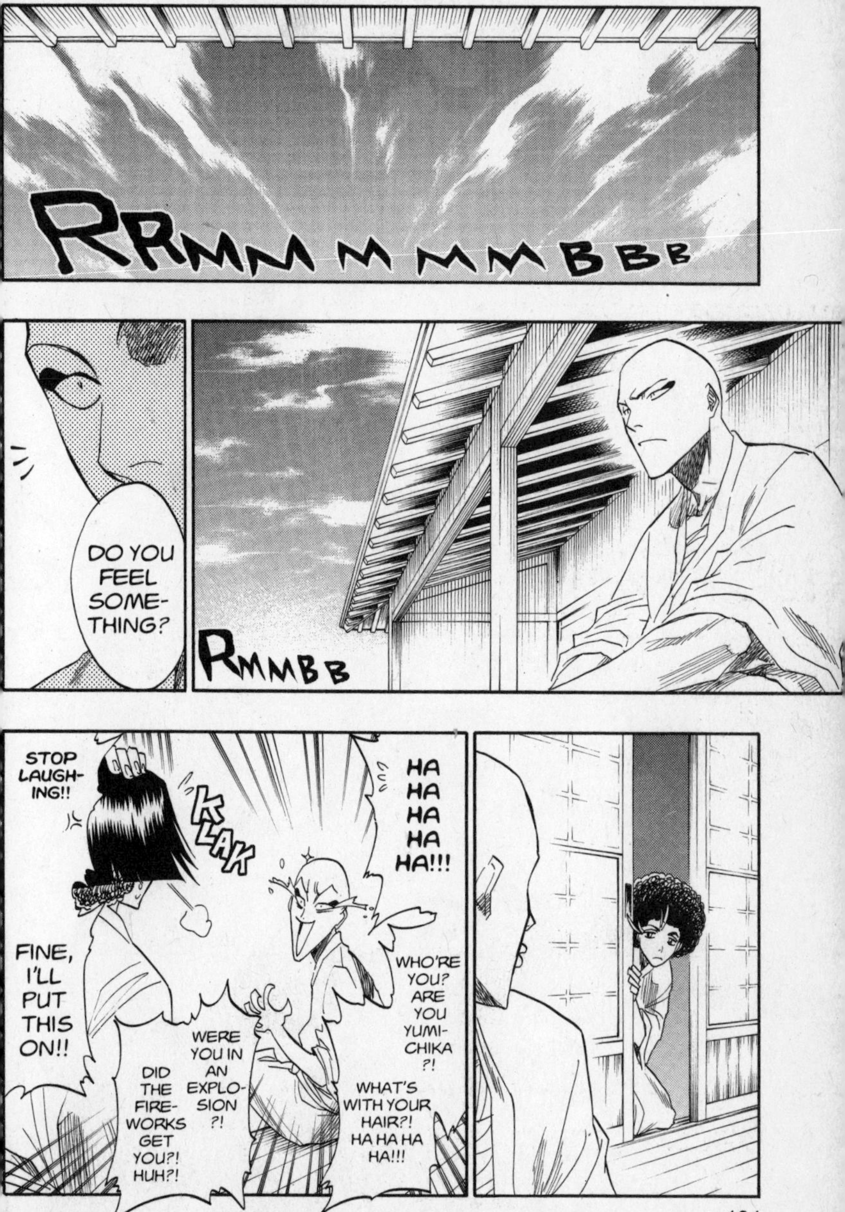
RRMMMMMMBBB
RMMBB
DO YOU FEEL SOMETHING?
HA HA HA HA HA!!!
KLAK
STOP LAUGHING!!
WHO'RE YOU? ARE YOU YUMICHIKA?!
WHAT'S WITH YOUR HAIR?! HA HA HA HA!!!
WERE YOU IN AN EXPLOSION?!
DID THE FIREWORKS GET YOU?! HUH?!
FINE, I'LL PUT THIS ON!!

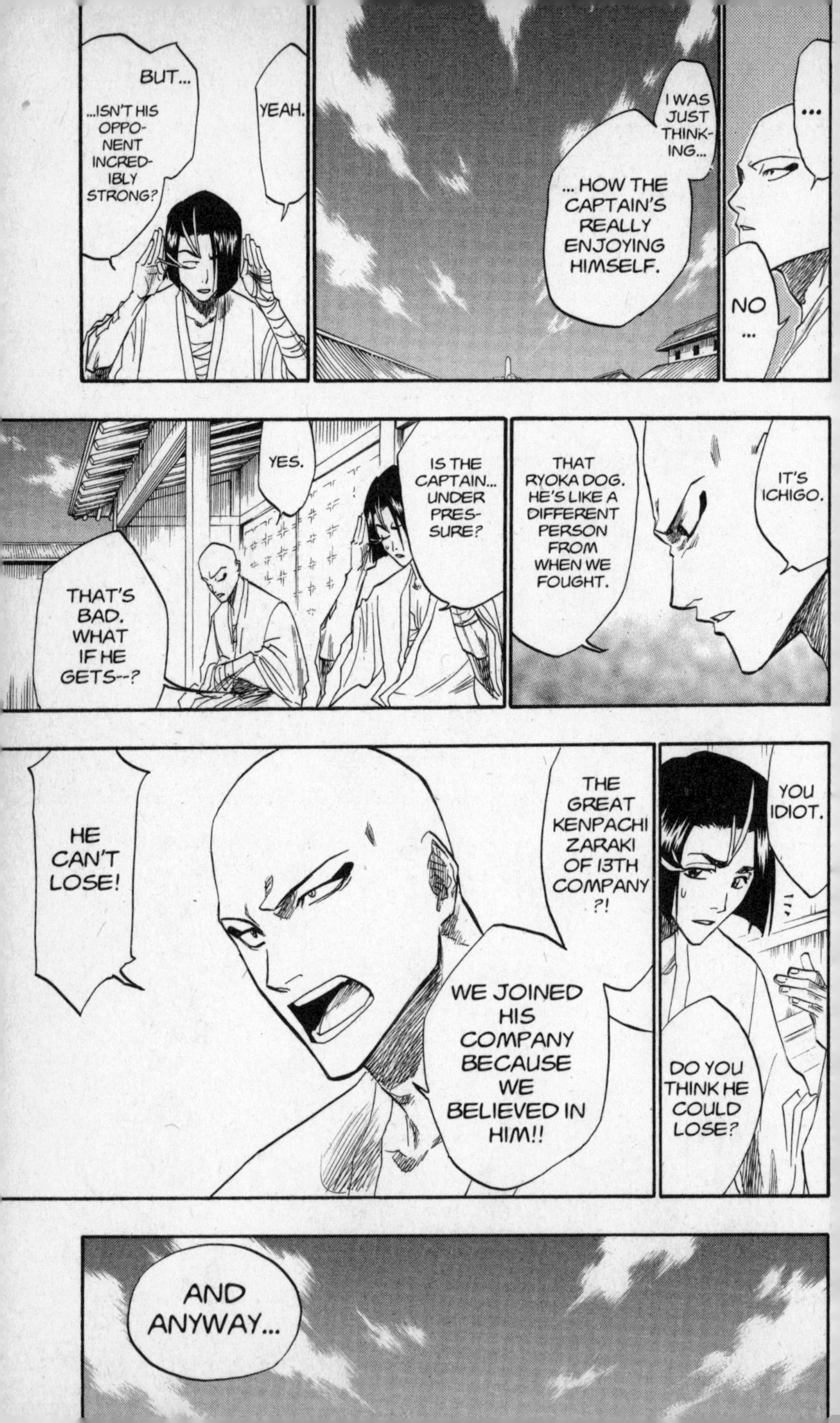
...
NO...
I WAS JUST THINKING...
... HOW THE CAPTAIN'S REALLY ENJOYING HIMSELF.
YEAH.
BUT...
...ISN'T HIS OPPONENT INCREDIBLY STRONG?
IT'S ICHIGO.
THAT RYOKA DOG. HE'S LIKE A DIFFERENT PERSON FROM WHEN WE FOUGHT.
IS THE CAPTAIN... UNDER PRESSURE?
YES.
THAT'S BAD. WHAT IF HE GETS--?
YOU IDIOT.
DO YOU THINK HE COULD LOSE?
THE GREAT KENPACHI ZARAKI OF 13TH COMPANY?!
WE JOINED HIS COMPANY BECAUSE WE BELIEVED IN HIM!!
HE CAN'T LOSE!
AND ANYWAY...

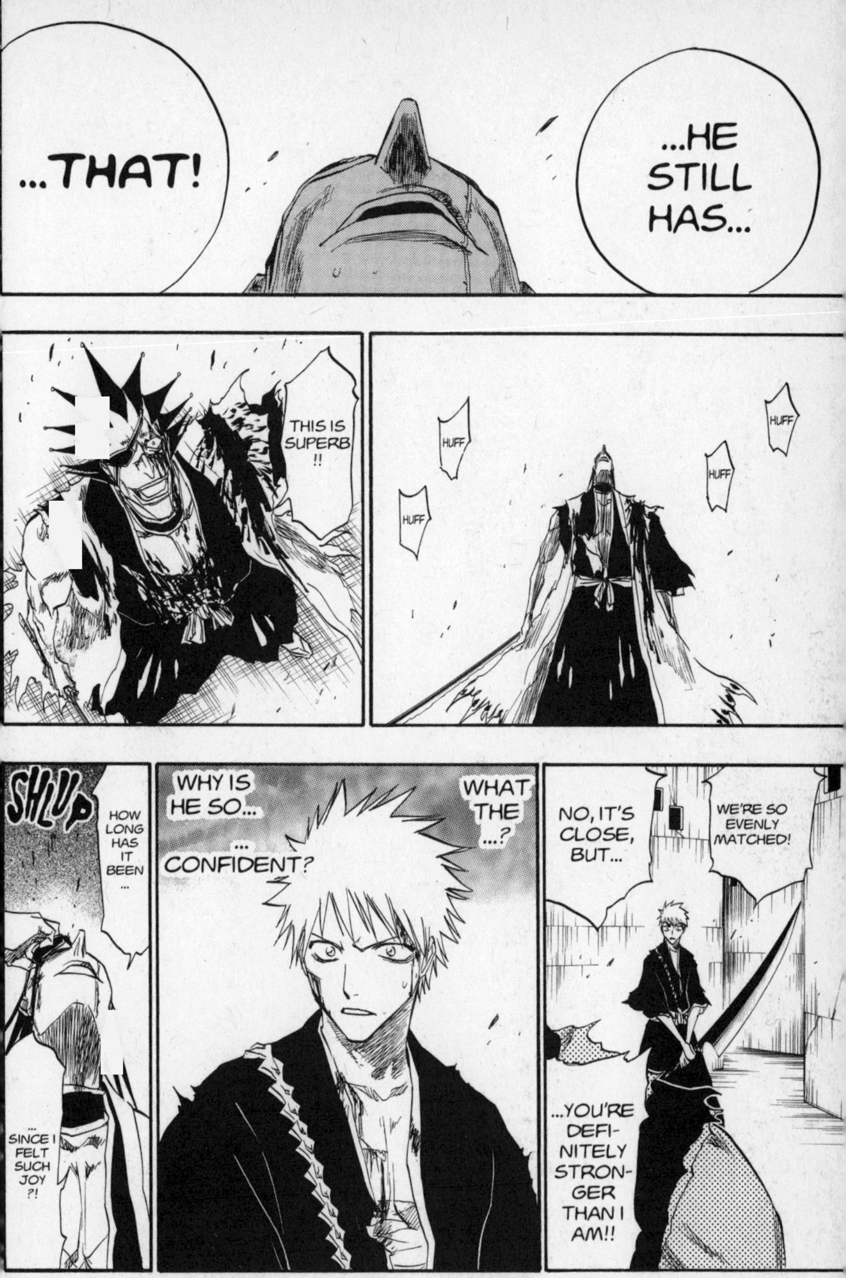
...HE STILL HAS...
...THAT!
HUFF
HUFF
HUFF
HUFF
THIS IS SUPERB !!
WE'RE SO EVENLY MATCHED!
NO, IT'S CLOSE, BUT...
...YOU'RE DEFI-NITELY STRON-GER THAN I AM!!
WHAT THE ...?
WHY IS HE SO...
... CONFIDENT?
SHLUP
HOW LONG HAS IT BEEN ...
... SINCE I FELT SUCH JOY ?!

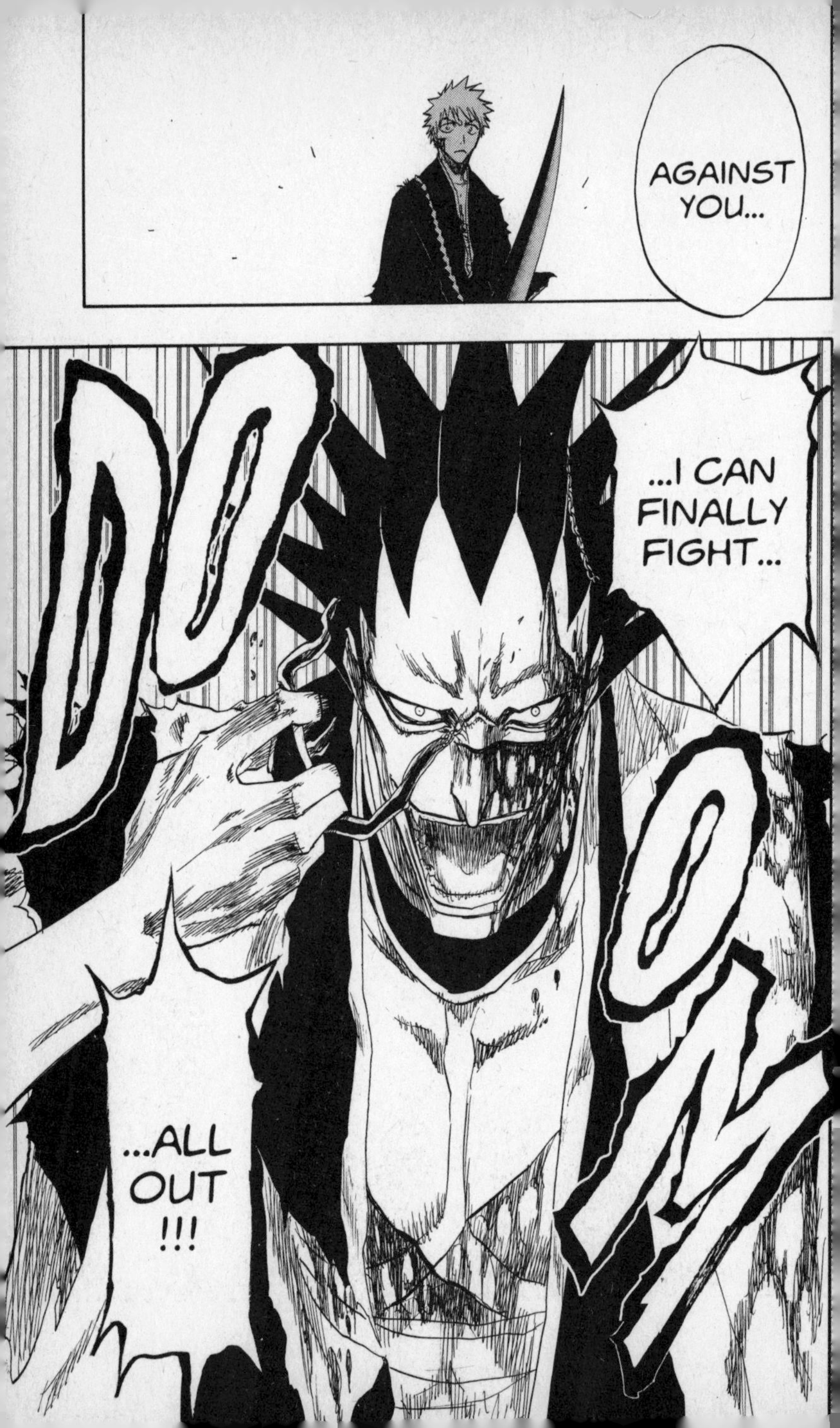
AGAINST YOU...
...I CAN FINALLY FIGHT...
DOON
...ALL OUT !!!

TODAY, MADARAME AND AYASEGAWA OF 11TH COMPANY IGNORED MY INSTRUCTIONS TO REST AND CHATTED IT UP ON THE VERANDA. I JUST WISH I COULD TELL THEM TO LEAVE IF THEY AREN'T PLANNING TO GET BETTER. YUMICHIKA'S LOWER THAN ME IN RANK, BUT HE BOSSES ME AROUND SAYING THINGS LIKE, "HEY, YOU. CAN YOU PASS ME THE NAIL-CLIPPERS?" THAT JERK. THEY WOULD GET BETTER SOON.

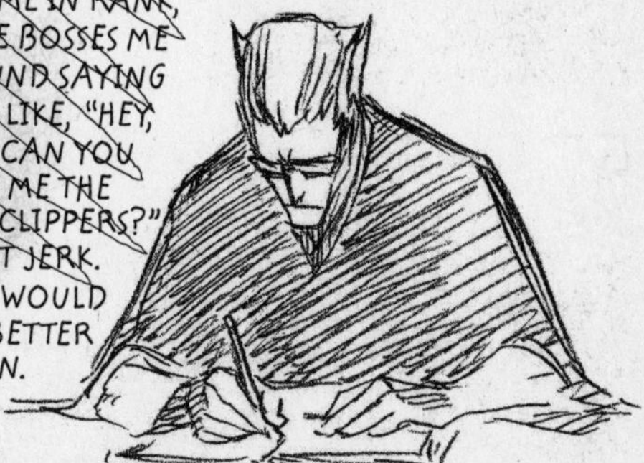

113. The Undead 3 (Closing Frantica)

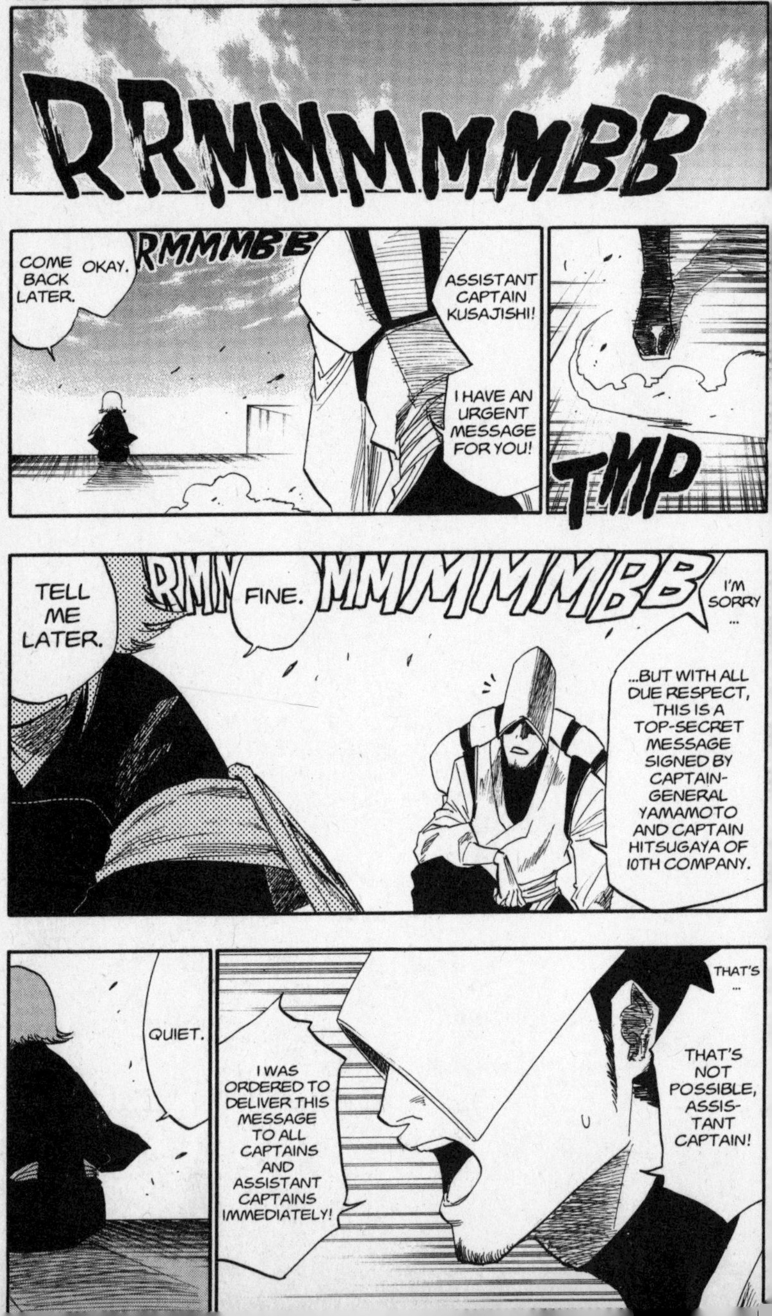
RRMMMMMBB
TMP
RMMMBB
ASSISTANT CAPTAIN KUSAJISHI!
I HAVE AN URGENT MESSAGE FOR YOU!
OKAY.
COME BACK LATER.
I'M SORRY...
...BUT WITH ALL DUE RESPECT, THIS IS A TOP-SECRET MESSAGE SIGNED BY CAPTAIN-GENERAL YAMAMOTO AND CAPTAIN HITSUGAYA OF 10TH COMPANY.
RMMMMMMMMBB
FINE.
TELL ME LATER.
THAT'S...
THAT'S NOT POSSIBLE, ASSIS-TANT CAPTAIN!
I WAS ORDERED TO DELIVER THIS MESSAGE TO ALL CAPTAINS AND ASSISTANT CAPTAINS IMMEDIATELY!
QUIET.

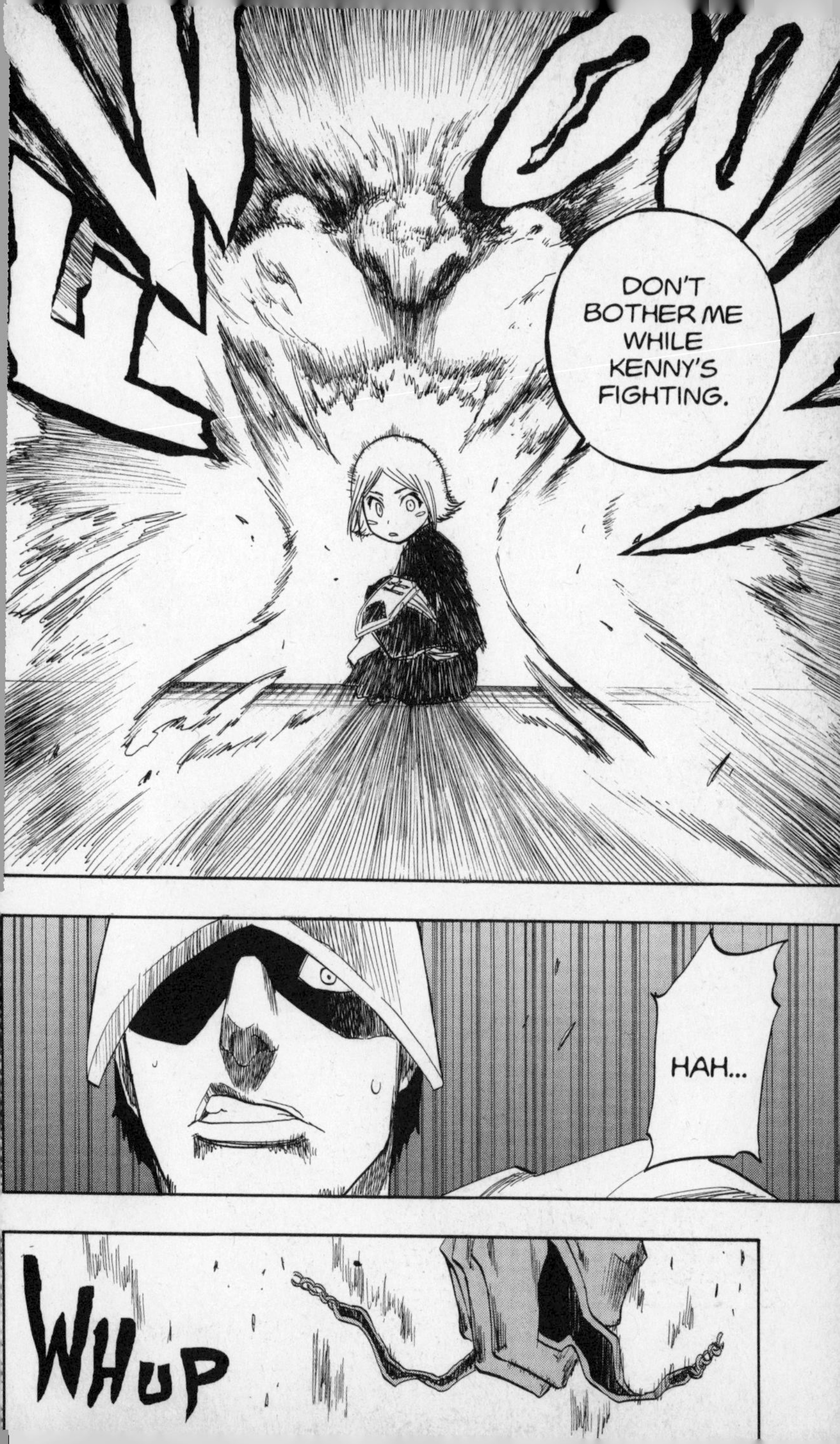
DON'T BOTHER ME WHILE KENNY'S FIGHTING.
HAH...
WHUP

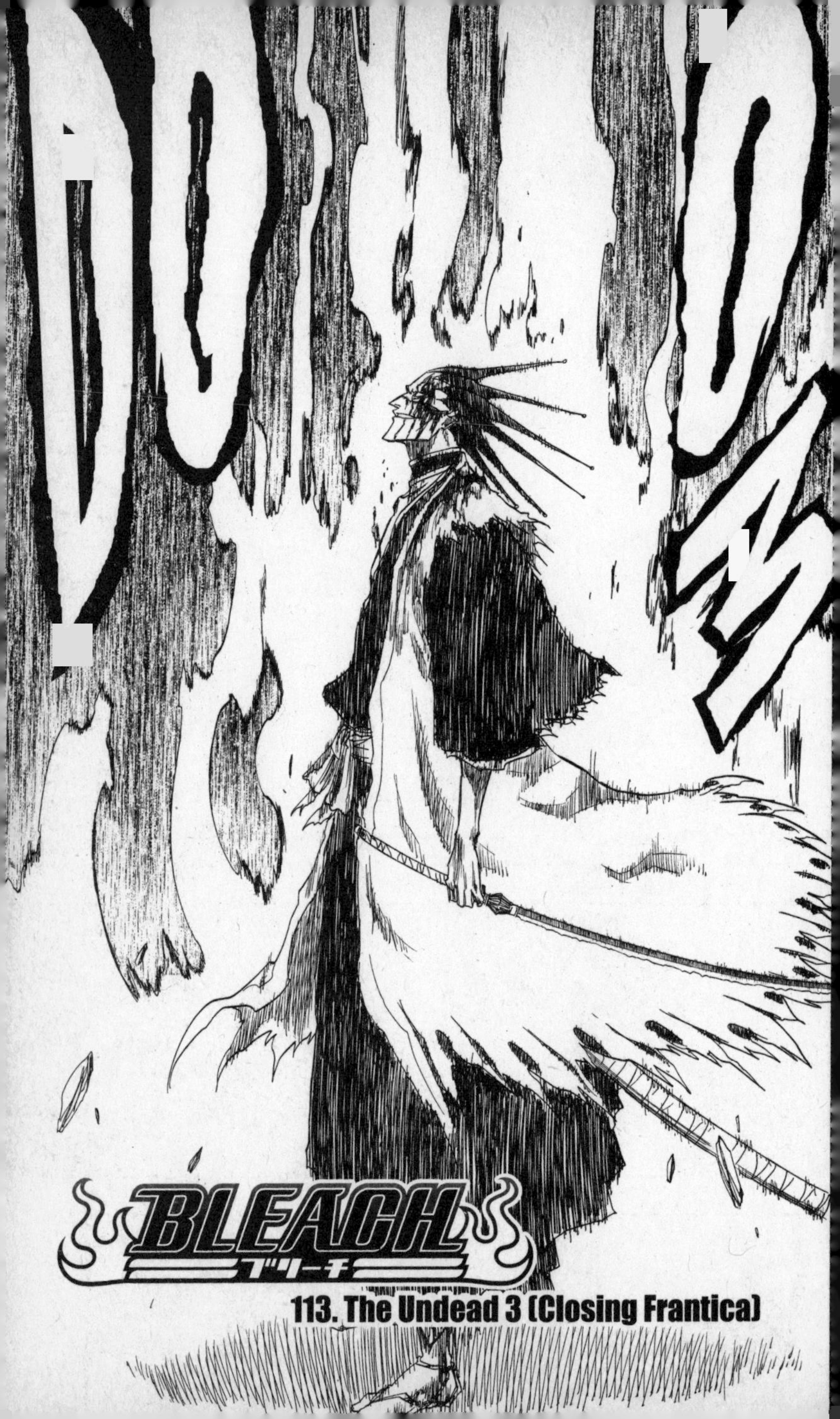

BLEACH

ブリーチ

113. The Undead 3 (Closing Frantica)

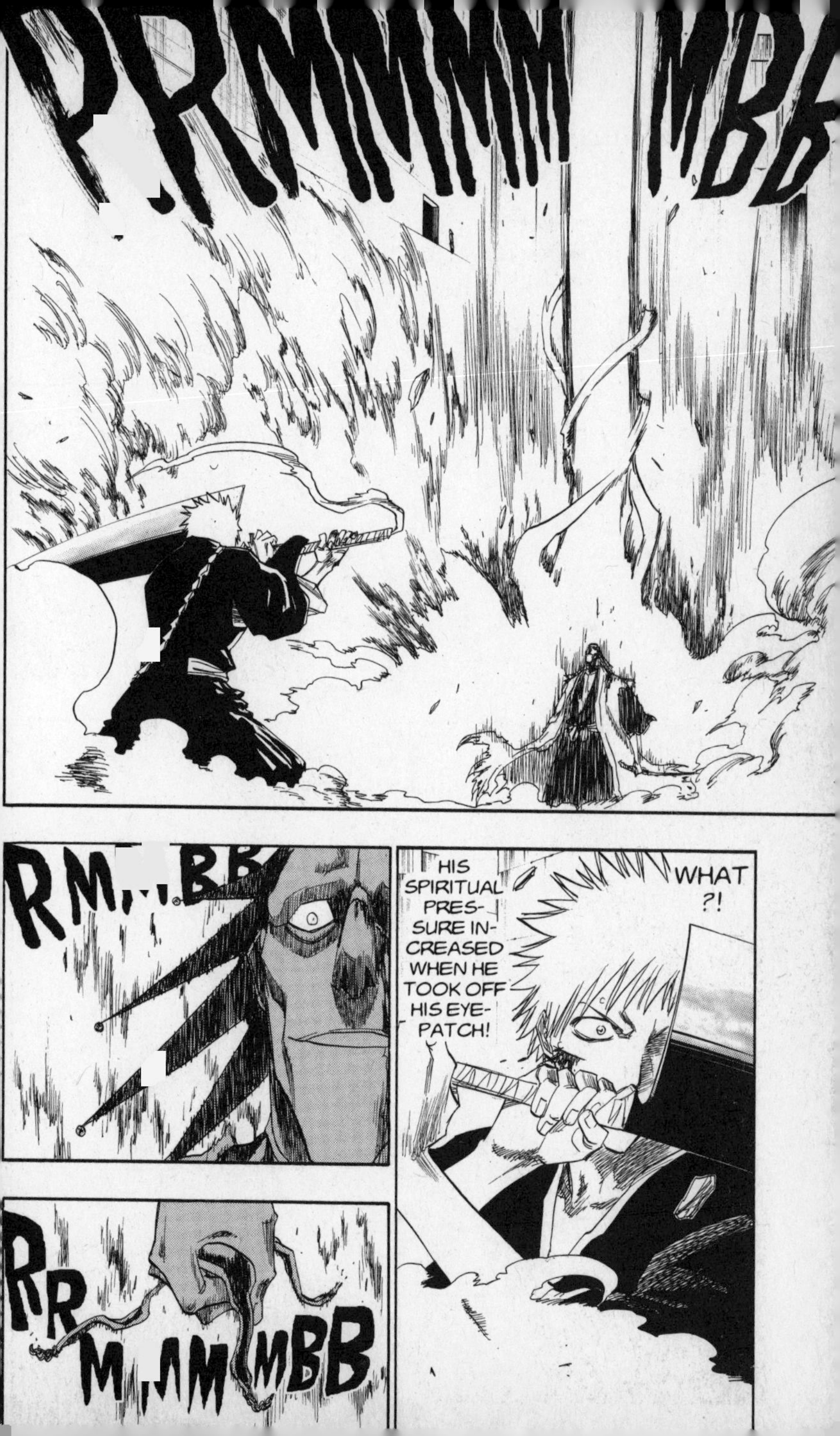
PRMMMMM MBB
WHAT ?!
HIS SPIRITUAL PRES-SURE IN-CREASED WHEN HE TOOK OFF HIS EYE-PATCH!
RMMBB
RRMMMMBB

READ THIS WAY

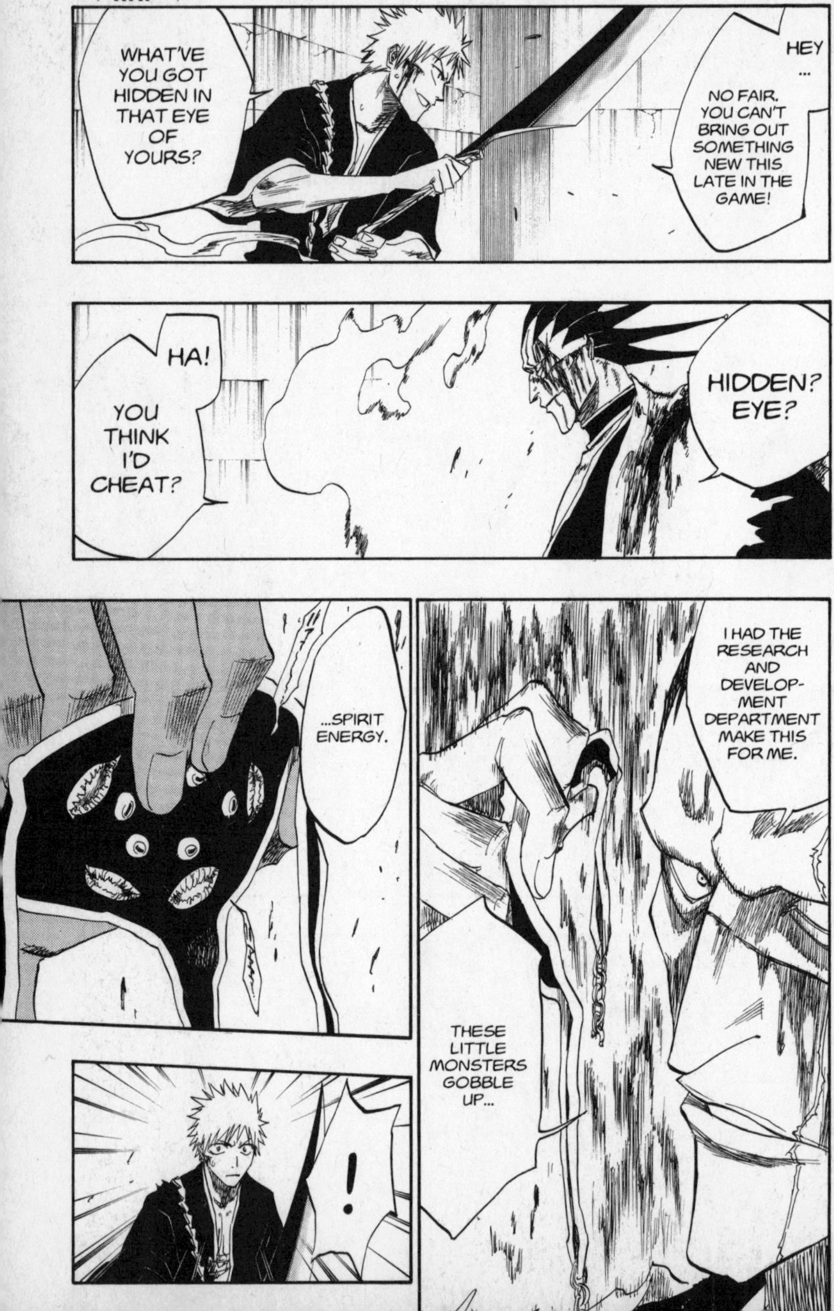
HEY ... NO FAIR. YOU CAN'T BRING OUT SOMETHING NEW THIS LATE IN THE GAME!
WHAT'VE YOU GOT HIDDEN IN THAT EYE OF YOURS?
HIDDEN? EYE?
HA! YOU THINK I'D CHEAT?
I HAD THE RESEARCH AND DEVELOP-MENT DEPARTMENT MAKE THIS FOR ME.
THESE LITTLE MONSTERS GOBBLE UP...
...SPIRIT ENERGY.
!

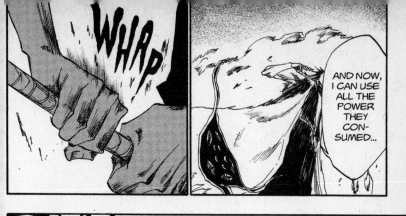

AND NOW, I CAN USE ALL THE POWER THEY CONSUMED...

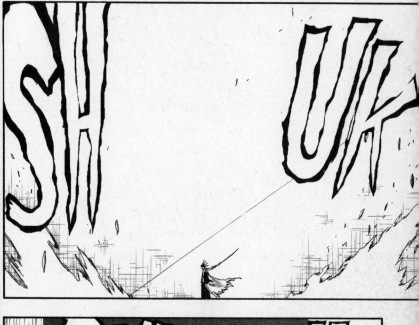

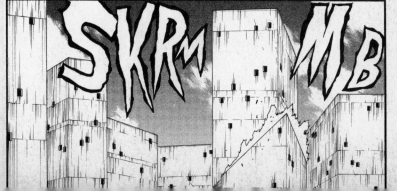

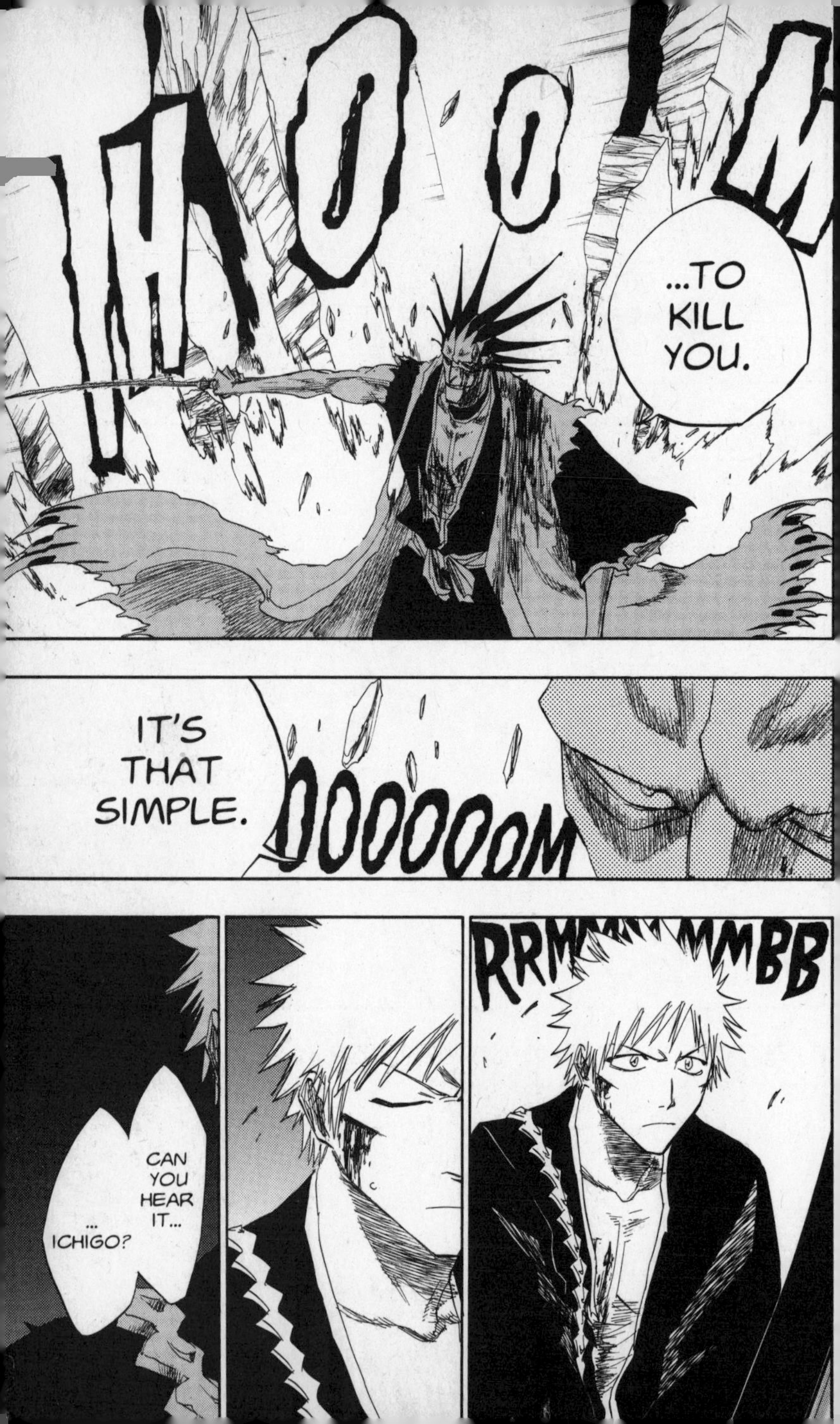
...TO KILL YOU.
OOOOOOM
IT'S THAT SIMPLE.
CAN YOU HEAR IT... ...ICHIGO?

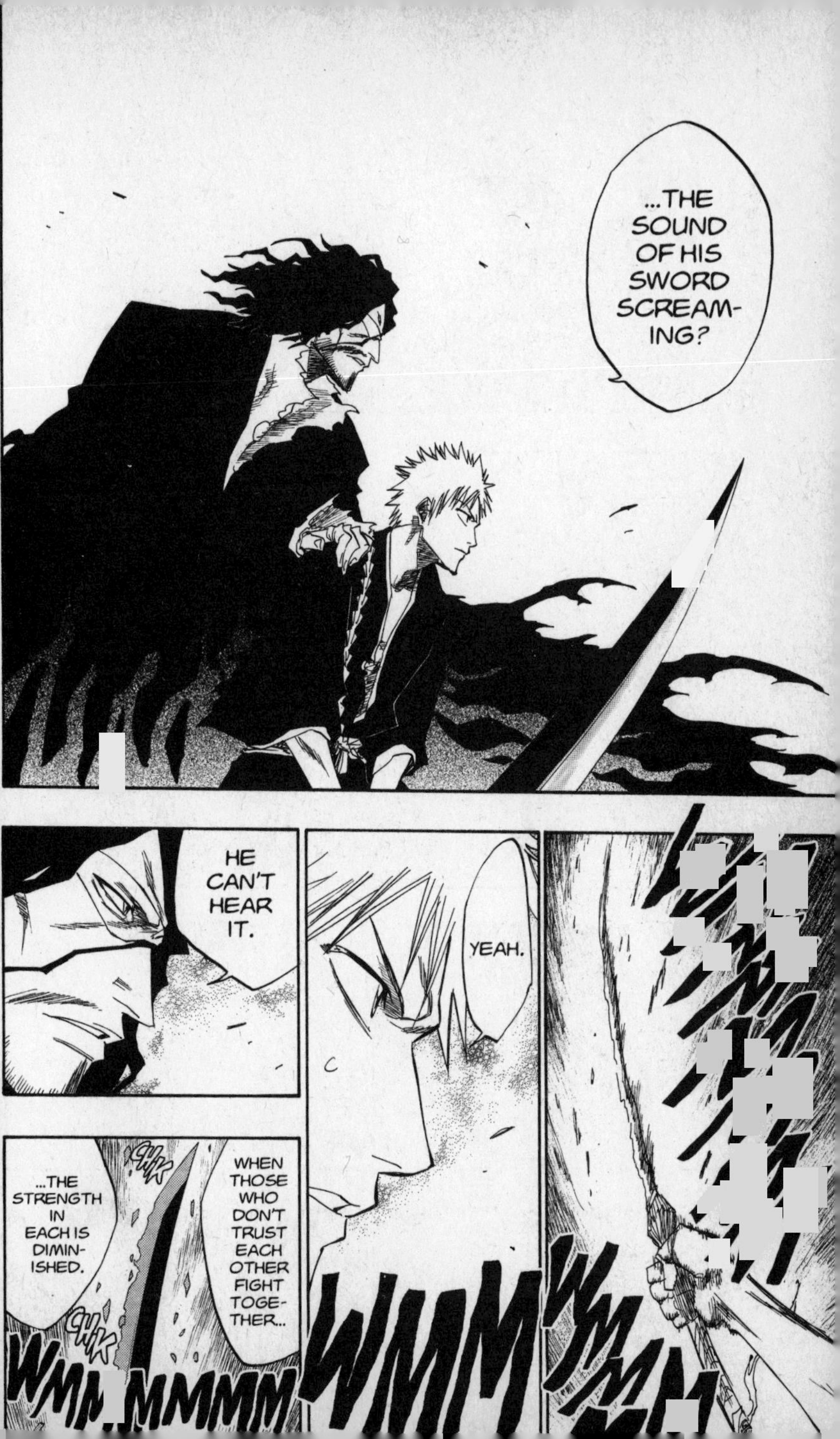
...THE SOUND OF HIS SWORD SCREAMING?
YEAH.
WMMM
HE CAN'T HEAR IT.
WHEN THOSE WHO DON'T TRUST EACH OTHER FIGHT TOGE-THER...
...THE STRENGTH IN EACH IS DIMIN-ISHED.
CHK
CHK
WMMMMMMMM

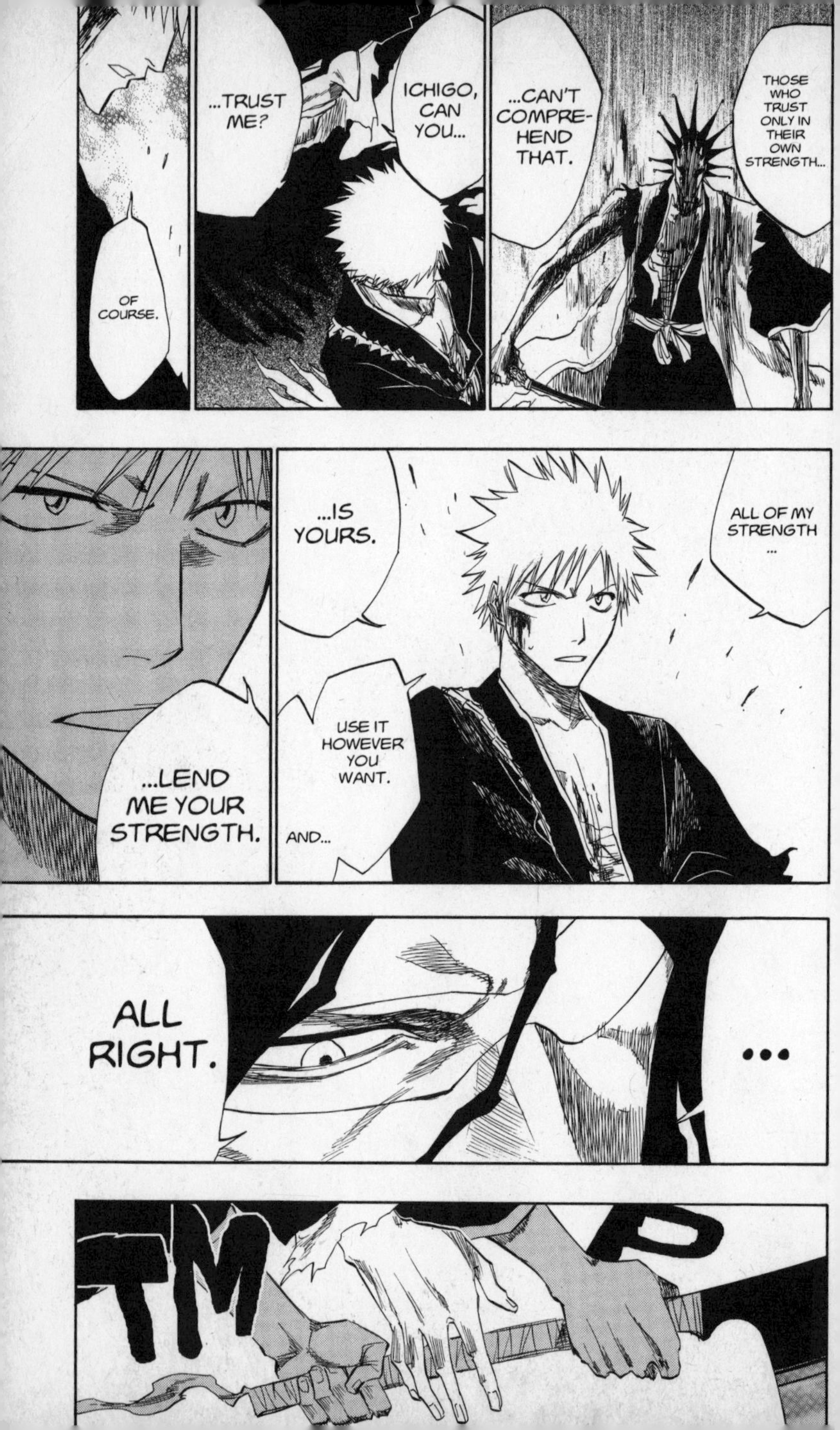
THOSE WHO TRUST ONLY IN THEIR OWN STRENGTH...
...CAN'T COMPRE-HEND THAT.
ICHIGO, CAN YOU...
...TRUST ME?
OF COURSE.
ALL OF MY STRENGTH ...
...IS YOURS.
USE IT HOWEVER YOU WANT.
AND...
...LEND ME YOUR STRENGTH.
...
ALL RIGHT.
TMP

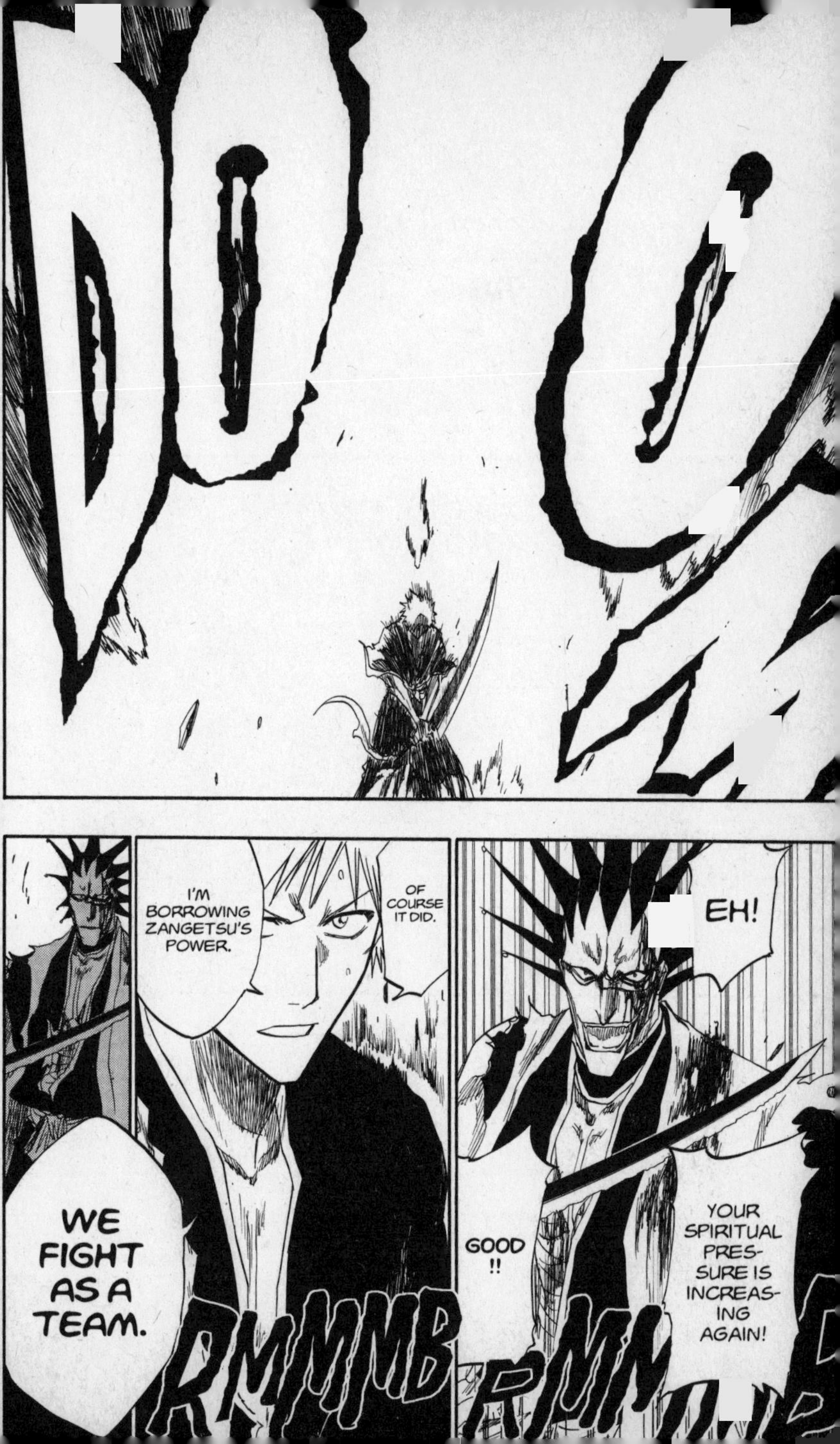
EH!
YOUR SPIRITUAL PRES-SURE IS INCREAS-ING AGAIN!
GOOD !!
OF COURSE IT DID.
I'M BORROWING ZANGETSU'S POWER.
WE FIGHT AS A TEAM.
RMMMB

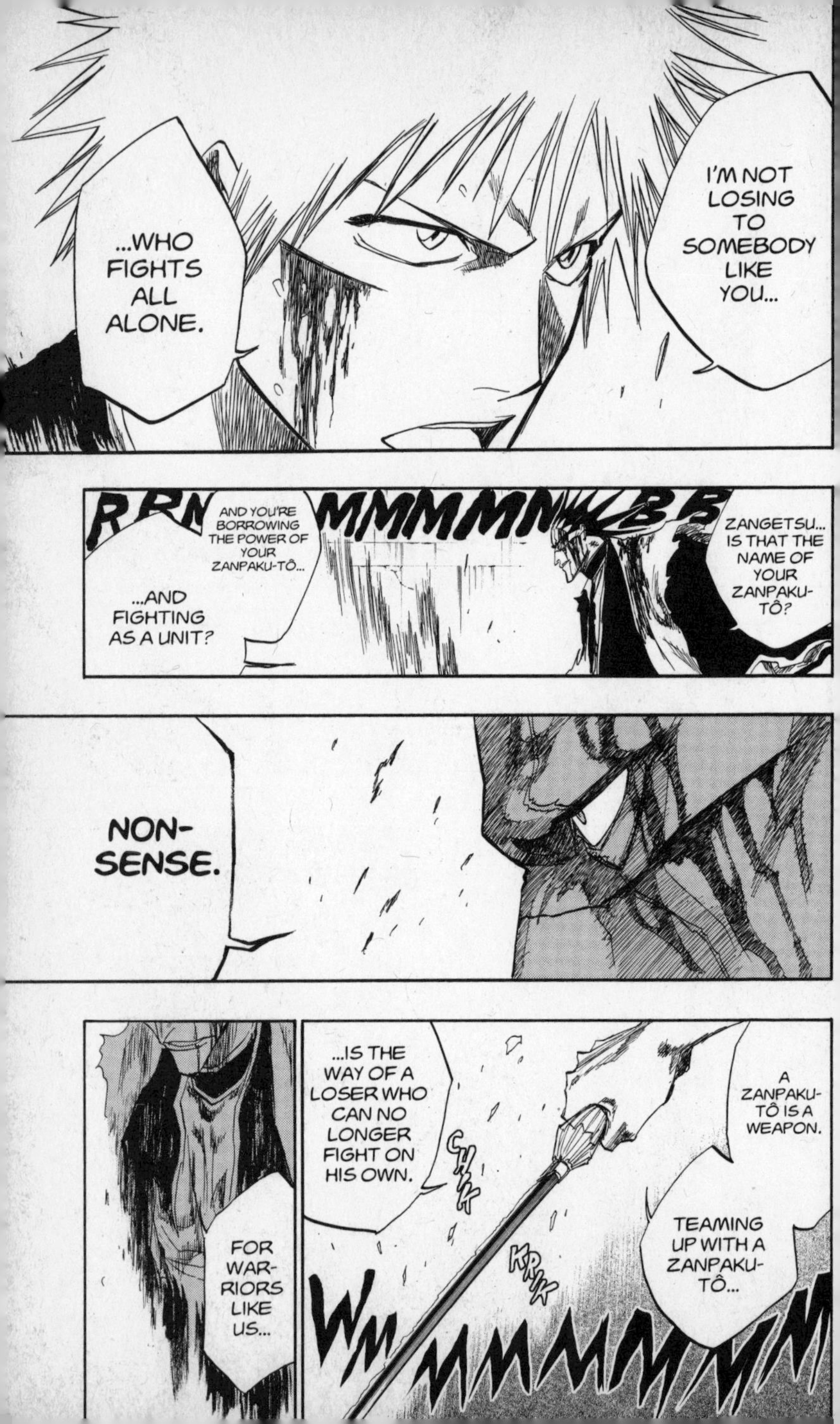

I'M NOT LOSING TO SOMEBODY LIKE YOU...
...WHO FIGHTS ALL ALONE.
ZANGETSU... IS THAT THE NAME OF YOUR ZANPAKU-TÔ?
RRN MMMMMN BB
AND YOU'RE BORROWING THE POWER OF YOUR ZANPAKU-TÔ...
...AND FIGHTING AS A UNIT?
NON-SENSE.
A ZANPAKU-TÔ IS A WEAPON.
TEAMING UP WITH A ZANPAKU-TÔ...
CHIK
KRIK
...IS THE WAY OF A LOSER WHO CAN NO LONGER FIGHT ON HIS OWN.
WMMMMMMMMM
FOR WARRIORS LIKE US...

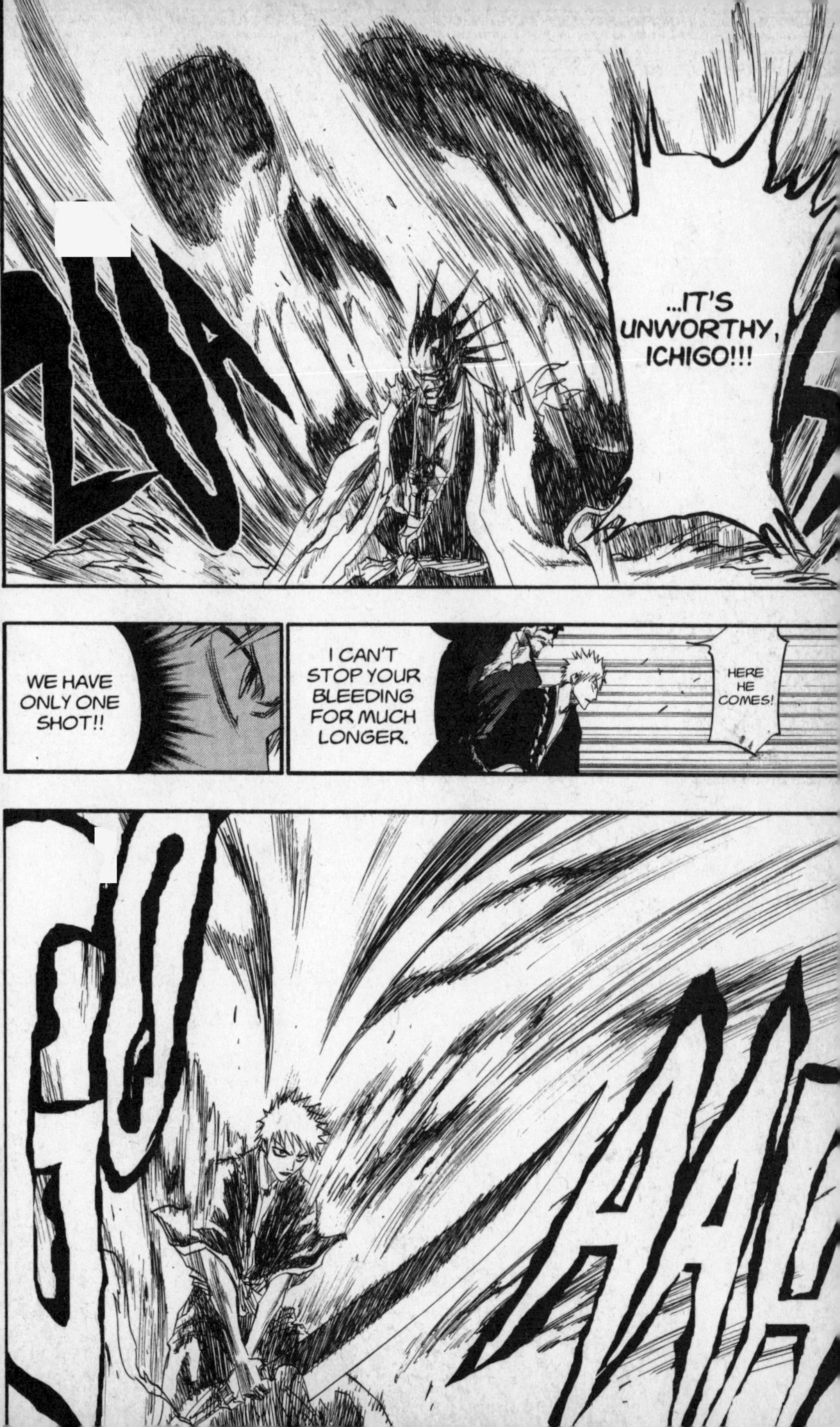
...IT'S UNWORTHY, ICHIGO!!!
HERE HE COMES!
I CAN'T STOP YOUR BLEEDING FOR MUCH LONGER.
WE HAVE ONLY ONE SHOT!!

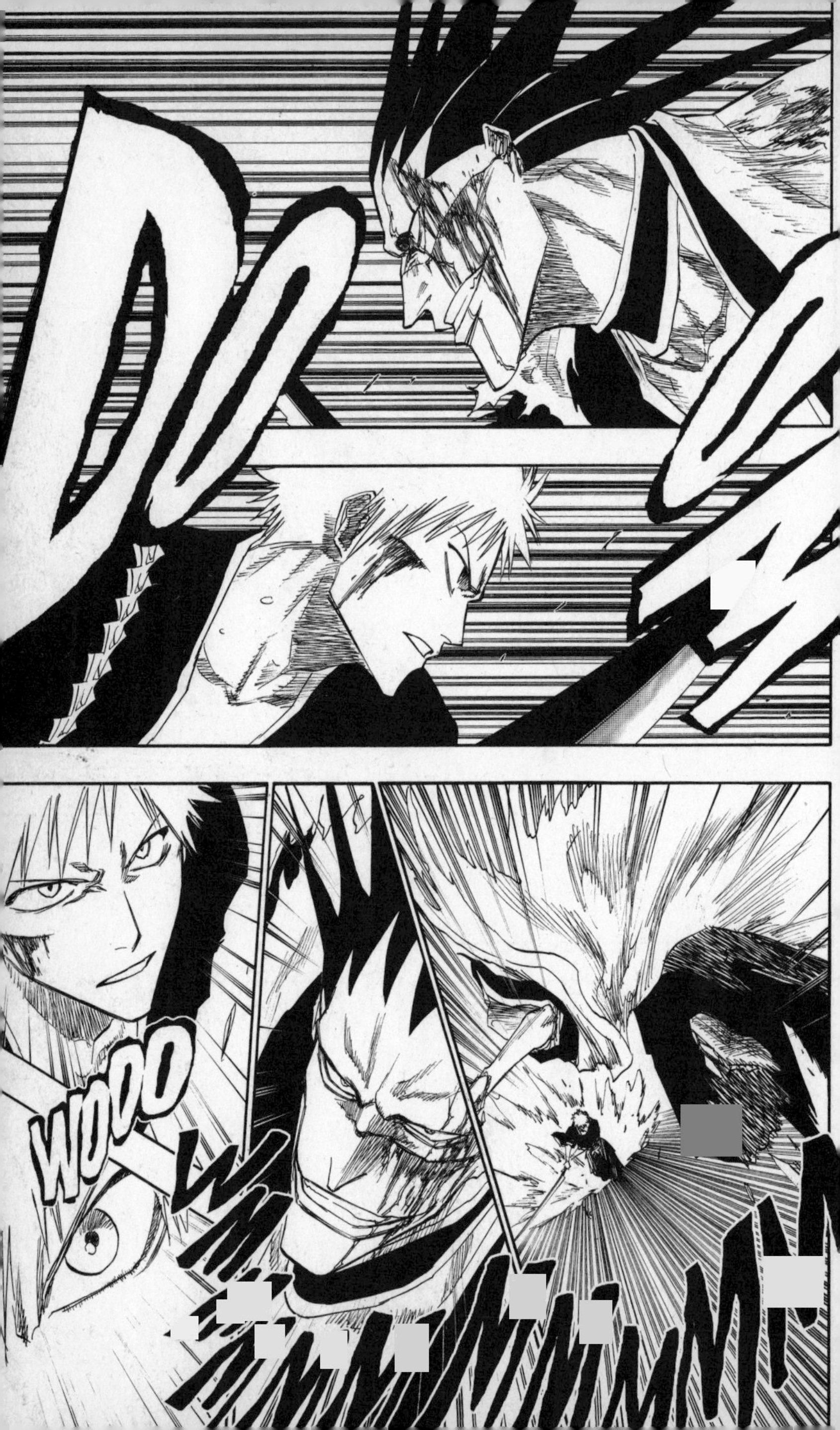
DOOM
WOOOWMMMMMMMM!

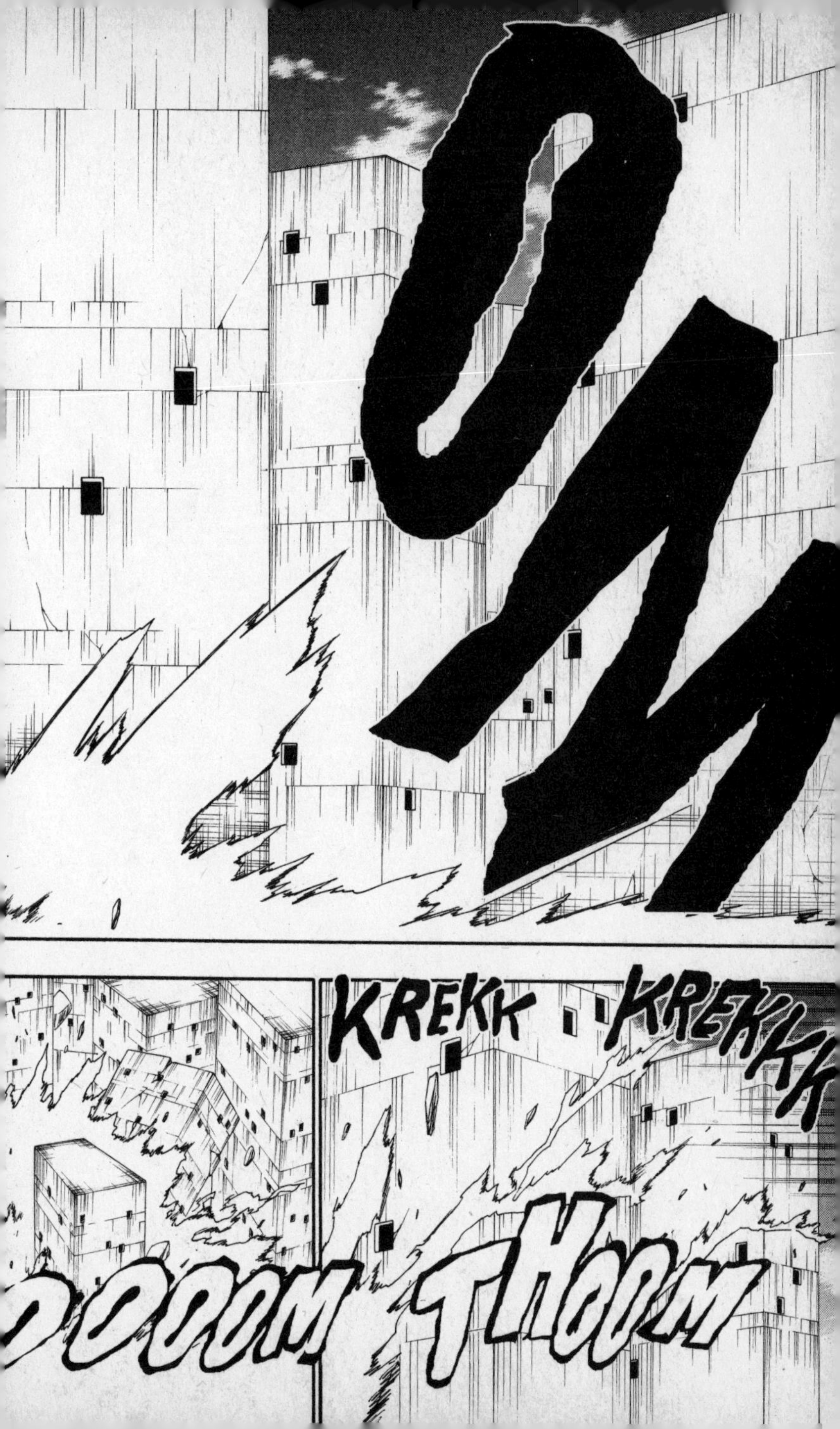
OM
KREKK KREKKK
THOOM
OOOOM

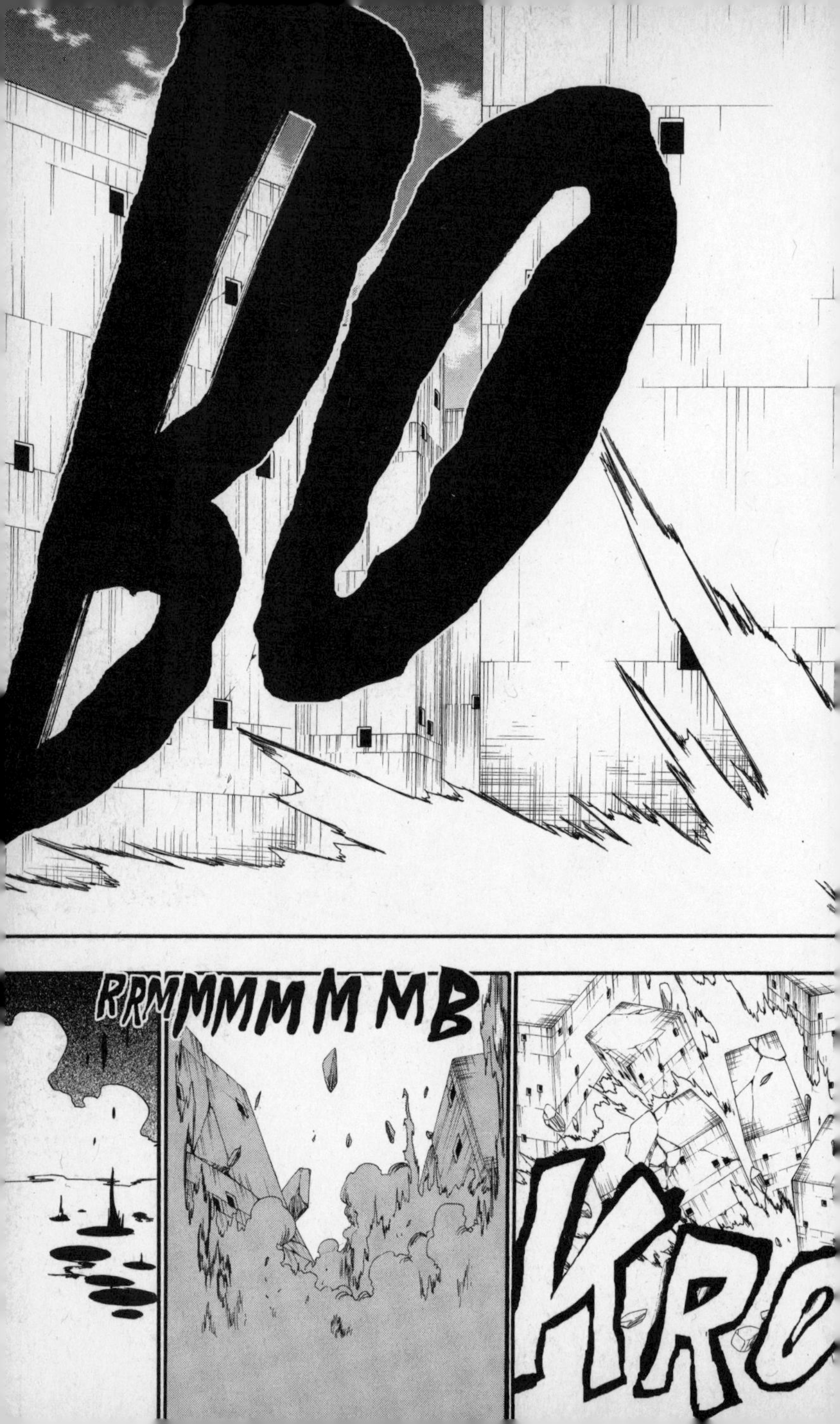
BO
KRO
RRMMMMMM M MB

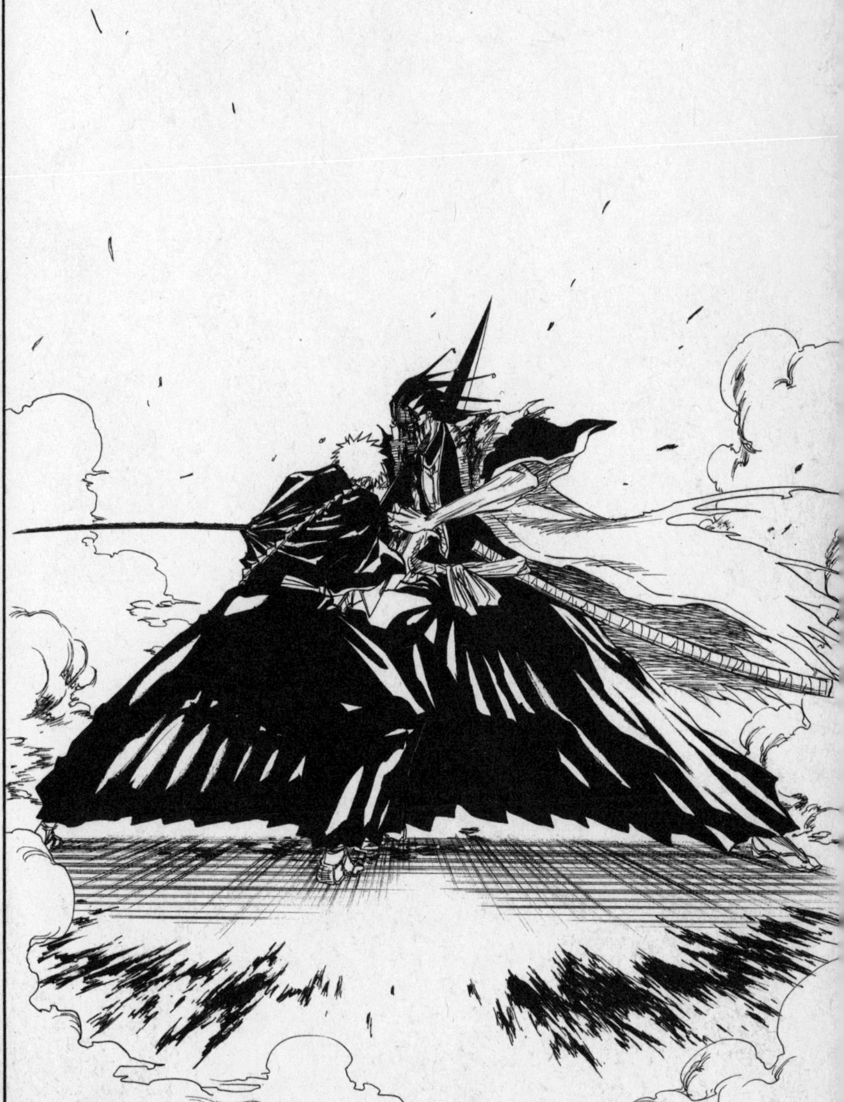

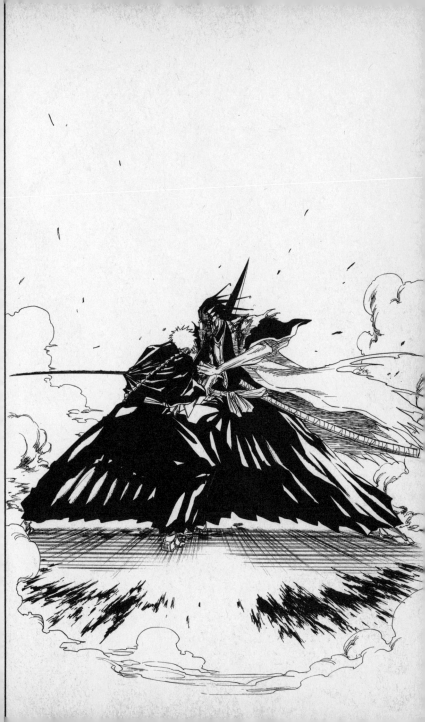

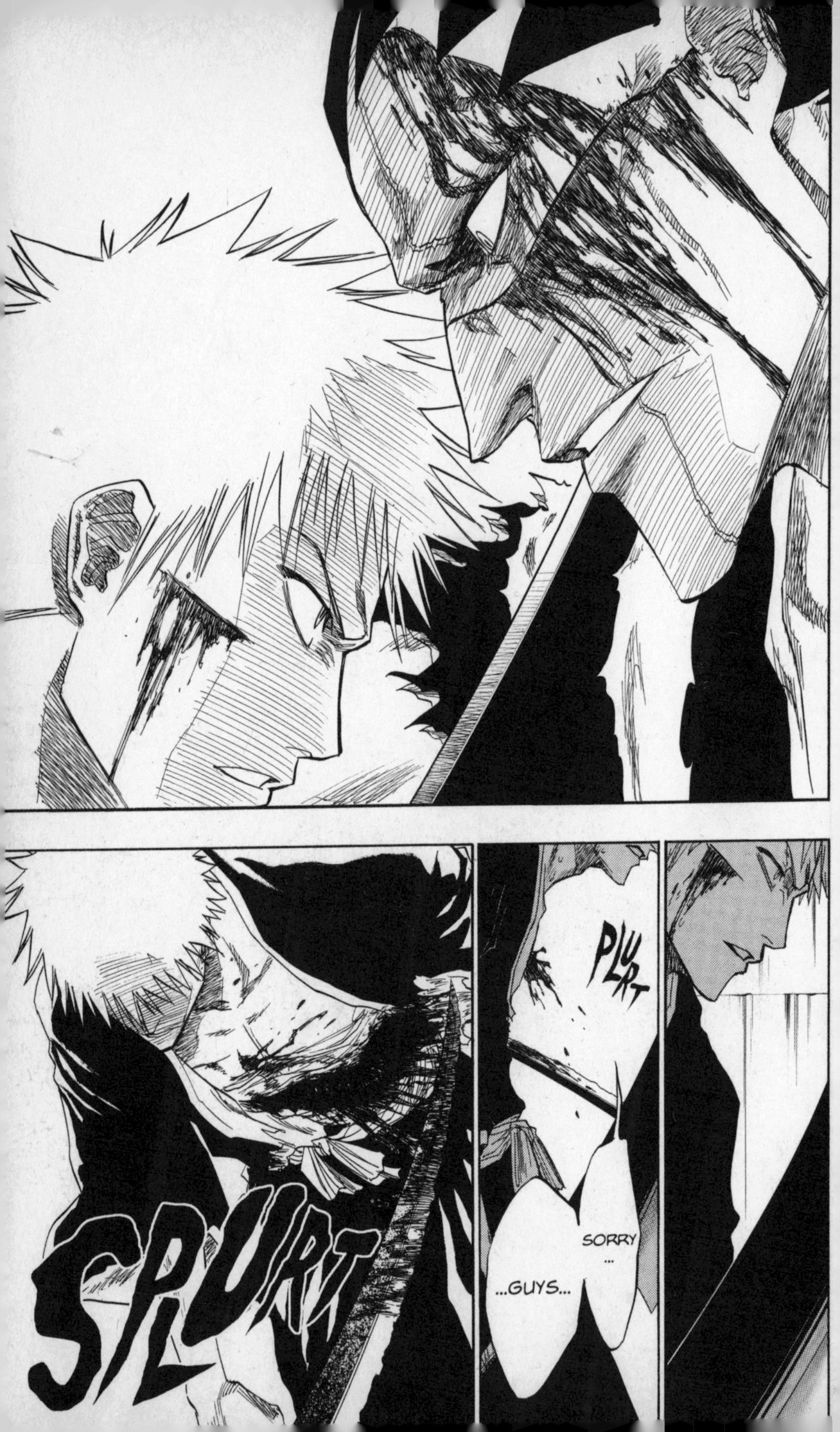
PLURT
SORRY ...
...GUYS...
SPURT

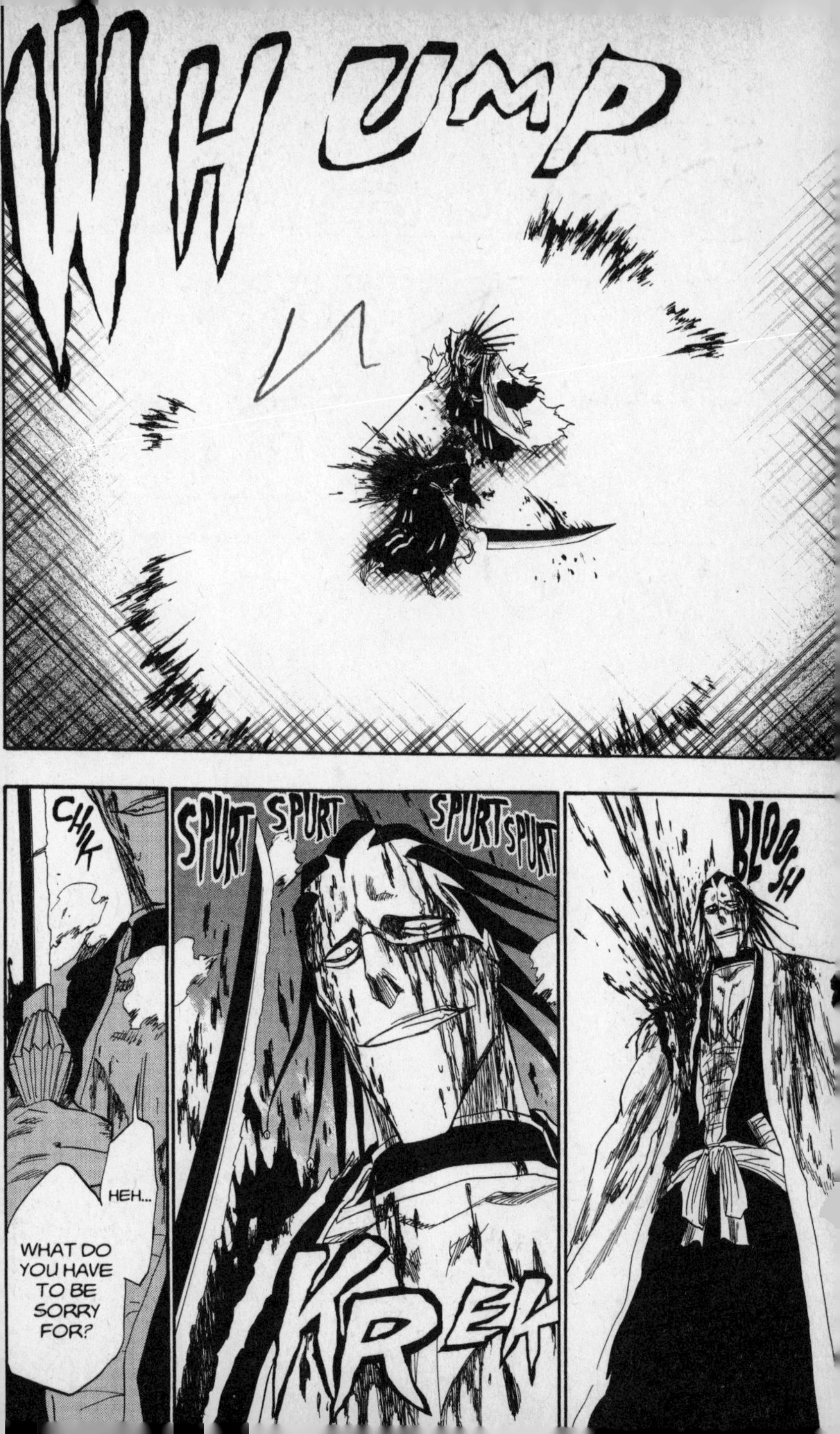
WHUMP
BLOOSH
SPURT SPURT
SPURT SPURT
KREK
CHIK
HEH...
WHAT DO YOU HAVE TO BE SORRY FOR?

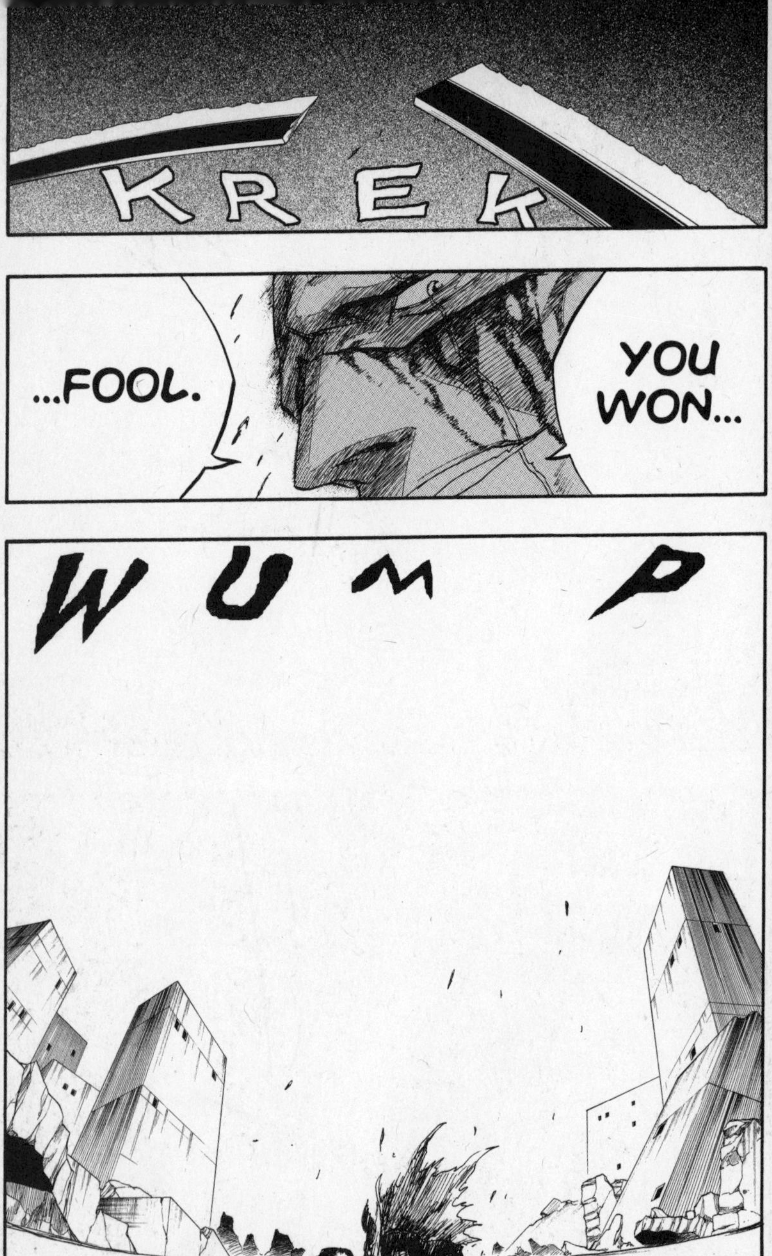
KREK
YOU WON...
...FOOL.
WUMP

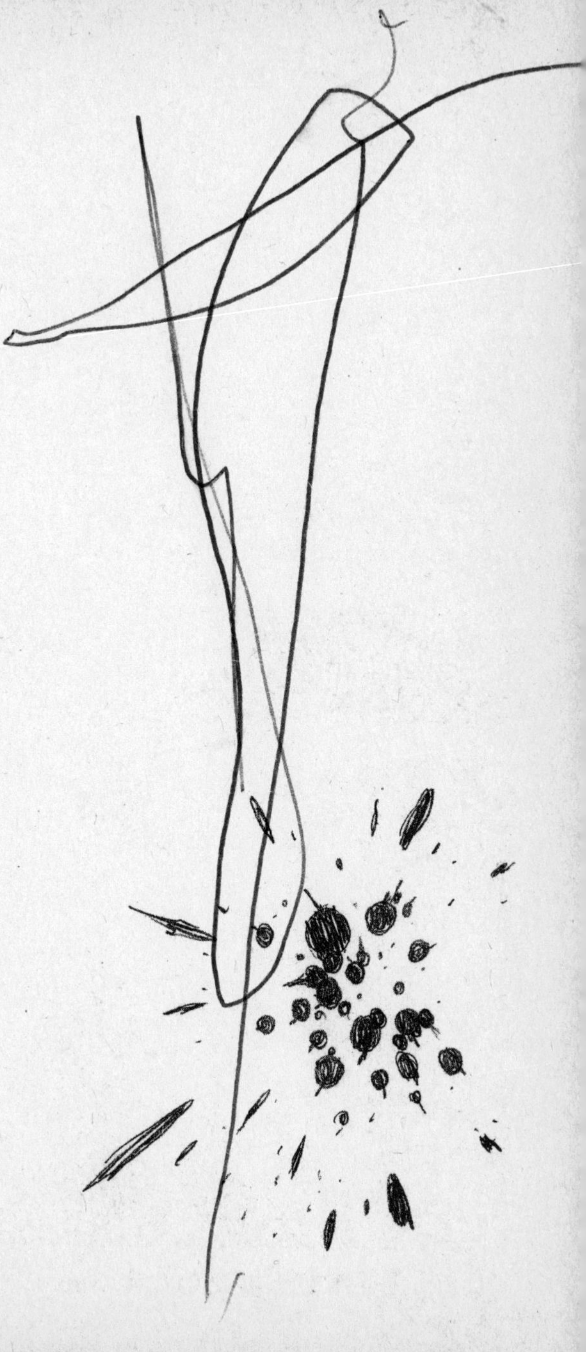

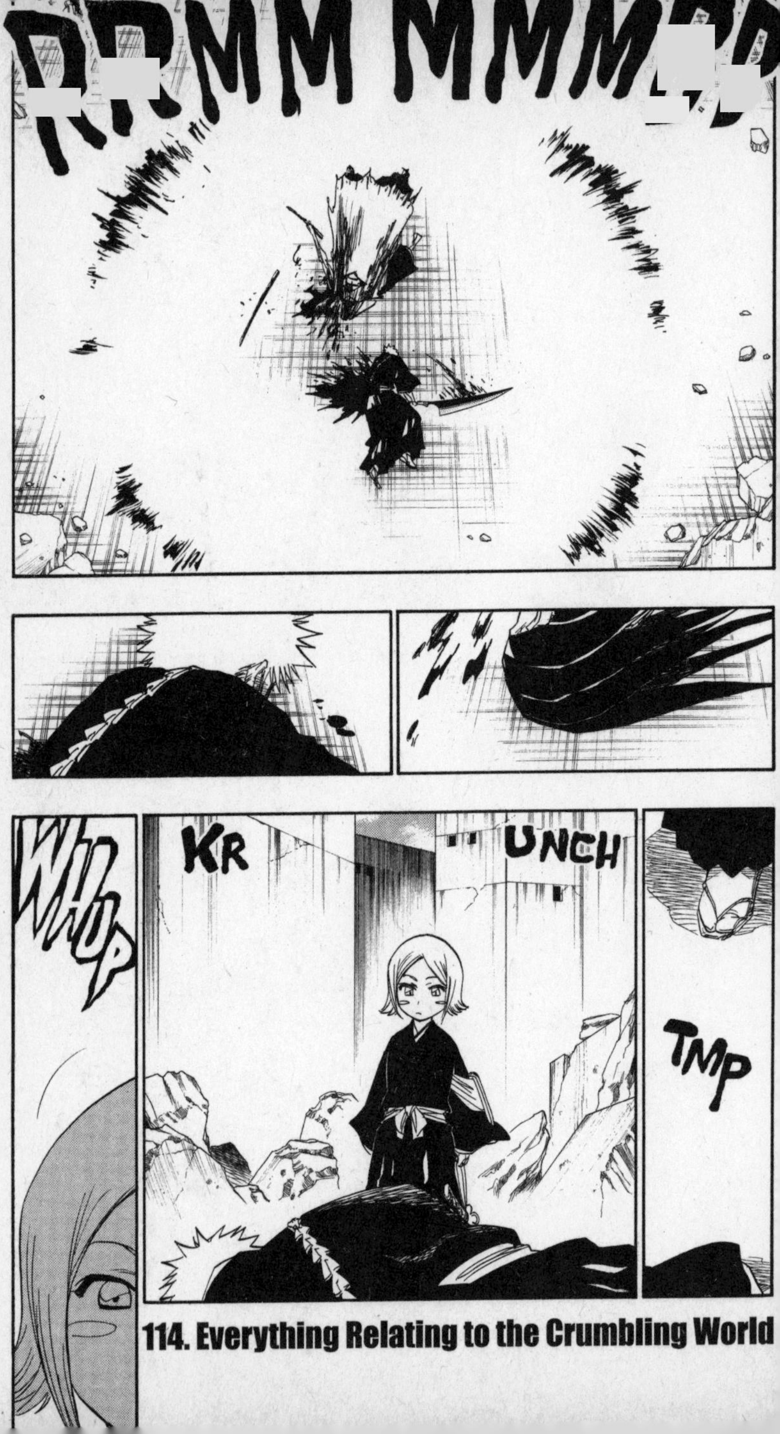
RRMM MMMBB
TMP
KR
UNCH
WHOP

114. Everything Relating to the Crumbling World

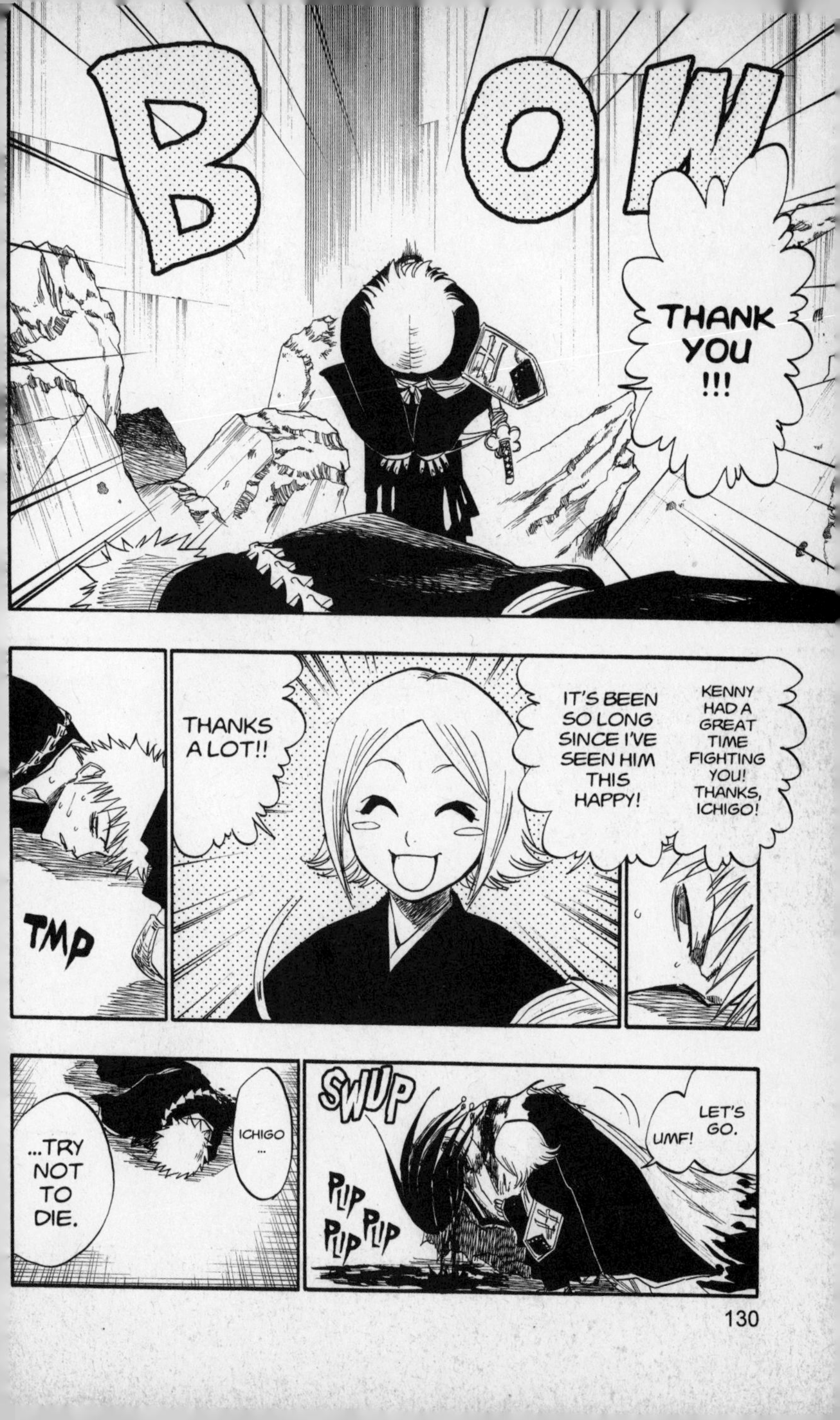
BOW
THANK YOU!!!
KENNY HAD A GREAT TIME FIGHTING YOU! THANKS, ICHIGO!
IT'S BEEN SO LONG SINCE I'VE SEEN HIM THIS HAPPY!
THANKS A LOT!!
TMP
SWUP
LET'S GO.
UMF!
PLIP PLIP PLIP
ICHIGO...
...TRY NOT TO DIE.

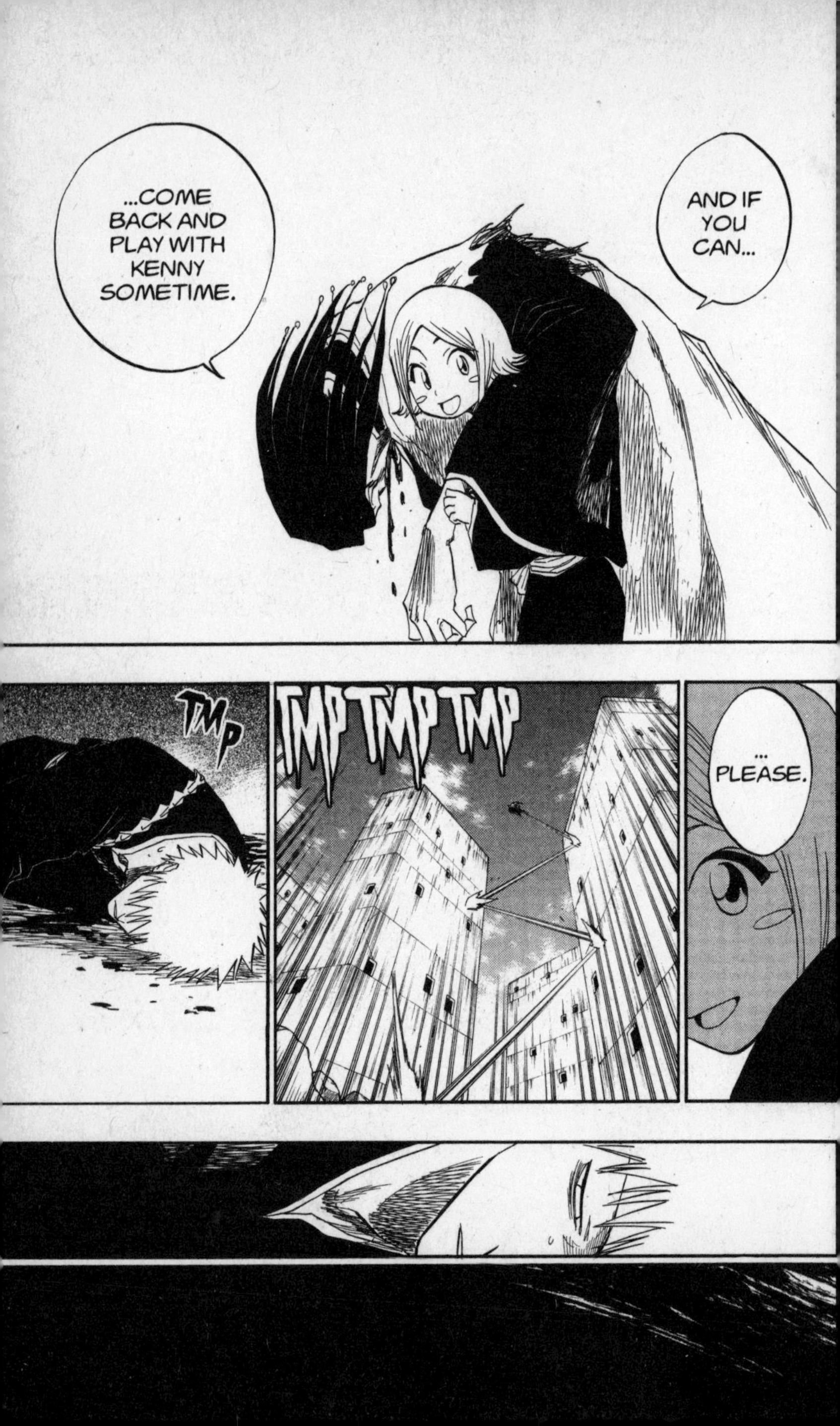
AND IF YOU CAN...
...COME BACK AND PLAY WITH KENNY SOMETIME.
... PLEASE.
TMP TMP TMP
TMP

BLEACH
114. Everything Relating to the Crumbling World

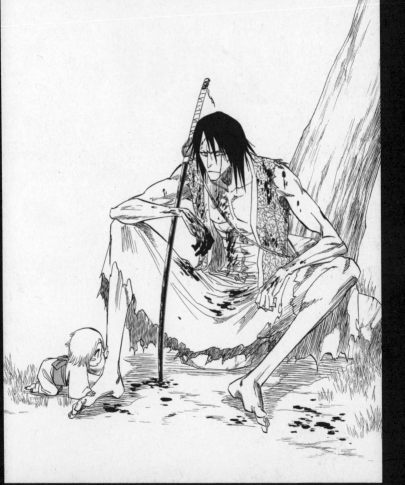

READ THIS WAY

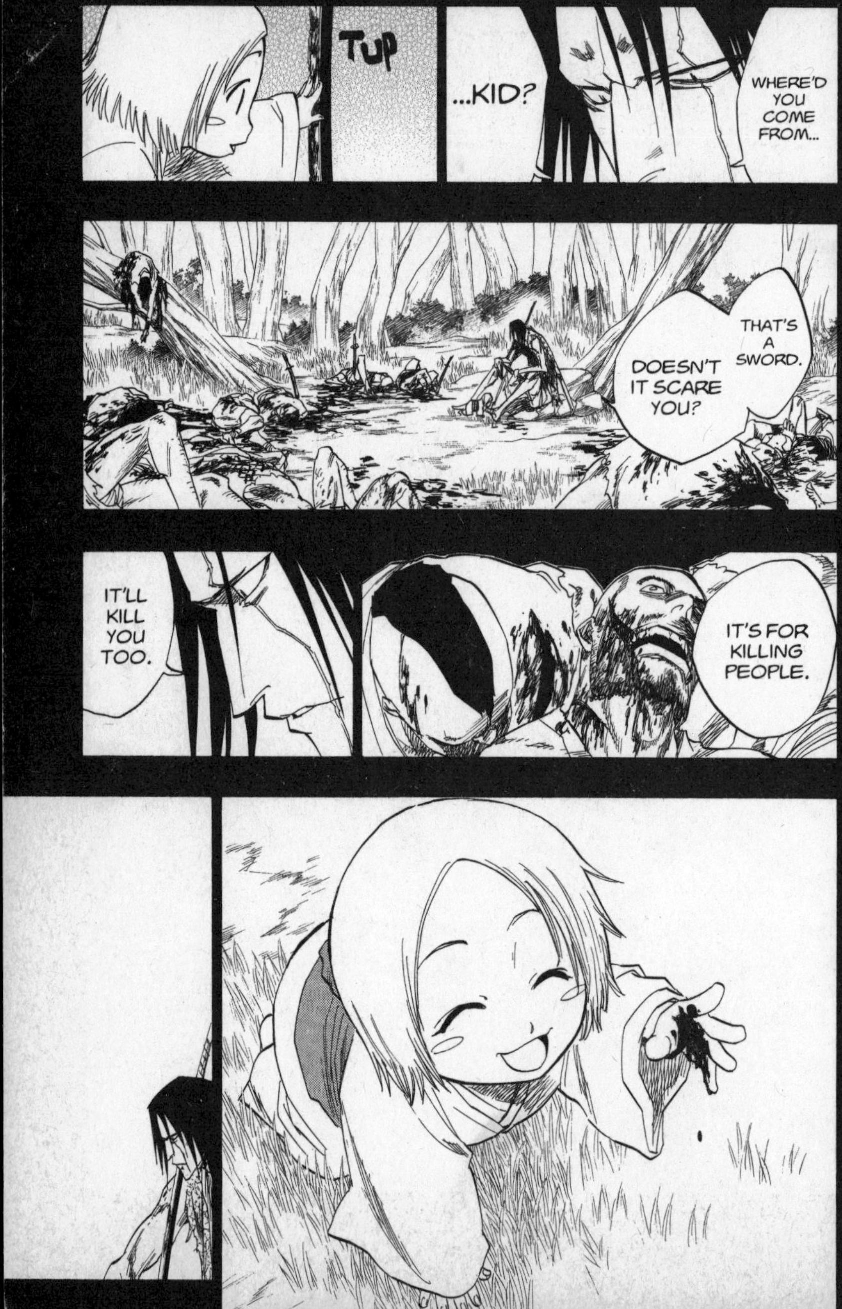
WHERE'D YOU COME FROM...
...KID?
TUP
THAT'S A SWORD.
DOESN'T IT SCARE YOU?
IT'S FOR KILLING PEOPLE.
IT'LL KILL YOU TOO.

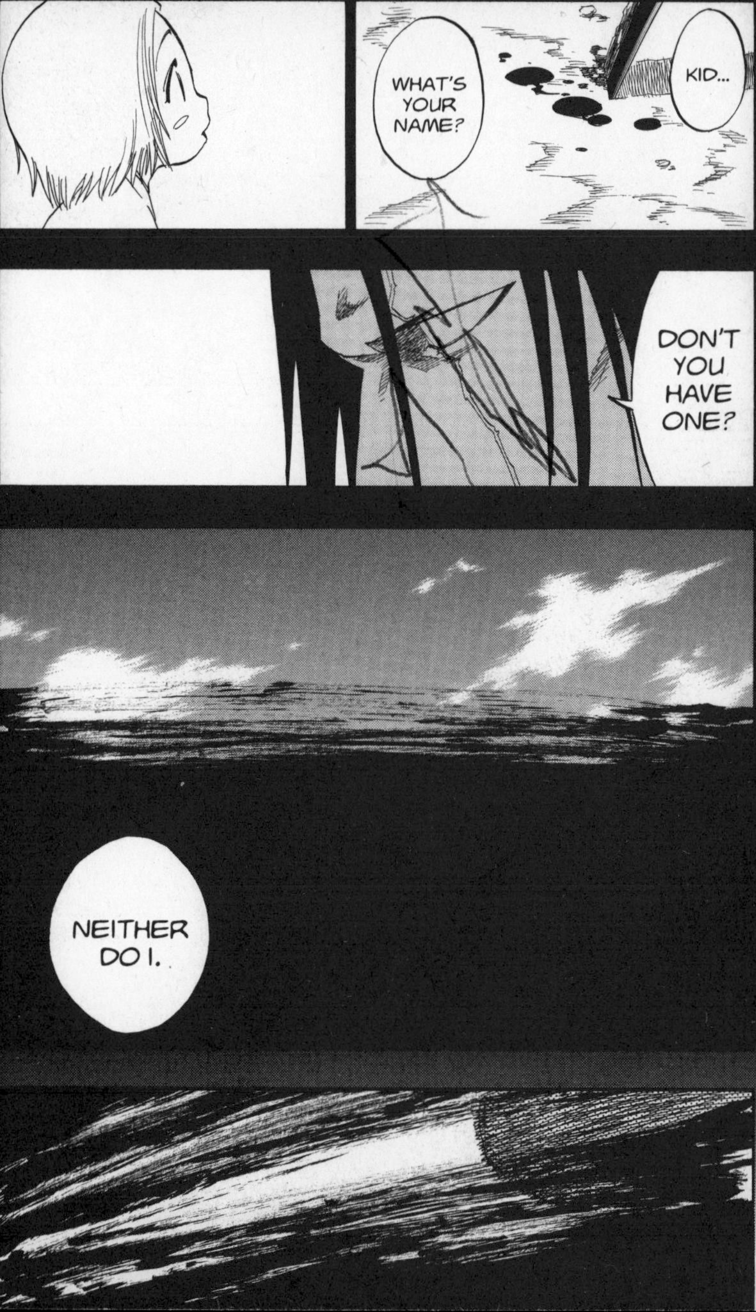
KID...
WHAT'S YOUR NAME?
DON'T YOU HAVE ONE?
NEITHER DO I.

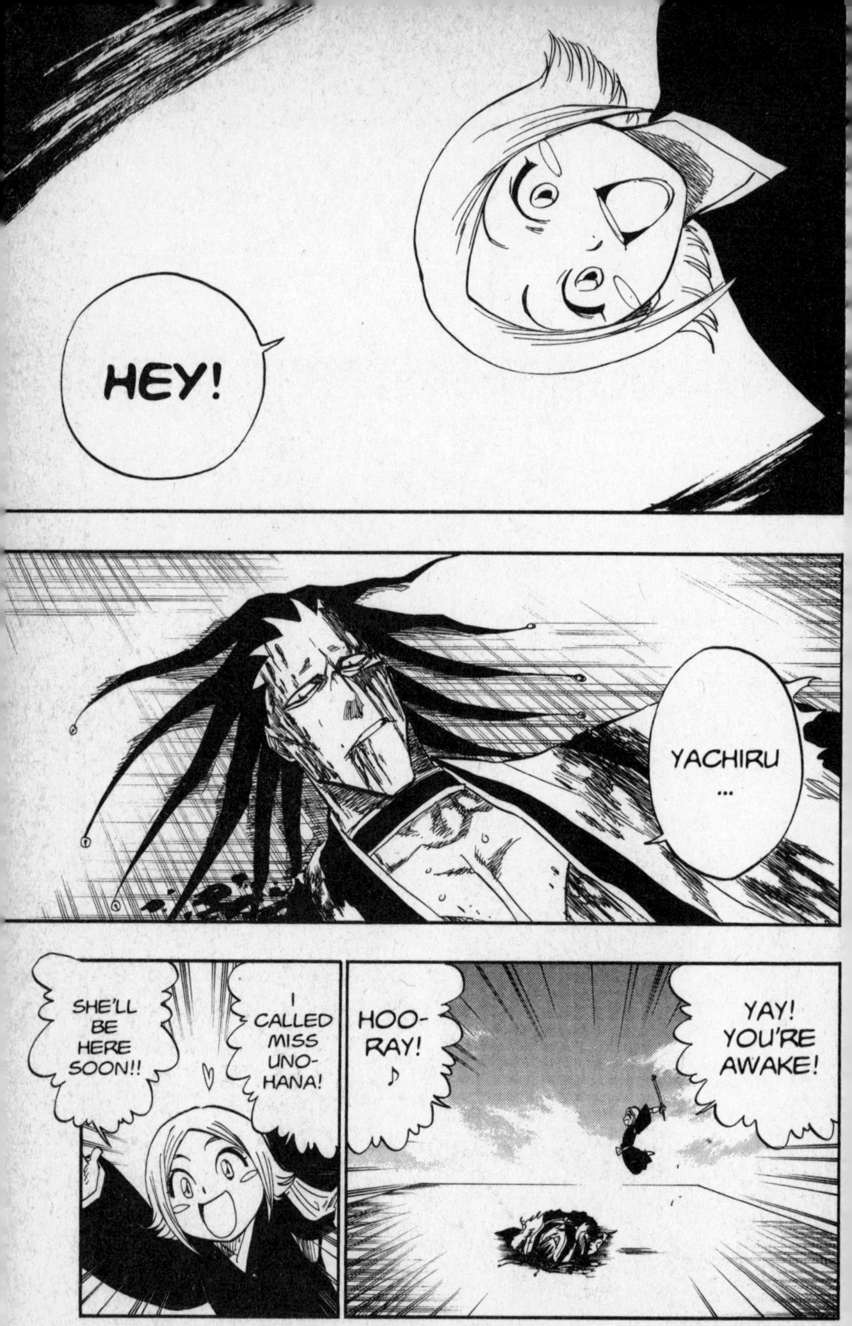
HEY!
YACHIRU ...
YAY! YOU'RE AWAKE!
HOO-RAY! ♪
I CALLED MISS UNO-HANA!
SHE'LL BE HERE SOON!!

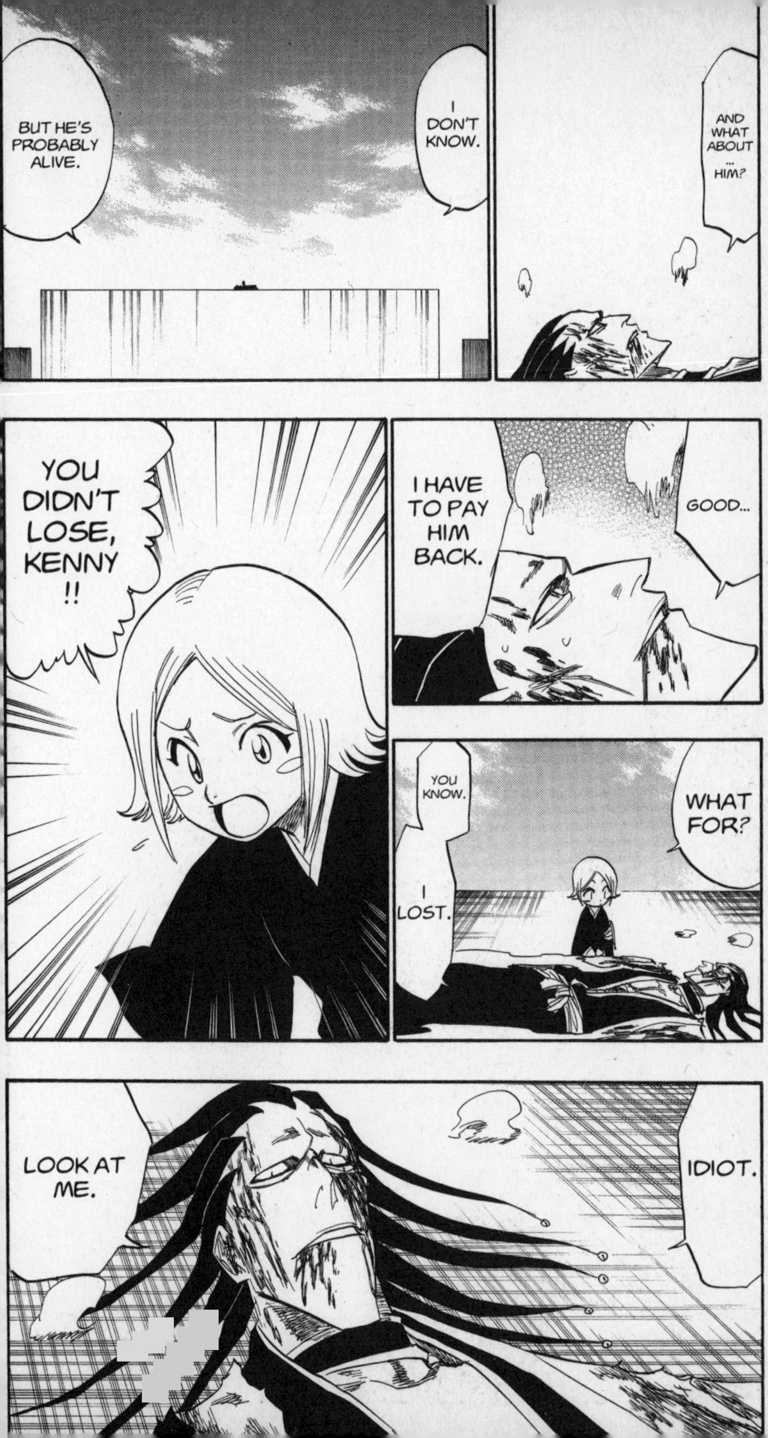
AND WHAT ABOUT ... HIM?
I DON'T KNOW.
BUT HE'S PROBABLY ALIVE.
GOOD...
I HAVE TO PAY HIM BACK.
WHAT FOR?
YOU KNOW.
I LOST.
YOU DIDN'T LOSE, KENNY !!
IDIOT.
LOOK AT ME.

READ THIS WAY

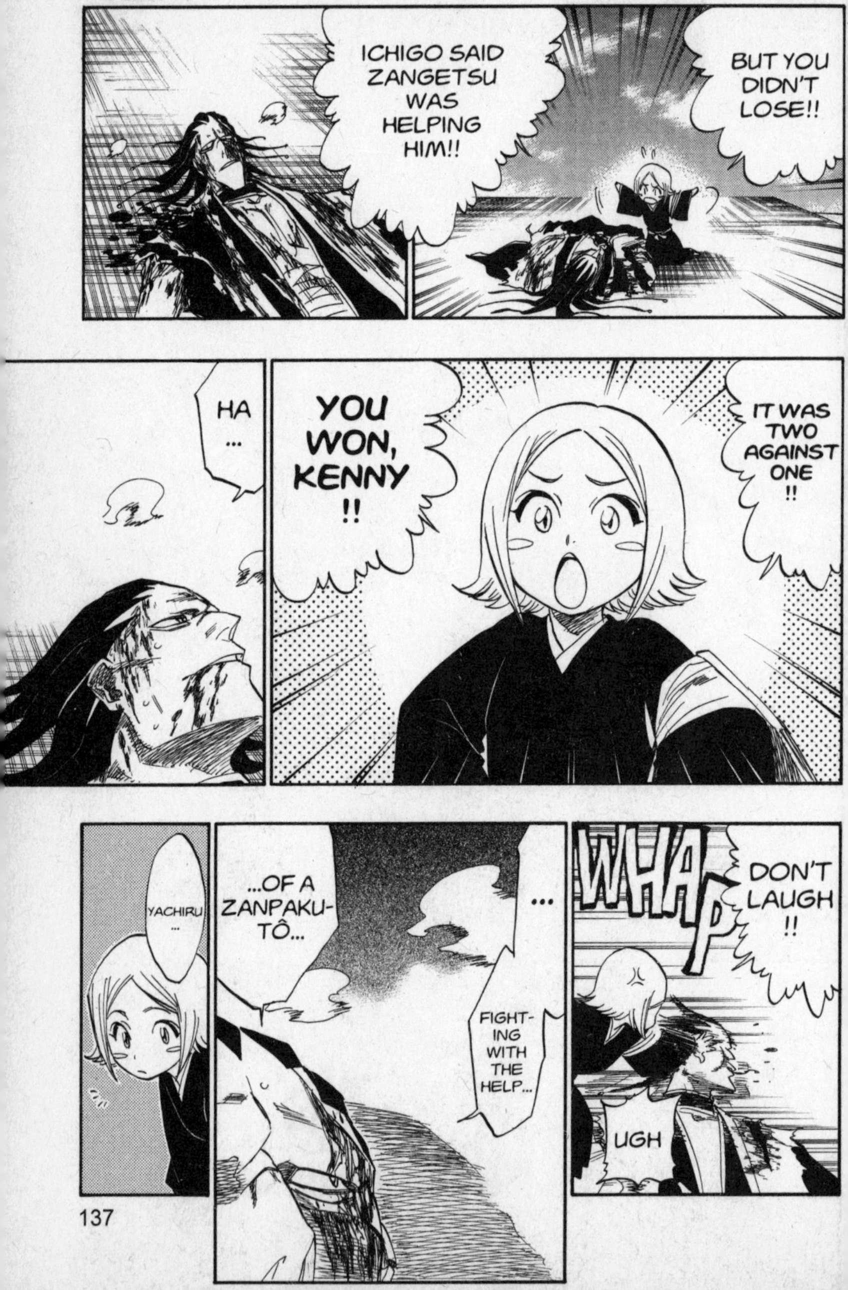

BUT YOU DIDN'T LOSE!!
ICHIGO SAID ZANGETSU WAS HELPING HIM!!
IT WAS TWO AGAINST ONE!!
YOU WON, KENNY!!
HA...
DON'T LAUGH!!
WHAP
UGH
...
FIGHTING WITH THE HELP...
...OF A ZANPAKUTÔ...
YACHIRU...

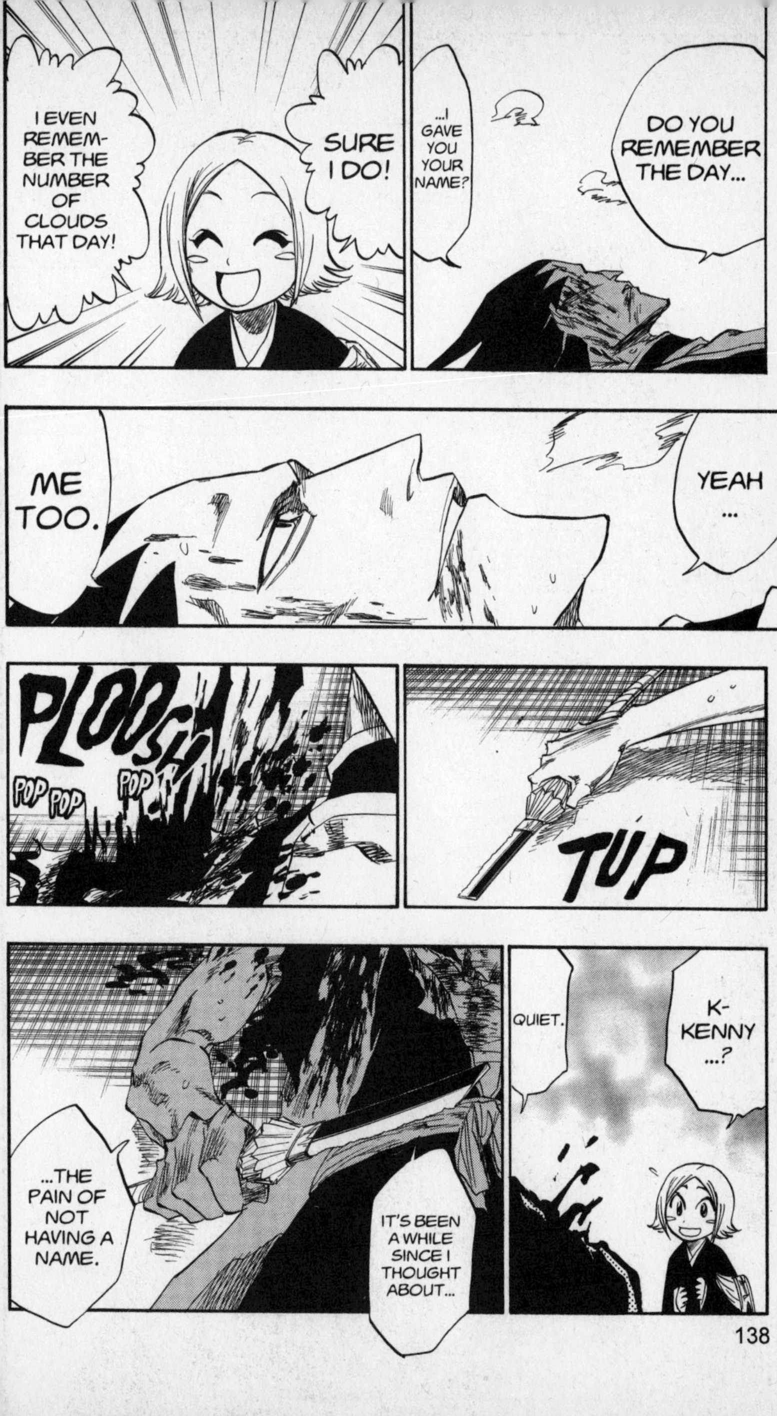
DO YOU REMEMBER THE DAY...
...I GAVE YOU YOUR NAME?
SURE I DO!
I EVEN REMEMBER THE NUMBER OF CLOUDS THAT DAY!
YEAH ...
ME TOO.
TUP
PLOOSH
POP
POP POP
K-KENNY ...?
QUIET.
IT'S BEEN A WHILE SINCE I THOUGHT ABOUT...
...THE PAIN OF NOT HAVING A NAME.

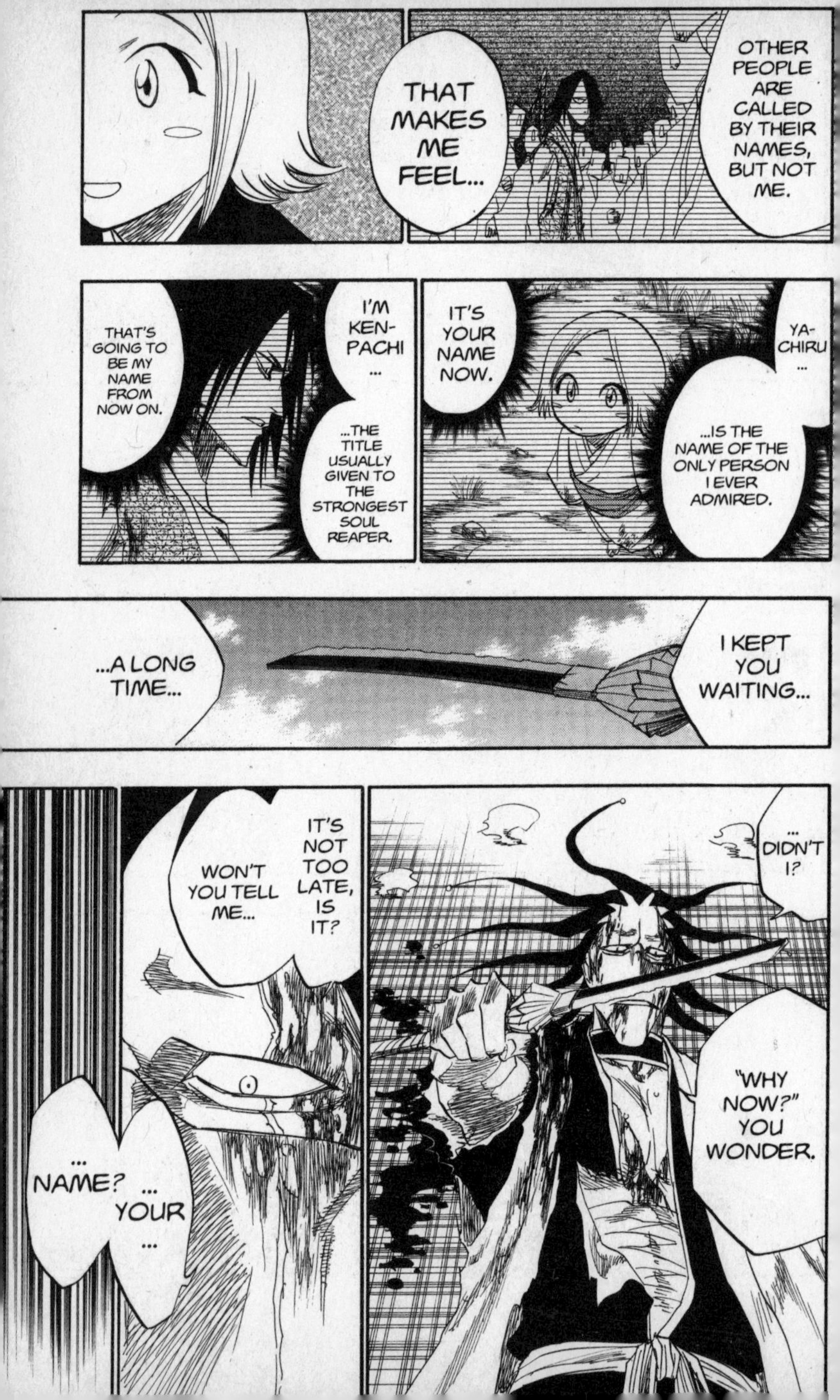
OTHER PEOPLE ARE CALLED BY THEIR NAMES, BUT NOT ME.
THAT MAKES ME FEEL...
YA-CHIRU...
...IS THE NAME OF THE ONLY PERSON I EVER ADMIRED.
IT'S YOUR NAME NOW.
I'M KEN-PACHI...
...THE TITLE USUALLY GIVEN TO THE STRONGEST SOUL REAPER.
THAT'S GOING TO BE MY NAME FROM NOW ON.
I KEPT YOU WAITING...
...A LONG TIME...
...DIDN'T I?
"WHY NOW?" YOU WONDER.
IT'S NOT TOO LATE, IS IT?
WON'T YOU TELL ME...
...YOUR... ...NAME?

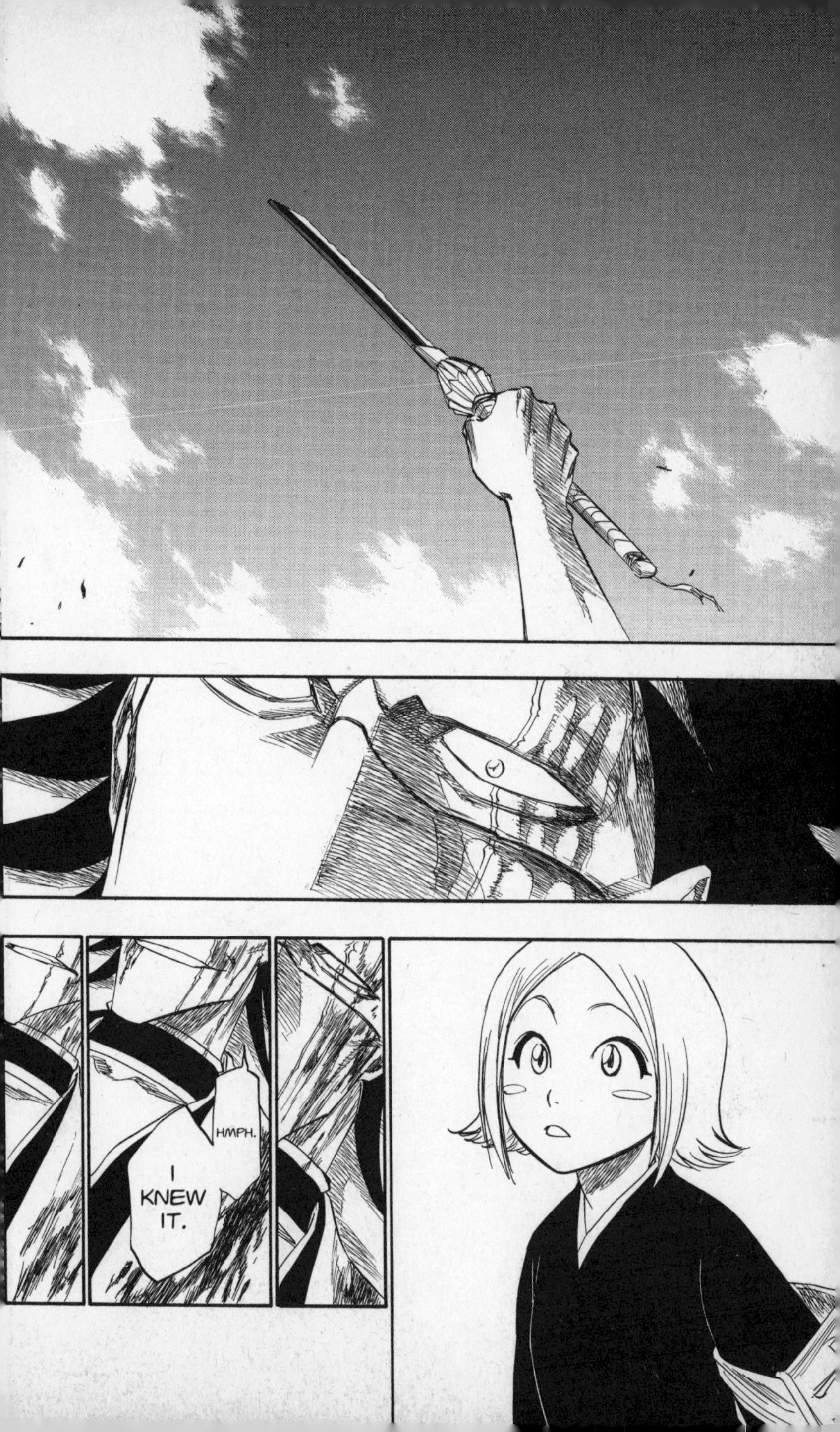
HMPH.
I KNEW IT.

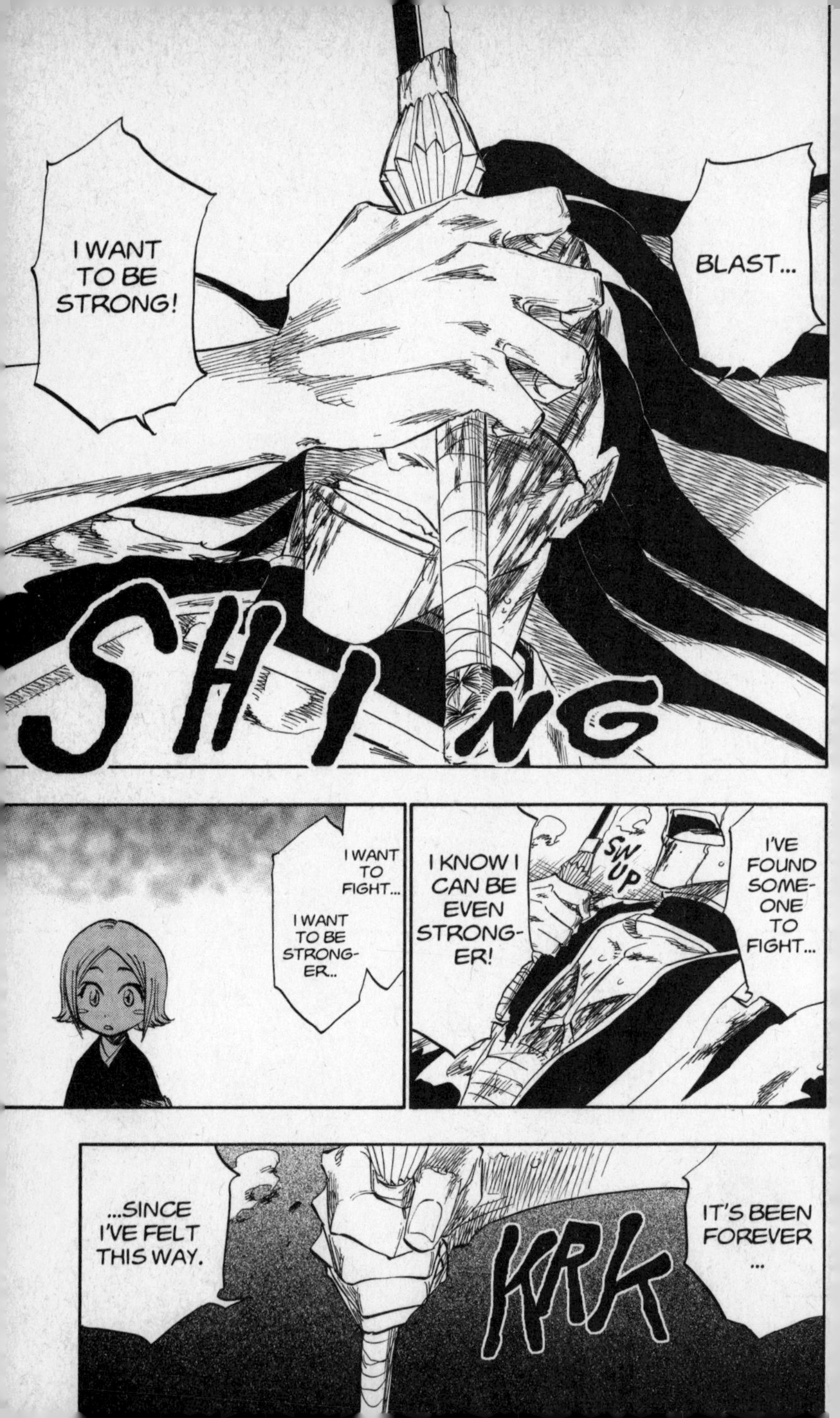
BLAST...
I WANT TO BE STRONG!
SHING
I'VE FOUND SOME-ONE TO FIGHT...
SWUP
I KNOW I CAN BE EVEN STRONG-ER!
I WANT TO FIGHT...
I WANT TO BE STRONG-ER..
IT'S BEEN FOREVER...
KRK
...SINCE I'VE FELT THIS WAY.

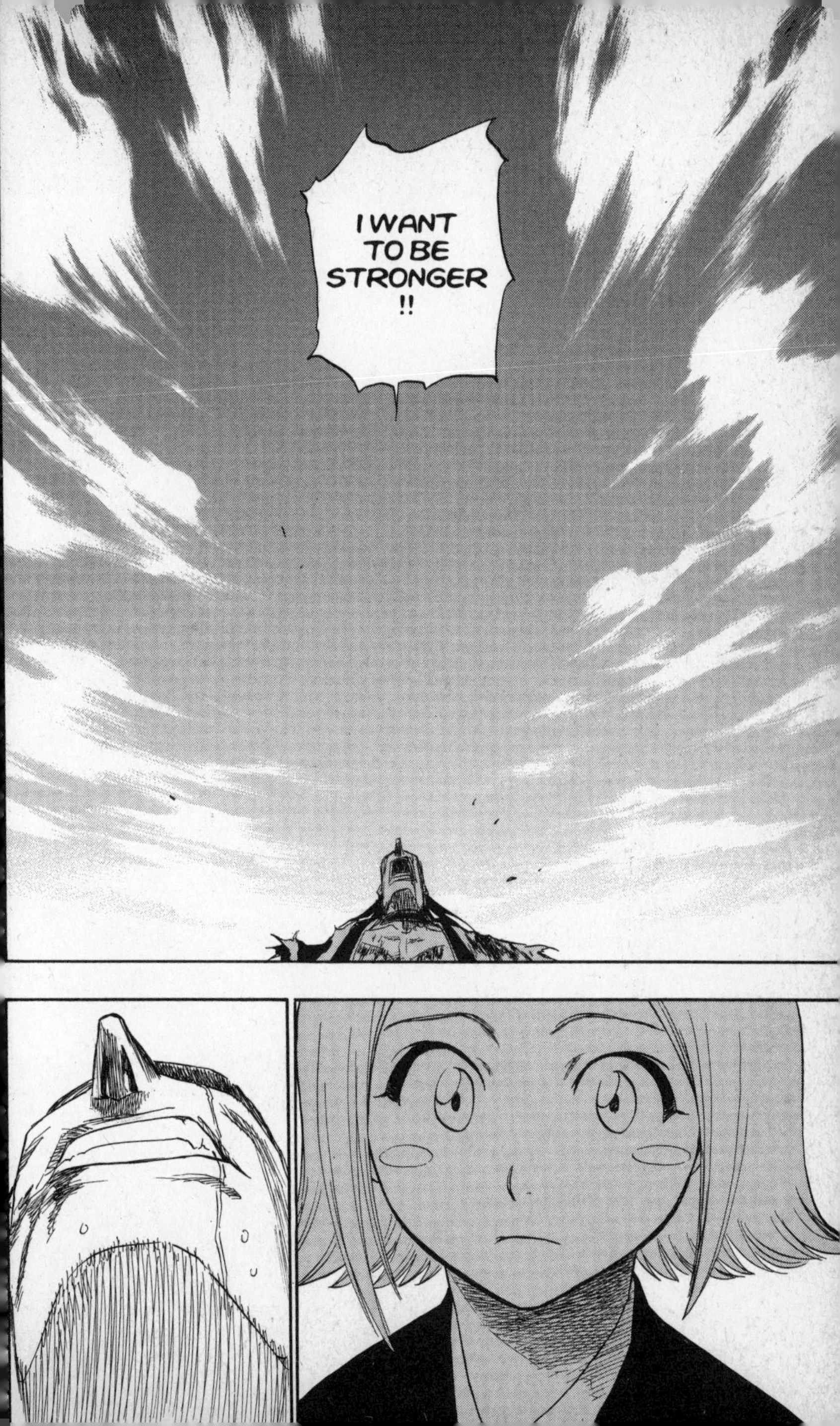
I WANT TO BE STRONGER !!

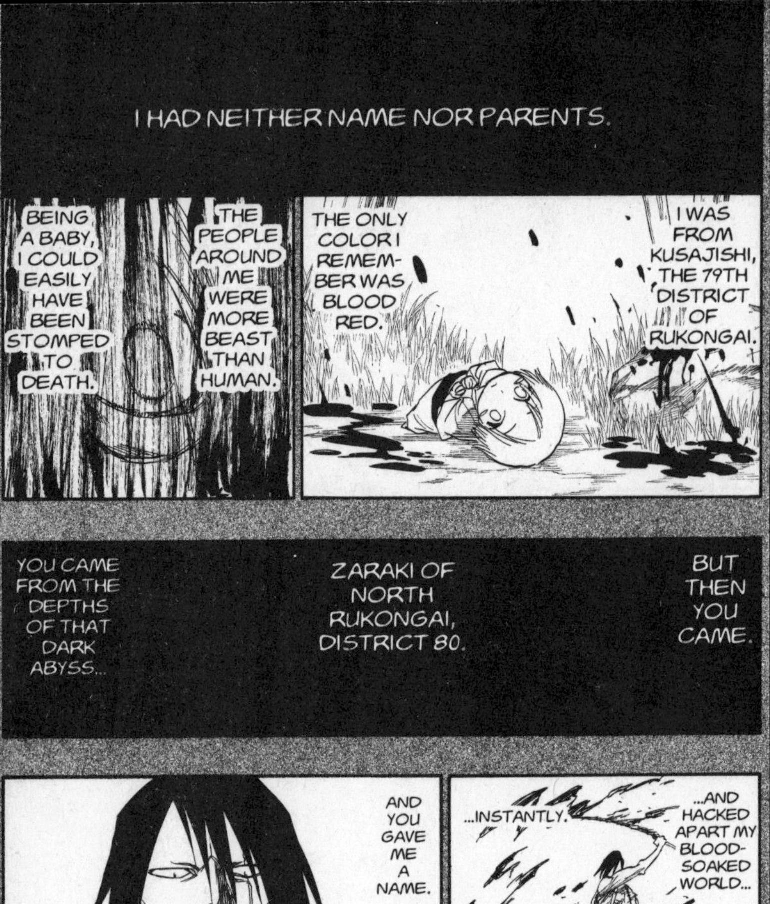
I HAD NEITHER NAME NOR PARENTS.
I WAS FROM KUSAJISHI, THE 79TH DISTRICT OF RUKONGAI.
THE ONLY COLOR I REMEMBER WAS BLOOD RED.
THE PEOPLE AROUND ME WERE MORE BEAST THAN HUMAN.
BEING A BABY, I COULD EASILY HAVE BEEN STOMPED TO DEATH.
BUT THEN YOU CAME.
ZARAKI OF NORTH RUKONGAI, DISTRICT 80.
YOU CAME FROM THE DEPTHS OF THAT DARK ABYSS...
...AND HACKED APART MY BLOOD-SOAKED WORLD...
...INSTANTLY.
AND YOU GAVE ME A NAME.
IF YOU HADN'T SHOWN UP...
...I WOULDN'T BE HERE NOW.

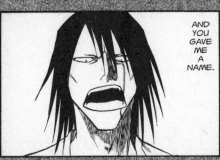

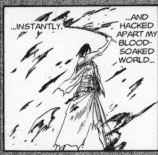

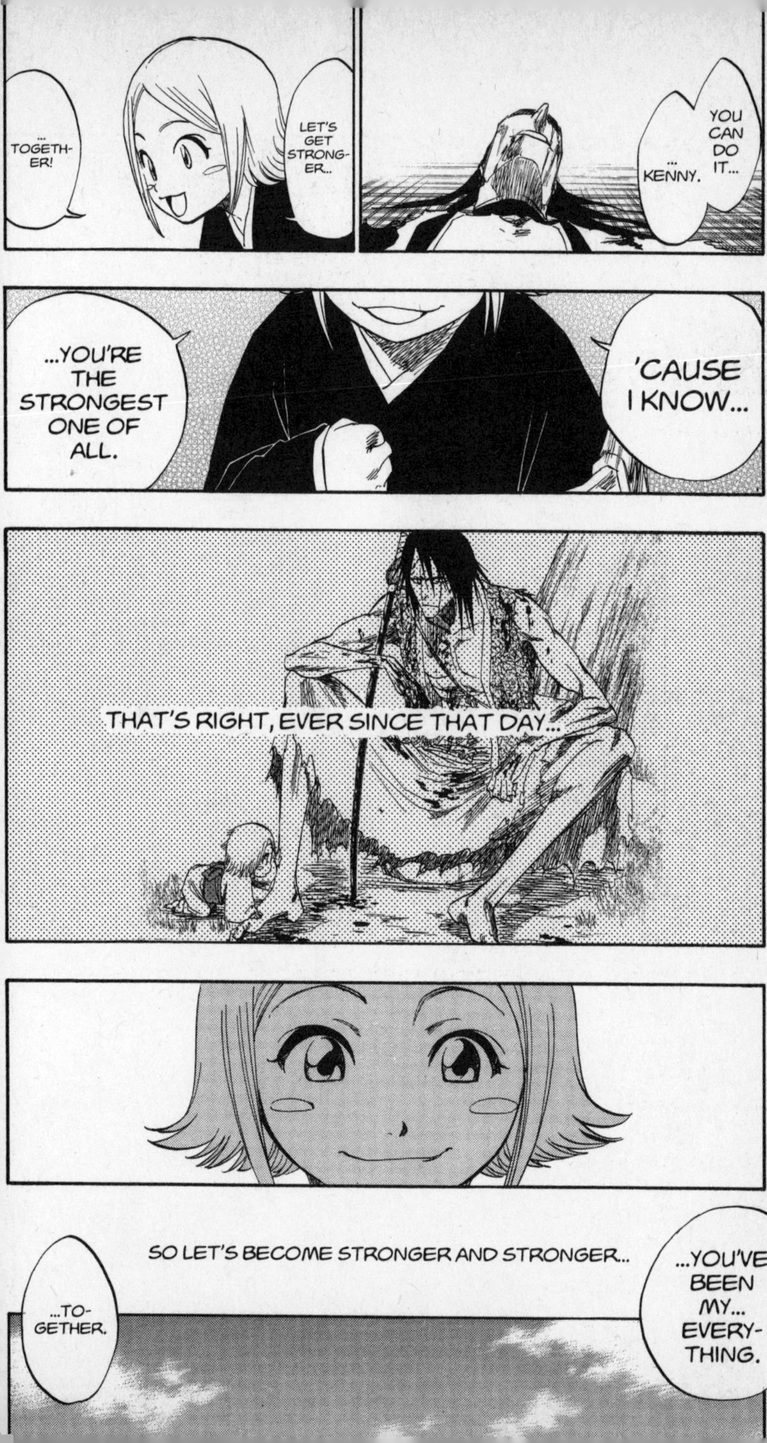
YOU CAN DO IT...
...KENNY.
LET'S GET STRONGER...
...TOGETHER!
'CAUSE I KNOW...
...YOU'RE THE STRONGEST ONE OF ALL.
THAT'S RIGHT, EVER SINCE THAT DAY...
...YOU'VE BEEN MY... EVERYTHING.
SO LET'S BECOME STRONGER AND STRONGER...
...TOGETHER.

READ THIS WAY

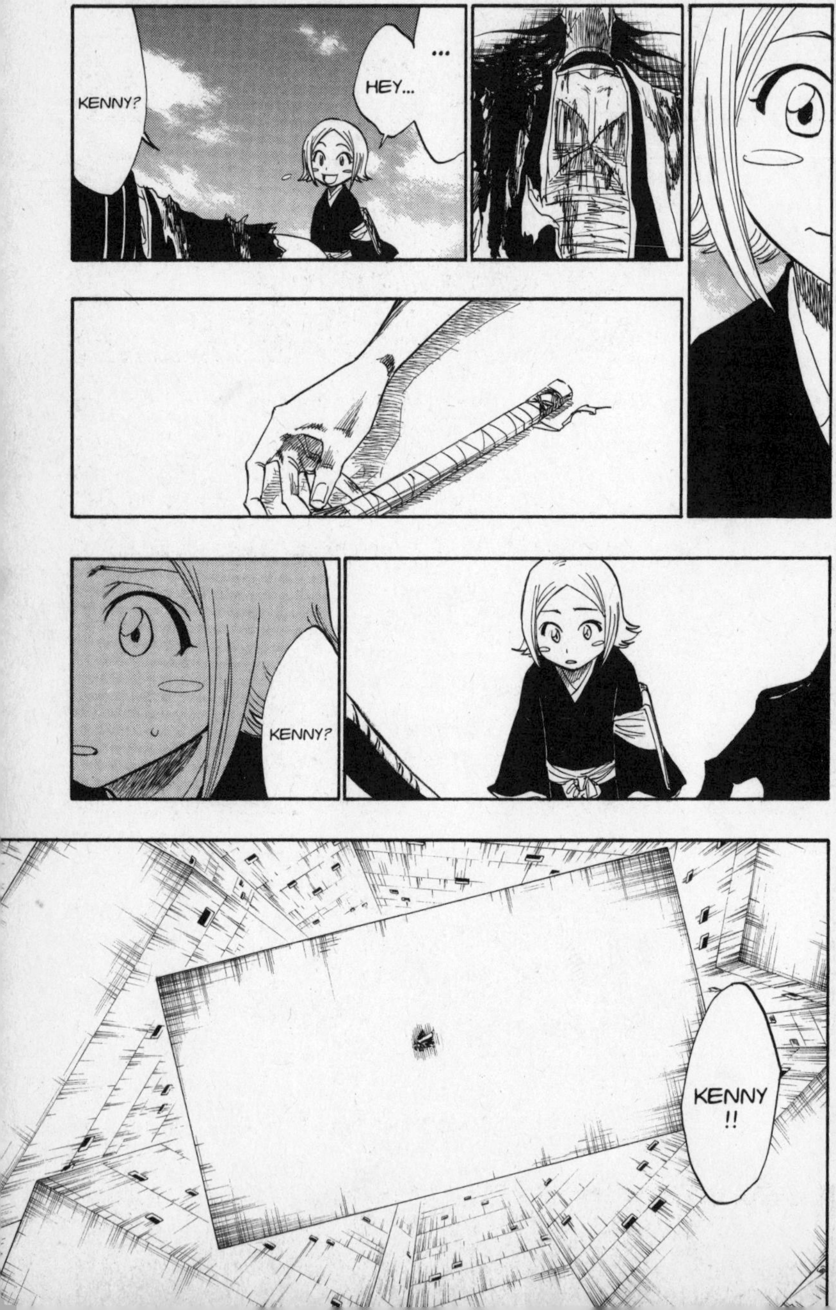
...
HEY...
KENNY?
KENNY?
KENNY !!

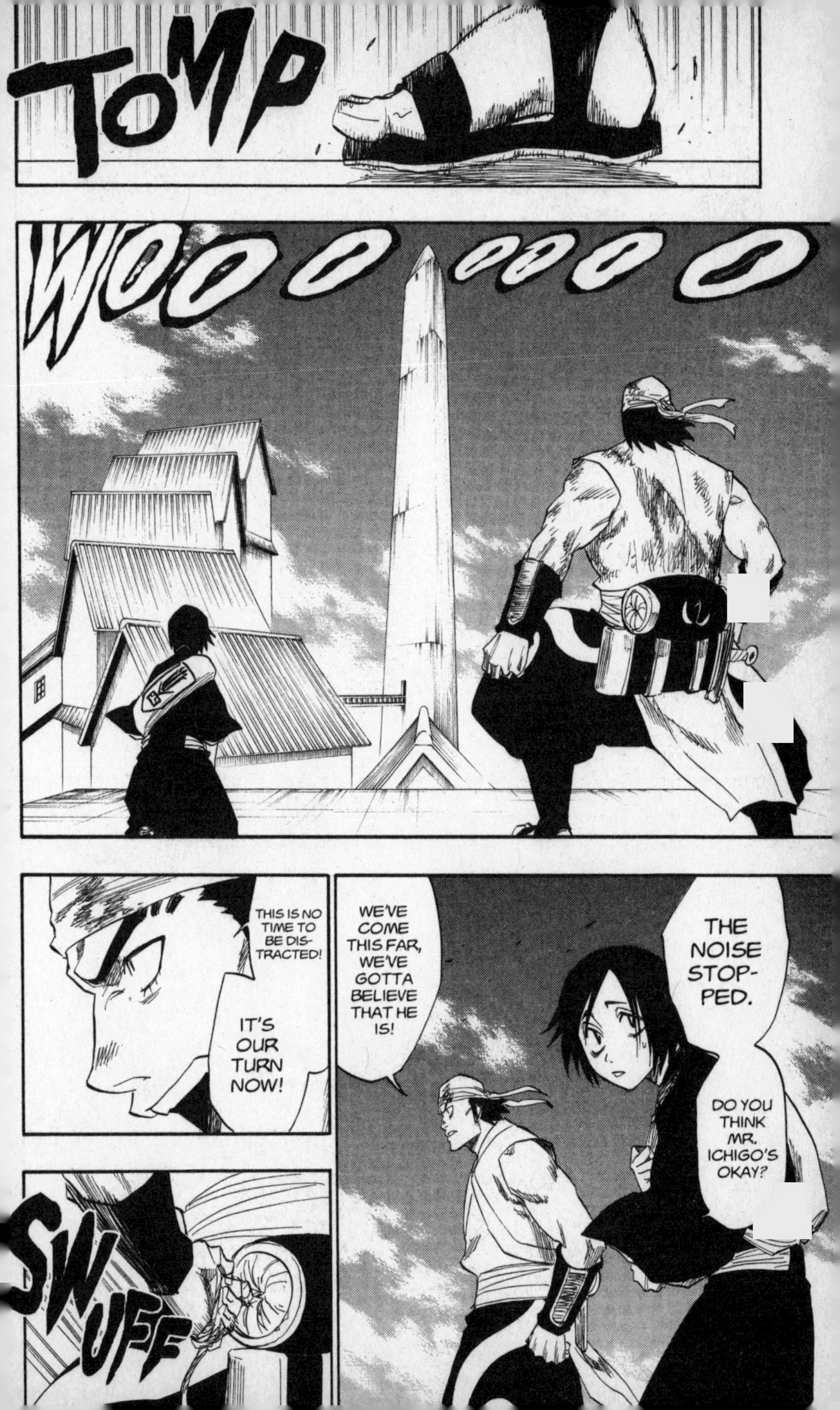
TOMP
WOOOOOOOOO
THE NOISE STOP-PED.
DO YOU THINK MR. ICHIGO'S OKAY?
WE'VE COME THIS FAR, WE'VE GOTTA BELIEVE THAT HE IS!
THIS IS NO TIME TO BE DIS-TRACTED!
IT'S OUR TURN NOW!
SWUFF

READ THIS WAY

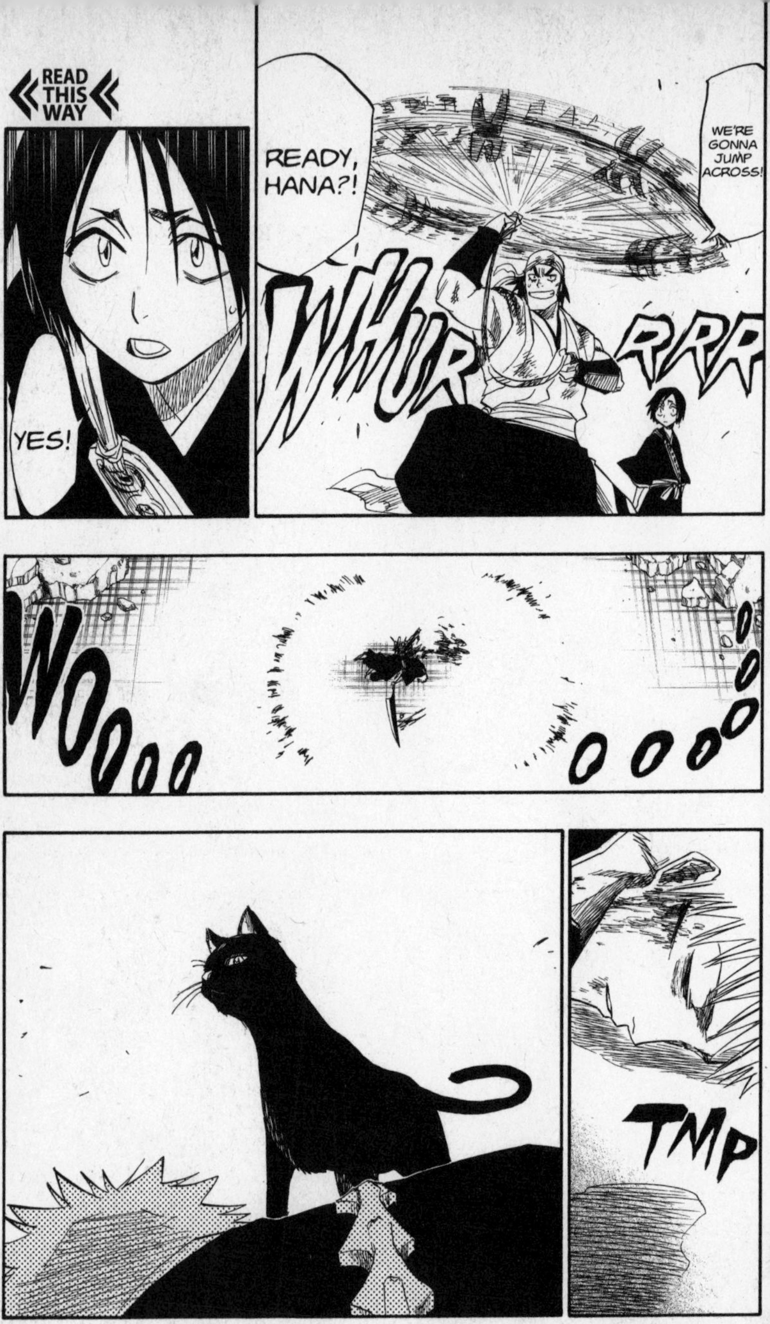
WE'RE GONNA JUMP ACROSS!
READY, HANA?!
WHURRRR
YES!
WOOOOOOOOOOOO
TMP

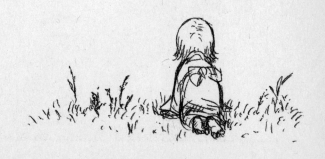

115. Remnant

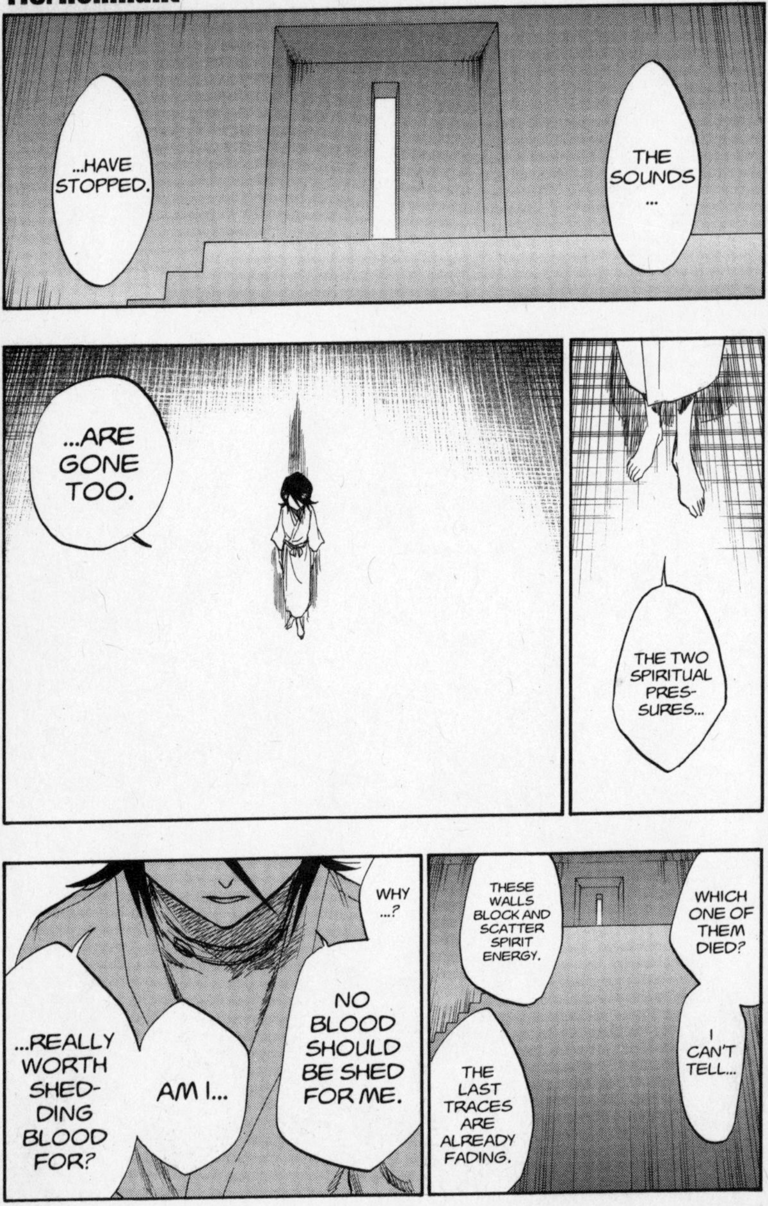
THE SOUNDS ...
...HAVE STOPPED.
THE TWO SPIRITUAL PRES-SURES...
...ARE GONE TOO.
WHICH ONE OF THEM DIED?
I CAN'T TELL...
THESE WALLS BLOCK AND SCATTER SPIRIT ENERGY.
THE LAST TRACES ARE ALREADY FADING.
WHY ...?
NO BLOOD SHOULD BE SHED FOR ME.
AM I...
...REALLY WORTH SHED-DING BLOOD FOR?

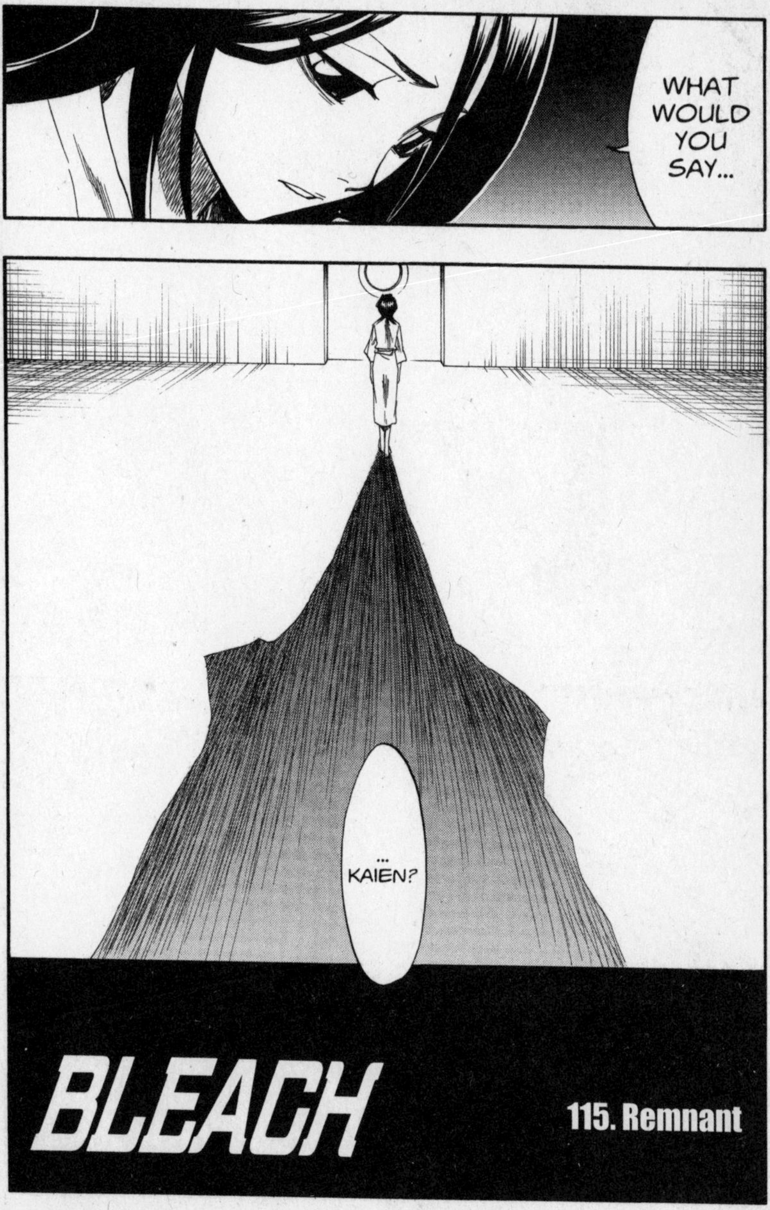
WHAT WOULD YOU SAY...
... KAIEN?
BLEACH
115. Remnant

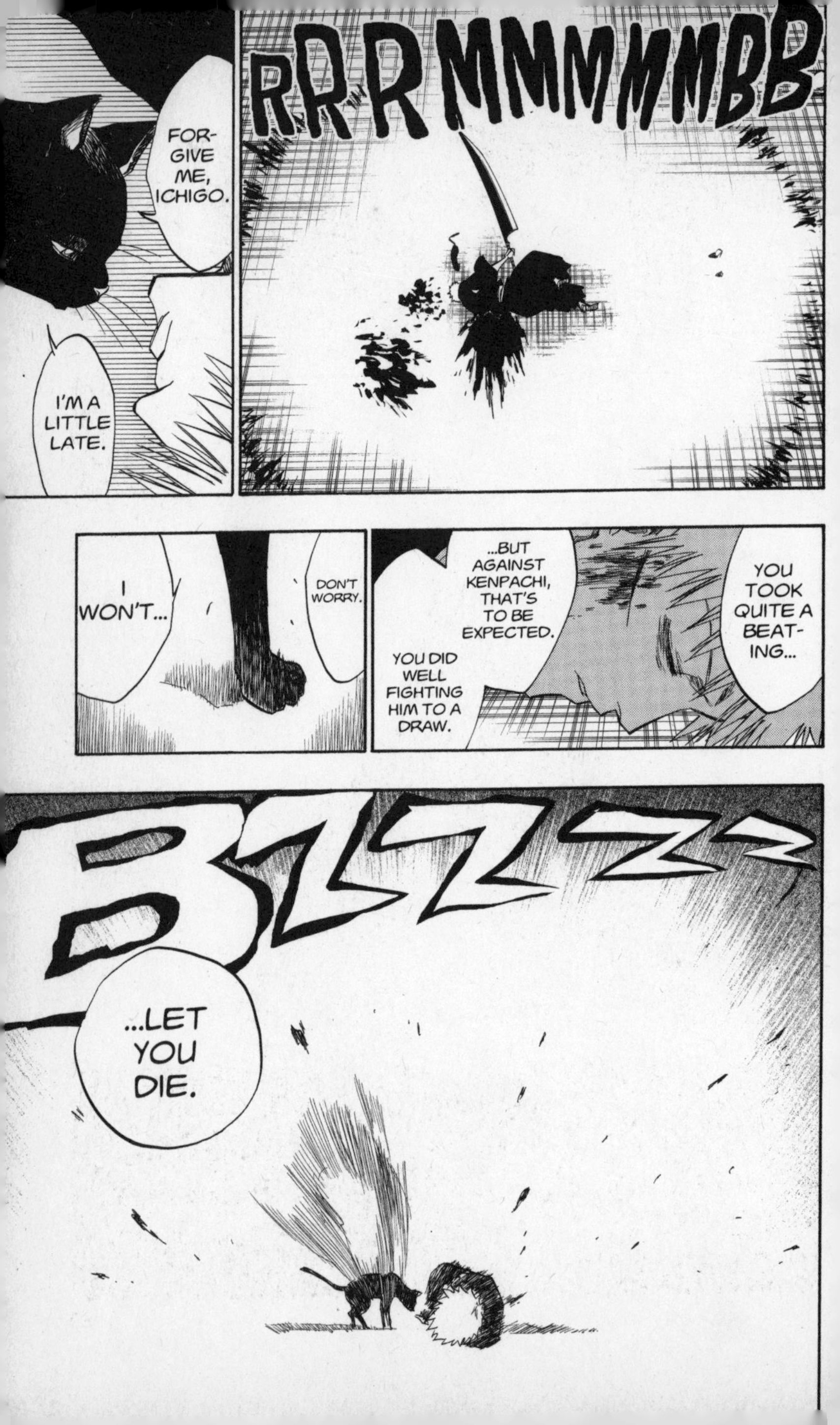
RRRMMMMMBB
FOR-GIVE ME, ICHIGO.
I'M A LITTLE LATE.
YOU TOOK QUITE A BEAT-ING...
...BUT AGAINST KENPACHI, THAT'S TO BE EXPECTED.
YOU DID WELL FIGHTING HIM TO A DRAW.
DON'T WORRY.
I WON'T...
BZZZZ
...LET YOU DIE.

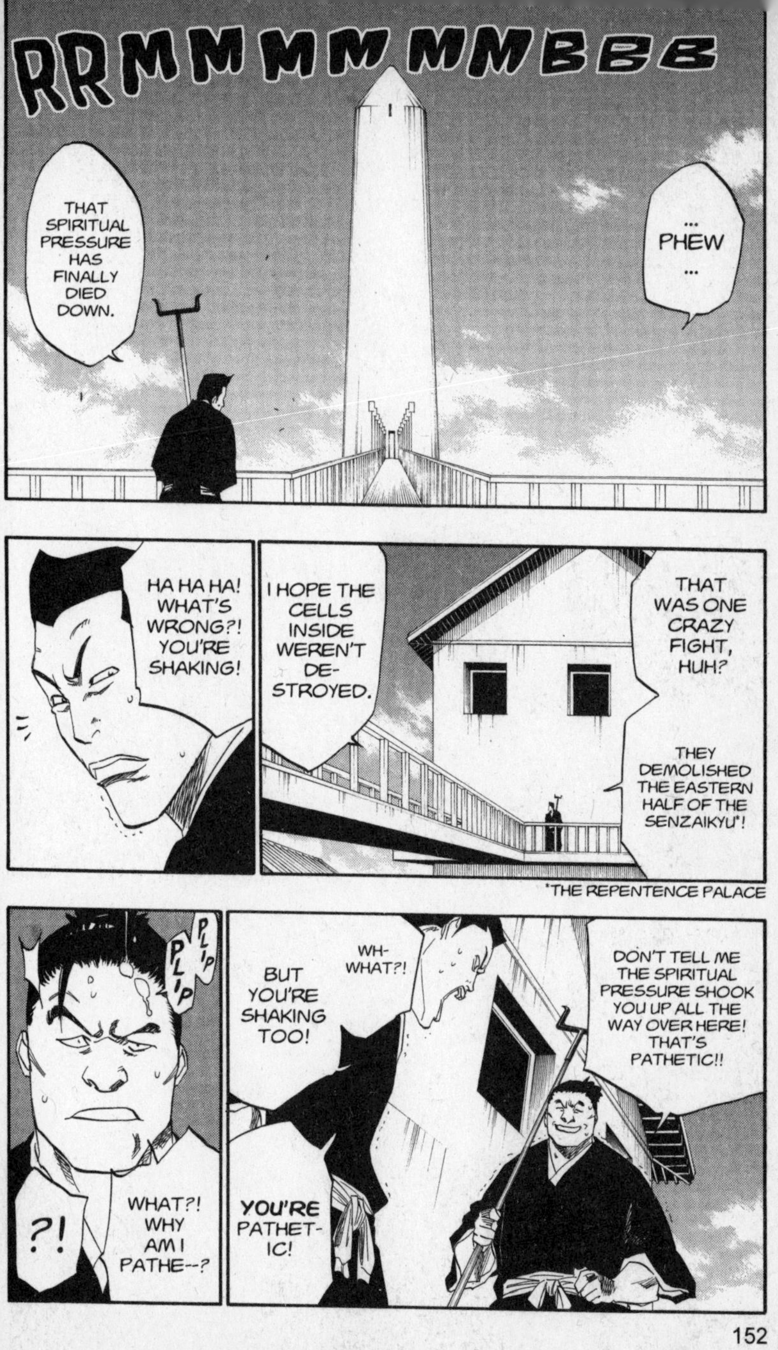
RRMMMMMMMMBBB
... PHEW ...
THAT SPIRITUAL PRESSURE HAS FINALLY DIED DOWN.
THAT WAS ONE CRAZY FIGHT, HUH?
THEY DEMOLISHED THE EASTERN HALF OF THE SENZAIKYU*!
I HOPE THE CELLS INSIDE WEREN'T DE-STROYED.
HA HA HA! WHAT'S WRONG?! YOU'RE SHAKING!
*THE REPENTENCE PALACE
DON'T TELL ME THE SPIRITUAL PRESSURE SHOOK YOU UP ALL THE WAY OVER HERE! THAT'S PATHETIC!!
WH- WHAT?!
BUT YOU'RE SHAKING TOO!
YOU'RE PATHET-IC!
PLIP PLIP
WHAT?! WHY AM I PATHE--?
?!

READ THIS WAY

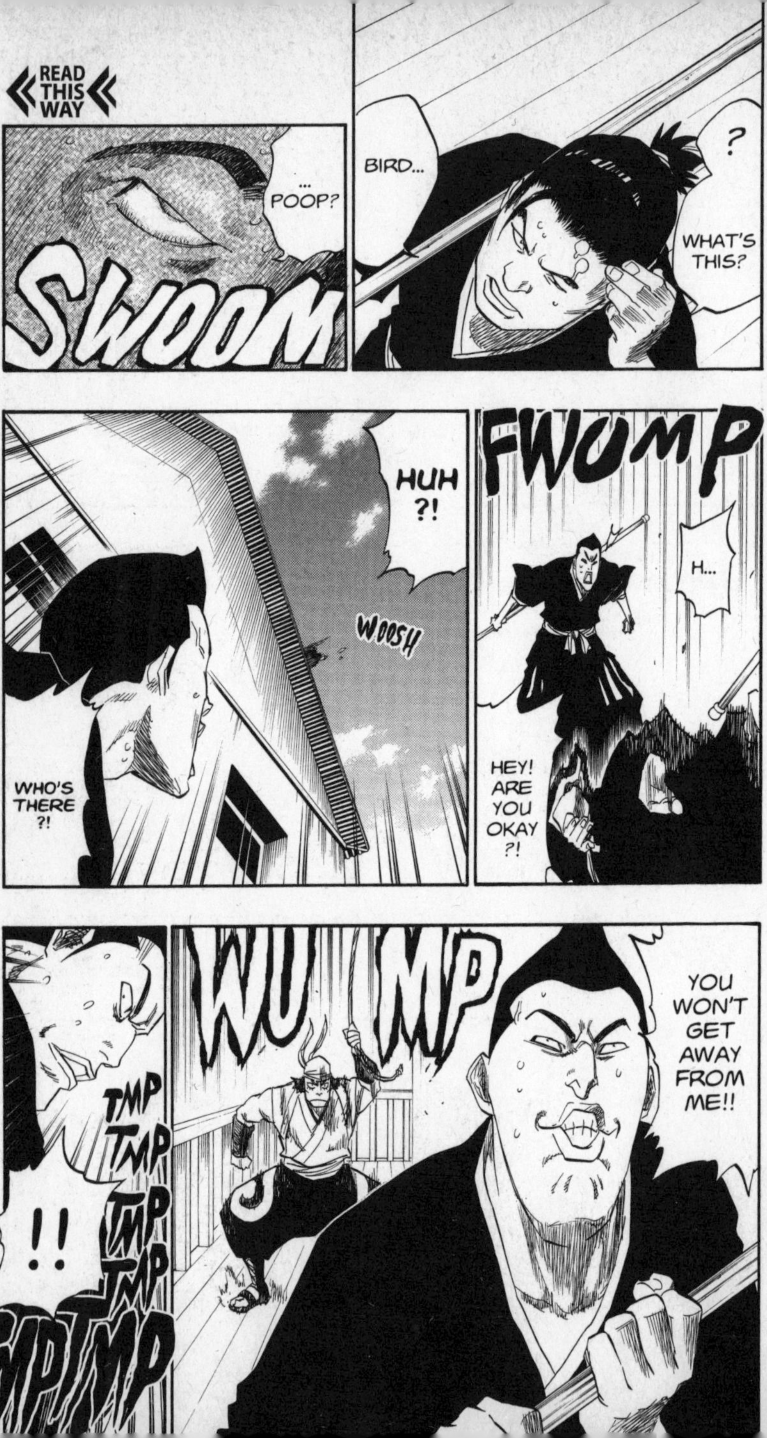
?
WHAT'S THIS?
BIRD...
... POOP?
SWOOM
FWOMP
H...
HEY! ARE YOU OKAY ?!
HUH ?!
WOOSH
WHO'S THERE ?!
WUMP
YOU WON'T GET AWAY FROM ME!!
TMP TMP TMP TMP
!!
TMPTMP

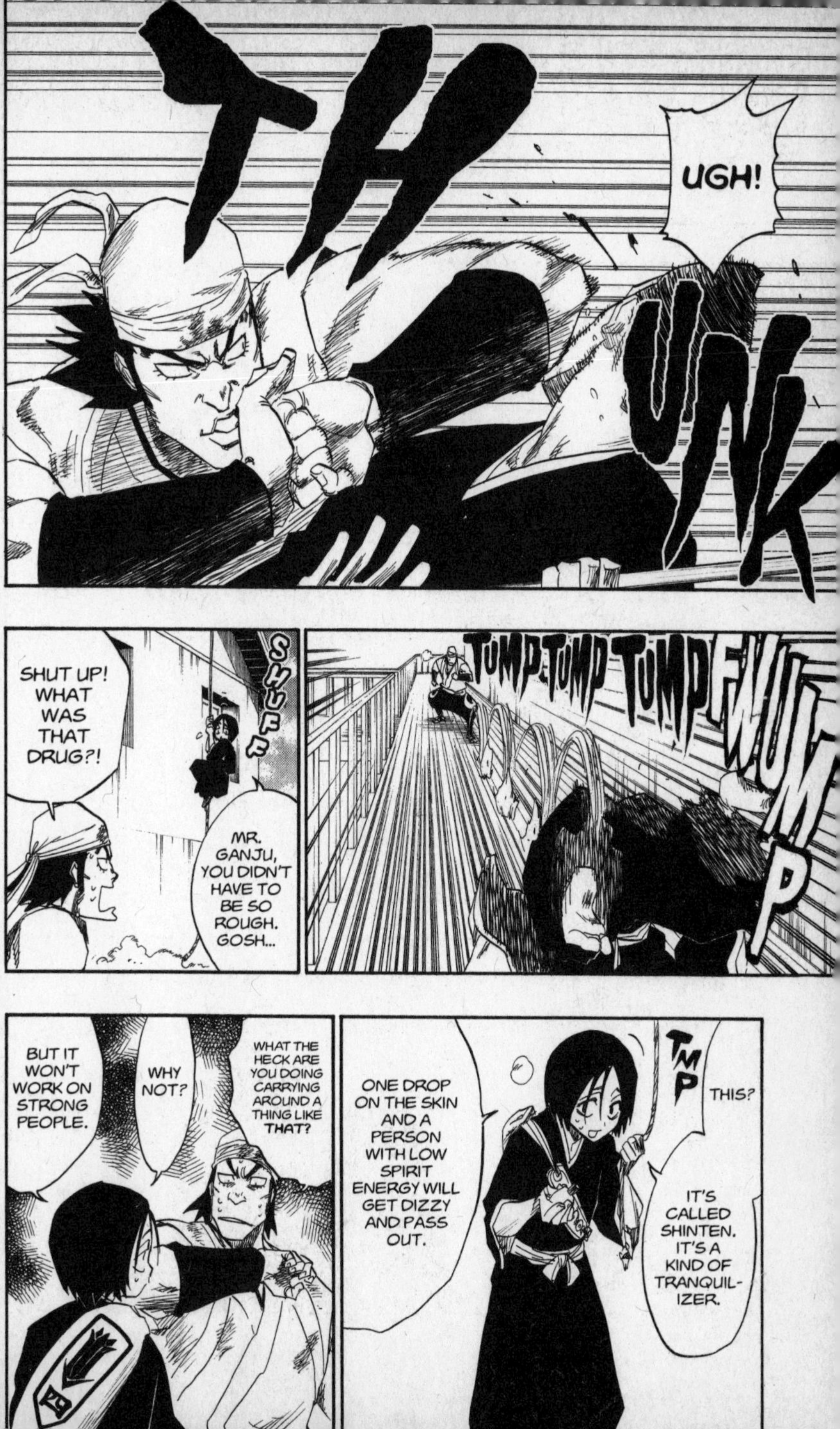
UGH!
THUNK
TUMP TUMP TUMP
FWUMP
SHUFF
MR. GANJU, YOU DIDN'T HAVE TO BE SO ROUGH. GOSH...
SHUT UP! WHAT WAS THAT DRUG?!
THIS?
TMP
IT'S CALLED SHINTEN. IT'S A KIND OF TRANQUIL-IZER.
ONE DROP ON THE SKIN AND A PERSON WITH LOW SPIRIT ENERGY WILL GET DIZZY AND PASS OUT.
WHAT THE HECK ARE YOU DOING CARRYING AROUND A THING LIKE THAT?
WHY NOT?
BUT IT WON'T WORK ON STRONG PEOPLE.

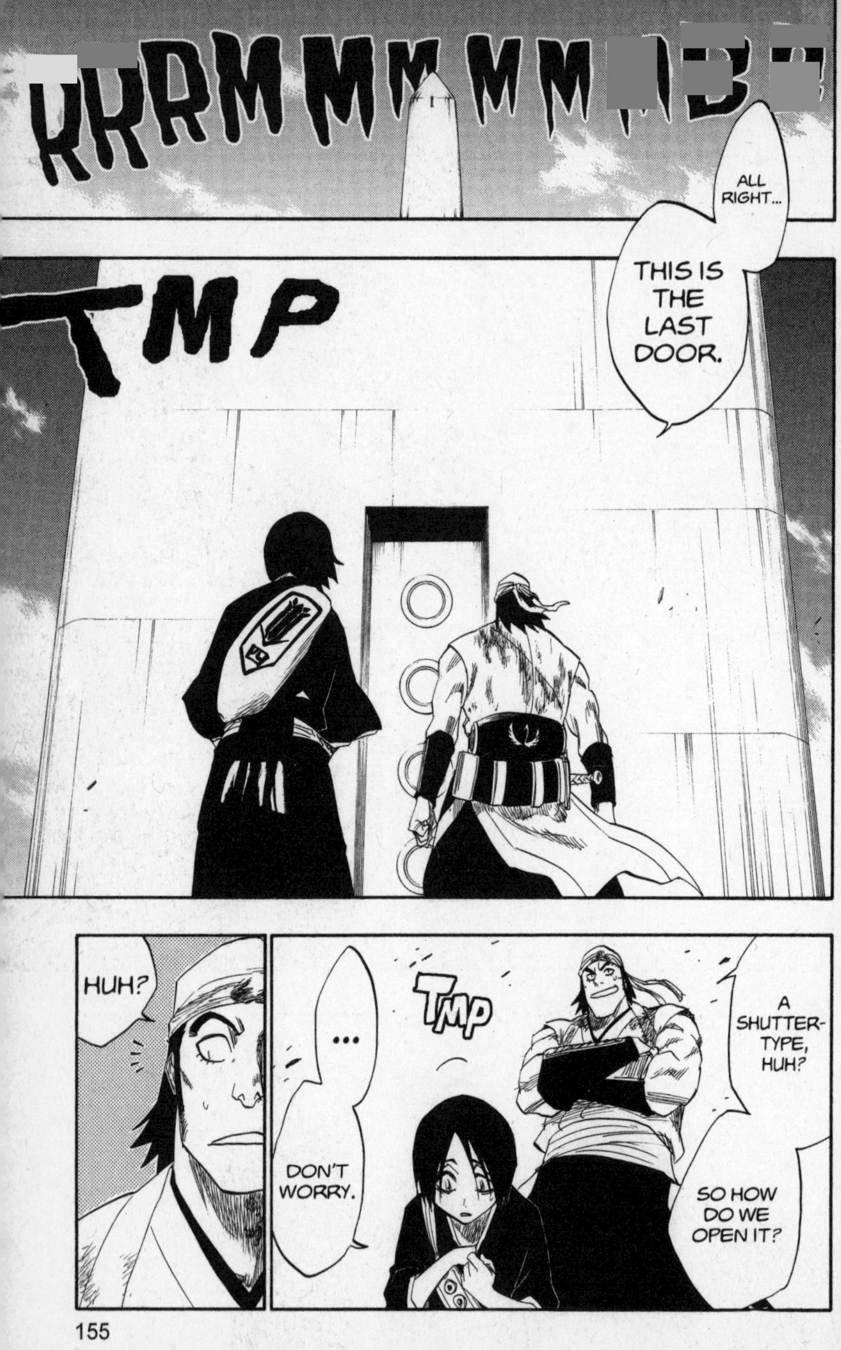
RRRMMMMMM[redacted]
ALL RIGHT...
TMP
THIS IS THE LAST DOOR.
A SHUTTER-TYPE, HUH?
SO HOW DO WE OPEN IT?
TMP
...
DON'T WORRY.
HUH?

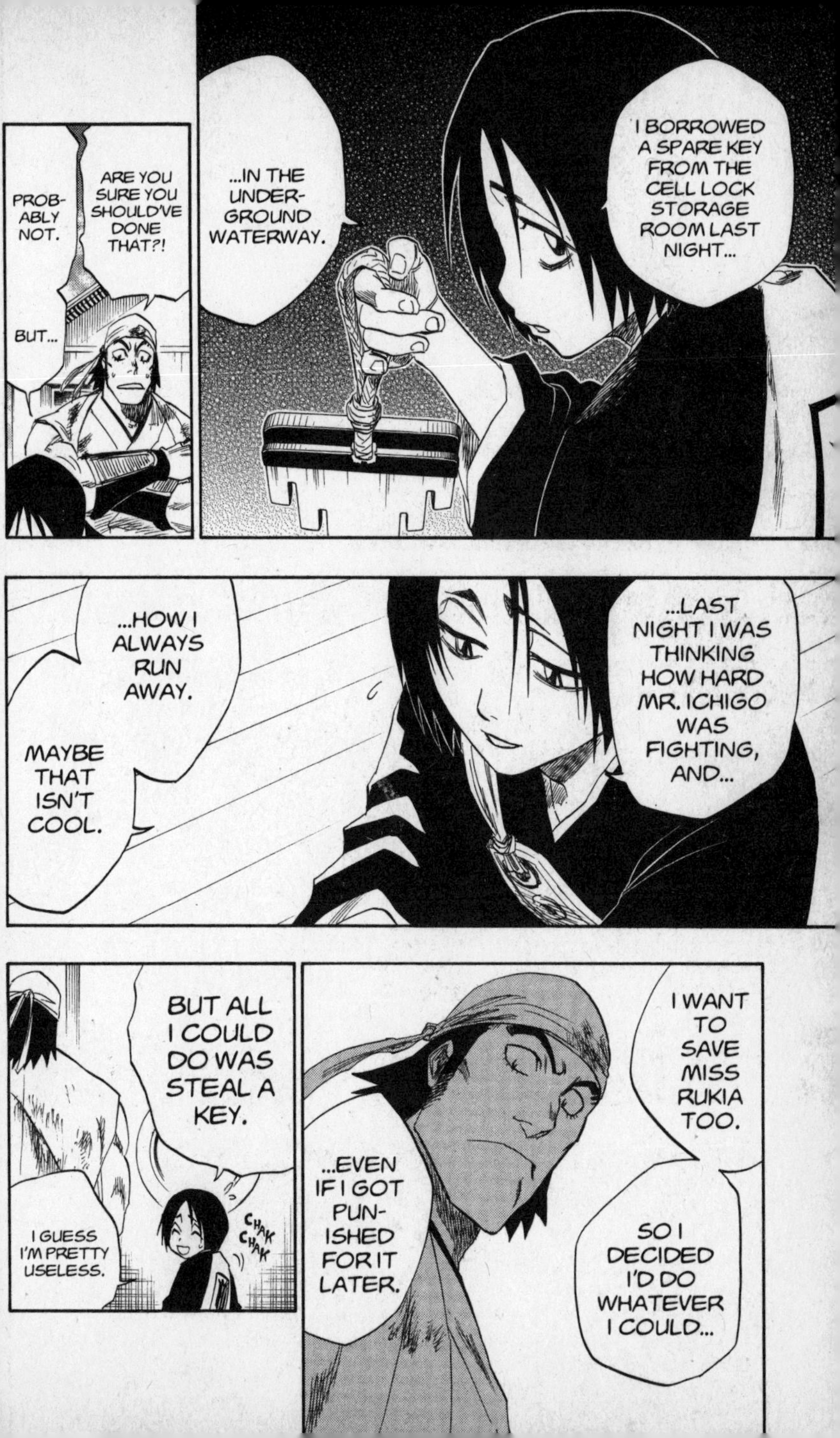
I BORROWED A SPARE KEY FROM THE CELL LOCK STORAGE ROOM LAST NIGHT...
...IN THE UNDER-GROUND WATERWAY.
ARE YOU SURE YOU SHOULD'VE DONE THAT?!
PROB-ABLY NOT.
BUT...
...LAST NIGHT I WAS THINKING HOW HARD MR. ICHIGO WAS FIGHTING, AND...
...HOW I ALWAYS RUN AWAY.
MAYBE THAT ISN'T COOL.
I WANT TO SAVE MISS RUKIA TOO.
SO I DECIDED I'D DO WHATEVER I COULD...
...EVEN IF I GOT PUN-ISHED FOR IT LATER.
BUT ALL I COULD DO WAS STEAL A KEY.
I GUESS I'M PRETTY USELESS.
CHAK CHAK

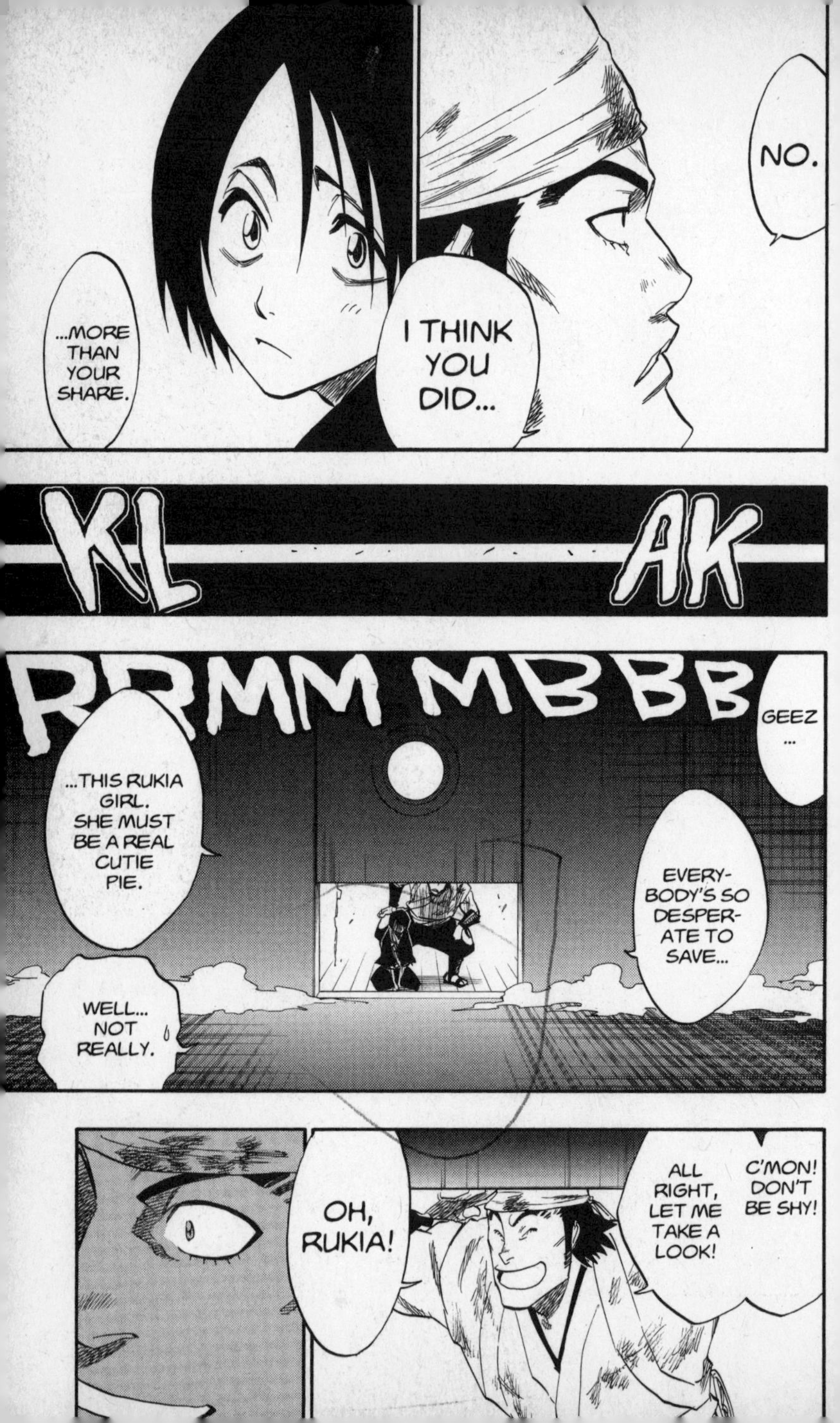
NO.
I THINK YOU DID...
...MORE THAN YOUR SHARE.
KL AK
RRMM MBBB
GEEZ...
EVERY-BODY'S SO DESPER-ATE TO SAVE...
...THIS RUKIA GIRL. SHE MUST BE A REAL CUTIE PIE.
WELL... NOT REALLY.
C'MON! DON'T BE SHY!
ALL RIGHT, LET ME TAKE A LOOK!
OH, RUKIA!

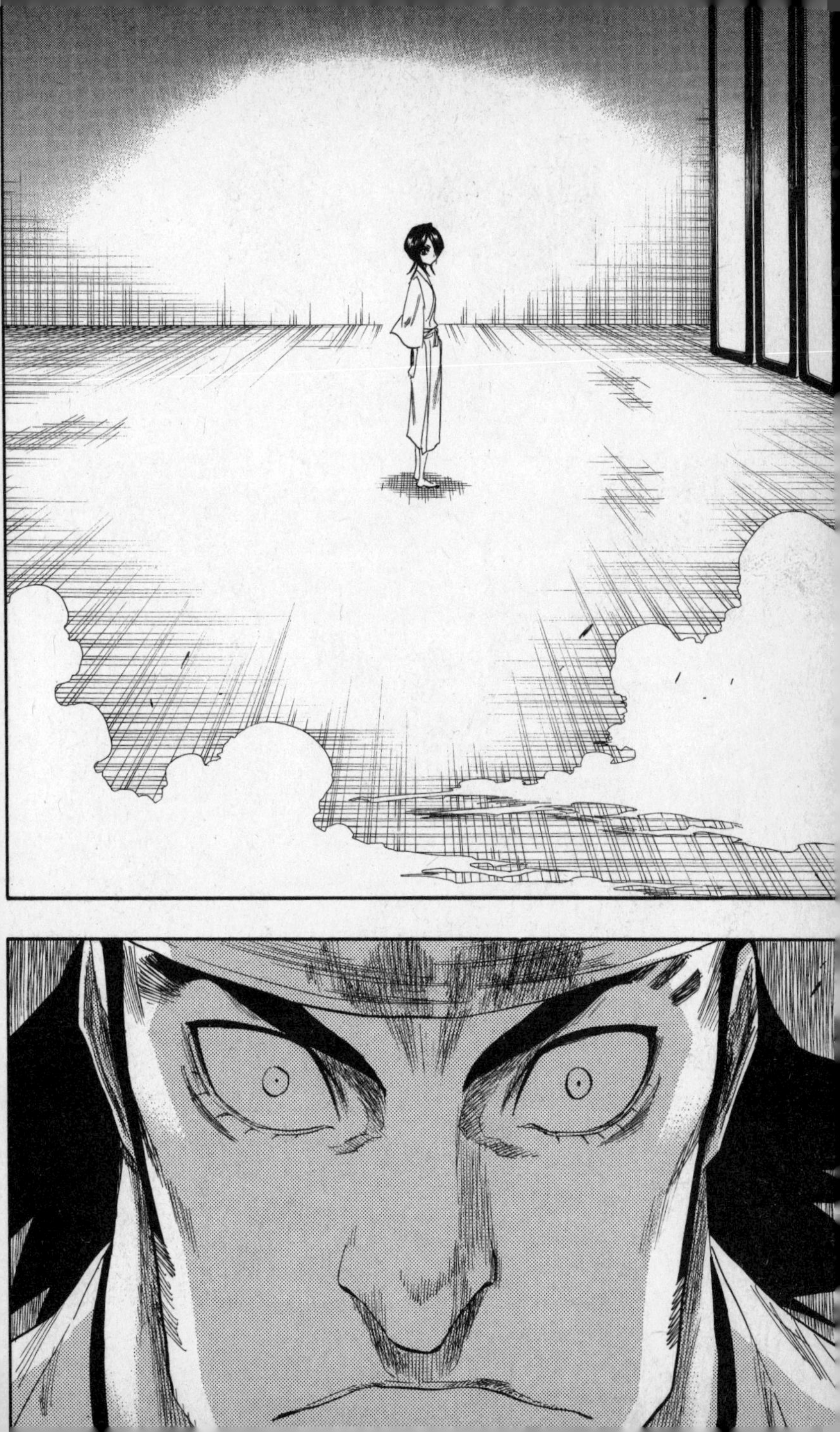

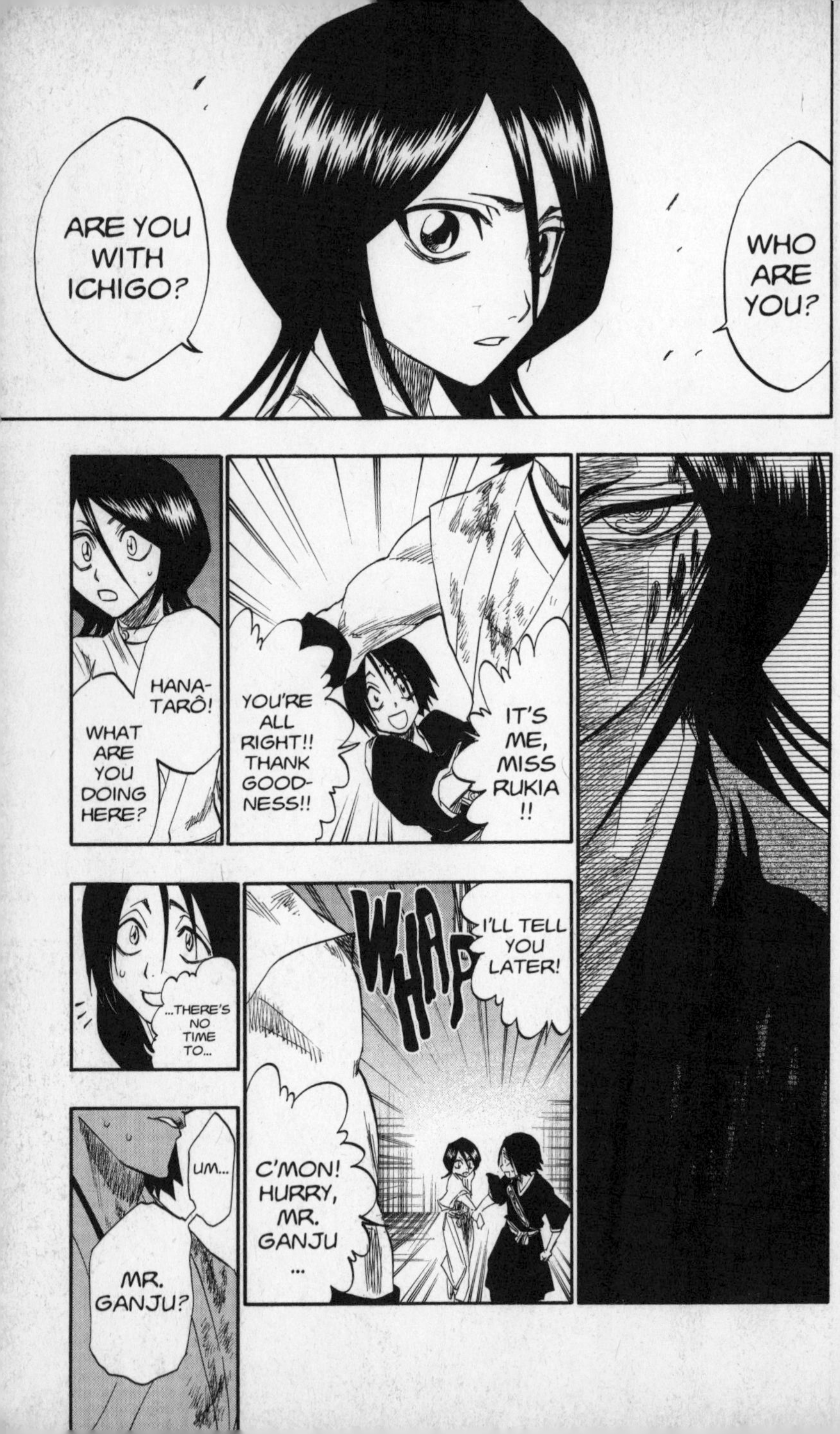

WHO ARE YOU?
ARE YOU WITH ICHIGO?
IT'S ME, MISS RUKIA!!
YOU'RE ALL RIGHT!! THANK GOODNESS!!
HANATARÔ!
WHAT ARE YOU DOING HERE?
I'LL TELL YOU LATER!
WHAP
C'MON! HURRY, MR. GANJU ...
...THERE'S NO TIME TO...
UM...
MR. GANJU?

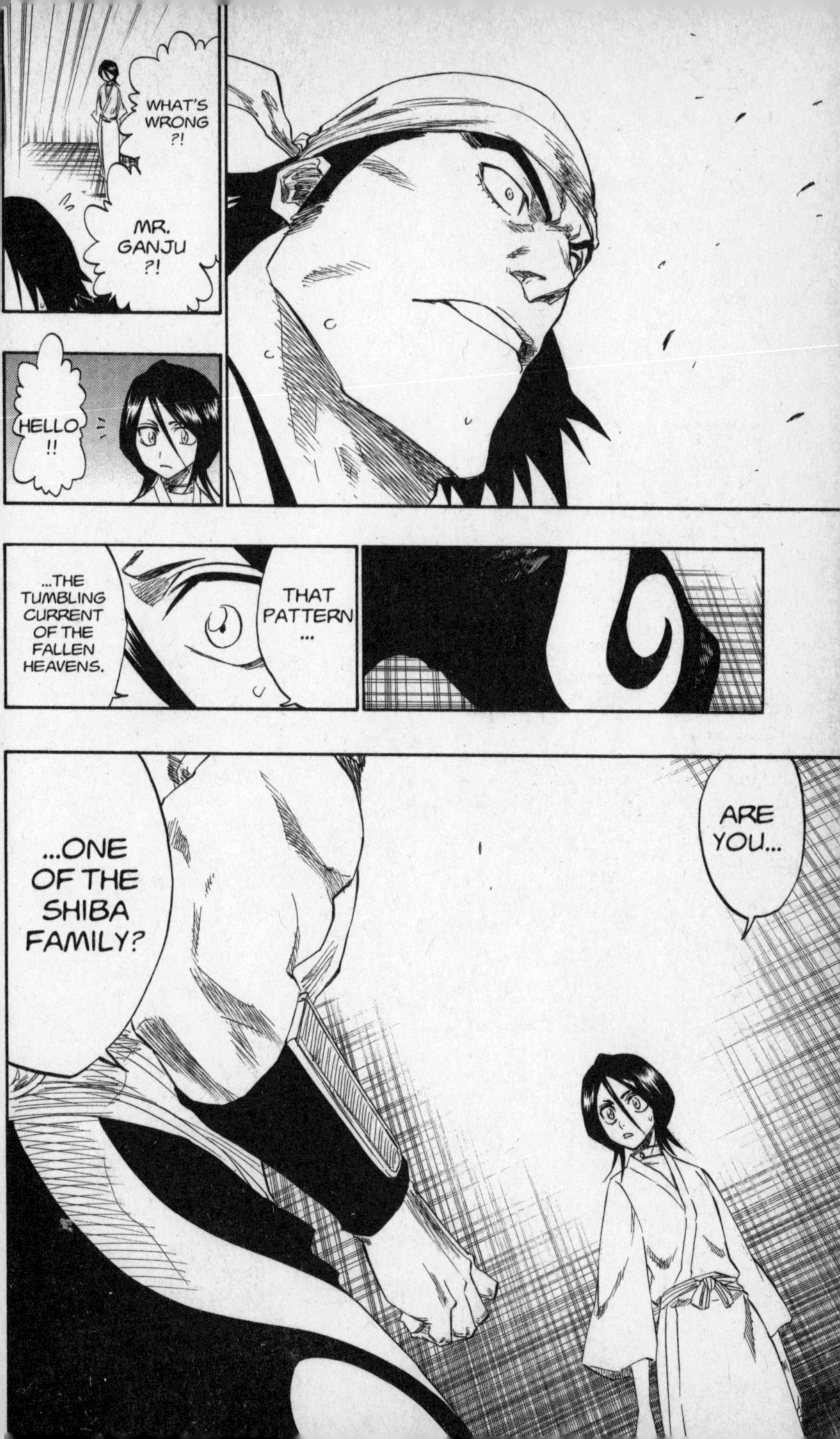
WHAT'S WRONG?!
MR. GANJU?!
HELLO!!
THAT PATTERN...
...THE TUMBLING CURRENT OF THE FALLEN HEAVENS.
ARE YOU...
...ONE OF THE SHIBA FAMILY?

READ THIS WAY

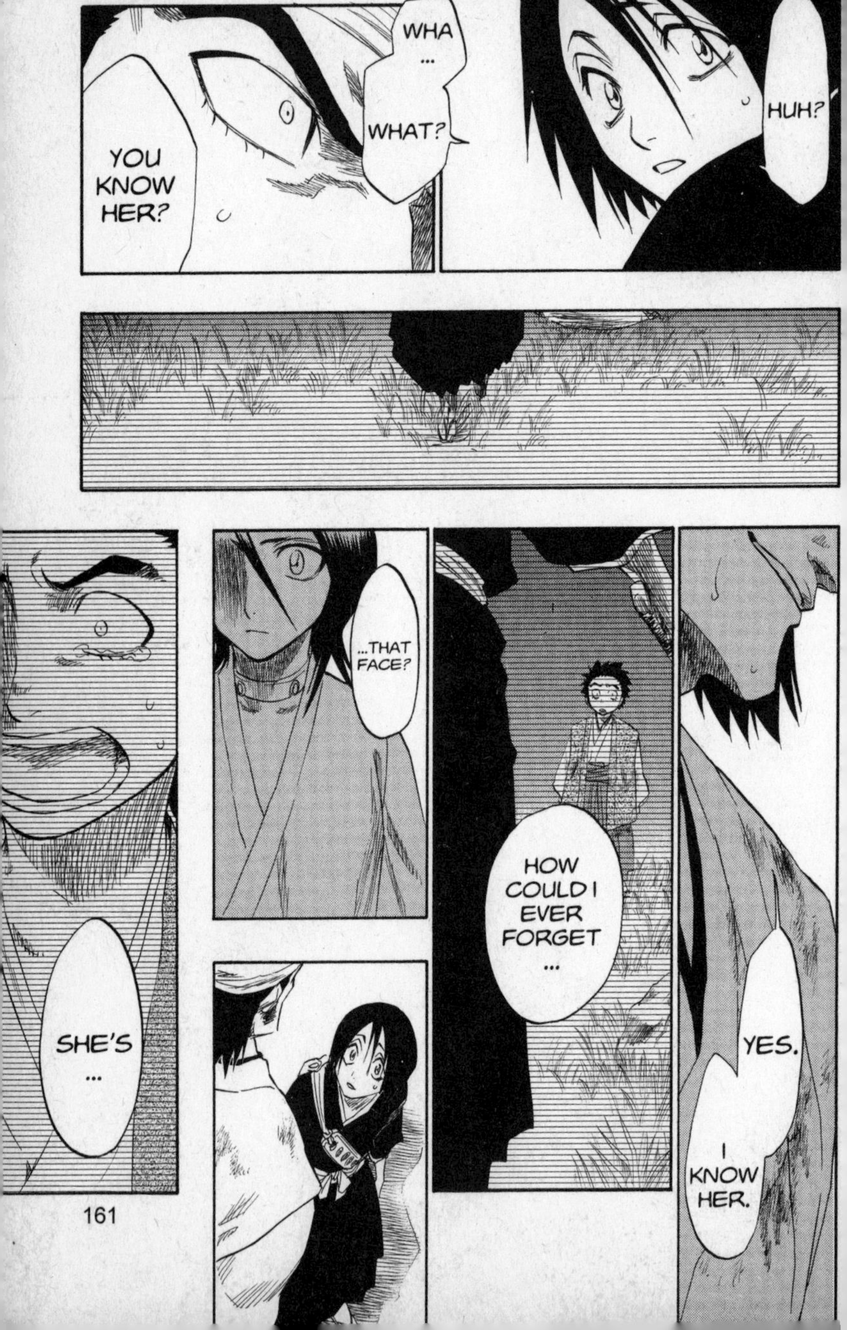
HUH?
WHA ... WHAT?
YOU KNOW HER?
YES.
I KNOW HER.
HOW COULD I EVER FORGET ...
...THAT FACE?
SHE'S ...

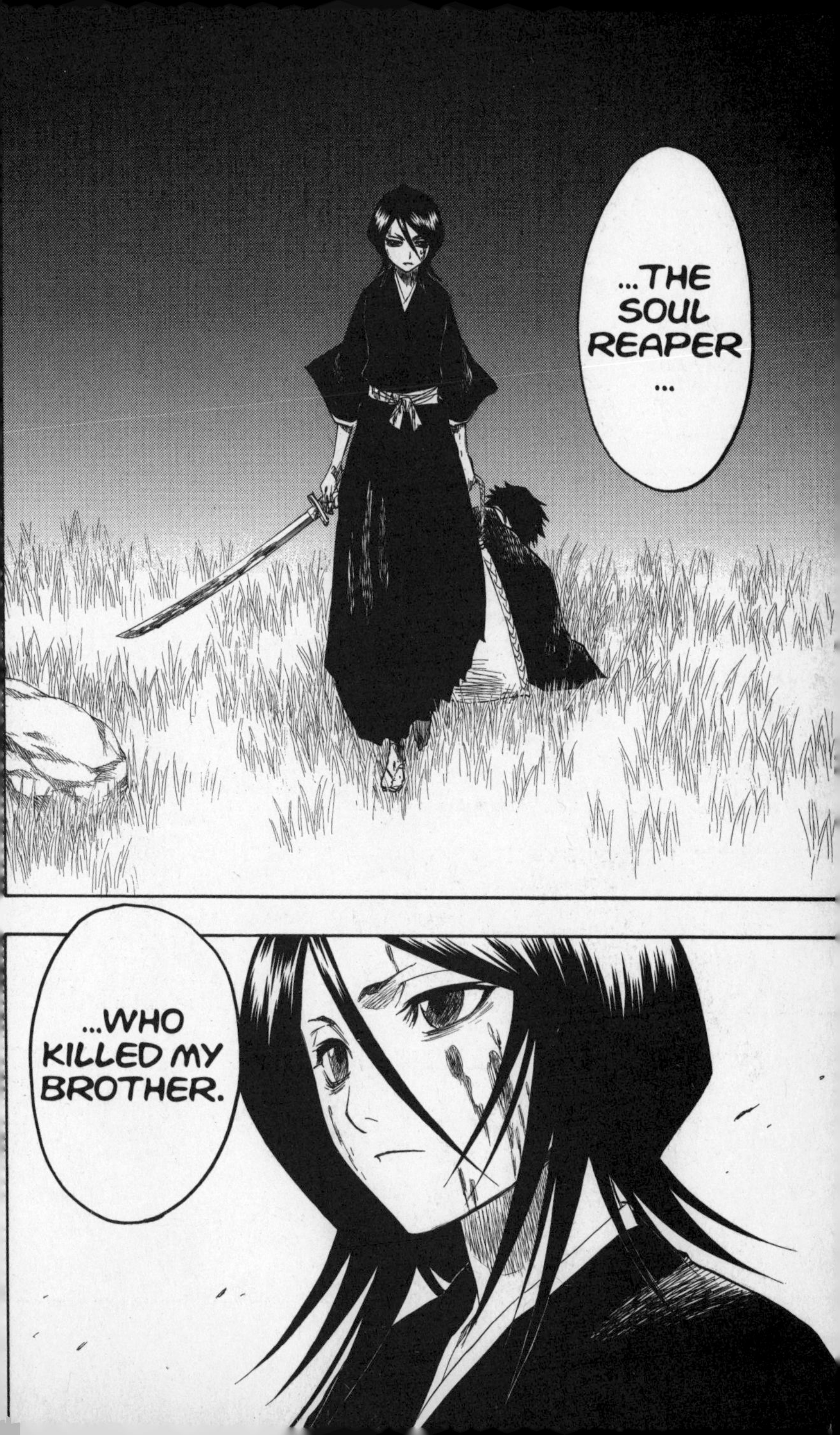
...THE SOUL REAPER ...
...WHO KILLED MY BROTHER.

READ THIS WAY

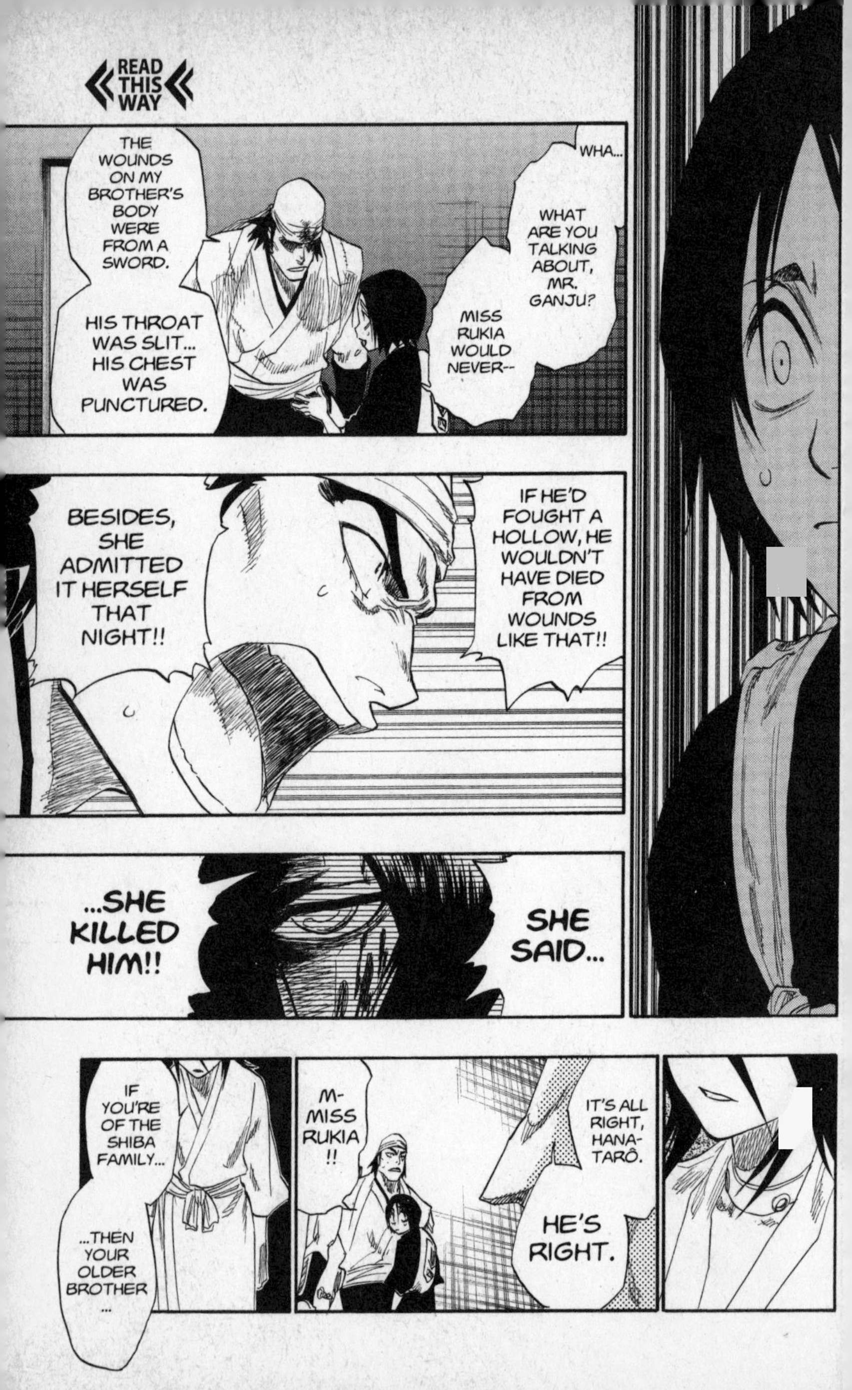
WHA...
WHAT ARE YOU TALKING ABOUT, MR. GANJU?
MISS RUKIA WOULD NEVER--
THE WOUNDS ON MY BROTHER'S BODY WERE FROM A SWORD.
HIS THROAT WAS SLIT... HIS CHEST WAS PUNCTURED.
IF HE'D FOUGHT A HOLLOW, HE WOULDN'T HAVE DIED FROM WOUNDS LIKE THAT!!
BESIDES, SHE ADMITTED IT HERSELF THAT NIGHT!!
SHE SAID...
...SHE KILLED HIM!!
IT'S ALL RIGHT, HANATARÔ.
HE'S RIGHT.
M-MISS RUKIA !!
IF YOU'RE OF THE SHIBA FAMILY...
...THEN YOUR OLDER BROTHER ...

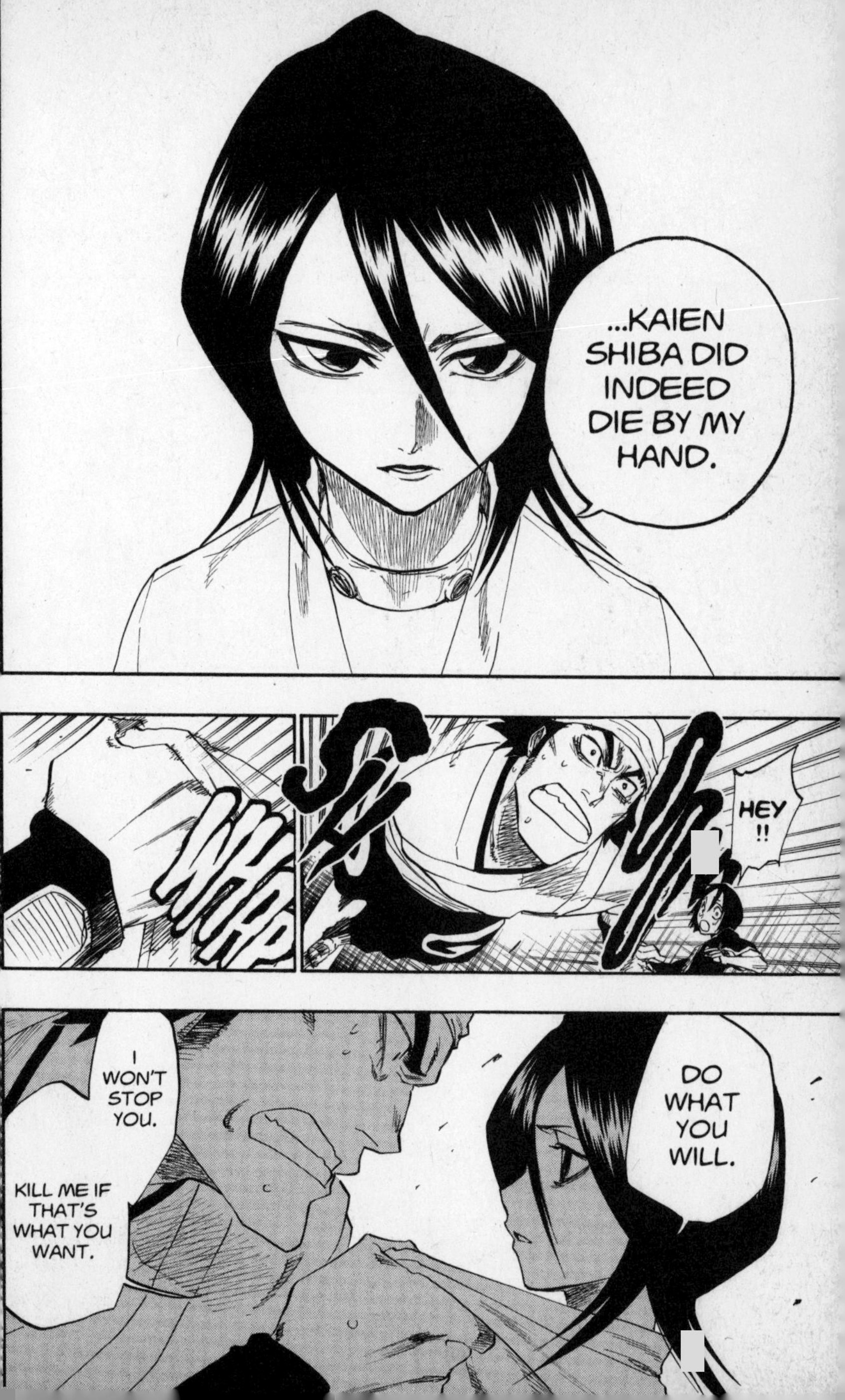
...KAIEN SHIBA DID INDEED DIE BY MY HAND.
HEY !!
WHAP
DO WHAT YOU WILL.
I WON'T STOP YOU.
KILL ME IF THAT'S WHAT YOU WANT.

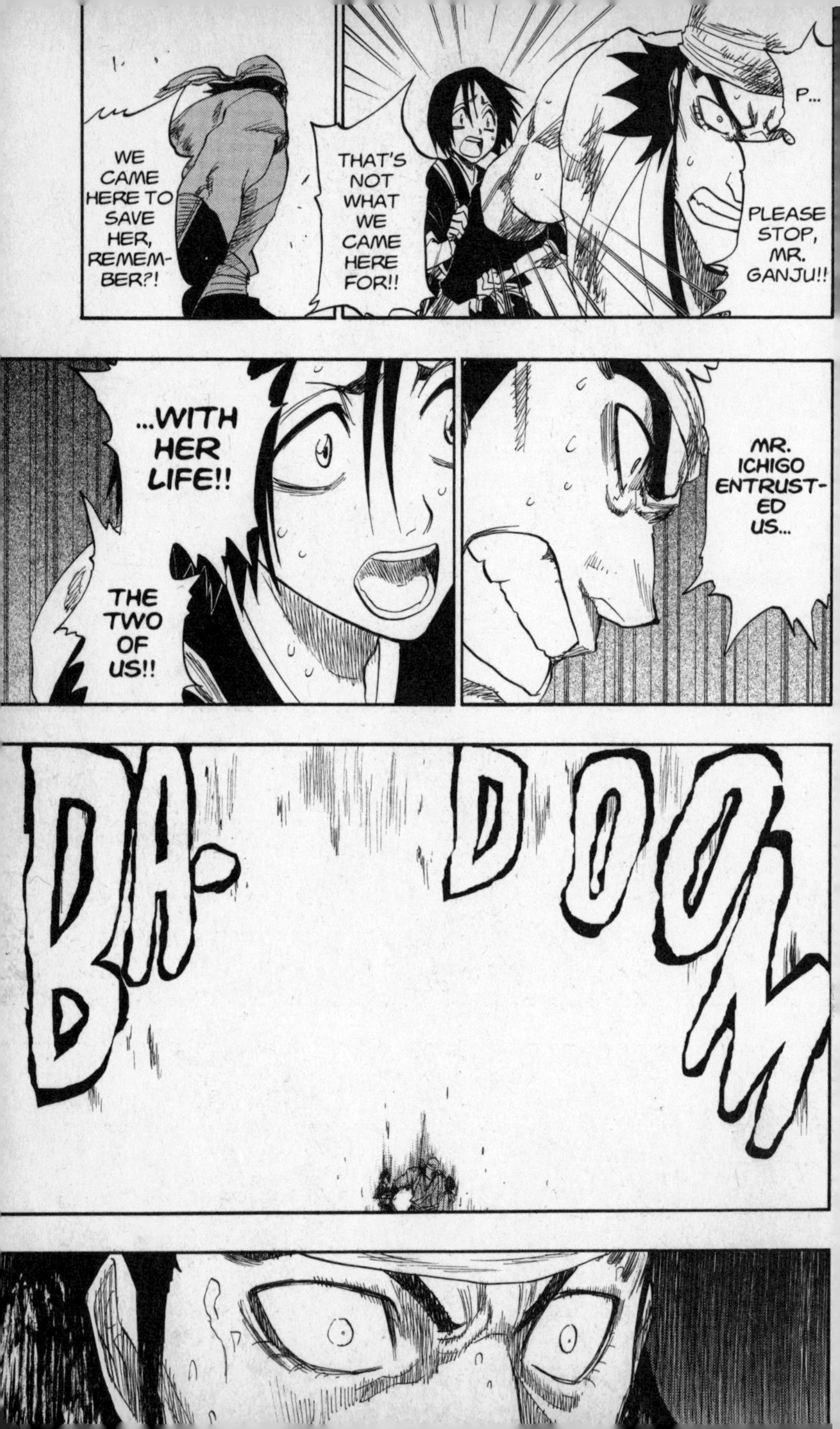
P...
PLEASE STOP, MR. GANJU!!
THAT'S NOT WHAT WE CAME HERE FOR!!
WE CAME HERE TO SAVE HER, REMEMBER?!
MR. ICHIGO ENTRUSTED US...
...WITH HER LIFE!!
THE TWO OF US!!
BA-DOOM

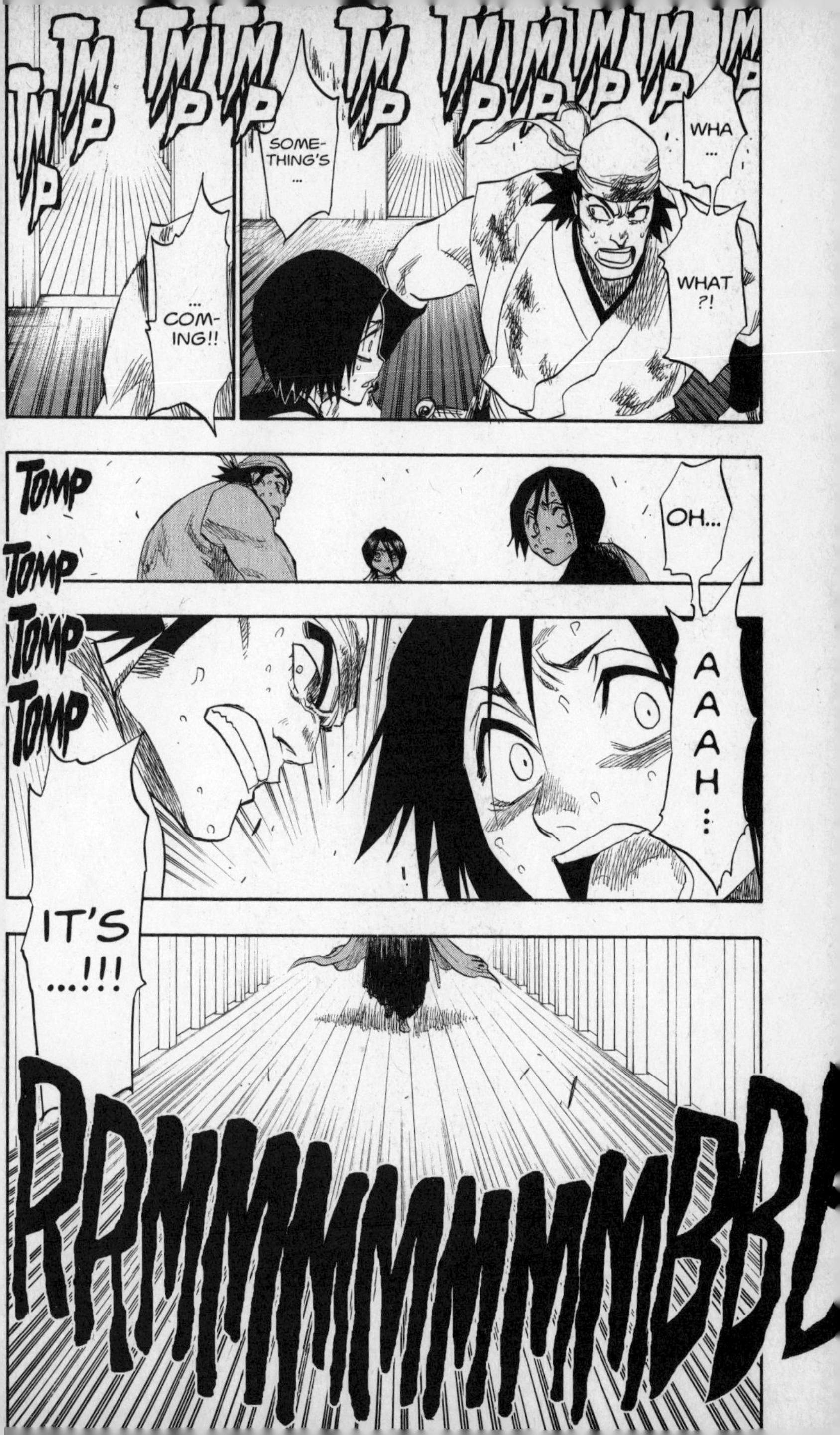
TMP TMP TMP TMP TMP TMP TMP TMP TMP TMP TMP
WHA ...
SOME-THING'S ...
WHAT ?!
... COM-ING!!
OH...
TOMP
TOMP
AAAH ...
TOMP
TOMP
IT'S ...!!!
RRMMMMMMMMMBBL

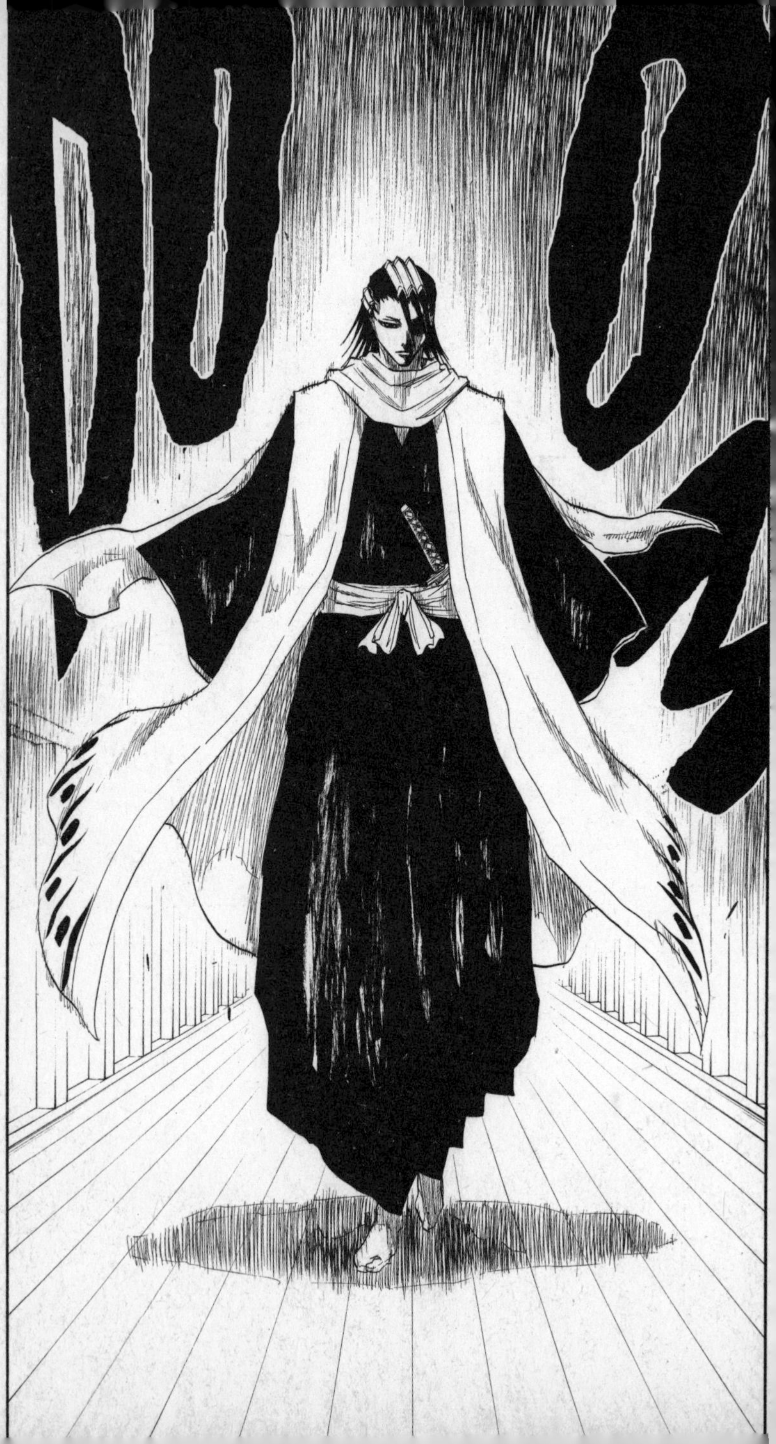

CONTI
NUED
IN
BLEACH
14

READ THIS WAY

BANNER: HAPPY 2ND ANNIVERSARY

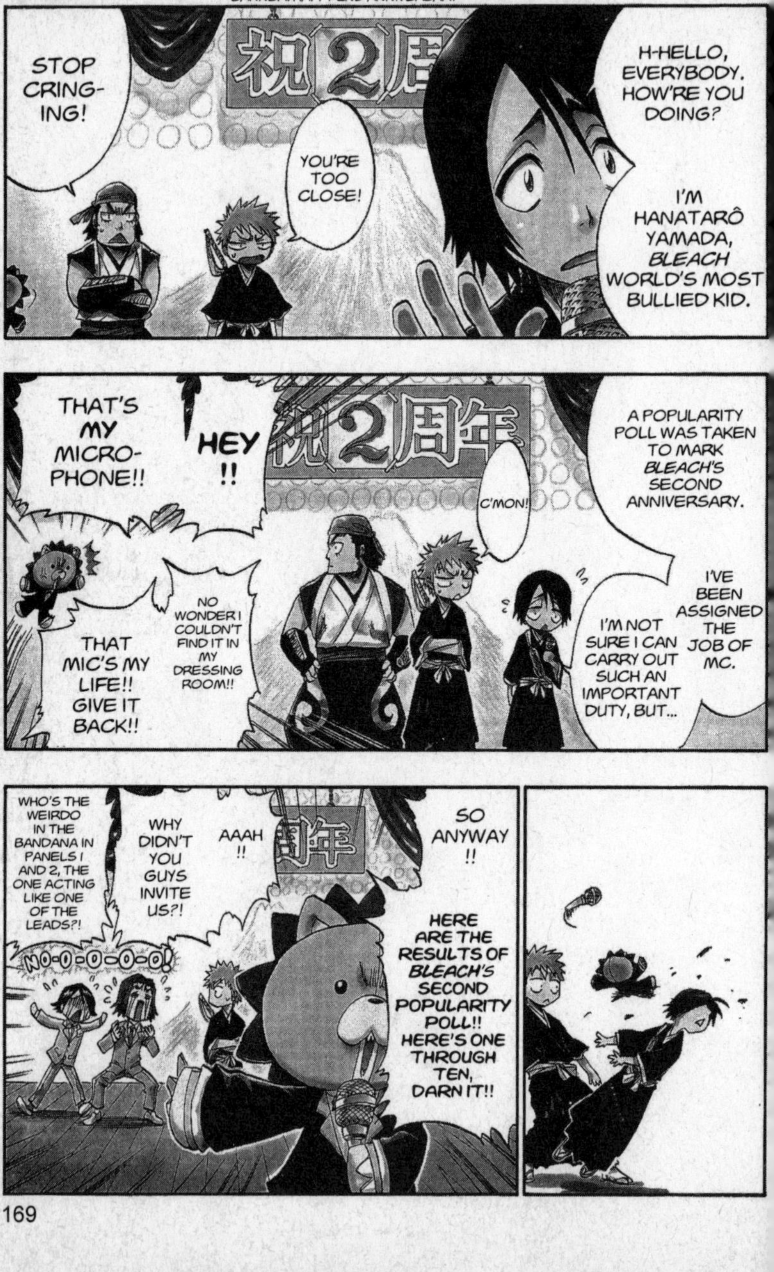

祝2周
H-HELLO, EVERYBODY. HOW'RE YOU DOING?
I'M HANATARÔ YAMADA, *BLEACH* WORLD'S MOST BULLIED KID.
YOU'RE TOO CLOSE!
STOP CRINGING!
祝2周年
A POPULARITY POLL WAS TAKEN TO MARK *BLEACH'S* SECOND ANNIVERSARY.
I'VE BEEN ASSIGNED THE JOB OF MC.
I'M NOT SURE I CAN CARRY OUT SUCH AN IMPORTANT DUTY, BUT...
C'MON!
HEY!!
THAT'S MY MICROPHONE!!
NO WONDER I COULDN'T FIND IT IN MY DRESSING ROOM!!
THAT MIC'S MY LIFE!! GIVE IT BACK!!
SO ANYWAY!!
HERE ARE THE RESULTS OF *BLEACH'S* SECOND POPULARITY POLL!! HERE'S ONE THROUGH TEN, DARN IT!!
AAAH!!
WHY DIDN'T YOU GUYS INVITE US?!
WHO'S THE WEIRDO IN THE BANDANA IN PANELS 1 AND 2, THE ONE ACTING LIKE ONE OF THE LEADS?!
NO-O-O-O-O-O!

POPULARITYVOTE 2: RESULT

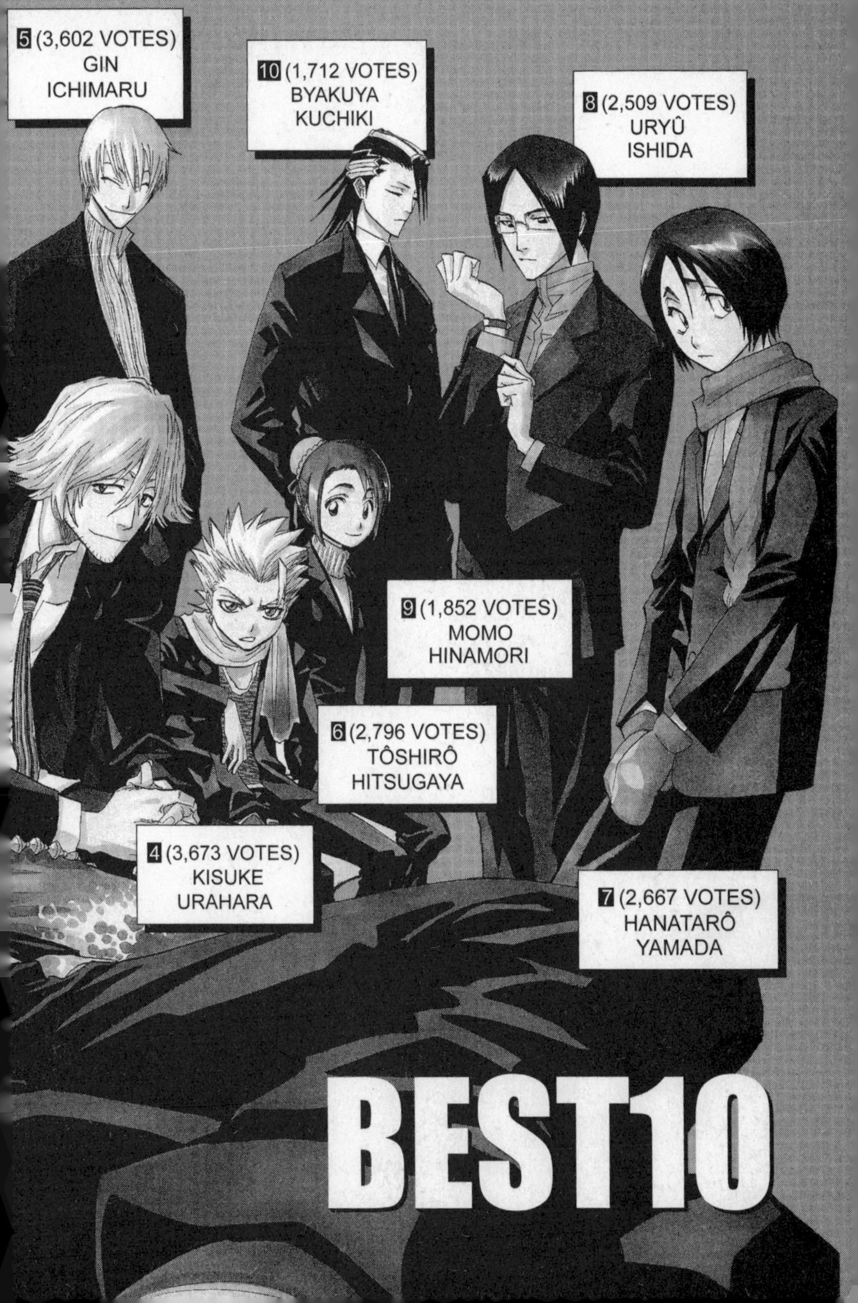

5 (3,602 VOTES) GIN ICHIMARU
10 (1,712 VOTES) BYAKUYA KUCHIKI
8 (2,509 VOTES) URYÛ ISHIDA
9 (1,852 VOTES) MOMO HINAMORI
6 (2,796 VOTES) TÔSHIRÔ HITSUGAYA
4 (3,673 VOTES) KISUKE URAHARA
7 (2,667 VOTES) HANATARÔ YAMADA
BEST10

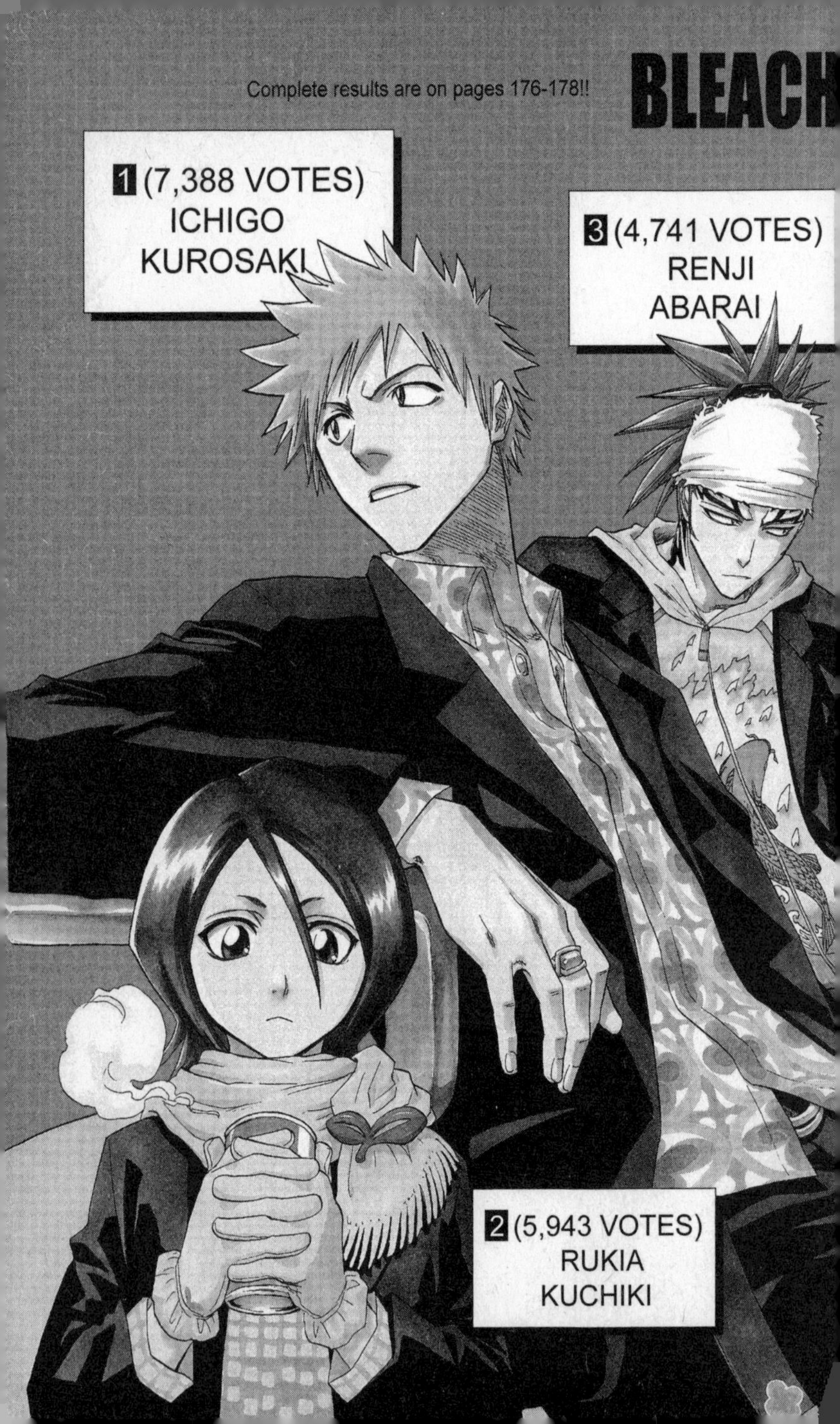
BLEACH
Complete results are on pages 176-178!!
1 (7,388 VOTES)
ICHIGO
KUROSAKI
3 (4,741 VOTES)
RENJI
ABARAI
2 (5,943 VOTES)
RUKIA
KUCHIKI

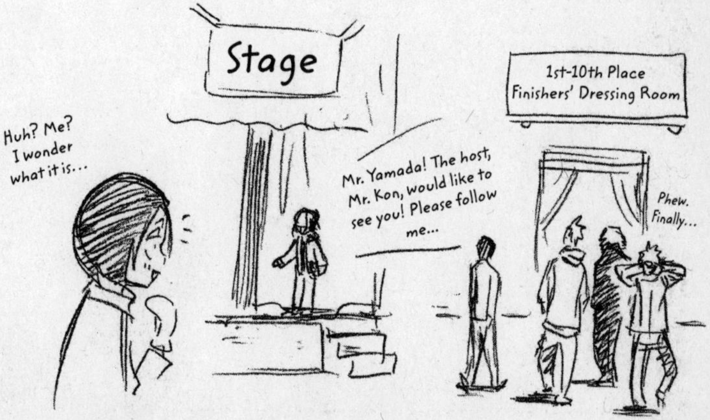
1st-10th Place Finishers' Dressing Room
Stage
Phew. Finally...
Mr. Yamada! The host, Mr. Kon, would like to see you! Please follow me...
Huh? Me? I wonder what it is...

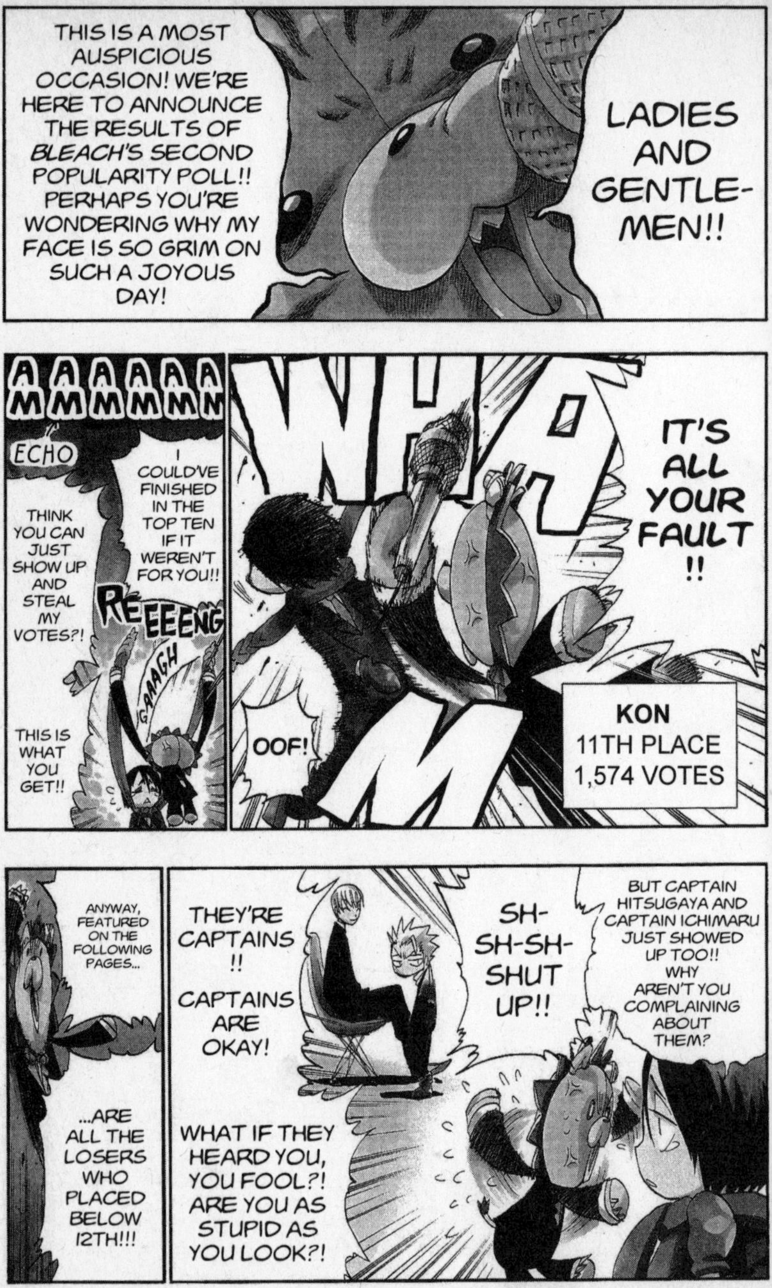
LADIES AND GENTLEMEN!!
THIS IS A MOST AUSPICIOUS OCCASION! WE'RE HERE TO ANNOUNCE THE RESULTS OF *BLEACH'S* SECOND POPULARITY POLL!! PERHAPS YOU'RE WONDERING WHY MY FACE IS SO GRIM ON SUCH A JOYOUS DAY!
WHAM
IT'S ALL YOUR FAULT!!
OOF!
KON
11TH PLACE
1,574 VOTES
AAAAAAMMMMMN
ECHO
I COULD'VE FINISHED IN THE TOP TEN IF IT WEREN'T FOR YOU!!
THINK YOU CAN JUST SHOW UP AND STEAL MY VOTES?!
REEEENG
GRAAAGH
THIS IS WHAT YOU GET!!
BUT CAPTAIN HITSUGAYA AND CAPTAIN ICHIMARU JUST SHOWED UP TOO!! WHY AREN'T YOU COMPLAINING ABOUT THEM?
SH-SH-SH-SHUT UP!!
THEY'RE CAPTAINS!!
CAPTAINS ARE OKAY!
WHAT IF THEY HEARD YOU, YOU FOOL?! ARE YOU AS STUPID AS YOU LOOK?!
ANYWAY, FEATURED ON THE FOLLOWING PAGES...
...ARE ALL THE LOSERS WHO PLACED BELOW 12TH!!!

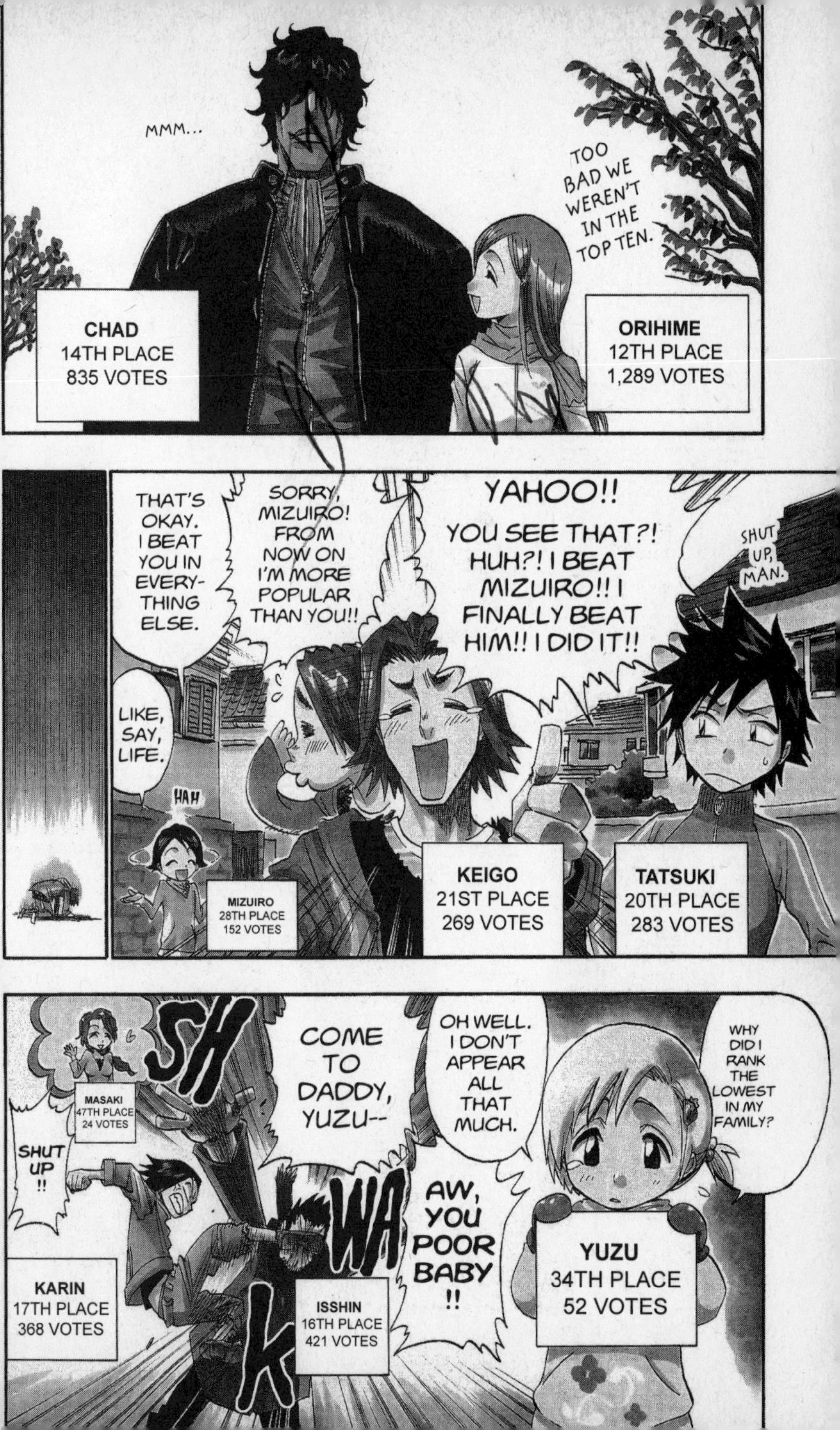

TOO BAD WE WEREN'T IN THE TOP TEN.
ORIHIME 12TH PLACE 1,289 VOTES
MMM...
CHAD 14TH PLACE 835 VOTES
SHUT UP, MAN.
YAHOO!!
YOU SEE THAT?! HUH?! I BEAT MIZUIRO!! I FINALLY BEAT HIM!! I DID IT!!
SORRY, MIZUIRO! FROM NOW ON I'M MORE POPULAR THAN YOU!!
THAT'S OKAY. I BEAT YOU IN EVERY-THING ELSE.
LIKE, SAY, LIFE.
TATSUKI 20TH PLACE 283 VOTES
KEIGO 21ST PLACE 269 VOTES
HAH
MIZUIRO 28TH PLACE 152 VOTES
WHY DID I RANK THE LOWEST IN MY FAMILY?
OH WELL. I DON'T APPEAR ALL THAT MUCH.
COME TO DADDY, YUZU--
SH
AW, YOU POOR BABY!!
YUZU 34TH PLACE 52 VOTES
WA
K
MASAKI 47TH PLACE 24 VOTES
SHUT UP!!
ISSHIN 16TH PLACE 421 VOTES
KARIN 17TH PLACE 368 VOTES

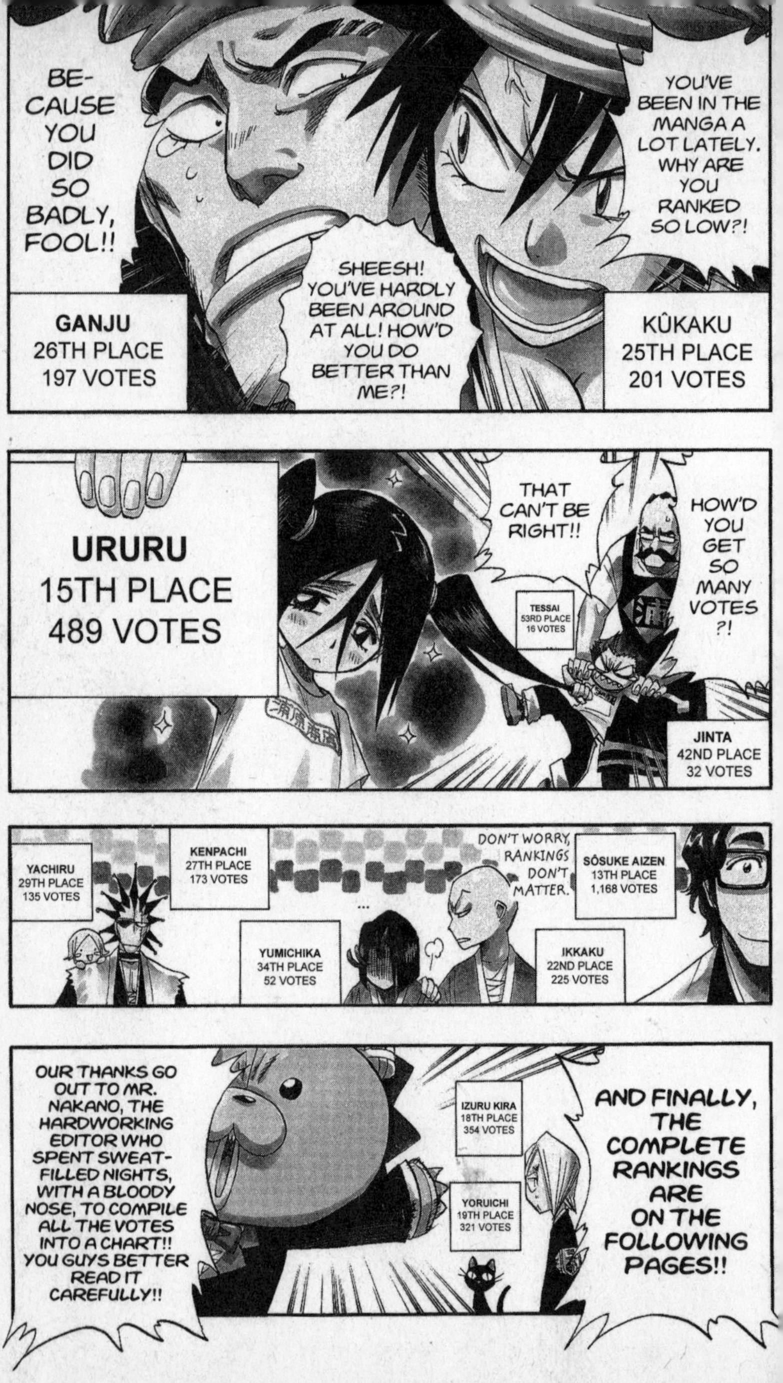
YOU'VE BEEN IN THE MANGA A LOT LATELY. WHY ARE YOU RANKED SO LOW?!
KÛKAKU 25TH PLACE 201 VOTES
BE-CAUSE YOU DID SO BADLY, FOOL!!
SHEESH! YOU'VE HARDLY BEEN AROUND AT ALL! HOW'D YOU DO BETTER THAN ME?!
GANJU 26TH PLACE 197 VOTES
HOW'D YOU GET SO MANY VOTES ?!
THAT CAN'T BE RIGHT!!
TESSAI 53RD PLACE 16 VOTES
JINTA 42ND PLACE 32 VOTES
URURU 15TH PLACE 489 VOTES
SÔSUKE AIZEN 13TH PLACE 1,168 VOTES
DON'T WORRY, RANKINGS DON'T MATTER.
IKKAKU 22ND PLACE 225 VOTES
...
YUMICHIKA 34TH PLACE 52 VOTES
KENPACHI 27TH PLACE 173 VOTES
YACHIRU 29TH PLACE 135 VOTES
AND FINALLY, THE COMPLETE RANKINGS ARE ON THE FOLLOWING PAGES!!
IZURU KIRA 18TH PLACE 354 VOTES
YORUICHI 19TH PLACE 321 VOTES
OUR THANKS GO OUT TO MR. NAKANO, THE HARDWORKING EDITOR WHO SPENT SWEAT-FILLED NIGHTS, WITH A BLOODY NOSE, TO COMPILE ALL THE VOTES INTO A CHART!! YOU GUYS BETTER READ IT CAREFULLY!!

BLEACH POPULARITY VOTE 2 RESULTS

第二回人気投票全結果

PERFECT LIST

1st	(7,388 votes)	Ichigo Kurosaki
2nd	(5,943 votes)	Rukia Kuchiki
3rd	(4,741 votes)	Renji Abarai
4th	(3,673 votes)	Kisuke Urahara
5th	(3,602 votes)	Gin Ichimaru
6th	(2,796 votes)	Tôshirô Hitsugaya
7th	(2,667 votes)	Hanatarô Yamada
8th	(2,509 votes)	Uryû Ishida
9th	(1,852 votes)	Momo Hinamori
10th	(1,712 votes)	Byakuya Kuchiki
11th	(1,574 votes)	Kon
12th	(1,289 votes)	Orihime Inoue
13th	(1,168 votes)	Sôsuke Aizen
14th	(835 votes)	Yasutora Sado
15th	(489 votes)	Ururu Tsumugiya
16th	(421 votes)	Isshin Kurosaki
17th	(368 votes)	Karin Kurosaki
18th	(354 votes)	Izuru Kira
19th	(321 votes)	Yoruichi
20th	(283 votes)	Tatsuki Arisawa
21st	(269 votes)	Keigo Asano
22nd	(225 votes)	Ikkaku Madarame
23rd	(212 votes)	Tite Kubo
24th	(207 votes)	Zangetsu
25th	(201 votes)	Kûkaku Shiba
26th	(197 votes)	Ganju Shiba
27th	(173 votes)	Kenpachi Zaraki
28th	(152 votes)	Mizuiro Kojima
29th	(135 votes)	Yachiru Kusajishi
30th	(63 votes)	Zennosuke Kurumadani
31st	(61 votes)	Bonnie
32nd	(54 votes)	Nemu Kurotsuchi/ Renji's attendant
34th	(52 votes)	Yuzu Kurosaki/ Yumichika Ayasegawa
36th	(51 votes)	Shunsui Kyôraku/ Chizuru Honshô
38th	(44 votes)	Tetsuzaemon Iba
39th	(40 votes)	Rangiku Matsumoto
40th	(35 votes)	Akon
41st	(34 votes)	"Handstand" sculpture
42nd	(32 votes)	Jinta Hanakari
43rd	(31 votes)	Tsubaki
44th	(29 votes)	Soi Fon
45th	(27 votes)	Zangetsu (sword)/ Don Kanonji
47th	(24 votes)	Masaki Kurosaki/ Shûhei Hisagi
49th	(22 votes)	Yûichi Shibata
50th	(21 votes)	Princess & Dragon

51st (18 votes) Menos Grande

52nd (17 votes) Keigo's older sister

53rd (16 votes) Tessai Tsukabishi/ "The Champion" sculpture

55th (15 votes) Jidanbô/the gorilla girl who beat Tatsuki in Nationals

57th (14 votes) Ryô Kunieda/ Misato Ochi

59th (13 votes) The school principal/ Rukia's drawings

61st (12 votes) Sora Inoue/Benihime

63rd (11 votes) Hironari Horiuchi

64th (10 votes) Enraku/Hawk (Taichi Miyamoto)

66th (9 votes) Tetsuo Momohara/ Shunô

68th (8 votes) Mayuri Kurotsuchi (Chief of R&D)/Ayame/Li'l Mitch/ Tadanobu Asano/C.T. Smith

73rd (7 votes) Ichigo's little sister, as imagined by Chad

74th (6 votes) Retsu Unohana/ Zabimaru/Justice headband/Tomohiro Conrad Odagiri/ "First Love" sculpture/the Hell Butterfly/ Tsujishiro Kurôemon III/the Hollow, Neen, who fought Rukia

82nd (5 votes) Shigekuni Genryûsai Yamamoto/the melon/the man who yelled at Ichigo/Yobi-Rin Mushi of the R&D Dept./the future Orihime/ Tinatina/Urara Kokumashi

89th (4 votes) Nanao Ise/Mahana Natsui/Michiru Ogawa/Shunshun Rikka/Lily/Cookie/So Waru Pin/the cat that served as Yoruichi's model/Hitomi Victoria Odagiri/ Tobiume/the star-shaped Hollow/ Top (Kenji Yamashita)/Gamma Akutabi/Richard Steddler Cricien

103rd (3 votes) Kaien Shiba/Uryû's master/Baigon/Hiyosu/Koganehiko/ Shiroganehiko/the pickled radish cut by Zabimaru/the killer who tried to off the champ in Orihime's fantasy/Magic Girl Megalon/the hairdo on the cover flap of volume one/the lucky charm that Masaki gave Isshin/the Soul Reaper in Rukia flashback/Shigeo/the guy Byakuya talked about/old man Ken, the vegetable seller/Reiichi Ôshima/ Dumbbell (Sadatomo Saionji)/ Fever (Mitsuru Ishino)/Felis Catus/ Ryûta Yokokawa

123rd (2 votes) Acid Wire/Grand Fisher/Urahara Shôten/Rukongai district elder/Wabisuke/Jirôbô Ikkanzaka/Midoriko Tôno/ Hollow/Kubo sensei's combo/ Shinsô/Hotarukazura/Madame Akiyama/Sôkyoku/Karin's doll/ Isshin's chicken whistle/Kon's microphone, which Hanatarô was using/wasabi & honey-flavored *taiyaki*-style ramen/Bruce Willis/ Kenichiro Nanbu/Tessai's glasses, when they were in critical condi- tion/Ichigo when he was about to turn into a Hollow/the girl with glasses in the R&D Dept./the Yumichika that Ichigo imagines/ Ichigo's wristband/Peetan, the one that's not Pooh/L'Arc de Triomphe whistle/Katsuhiko Hino/keeper of the Gates of Hell/Chain of Fate/ Satoru Kudô/Nancy/Wolfina/ Balmunk/Jade Hermitage's mother (a 52-year-old wrestler)

BLEACH POPULARITY VOTE 2 RESULTS 第二回人気投票全結果 PERFECT LIST

157th (1 vote)
Shibata's mother/Soul Candy Yuki/Orihime's father/Akane Aki/Ginpaku Kazanohana no Usuginu/Kôtotsu/the author and friend who are busy moving/the row of ants that Kon protected/the Hollow masks/the vase that fell in chapter one/the dog that Kon was about to be put into/the beetle that went after Rukia's chocolate/the guy in Yokohama who bought Orihime sushi/Mr. Kagine/Bostav/Valley of Paradise/Hoteiya's gourmet rice dumplings in sweet bean paste/Captain of 13th Company/Katsuhiko Hino/Ichigo's scissors that were used to cut Keigo's headband/the zanpaku-tô's hilt/Ichigo's zanpaku-tô, which Kisuke broke/the box containing Soul Reaper powers/Kenpachi's eye patch/Sôsuke's glasses/Randy Johnson/Ewan McGregor/Tyrano Inoue/the ghosts that were making out in broad daylight/the cat that's in constant heat/the entire staff/the Hollow that fixed Grand Fisher/the Hollow that was talking excitedly behind Tatsuki/the window from which you can see Sôkyoku/Yuzu's banana/the girl watching "Spontaneous Trips"/the Soul Reaper cleaning crew/John Travolta/Keanu Reeves/Marie Hatsue/nerdy glasses/nerdy headband/Bostav used as a Girl's Festival doll/Orihime's homemade red bean paste-filled bread/Yuzu's codes/Renji's eyebrows/Ichigo, when he was wearing the wrong outfit in Orihime's vision/the host of "Spontaneous Trips"/the special desk for throwing/Don Kanonji's glasses/Bankin Taihô/Kenseikan/Uchû-dama/Karakura Superheroes/the doll that Uryû fixed/Mr. Goofy Tattooed Eyebrows Man/Soul Candy Alfred/Marie/Marie's friend/Mr. Kubo's parents, who sent a letter to "Radio Kon Baby"/Kaname Tôsen/Makoto Senô/Komamura/Hôzukimaru/Soul Candy Chappy/Marianne/the male ghost in chapter 2/the Kurosaki parents/Byakuya's attendant/the mask Isshin wore/Masaki's poster/"The Scream" T-shirt/the three students in Karin's class/the Soul Reaper who takes care of Renji/Gonzales Gym/Hinagiku/Fishbone D/the Soul Reaper who gets his zanpaku-tô broken by Chad/Urahara Shoten's summoning cannon/the grandfather and boy during the blackout/the watermelon poster/Mizuiro's souvenir from Phuket/a woman's bulge/the Mod Konpaku with the uselessly beautiful voice/all the zanpaku-tô/the leeches that Shrieker spits out/Kojaku/Mikami/the guy who wonders if Orihime has a boyfriend/Rukia's gigai/the dying message-like summons method/the author's self-portrait in volume one/the warrior behind Kon/the guy who was eavesdropping on Renji and Sôsuke/Toshi-rin/the Soul Reaper on the right in panel 4 of the third page in chapter 86/the good-looking Soul Reaper in the front on the right in panel 4 of the 16th page in chapter 92/the Hollow that Uryû defeated/Kaneda/the moaning patient/Li'l Yama/the Soul Reaper that Ichigo steps on/Hiroyoshi Kato/Hama-ya/Kazuya Usaka/Takeshi Nakadaira/Morita/Ryôhei Toba/Shorty (Yachiru's nickname)/Kei Uehara (Donny)/Heita Tô-jôin (Pinta)/Sakari Takami/Jaguar Junichi/Elwood/Amantine/Emilio/Joanne/Kotono Tsujigami/PD-Type 25 (Rachel)/Shimizu Akai

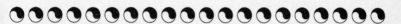

So there you have it, the results of the 2nd *Bleach* popularity poll. The higher rankings fluctuated a lot due to the appearance of the Soul Society's Soul Reapers. Yet Ichigo and Rukia's popularity was firmly set. As the author, I'm pleased. Like last time, someone voted for Kisuke several hundred times (there were so many votes that we couldn't get an accurate count). Someone also voted for Keigo 50 times by sending in 50 handwritten, hand-drawn illustrations and messages. There were countless votes for rare characters who didn't even have names. It was fun for me, but Mr. Nakano, who had to check them, was seriously about to cry. Personally, I thought the vote for Jaguar Junichi was funny, but it's obviously against the rules, so those won't count in the future. Okay, until next time!!

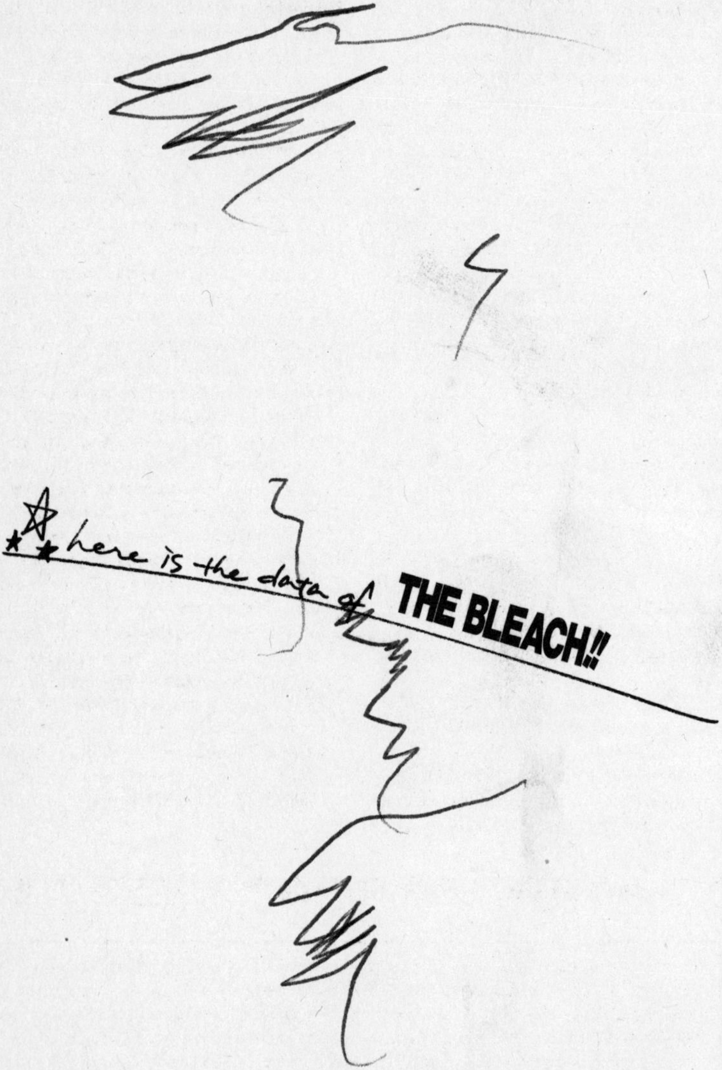
here is the data of THE BLEACH!!

THIRTEEN COURT GUARD COMPANIES	更木剣八	KENPACHI ZARAKI 11TH COMPANY

202 CM
108 KG
D.O.B. NOVEMBER 19

• THE CAPTAIN OF THE FIERCE 11TH COMPANY. TALL, WITH STRANGE HAIR, HE WEARS AN EYE PATCH AND HAS AN INTIMIDATING PRESENCE.

• FROM ZARAKI, NORTH RUKONGAI'S 80TH DISTRICT. THE ONLY PERSON EVER TO BECOME A CAPTAIN OF THE THIRTEEN COMPANIES WITHOUT TAKING THE ENLISTMENT EXAM. MORE ABOUT THAT IN THE FUTURE.

• SETS HIS HAIR HIMSELF EACH MORNING. SOMETIMES YUMICHIKA TRIES TO DO IT FOR HIM, BUT HE ALWAYS REFUSES BECAUSE HE THINKS THAT'S GROSS. THE BELLS ARE BRAIDED INTO HIS HAIR SO THEY WON'T FALL OUT.

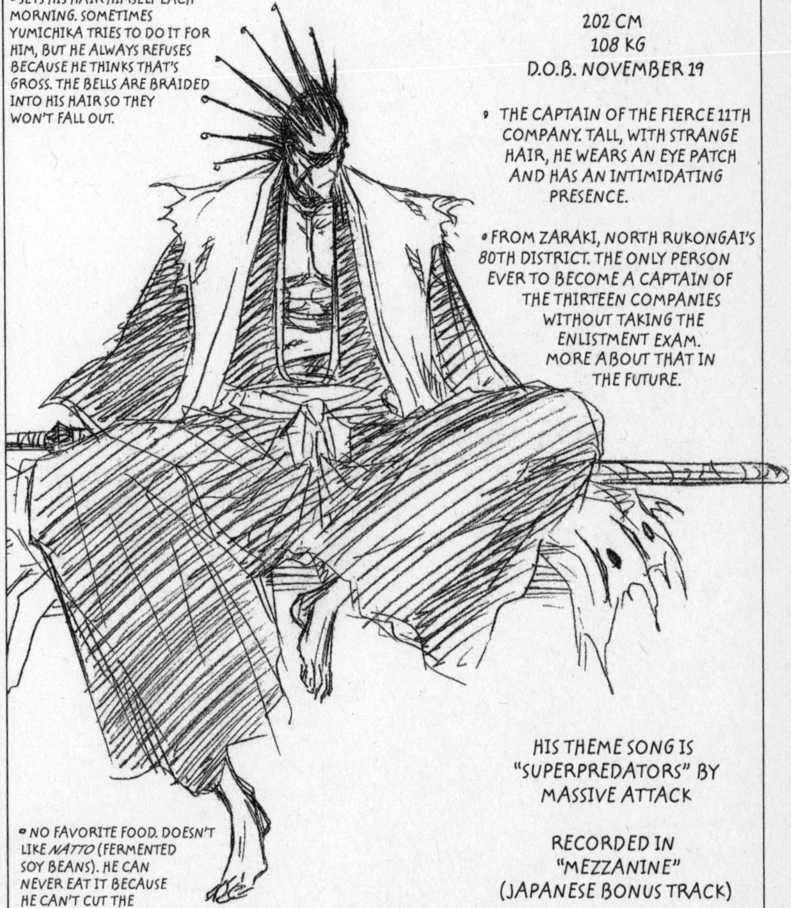

HIS THEME SONG IS "SUPERPREDATORS" BY MASSIVE ATTACK

RECORDED IN "MEZZANINE" (JAPANESE BONUS TRACK)

• NO FAVORITE FOOD. DOESN'T LIKE *NATTO* (FERMENTED SOY BEANS). HE CAN NEVER EAT IT BECAUSE HE CAN'T CUT THE STICKY THREADS.

| **THIRTEEN COURT GUARD COMPANIES** | 草鹿やちる | YACHIRU KUSAJISHI 11TH COMPANY |

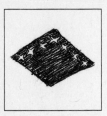

11TH COMPANY CREST
SYMBOL:
"NOKOGIRISÔ"
(YARROW PLANT)
MOTTO: "FIGHT"

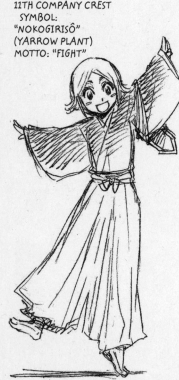

109 CM
15.5 KG
D.O.B. FEBRUARY 12

• THE SHORTEST AND LIGHTEST MEMBER OF THE THIRTEEN COURT GUARDS COMPANIES.

• FROM KUSAJISHI, THE 79TH DISTRICT OF NORTH RUKONGAI.

○ SIMILAR TO KENPACHI, SHE'S THE ONLY PERSON EVER TO BECOME AN ASSISTANT CAPTAIN OF THE THIRTEEN COMPANIES WITHOUT TAKING THE ENLISTMENT EXAM.

• HER SWORD ISN'T VERY LONG, BUT ITS SCABBARD HAS TRAINING WHEELS BECAUSE SHE PULLS IT BEHIND HER WITH A STRING, INSTEAD OF WEARING IT AT HER WAIST. IKKAKU, WHO IS GOOD WITH TOOLS, MADE IT FOR HER AFTER SHE PESTERED HIM FOR IT.

• HER FAVORITE FOOD IS *KONPEITO* (A CANDY MADE BY CRYSTALLIZING SUGAR AROUND A POPPY SEED CORE). GIVEN THE CHANCE, SHE'LL GULP IT DOWN LIKE IT'S WATER.

THEME SONG
"YOO-HOO!"
SORA IZUMIKAWA.
RECORDED IN
"SORA HE."

YOU'RE NOT WORTHY OF GOLD!!
17TH
45TH
GIVE UP YOUR GOLD STATUS!!
42ND
JINTA, HIS RANKING'S ONLY SLIGHTLY LOWER THAN YOURS.
15TH

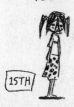

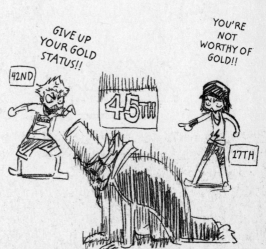

Next Volume Preview

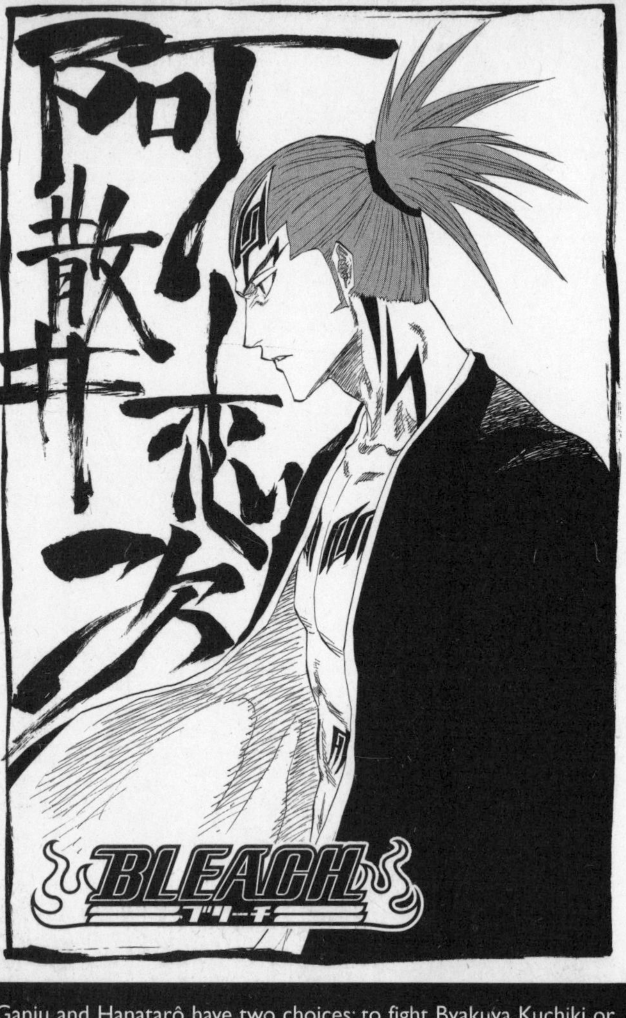
阿散井恋次
BLEACH
ブリーチ

Ganju and Hanatarô have two choices: to fight Byakuya Kuchiki or flee. But now that Ganju knows the horrible truth about Rukia, will he abandon their rescue mission altogether? Meanwhile, a battered Ichigo awakens to the sight of a familiar face, but it's not exactly who he thinks it is!

Available now!

HOSHIN ENGI™

$7.99

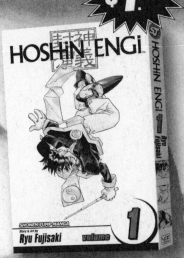

MANGA ON SALE NOW!

WHO IS BEHIND THE MYSTERIOUS HOSHIN PROJECT?

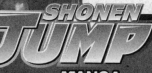

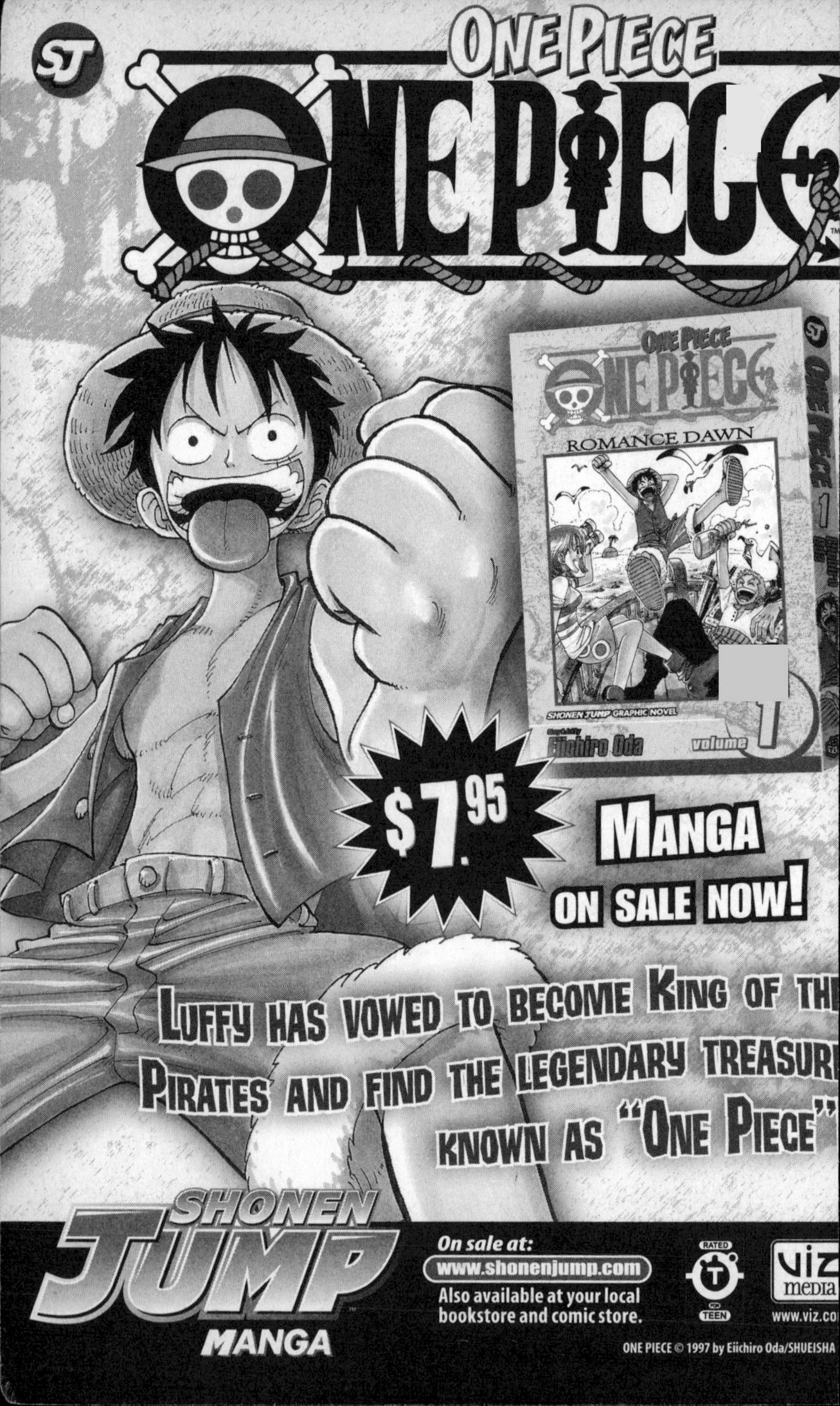

SJ
ONE PIECE
ONE PIECE
ONE PIECE
ONE PIECE
ROMANCE DAWN
SHONEN JUMP GRAPHIC NOVEL
Eiichiro Oda
volume 1
$7.95
MANGA
ON SALE NOW!
LUFFY HAS VOWED TO BECOME KING OF TH
PIRATES AND FIND THE LEGENDARY TREASUR
KNOWN AS "ONE PIECE"
SHONEN JUMP
MANGA
On sale at:
www.shonenjump.com
Also available at your local bookstore and comic store.
RATED T TEEN
viz media
www.viz.co
ONE PIECE © 1997 by Eiichiro Oda/SHUEISHA

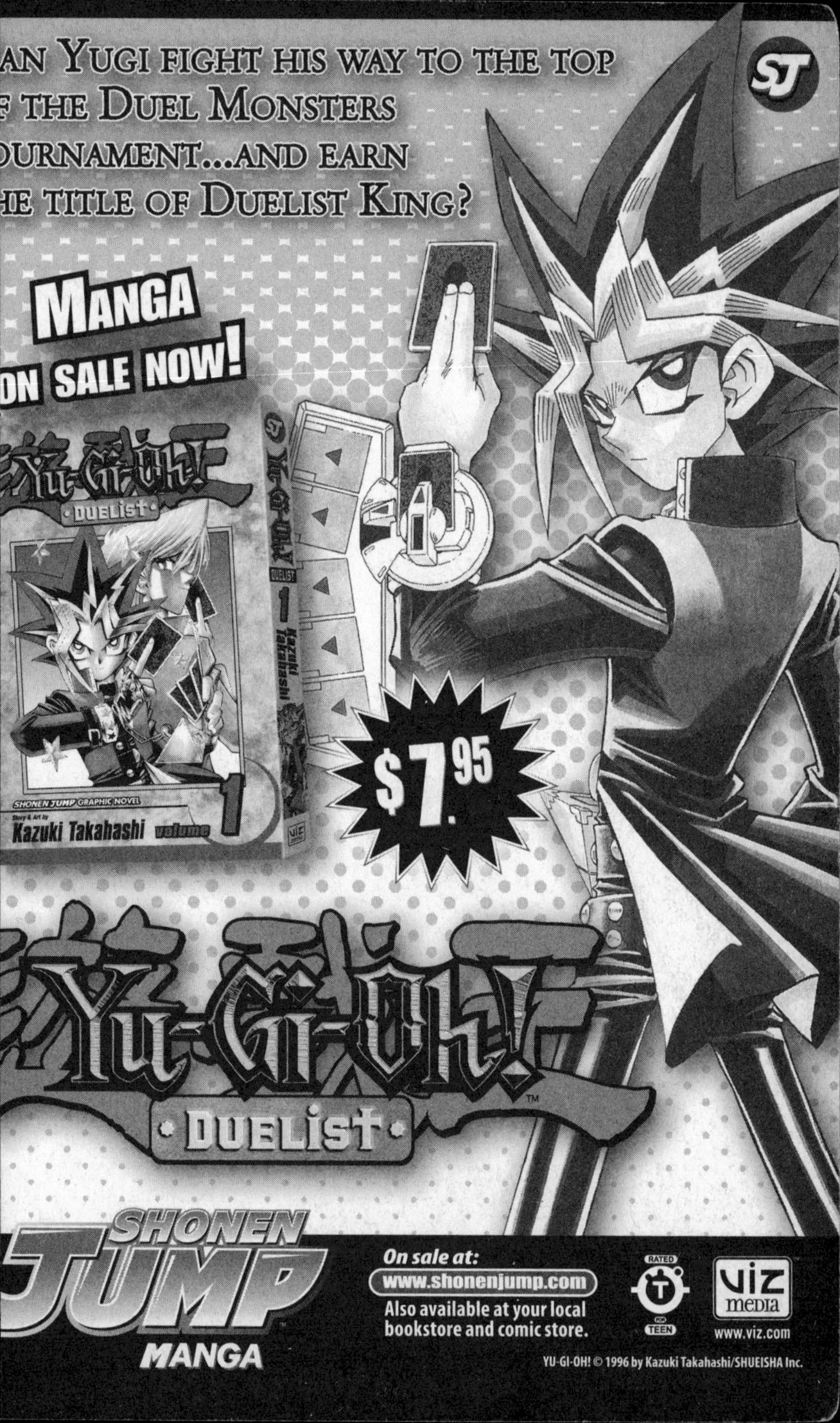

AN YUGI FIGHT HIS WAY TO THE TOP
F THE DUEL MONSTERS
OURNAMENT...AND EARN
HE TITLE OF DUELIST KING?
SJ
MANGA
ON SALE NOW!
YU-GI-OH! DUELIST
SHONEN JUMP GRAPHIC NOVEL
Story & Art by
Kazuki Takahashi volume 1
$7.95
YU-GI-OH! DUELIST™
SHONEN JUMP MANGA
On sale at:
www.shonenjump.com
Also available at your local bookstore and comic store.
RATED T FOR TEEN
viz media
www.viz.com
YU-GI-OH! © 1996 by Kazuki Takahashi/SHUEISHA Inc.

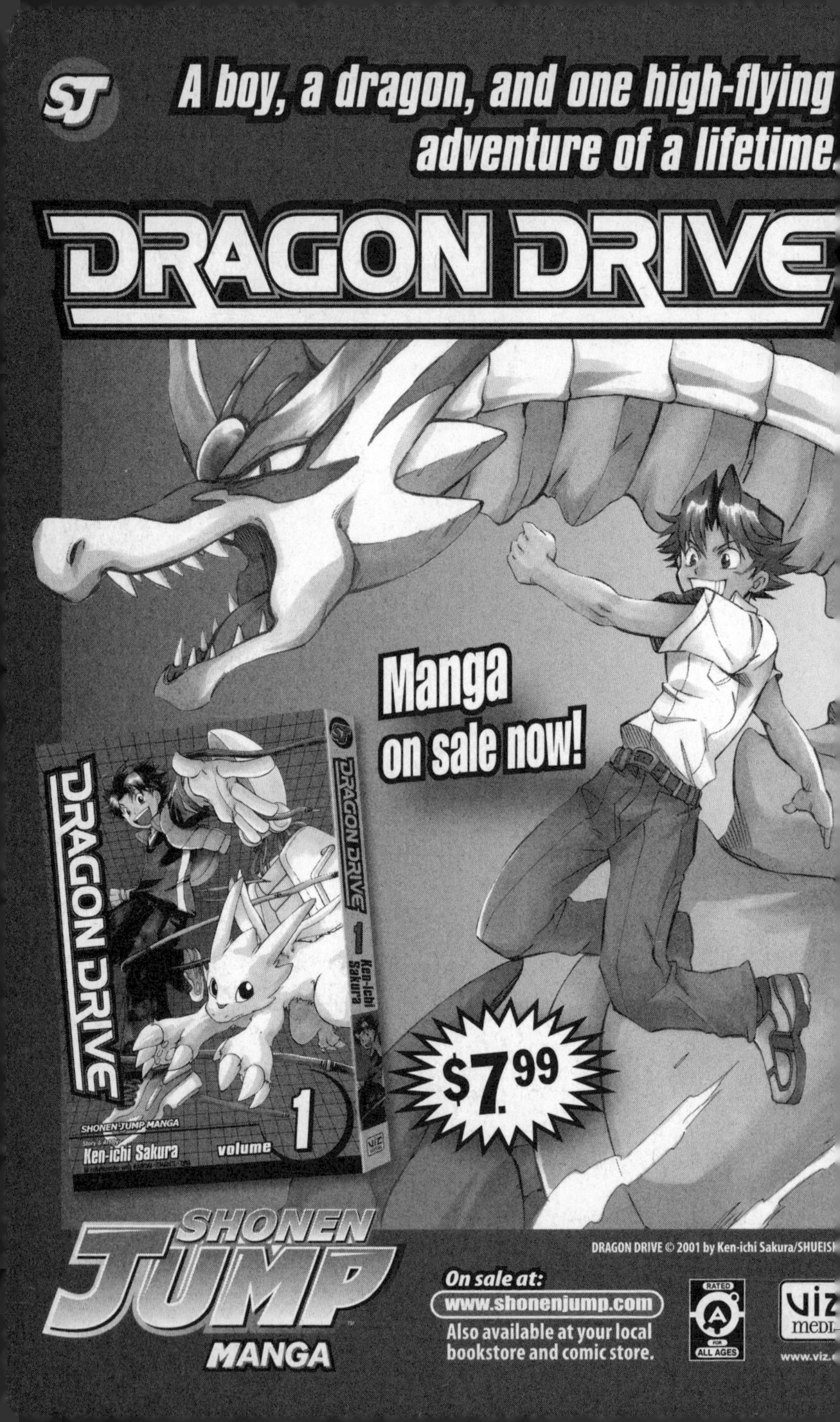

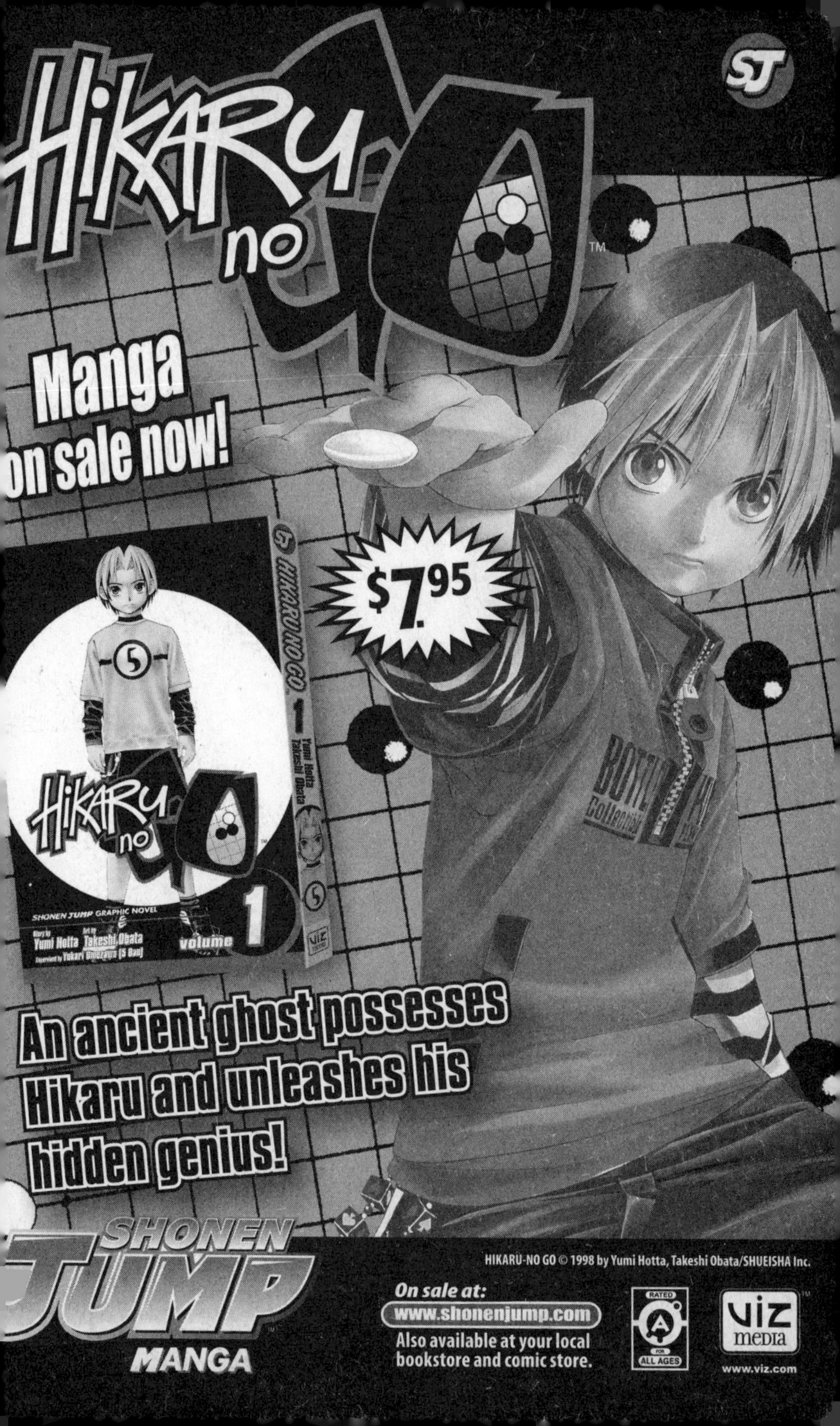

SJ
Hikaru no Go™
Manga on sale now!
$7.95
SHONEN JUMP GRAPHIC NOVEL
Yumi Hotta Takeshi Obata
volume 1
HIKARU NO GO 1 Yumi Hotta Takeshi Obata
An ancient ghost possesses Hikaru and unleashes his hidden genius!
SHONEN JUMP MANGA
HIKARU-NO GO © 1998 by Yumi Hotta, Takeshi Obata/SHUEISHA Inc.
On sale at:
www.shonenjump.com
Also available at your local bookstore and comic store.
RATED A FOR ALL AGES
VIZ media
www.viz.com

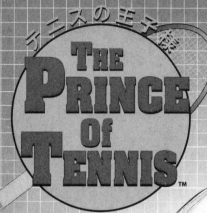
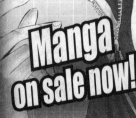

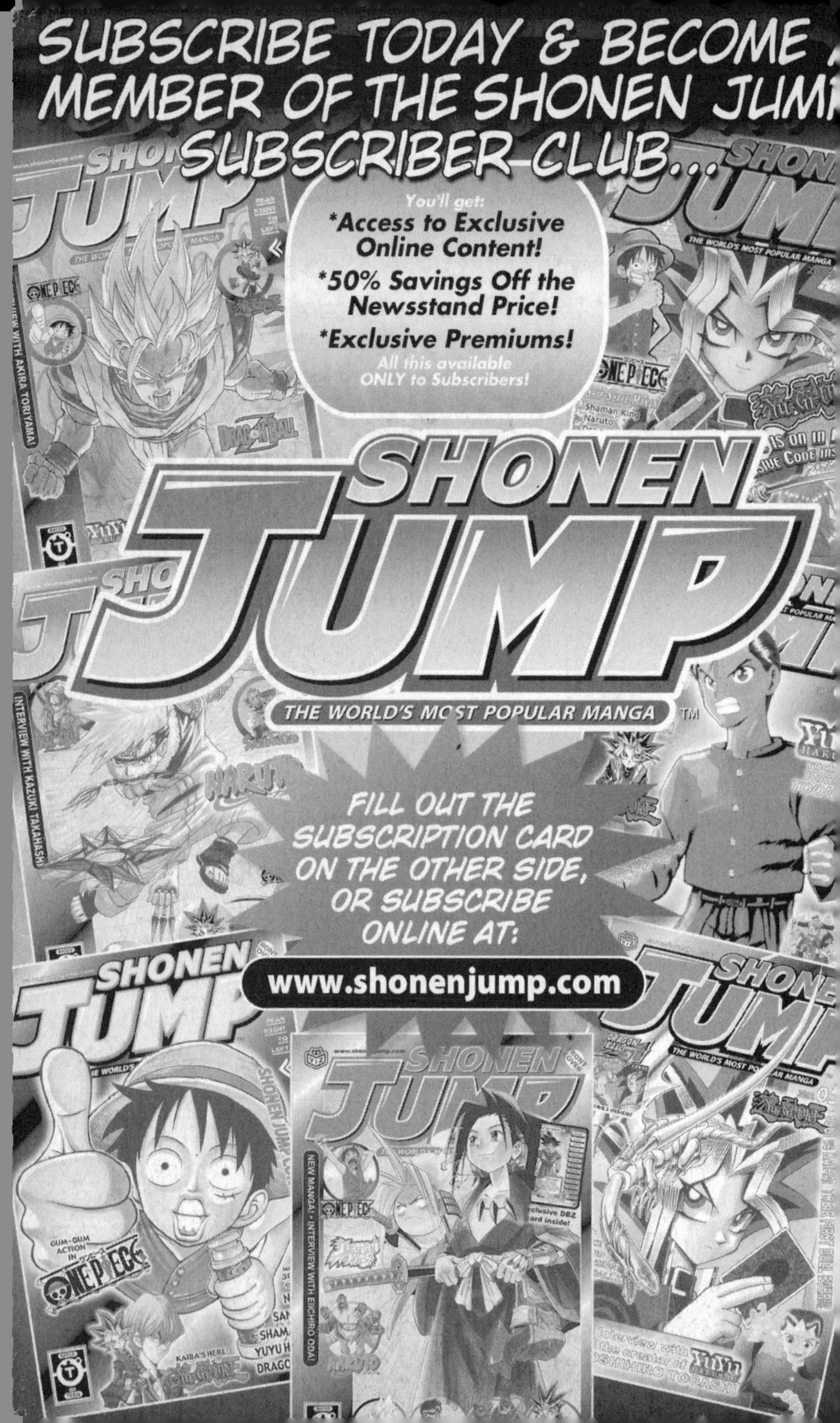
SUBSCRIBE TODAY & BECOME A MEMBER OF THE SHONEN JUMP SUBSCRIBER CLUB...
You'll get:
*Access to Exclusive Online Content!
*50% Savings Off the Newsstand Price!
*Exclusive Premiums!
All this available ONLY to Subscribers!
SHONEN JUMP
THE WORLD'S MOST POPULAR MANGA ™
FILL OUT THE SUBSCRIPTION CARD ON THE OTHER SIDE, OR SUBSCRIBE ONLINE AT:
www.shonenjump.com

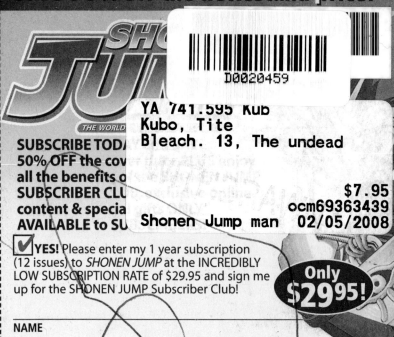